WAKE UP,
WHITE AMERICA

WAKE UP, WHITE AMERICA

Anne!
You Are Still The Best!

John Stephen Parker

Rev. date: 02/28/2019

To order additional copies of this book, contact:
Xlibris
1-888-795-4274
www.Xlibris.com
Orders@Xlibris.com
775894

ABOUT THE BOOK

Wake Up White America comes from the mind of controversial author, John Parker. Filled with experiences, anecdotes, statistics, and social commentary, Parker shines a light on racism and the attitudes he and much of the black population of this country feels white America displays toward this often sensitive and polarizing topic.

Parker understands that much of white America chooses to reject race as a reason for inequality because it frees them from the reality of guilt, even though these same people continue to benefit from said inequality. He also draws some very clear patterns of these attitudes and shows why, if the United States of America is to ever evolve into what it can be, it must first hold itself accountable for the treatment of its own citizens, which up to this point, it never has.

This book is a much needed read for everyone, regardless of race. Parker makes it clear, on many levels, that it is time for white America to WAKE UP.

ABOUT THE AUTHOR

John Parker is a father, author, successful entrepreneur, professional motivational speaker and social activist. He is a former college and professional football coach of twenty-five years and an award-winning television and radio talk show host. He is currently the Director of Corporate Communications and Media for St. Louis Development Corporation in St. Louis, Missouri and the publisher of Evolution Magazine.

He has authored two previous books on the subject of racism and social justice (From Sheets to Suits: Embedded Racism in American Society and A Cold in August: The Controversial Killing of Michael Brown Jr).

Often labeled as a "controversial figure," Parker has delivered speeches to national organizations such as the International Association of Police Chiefs and Law Enforcement Officers, and has been on the forefront of social and racial change. He is a long time cultural activist, often being the voice of, and fighting for the rights of black people and the socially under served.

CONTENTS

DEDICATION

Every time I write a book, I always look for something or someone to dedicate my work to. Often it is a person who has touched of influenced me or my writing. Sometimes it is a passion that hits me out of the blue and just never leaves. In this case, it is a bit of both.

This book is dedicated to young people, both black and white, who have taken up the torch of making this world a better place. Never believe that a small group of like-minded individuals or even one person screaming in the middle of nowhere can't change the world, because, truthfully, it is the only thing that ever has.

To my children, Andrea and Jordan, who are by far the greatest achievements of your mother and me, I don't have much to leave you in this world. You are both smarter than your father. But, I will leave you with this.

No matter what decisions you make in your life, always remember, they are never based on right or wrong. They are truly based on if they were yours or someone else's. The world is a cruel place and it will beat you to the ground some days, but the sooner you stop being concerned about what people think, the faster you figure out who you really are. Remember, opinions are like assholes; Everyone has one and they all stink. Live your life and nobody else's. Always keep your head to the sky, find your own passion and know that love is the key to life.

Don't ever give up on the hope that the good people of the United States of America will wake up and come together. And, by all means, Remember, your dad loves you!

STAY WOKE, PLEASE!

PREFACE

WITHOUT MAKING A huge deal out of this, I want to make this crystal clear. This is not an "I hate white America" book. Quite the contrary. I have been able to achieve many things in my life and none of those would have been accomplished without the love, guidance, and support of many people in my life, both black and white. I was married to a beautiful white, polish-catholic woman for fifteen years. She gave me two wonderful children that I am incredibly proud of. If I hated white America, none of that would have ever been possible. Thank you, Laura.

Not so long ago a member of white America called me a racist. In fact, it happens nearly every day and all I can do is laugh. It is at these moments that I realize that many in white America have really become delusional if they believe that any black person could actually be racist. At the core of my being, I'm a good person! I have insisted on this, but I just don't have time for bullshit anymore. I have finally reached an age where I can say what I want to say. I do see color in my life every day, and I don't have a racist bone in my body. I have felt insulted and misunderstood and have stomped off to lick my wounds many times in my life. That's because I thought being me meant not being liked by people who didn't look like me. That is not me anymore.

For years I have struggled silently to understand race and racism. I had no way to make sense of debates in the media about whether the white guy I was talking to was "being a racist" or me as the black guy, was "playing the race card." I had and have always wanted close friends regardless of color but kept ending up with mostly white people as my closest friends. When I am with black people, I have often felt an inexplicable tension that I didn't always fit in or that I would do something offensive or embarrassing. This comes from being raised in a predominately white atmosphere of the North County of St. Louis, Missouri, in the 1970s.

When I was younger, many white people made blatantly racist jokes or remarks around me. I felt upset but had no idea what to do or say. I didn't understand why—if historical laws supporting slavery, segregation, and discrimination had been abolished—because lifestyles still looked so different across color lines. Most confusing were unwanted racist thoughts toward many white people that made me feel like a jerk. I felt too embarrassed to admit any of this, which prevented me from going in search of answers.

It turns out stumbling block number one was that I knew I was black and that I was always going to be behind the eight ball for the rest of my life, so I never thought to look within myself for answers. The way I understood it as a kid was that success and privilege were for other people—white-skinned people. Don't get me wrong, if you put a census form in my hand, I would know to check "black." It's more than I thought all those other categories—like Asian, American Indian, and Latino—were the real races. I thought white was the "raceless" race, just plain, normal, the one against which all others were measured.

What I've learned is that thinking white people are raceless has allowed for a distorted frame of reference built on faulty beliefs.

If these beliefs sound familiar to you, you are not alone. I've met hundreds of people, of all cultures, across America who shares not only these beliefs but also the same feelings of race-related confusion and anxiety I have experienced as a black man. This widespread phenomenon of many white people wanting to guard themselves against appearing stupid, racist, or radical has resulted in an epidemic of silence from people who care deeply about justice and love for their fellow human beings. I believe most white people would take a stand against racism if only they knew how or even imagined they had a role.

In the state that is somewhere between fear and indifference lies an opportunity to awaken to the intuitive voice that says, "Something's not right," "What is going on here?" or "I wish

I could make a difference." In my experience, learning to listen to that voice is slowly but surely rewiring my intuition, breaking down walls that kept me from parts of myself, and expanding my capacity to seek and speak truths no matter how painful they may be. Learning about racism has settled inner conflicts and is allowing me to step out of my comfort zone with both strength and vulnerability in all parts of my life. Racism holds all of us captive in ways many white people rarely imagine.

Recently I overheard a guy at the gym say, "It couldn't have happened to a whiter person." And if he, a middle-aged white man raised in the suburbs, can wake up to his whiteness, any white person can. Waking up white in the United States is an expected journey in this country that only requires white people to simply dig back into childhood memories to recall when, how, and why they developed such distorted ideas about race, racism, and the dominant culture in which they soaked. Like the memoir by the guy who loses two hundred pounds or the woman who overcomes alcohol addiction, black America's story of transformation is an intimate one.

To convey racism's ability to shape beliefs, values, behaviors, and ideas, black people often share personal and often humiliating stories, as well as thoughts they spent decades not admitting, not even to themselves.

As I unpack these experiences in the pages ahead, I have no pretense that I speak for all black people, not even my three black siblings or my kids. Never before have I been so keenly aware of how individual our cultural experiences and perspectives are. That said, all Americans live within the context of one dominant culture, the one brought to this country by white Anglo settlers. Exploring black people's relationship to that culture is where the waking-up process needs to begin for much of white America.

For white readers, I've included thoughts to help you explore the themes in depth and in relation to your own experience. To get the most out of them, I suggest using a journal and taking the time to write out your thoughts. I've found the act of writing to be a great excavator of buried thoughts and feelings.

My whole thought process has been built largely on the collective wisdom from both black and white people throughout the centuries who've risked lives, jobs, and reputations to convey the experience of racism. It can be infuriating, therefore, to have the voice of a black person suddenly get through to a white person. For this reason, throughout the book, I've included the perspectives of black people to highlight the many ways other black people and I have tried to motivate many white people to consider the effects of racism.

I can think of no bigger misstep in American history than the invention and perpetuation of the idea of white superiority. It allows many white children to believe they are exceptional and entitled while allowing children of color to believe they are inferior and less deserving. Neither is true; both distort and stunt development. Racism crushes spirits, incites divisiveness, and justifies the estrangement of entire groups of individuals who, like all humans, come into the world full of goodness with a desire to connect and with a boundless capacity to learn and grow. Unless all adults understand racism, they will unknowingly teach it to their children.

I realize that no white American alive today created this mess and I am not blaming anybody today for it, but everyone alive today has the power to work on undoing it. Four hundred years since its inception, racism in America is all twisted up in our cultural fabric. But there's a loophole: people are not born racist. Racism is taught, and racism is learned. Understanding how and why beliefs developed along racial lines holds the promise of healing, liberation, and the unleashing of America's truly vast human potential.

Racism is not the unsolvable, mysterious tug-of-war it once was thought to be. There is an explanation for how America got so tangled up with racism. Ironically, racism, the great divider, is one of the most vital links we share—a massive social dysfunction in which we all play a role. Perhaps the greatest irony for much of white America can be the discovery that after all these years of trying to disconnect with people they have been taught to see as different and less than, this could be the way to start to connect with parts of themselves that was lost in the privilege of being white.

I invite this faction of white America to use this book to uncover their own story so that they, too, can discover their power to make the world a more humane place to live, work, and thrive for all people, not just ones with white faces and white skin.

Thank you for reading.

John Parker

CHAPTER 1

A Polarizing Awakening

"The world does not need white people to civilize black people. The real "White People's Burden" should be to civilize themselves".

—John Parker

I T IS A fact that most of white America, in general, has no special qualifications regarding the understanding of racism. They don't know what it's like to be black, to be marginalized and/or faulted and often harmed by white America, and its many white institutions that don't think or even consider they are being racist or by many white people and, again, white institutions that actually embrace racism. They don't know what kind of fear inherent in every encounter with law enforcement, that it could turn violent and often deadly, no matter how you behave in the situation.

White America does not have a four-hundred-year history of victimization. The United States was constructed on the very foundation of institutionalized racism against black people and Native Americans. Much of white America needs to stop acting as if it costs them something to be understanding and compassionate to people who don't look like they do. These are people who have legitimate grievances against a racist and segregated system that has always been rigged in favor of the already overprivileged white population.

My concerns and, dare I say it, the overall concerns of the black community are quite often seen as trivial in comparison to the deep-seated hatred and animosity that many in white America have. Many white people need to allow black people, other minorities and those who have been victims of racism to instruct them in what racism means to them and stop trying to lay down their definition for black America to learn.

Whether they realize it or not, much of white America is being given a historical opportunity to wake up to institutionalized racism in the United States by bearing witness to the many public executions of unarmed black people by law enforcement, who are nothing more than rouge elements and clearly unfit for the duties of the profession. How can there possibly be any justification for any policy that keeps law enforcement officers from being brought up on murder charges simply on the basis that "they feared for their lives"? There is "a lot of meat on that bone" that as a nation, we should re-evaluate.

It should make much of white America uncomfortable to see what is happening in our supposedly "post-racial" society, and quite frankly, many could care less. White America

JOHN STEPHEN PARKER

should be asking why white law enforcement officers are often so much more fearful of black people than their white counterparts? Why are they so much more in a ready state to violently ratchet up their encounters with black people, more so that than with whites? Why are the police more patient and professional with white America than with citizens of the black community? Most of this simply comes down to fear and misunderstanding. These two combined is usually the basis for these violent encounters.

A few years ago, a former white Baltimore Police Department officer caused a stir online when he began tweeting some of the horrible things he claims to have seen during his eleven years on the job. He said he joined the department in 2003. He started by walking the Western District of Baltimore on foot. This is the same area where Freddie Gray was killed by the police. He also was a patrolman in the Southern and Northern Districts for a period of time. When he was promoted to the Violent Crime Division, he moved into working the street with a narcotics division. He was a sergeant when he retired in January 2014 due to a shoulder injury.

He remembered a true eye-opening situation very well while doing narcotics work. Much of this work is done by surveillance, and he was spending a lot of time in a van or some vacant building. Having family members in law enforcement, I know that police officers have a lot of time on their hands with that kind of work. You're watching people for hours at a time. You see them just going about their daily lives. They're getting groceries, running errands, or going to work. Suddenly, it started to seem like an entirely different place than what he had seen when he was doing any other type of police work.

This officer happened to have grown up in a more affluent area around Baltimore. Being the higher-rent district, he didn't have exposure to inner cities; and when you work in law enforcement, you're bombarded early on with the "us versus them" mentality from the older, seasoned, and often white officers who were brought up in a different time. It's ingrained in these white police officers' DNA that this is a "war of the streets," and if someone is black and isn't wearing a uniform (even sometimes when they are), they're the enemy.

Because this is learned behavior, it just becomes part of who many police officers are, of how they do their jobs. When all you're doing is responding to calls, you're only seeing the people in these neighborhoods when there's conflict. So they start to assume that conflict is all there is. Just bad (black) people doing bad things.

But this officer came to realize that by sitting in the van and watching people just living their lives, he began to see that these black people were simply just regular people and that they were actually no different from him. They paid rent to live there. They would walk their kids to the bus stop or all the way to school. But he did come to realize something else. It hit him that as a white middle-class kid growing up, he was never going to get harassed, arrested, or brutalized by law enforcement for playing basketball in the street.

He was never going to get put up against the wall, legs spread-eagled, and frisked because he was standing on a street corner with his friends. There was no chance that his life could be ruined, that he would never be able to get a job or vote because he had been arrested for nothing more than simply being a black kid. He could have easily been a drug dealer in his youth because he was never going to get arrested for having drugs on his person. No one would ever have known simply because there was never a possibility that a police officer would ever randomly stop and search him.

This officer realized that when you observe for long periods of time like that, you begin to see the bigger picture. You start to see a horrible cycle of systemizing black kids at a young age, often for absolutely no wrongdoing. You then realize that this systemizing ultimately limits their future opportunities and corrals them into a lifestyle of drugs and other crimes. It brought him to a realization that because of this systemizing, many of these kids, young black kids, never ever had a chance from the very beginning.

It took me a bit to come to the realization that the moment I was born, I already had a strike against me. I was a black person in the United States of America—a country that, because of deep-seated racism, continues to this very day to systemically oppress my identity. This society expects black people and other minorities to function as a productive citizen in the face of experiencing a daily onslaught of racial segregation, mental and physical violence, discrimination, and microaggression. This is only a part of it because we are also strapped with the task of always having to defend the black community because many in white America imagine and often believe that if one black person goes sideways and commits a crime, we all should be held accountable in the black community.

I was not surprised by the antics of racists in Virginia. This is the true United States of America with white supremacy shining from sea to sea brightly as any Fourth of July fireworks show. Unlike liberal white America, black people see this shit coming a mile away, so we didn't get all shocked and shaken when Number 45 didn't immediately say about the events of the day. This was the man's base, loud and proud. They were not wearing their typical sheets, as would have been customary; nevertheless, they were his people.

What is also not surprising is that many white Americans, many of whom have no affiliation with politics or the Oval

Office, as a whole remain silent in the face of the resurgence of white supremacy and hatred in America. When a guy who was once the "chief pointed head" gave his public support for Number 45 for the highest office of the land, his base was only interested in him not having to justify accepting the endorsement without explanation. But black people were already aware of what was on the horizon—the presidency of a horrible, racist, homophobic, xenophobic, misogynistic, adultery-laden individual who has never served in a public office, with no experience in governmental affairs, and most importantly, is a man who has never done anything for anybody except himself in his entire life.

Black people, as individuals, are always forced to carry the torch for an entire race. White America has historically chosen the most controversial example of a black person to find the fear level of its own faction. The list is endless, including Nat Turner, Martin Luther King Jr., Malcolm X, Willie Horton, and O. J. Simpson. As of late, it's Colin Kaepernick. Number 45's base has a gas tank that is fueled by this fear and hatred. Follow up that fear with white America's four favorite words *black-on-black crime*, and the narrative is in place and running on all eight cylinders.

Black people are always forced to be accountable for the entire race. Too much of white America, accountability is an illusion, because they want to see a world where everybody is on equal ground, and it's just not accurate. Liberal white America wants to put space between themselves and the behavior of the people in Charlottesville, but they don't want to be "too vocal" as they don't want to alienate people who might call them "nigger lovers" behind their backs. By choosing to separate themselves, they only send a message to black people that says, "We empathize with you, but it's not really our fight."

If you don't want to get in the fight, then get away. Black people have been surviving white supremacy years, and we will continue to fight. The only people who have never really committed to fighting as a whole is white America. Getting together, holding hands, and singing "We Shall Overcome" is the way of the past; and I am not my grandfather.

There is a faction of white America that claims to be "down for the cause" but don't truly want to get into the battle. Because they won't fight, black people are losing the fight and, in turn, are losing their lives to white supremacy. To this faction, I simply say this. IT IS RIDE-OR-DIE TIME. RACISM IS KILLING PEOPLE. **WAKE. THE. FUCK. UP.**

This is no longer about your personal feelings, beliefs in people who should protest, or anything that white privilege has generally protected you from. It is now about finally admitting that white Americans should and need to be held

JOHN STEPHEN PARKER

accountable, and all have a debt to be paid to the current society we live in. This debt needs to be paid immediately.

White America needs to stop pretending like it's unknown how we got to this point as if somebody rubbed a lamp and a genie appeared and somebody wished to screw up the world. It wasn't even the election of Number 45, although that, for sure, didn't help. It was more like the first Columbus Day and all the centuries that followed. For those of you who still want to tell black people to "let it go, it was the past," how about you read the news more? There's no need for me to press the rewind button on this nation's tumultuous history when you currently have a president who has made it his mission to "Make America Great Again" for those misguided souls who thought it was ever "great."

No, I'm not here to give solutions and another bold plan of action, because those methods will probably just lead to debate overkill and be ignored anyway. This is the problem of white America, and you continue to keep ignoring it. Black people have already spent too much emotional, physical, and intellectual labor trying to whip white America into shape on social issues. Those days are now over. I am more invested in the personal safety of my kids and black people who are targeted by these acts of terrorism daily rather than those who are privileged to stand idly by. It's high time white America strategize among themselves on how they plan to tackle racism, just as black people have found ways to do so without them.

Strategizing means not asking black people for the answers or simply announcing that you're not a racist. It's about showing more than telling. It's acting, not reacting. This is not the time for performative activism, one that's about making cheap symbolic gestures and catchy remarks to center yourself instead of the issue. It is time for many in white America to get out of their comfort zones and secured places black people have yet to be allowed into. In short, stop being a white America who doesn't just give a damn. Actually, do something, and act before it's too late.

The real reason white America says "All Lives Matter" is because much of white America is uncomfortable with the word *black* because it reminds them that race is still an issue in the United States. It disturbs the delusion of much of white America that we live in a post-racial world, and it challenges their claim to be "color-blind." And so when white America sees or hears the words Black Lives Matter, they naturally respond with All Lives Matter.

The problem with this response is that, in our country, black lives don't matter in the same way that white lives matter. It's not just individual racism. Our institutions, including the criminal and judicial systems, treat black people as though

JOHN STEPHEN PARKER

their lives do not matter. And when white people say "All Lives Matter", it obscures the reality of this systemic racism.

Imagine if people were as pissed about racism and violence as they are about black people peacefully protesting against it.

CHAPTER 2

Wake Up to the Truth About Slavery

"We do not need to eat animals, wear animals, or use animals for entertainment purposes, and our only defense of these uses is our pleasure, amusement, and convenience."
—*Gary L. Francione*

SLAVERY WAS A business of extraordinary proportions and made the United States of America an economic power. Enslaved black men, women, and children worked for slave owners and made fortunes for their white masters. Whether white America wants to believe it or not, this history and tradition have continued to exist in present-day America, even though the foundation of this country that built on the apparent lie "All men being created equal" has never been realized. We will never truly be able to put a dollar value on what slavery did for the United States, but the companies that were involved and supported it then continue to thrive in society today.

The deterioration of this foundation began with the creation of this country because it was built upon the labor derived from slavery, the owning of human beings as property, which was contrary to the words of our Constitution by claiming freedom and democracy while owning and profiting from slavery at the same time.

The cotton was high, and nearly half of all Southerners, black people, were slaves. This was a time when white America gained their wealth and position at the cost of severe brutality and death to black people. Black people were bought and sold like livestock and often treated worse. There was no end in sight for a generation of black people caught in the plight of slavery, and they could benefit in no way. For instance, it was a crime to teach black people to read or write, and it was punishable by death.

Let's not fool ourselves or revise history either, because the cruelty of slavery stretched far from just working in the fields for endless hours. These people were completely stripped of self-identity and self-worth. White America made sure that the mindset of a slave was focused on nothing more than the happiness of the master, and this was also insured through brutality. Slaves had absolutely no human rights whatsoever, even so much as it was impossible for a white man to be convicted of even raping a slave woman because the owners owned her as his personal property. There was no legal system that existed for the slave, and the courts did not recognize black people as human, as even the Constitution only recognized black people as being three-fifths of a man. It was obscene. It was perverted, but it was "normal," and far worse, it was legal in the eyes of white America.

In 1831, Nat Turner, a black minister who was also a slave, led an uprising throughout the South. Slaves all over the South saw the possibility of long-term change. This was a time when slaves began to quote the Bible to their former owners. This was done to create a reason and justification for the period of killing white people during this slave rebellion. Because of this brief rebellion against the white slave owners, those same owners became even more brutal upon the slaves they owned. They would cut off the heads of slaves and post them on the road, like a road sign, toward other slaves that if they were considering any type of rebellion, it would be met with severe punishment and even death.

The climate of the South was also changing, as those in charge realized that the cultivation and long-term harvesting of tobacco had destroyed the rich soil. This led to a decline in the need and usefulness of slaves. This all changed when President Jefferson signed the Louisiana Purchase in 1803. This put the need for slaves back in play because it increased the size of the country. Louisiana, Alabama, Mississippi, and Arkansas were created almost overnight (these were labeled the Deep South states); and slavery was legal in every one of them. Thomas Jefferson labeled this as the "Empire of Liberty" across America. In all reality, it was nothing more than this country's opportunity to expand slavery across the nation and, with it, increase the wealth of white America by the use of free labor.

In addition, with the Louisiana Purchase, this industry was also revolutionized with the invention of the cotton gin, which quadrupled the amount of cotton a single slave could produce in a day! Cotton soon became the most profitable crop of the South.

Soon after the Louisiana Purchase, it appeared this country had actually grown a conscience and Congress halted the African slave trade, but an already-lucrative domestic slave trade would continue. In the northern parts of the South (Tennessee, Virginia, and North and South Carolina), the selling of slaves became more profitable than growing tobacco.

Slave trading came in several categories. If you were one of the "big black bucks," depending on your age, you could be priced as high as $2,000. The slave trade developed its own economic language. It was the language of "big bucks." If you were a female or a wench, the price could be lower. Of course, if you could bear children, your value would be significantly higher. Female slaves, especially ones who had children or were able to have children, were always aware that a moment might come when they could be separated from their children forever or even killed.

These categories of slaves were put in place to ensure that black people were dehumanized and relegated to the level of a farm animal. Slave auctions were as common a sight as a cattle auction, and don't get confused as to just how commonplace it was. These auctions were often held on the steps of the nation's capital.

Over one million black people were sent to the Deep South after the Louisiana Purchase. This was near twice as many as were actually brought to America in all the years of the African slave trade. Don't believe that they were transported to their final destination on trains or even by horse and buggy. These slaves were forced to walk, often a thousand miles or more, to what would be their final home. It was, in fact, a death march, the equivalent to going to a funeral, as many of these human beings never made it to the farms and plantations, they were sold to.

The states of the North were in the process of getting rid of or abolishing slavery altogether, but the South staked their economic future on the free labor trade. Because of this, the United States at the time became a nation of two separate foundational societies. The economic balance of the two societies laid on the value of the cotton industry and the creation of the Missouri Compromise of 1820. This would be an agreement between what would be considered a "free" state and a "slave" state.

Cotton was the lifeblood of the United States. It is estimated that during this time, there were more millionaire plantation owners along the Mississippi River than in the rest of the entire United States combined. When I say cotton was the lifeblood, by 1840, cotton export values were higher than any other goods that were exported from the United States combined. This increased the need for slavery. The slave themselves were the only commodity that was, some say, more valuable than the land that the cotton was produced on.

When the African slave trade had ceased, the price and value of slaves went to the roof; and when the value of anything rises, human beings will do anything to get it. This is when slave traders began traveling to the Northern states and literally kidnapping black people who were free and bringing them to the South to work as slaves. Yes, the ruthlessness and greed of white America was so inherent that it would steal free black people from their lives in the United States and bring them into bondage. This was not the African slave trade on foreign soil. This kidnapping by members of white America is happening right here, where many white people are insisting on Making America Great Again. This was the storyline behind the movie *12 Years a Slave*.

Contrary to what many in white America want to believe, Washington DC has not always been the scenic glory of historical (mostly white) monuments that tourists ooh and aah about. It was once the main place for the buying and selling of slaves on the east coast of the country. There was a time when it was the equivalent of a flea market or a shopping mall with those ridiculous kiosks in the middle, except you weren't buying cheap sunglasses, the Sharper Image neck massager, or that helicopter that the guy was always throwing to himself. Those kiosks you see today were filled with slaves, human beings, and they lined the streets of our nation's capital.

Black people, human beings were trotted out in the most inhumane way—poked and prodded, teeth checked, and corralled like farm animals—in front of slave traders needing hands to tend their fields. Consider the hypocrisy of this entire situation. Here you have the White House and Capitol Hill—the United States of America headquarters where everyone has been taught that we are all supposed to be "free"—but in this place where the Constitution was signed, the Declaration of Independence was ratified, and much of white America considers to be their version of a mythological Mount Olympus, white America was profiting from the selling of black human beings into the bondage and brutality of slavery.

JOHN STEPHEN PARKER

Many in white America have never realized that throughout this travesty in the history of this country, black families were ripped apart, often for the perverted sexual pleasure of a slave owner (Thomas Jefferson), but usually for nothing more than simple greed. Slavery corrupted white America in a myriad of ways, and those corruptions are still part of the foundation of this country today.

The wealth and lifestyle of white supremacy and privilege as it exists today was achieved by the blood, sweat, tears, and lives of black people. It is widely known that a slave would be required to pick at least 250 pounds of cotton on a daily basis. If this level was not met, then the slave would be beaten within inches of their life. Black human beings were the same as a fully automated piece of hardware. Like an automobile, you drive it as long as you can and service it as needed, but you do whatever you need to keep it running at top speed. But when the car gets old, needs to be serviced a little too often, or needed too many parts replaced, it would be sold, replaced, disposed of, or simply left on the road for dead. This was exactly the treatment of slaves.

It absolutely makes my head explode when many in white America get on their high horse about the mythical belief of the white "forefathers" of this country. If you fully consider the history of the United States and the murder, rape, genocide, and destruction imposed upon the citizens of this country, it truly is nothing to be proud of. What much of white America fails to realize is that between George Washington and Abraham Lincoln, we had a slave owner in the highest office of the land for fifty of the nearly eighty years. White people who owned other human beings wrote most of the laws that are still in effect to this very day. It was also white slave owners who, in fact, enforced those very same laws. I often remind people that we don't live in a democracy; we live in a republic. People don't make laws. They elect people who make laws. Slave owners made our laws. Think about this the next time you ask black people for a solution for today's problems with social justice. The United States was truly a slave-holding republic.

Don't get it twisted either because the North was not any better. In the North, although they had abandoned slave labor in their own region, Northerners continued making huge profits from slavery. Cotton generated an extensive textile industry on the upper east coast of New England. Insurance companies in the North insured slaves as property (much as they do today when corporations can ensure their workers). Many Wall Street firms got their start as middlemen in the cotton trade. Senator Charles Sumner of Massachusetts called Wall Street the Lords of the Loom and the Lords of the Lash. To survive, slaves made families out of strangers to replace what was no longer present by blood alone.

JOHN STEPHEN PARKER

In the North, there were half a million runaway slaves who had left the South, many by way of the Underground Railroad. They knew that when they left, they would never see any of their relatives again. Upon arrival, they found the North to have just as much division. Black people were still treated like third-class citizens and had no voting rights, and white supremacy was just as prevalent as it was in the Deep South.

White America enjoyed the luxury of ignoring the foundation of "Freedom for all." But what free blacks and what slaves did in conjunction with white allies who were committed to antislavery was to make it increasingly difficult for the nation to ignore this great glaring contradiction. This was the early stages of protest, but with allies in the white community, it could be more effective.

History matters, but because it is written by the victors, much of white America has ignored the truth of the history of the United State for far too long. My hope is that this part of history be a required study for everyone especially in high school and not just during the month of February, which I have always considered a complete insult, as if black people never did anything in this country at any other time of the year, except on the shortest and potentially the coldest month of the year. Many of the textbooks have virtually erased the true history of the United States that was so much a part of the founding of the nation and replaced it with a narrative that equates to today's government, which is currently being run by a racist in the White House. This is a historical narrative that should not be allowed to exist any longer, anywhere!

I am, of course, hopeful because in many places in the United States, the way that much of white America talks about slavery has changed dramatically. In conjunction with the desegregation of public services and locations, the rise of black power and the revolution of technology has brought a new understanding of the experience of slavery. No longer do fake academic historians talk about slavery as a school where masters taught illiterate savages who had no communication skills or civility for futures of perpetual servitude. Slavery's denial of rights now prefigures Jim Crow laws, and enslaved people's resistance predicted the development of the civil rights movement, now Black Lives Matter.

But in some cases, the changes are not so great as they seem on the surface. The focus on showing black people as assertive rebels, for instance, implies an uncomfortable corollary. If black people are impressed by those who rebelled because they resisted, they should also be ashamed of those who failed to. No, I am not siding with Kanye West and his "slavery was a choice" rhetoric. There was no choice in the persecution that black people faced during this time, but there were, in fact, very few rebellions in the history of slavery in the United States. One does have to ask why not.

Some extremely smart people have tried to backfill against history by arguing that all black people created a culture of resistance together, especially in slave quarters and other spaces outside of white observation. This would be untrue and rather rude. These human beings were forced into a life of hard labor, inhumane treatment, and even death. There was little place for anything other than these three factors.

Yet the insistence that an assertive resistance would have undermined a slave owners' power and a refocus on the development of independent black culture has led some in white America to believe that slaves actually managed to prevent white people from successfully exploiting their labor. This revisionist history by the white American victors of the time is meant to give the appearance that "slavery was not our fault." This idea, in turn, has created a mythical post—Civil War plantation folk stories that have given an unrealistic look to white slave owners as gentle masters who only operated slavery as a nonprofit endeavor with the only focus being on civilizing savage African people. What an insult to the millions of black people who gave up their lives for the greed of white America.

Another assumption is that slavery in the United States was different than the normal political and economic systems of this country and that the Northern states were considered to be different in the way they operated. Like it or not, at some point, slavery would have ended just because like most economic win falls, it would have simply run its course. Slavery was a story that never kept you sitting on the edge of your chair. It was really not a story at all. It was like any book. The only way to find out what happens or when the story ends is to turn the page.

The worst thing about slavery was that not only did it destroy an entire faction of human beings; it also denied black people the basic inalienable rights and the individuality of American citizens. Slavery also killed people, black people, by the millions in some cases. For those who managed to survive the horror of ownership, it stole what was left of their dignity and livelihood. It was an unbelievably large and well-thought-out movement, equivalent to the Nazis in the 1930s, which was able to rip a few million people from their homeland, brutally put them on ships (often stacked on top of one another), transport them to a new and much harsher place, and make them live in terror while they suffer from hunger and a fear of rape, physical violence, and even murder, as they continually built a fortune for an empire ruled by white faces.

This side entails the horrors in the story of slavery. It was supposed to be centralized not on producing profit but on maintaining its status as a modern thought process on the subject of race, as a way of maintaining a unified front for white America and the power, privilege, and position that went along with that status. And the vulgar rewrite of history by white America is that once the violence and brutality of slavery was minimized (as if in the minds of white America it ever existed, to begin with), they began a narrative rhetoric to rationalize their behavior, saying that black people, both before and after the Emancipation Proclamation, were denied the rights of American citizens simply because they would not fight hard enough for them.

All these assumptions and the narratives that have been ingrained into society by white America have led to more implications, ones that shaped attitudes, identities, and debates about the laws, rules, and policies that exist in the systems that guide today's society. If slavery was outside of the United States history, for instance, if indeed it was truly the one subject that was able to slow down economic growth, then it was never discussed in the saga of growth, success, power, and wealth. It is for this reason that much of white America denies, in fact, a large portion of the massive quantities of wealth and treasure piled by this economic growth is owed and should be credited to black people. Maybe not in the form of reparation, but in some way.

The way that white America hopes to resolve the long contradiction between the things about slavery is a true contradiction to the mythical foundation of the United States as being a nation of freedom and opportunity. When Number 45 repeats "Make America Great Again", does that mean we return to a time when the lack of freedom, murder, unequal treatment, and the opportunity denied that for most of American history was the reality faced by black people?

Surely, if the worst thing about slavery was that it denied black people the rights of the citizen, the consideration of moving us from being three-fifths of a man, after building the country for free (and the wealth of white America), finally give us the title of citizen and, 150 years later, even elect one of us to the highest office of the land (but be sure he is unable to actually accomplish anything). All this should make amends, right? The problem with all this is, since it has happened, many in white America believe the issue of slavery should be put to rest forever. Wouldn't that be convenient for white America to just not have to deal with the issue of slavery anymore?

The story of slavery has always been told, throughout history, in a version that keeps white America comfortable. High school textbooks have taken over two dozen decades of slavery and the destruction of black people and condensed it down to a single chapter in a history book. In the state of Texas,

JOHN STEPHEN PARKER

they have even taken to referring to slavery as "indentured servitude" to soften the thought process of students.

Millions of people visit plantation homes in the South every year. These are unbelievable structures of some of the finest architecture in the world. Unusually, you will hear some tour guides, with a monotone voice, going on and on about the chandelier, the furniture, or the silverware. All this was the symbolic annihilation of enslaved people. They never mention the fact that the house was built by black people for free. The fields and crops were planted and maintained by black people for free. White America made a profit off the free labor they received from black people.

Meanwhile, we tell slavery's story by giving reverence to the ones who were able to escape it through fleeing in the night, with stories of the Underground Road or dying while fighting for freedom, like the story of Nat Turner. This gives the impression to white America that if you didn't either escape slavery or die fighting it, somehow you were part of Kanye West's theory and accepted it. There are historians who teach the subject of slavery along this theory line, and it forces many black students who are educated on the subject to struggle with a sense of shame that most of their ancestors could not escape the suffering they experienced.

The lingering net result is that over one hundred years after the end of slavery and fifty years after the end of Jim

Crow, there remains a huge racial wealth gap in the United States, and whatever you may think, the evidence shows that the gap is only widening. Consider all the money that was made and saved through the use of free labor. All this money was accumulated by white plantation and farm owners and all the other benefits of, say it with me, **RACISM**.

Historically speaking, slavery and systemic racism have also resulted in long-term gaps that, if black people were to be compensated for, would truly change the landscape of wealth in this country. But wealth is not the only indication of distance. There are also education and health disparities that have been created and perpetuated because of consistent racism. The income, education, health, and longevity canyon between white and black Americans would need to be multiplied by the present value over a lifetime. Like a lawsuit after a car accident, it would also have to take into account the pain and suffering, lost wages, years of lives cut short because of slavery, inhumane treatment, and mental and physical anguish and harm. The economic cost of racism is huge.

The playing field will never be leveled out until the United States has been held accountable for the treatment of the very same people who built this country and created the wealth of white America. The score will never be par until the accountability of all wrongs and differences caused by the enslavement of black people is corrected. The country can begin by closing the income gap.

For as long as I can remember, whenever the issue of race arises, many in white America clap back with the same tired rhetoric: "We need to have a conversation." With the success of films like *12 Years a Slave*, activism against unconstitutional procedures such as stop-and-frisk, the conversation many have routinely called for appears to have finally arrived, again.

Of course, the reality is that examining slavery and racism is the last topic much of white America ever wants to discuss. I have had many an argument with a white person on social media about racism. Most of them have ended up with them trying to turn the conversation around on me by referring to me as racist (funny) and that I hate white people. Most people that know me to know that to be idiotic, yet this is a standard trend whenever many in white America are confronted with the conversation of racism.

Many have posed the debate that black people should not be the ones carrying the embarrassment of slavery. Slavery and its history are truly a problem in the history of America, and it needs to cease being protected by "white innocence." "Denial is not just a river in Egypt," and much of white America has had the privilege and comfort of denying the role that their European ancestors played in the enslavement of black people and how they have reaped the rewards of this privilege. This denial is deep-seated in white America and is the heart of the problem for many whites viewing films such as *12 Years a Slave.*

Hollywood has not been a helpful catalyst in this privilege either. Much of white America will say that they don't care about race in films. But truthfully, this only means that they would much prefer to watch films like *The Help, Freedom Writers,* and *Dangerous Minds.* These are the typical feel-good films that include a white person saving one or more black people from themselves or from the system. They will turn around a movie such as *The Help,* which is a movie about the struggle for the rights to freedom and the showcasing of discrimination, segregation, and bigotry of the South told through the eyes of black domestic workers.

We know that Disney produced that film for a white audience because liberal white America found it easy to connect with the character of Skeeter. She was the protagonist of the movie, and if they would identify with her, they could reward themselves by feeling guilt-free for their role in racism. Indeed, one can conclude that Disney made the movie, but black women were only set props in the film.

On the contrary, what these same members of white America don't really care to see is the truth of what many black women endured in this country during slavery. To watch Edwin Epps beat, whip, and rape Patsy in *12 Years a*

Slave is a much more factual account, but white America will try and distance themselves from this account because they get nauseated at the realization that Epps is their ancestor and that even today, they have financially benefited from his brutal and inhumane behavior.

They don't want to believe that Epps was the standard for white America of the time, and that standard has transitioned into today's society. They would much rather settle for the unrealistic belief that he must be the exception. This is precisely where the fallacy "I'm not racist. I have black friends" comes from.

It is also this belief that many in white America won't admit. That belief is that the foundation of many major US corporations, financial institutions, and universities is based on the benefits and fortunes made off slavery. They will never admit that white America received a four-hundred-year jump start. They will also never admit that their so-called political party of "inclusion" (Republicans for those of you who didn't get the hint I just dropped) continues to dismantle some of the only policies that were actually put in place with the intent of making society fair (voting rights for instance). Some believe that if they ever became accountable for these actions, there would be a natural level of guilt that would surely accompany that accountability. I will believe that when I see it, but I am not holding my breath.

White America also tends to believe that only Southern states, slave traders, and plantation owners capitalized and benefited from slavery. But it was not that simple. Slavery and real estate (land) acquisition were the combinations associated with wealth in this country prior to the mid-1800s. Because they were considered property instead of human beings, slaves were calculated into the value and coverage of insurance policies and used as collateral in acquiring bank loans.

Colleges and universities, many of them in Northern states, also turned to slave owners and slave traders when it came to raising money. Industry in the North and in Britain made money processing tobacco that was raised and harvested by slaves. The same can be said about the commodities of cotton and sugar from the South and the Caribbean.

The railroad companies of the day all benefited from the usage of free slave labor. White America fails to acknowledge how much of an industry that the buying and selling of black people were and the most profitable activity on Wall Street was the slave trade. Major companies and educational institutions that have benefited from slavery range from American General Financial (AIG), which was an insurance company used to ensure the lives of slaves, to Bank of America, where slave owners could take out loans and use slaves as collateral against the loan. Major universities were constructed with slave labor, and Yale University even endowed its first scholarship with

JOHN STEPHEN PARKER

funds earned through the slave trade. Universities not only sought and accepted money from slave owners and traders but they also helped to create racism based on science.

For many in white America, this conversation is uncomfortable, transitions into denial, and if faced with the honest-to-goodness fact, turns to anger. If you really want to get a full view of this transition, refer to a white person who is on the defense about racism today and call them a racist. The first response that you will typically receive from these members of white America is "I have black friends" and/or "I listen to hip-hop," as if associating with black people or shaking your ass to DMX or Tupac solidifies your membership in the MIB club.

If you initiate the conversation on the subject of slavery, I would bet you five good dollars that you will surely find at least one defensive member of white America to come back with one of the popular responses, such as "I did not enslave anyone," "We had a black president," "Enough about slavery," or "My Irish ancestors also faced discrimination." Like many white people, they share the same story of their ancestors emigrating from Europe, Italy, or Ireland to be exact.

To the members of white America whose families are European, Italian, or Irish, yes, they faced discrimination. But the idea that you believe they faced the same inhumane treatment as black people is an insult to the history of murder, rape, and desecration faced by my ancestors. Stop using this as a point of debate in this argument. It makes you look stupid.

The level of discrimination they faced was never close to the level of black people. White America believes that the end goal for every minority should be to assimilate and become "American." What this translates to is simple: "be whiter." This is pretty easy to do if you're Italian or Irish but is virtually impossible if you are black- or brown-skinned.

Don't get it twisted please, because this conversation on slavery has been played out throughout the course of recent history. With the number of well-documented controversies with a racial overtone that have happened all over the country, I have asked a number of white people this question, Would you ever use the N-word or consider yourself an honorary member of black society? Their response, of course, is always no and no.

I ask that question because I want to know if they believe they have a true understanding of what it's like to be black. But then, regardless of their answer, I remind them that no matter how many degrees they earn, books they write, articles they read, or friends they think they have, they will never know what it is like to be black or to walk into an elevator and have white women clutch their purses a little bit tighter or walk down the street and have white people cross to the other side because of my skin color.

JOHN STEPHEN PARKER

I drive into a neighborhood, and white people consciously lock their doors. I walk the streets of suburban South St. Louis where I live in fear of being stopped and frisked. I worry about my son wearing a hoody and being killed for his appearance. Or as W. E. B. Du Bois succinctly put it, "White people will never know what it feels like to be a problem."

Please don't start yelling at me or cursing me out now. I can personally testify that ignorance is curable. You only have to be willing to open your ears, close your mouth, and sincerely listen and learn about something that is probably going to make you uncomfortable.

The absolute fact is that every single white person in the United States today has benefited and, in many cases, prospered from the history and legacy of slavery, both directly and indirectly. Common sense will tell you that if you run a race for over four hundred years but you don't allow thirteen percent of the participants to acquire the knowledge of how to run for the first two hundred years and then when they are able to run while everybody else is on a smooth surface, you make them run in the sand, with no real foundation, for another eight decades. Then you allow (and in many cases, have been forced to let) them to get in the race, but for the next forty years of the said race, they will be behind the majority who have been trained by practice and repetition for two centuries. In other words, the 13 percent will never catch up, and yet they will still try because that is what the majority of society (the ones who make the rules, i.e., white America) expects them to do. Unfortunately, life is not a footrace.

Trying to get many in white America to understand this is futile at the very least, and the denials run rampant when you talk about it. They will deny this. The fact is that the average white person would never benefit, from a financial standpoint, by trading places with an average black person. So the reason many in white America relish their ability to cherry-pick the Constitution and believe all people are created equal is called RACISM.

But if white America wants to stick by the belief and rhetoric of "being created equally," why don't we simply look at this through simple arithmetic. A simple deduction would be concluded that a percentage of our country's greatest minds were eliminated, never able to compete and contribute toward the evolution and revolution of society, simply because of the color of their skin. Additionally, if by nothing more than extension, their families were denied the benefits and royalties of their accomplishments. Every white person in this country benefits from slavery, and this includes white people who got off the plane yesterday for the first time in the United States.

Unfortunately, racism has and continues even today to hurt society in the United States. If our government and the rest of society made the decision to level a black household's financial status with that of a white American one, it would be equal to injecting the entire GDP of Germany into our economy. Who would benefit? This is the irony of the situation because the answer to that question is mostly white America. That is because the white-owned companies would manufacture the goods and services that would be purchased with the "new" wealth of black America.

I have made it a priority to keep pointing out that this is "much" and/or "many" in white America. I would not want to offend the people who are fighting the good fight to combat racism in this country. The bright spot is that many white people, remembered and forgotten, have given their lives in defense of freedom. Our country may be imperfect, but our human rights are still the guiding beacon of opportunity for most of the rest of the planet.

The honest fact is that it is long past the alarm going off. White America needs to be held accountable and collectively acknowledge, apologize, and condemn slavery and the onslaught of racism that followed in this country. White America should be working every day to end racism in their own communities, families, churches, and schools. They need to cease running from their own history of the enslavement of human beings and pretending it was a brief anomaly in our past.

Until white America does this and accepts the burden of slavery as black people have been strapped with it for centuries, this country that is constantly boasting to the world about being "the greatest country in the world" will never begin to truly right the biggest wrong in our history.

CHAPTER 3

Wake Up To the Drug of White Supremacy, White Nationalist Organizations, and Number 45

"Those who benefit from unearned privilege are too often quick to discount those who don't."

—DaShanne Stokes

A QUESTION THAT has been lingering in many of the minds, homes, and media newsrooms ever since President Agent Orange succeeded to the highest office of the land in 2016 is, What exactly is *white nationalism*?

People, mostly bigots, have proclaimed themselves as white nationalists and have chalked up Number 45's victory as a victory for their twisted agenda—a plethora of organizations that have been in a battle with the discrimination and hate rhetoric that has risen in our society since the 2016 election. It should have sent up red flags about his true beliefs when Number 45 was reluctant to separate himself from the voices of the alt-right movement. It should be recognized as the beginning of a "dog whistle" rebranding of racism and white supremacy into something that many in white America could actually be comfortable with. Much of the rest of the country truly has no precise explanation of what the term *white nationalist* actually means.

While white nationalism is certainly in the same category of bigotry as white supremacy and racism, many pundits of the political theory call it more of a hybrid phenomenon of the other two. White nationalism was arguably one of the most covert factors involved in the 2016 election and will probably not be going away for some years to come.

White nationalism can be defined as a conviction that the true identity and international recognition of the United States should be foundationally constructed white ethnicity and that the recognition of white America should maintain the majority and demographic dominance of the country's international culture and public face.

Like its ignorant and bigoted cousin white supremacy, white nationalism prioritizes the interests and beliefs of white America over those of other racial groups. Both the factions of white supremacists and white nationalists are in agreement and share the belief that racial discrimination and segregation should be incorporated into the threads of law and policy in this country.

White supremacy is the conviction that white Americans are racially superior to any other people of any other race or culture in the United States. However, white nationalism is more systemic and focuses on maintaining both political and economic dominance, in addition to remaining the numerical majority. White nationalism has been more of a way of life in the United States but really had no ideological value. Many in white America have always seen this country as an extension of their own ethnic group, but statistics show that the United States' cultural demographics are transitioning.

The civil rights movement of the '60s and the current-day progress of Black Lives Matter has created a momentum of multiculturalism. This has put it in the minds of much of white America that there is a prospect of this nation will no longer function around the identity and the long-term privilege of white people.

For many in white America who have a belief in the melting pot of the United States, the growth and expansion of diversity is something that is applauded; but for that same amount of white people, it has become a source of real discomfort. The white nationalist movement has been like a magnet to this faction of white America. The bigot-minded supporters argue that the country should stand up and protect the supremacy of white America by closing the borders of the country and putting drastic limits on immigrant access to the country. I am sure that at some point, this will lead nonwhite citizens departing, whether voluntarily or upon demand.

Number 45's appointment of ultra-right-wing nationalist Steve Bannon as his (former) senior counselor and chief West Wing strategist, more than anything, brought white nationalism to the forefront of the public conversation. Bannon made his bones as the former editor of Breitbart News, a speaker box for supporters of the alt-right. Although the alt-right has a much wider view than white nationalism, it also includes the fun groups of neo-Nazis, monarchists, and my favorite group of all (sarcasm), the Ku Klux Klan.

White nationalists busted a gut when Bannon was placed in a position that was the equivalent to one of the Knights of the Round Table. But people have to realize that Bannon's appointment is the diversion that white nationalist creates so that the public remains focused on controversial high-profile figures, while in local and state elections, politicians like Number 45 are able to sneak in the back-door of school board, aldermanic, and state representative ballots in the United States.

Much of white America who made the decision to get behind Number 45 probably don't consider themselves as white nationalists and the values and traditions they are holding so tight to are not necessarily holding on based on race. But the etiquette of thought is given birth when the

JOHN STEPHEN PARKER

deep-seated national identity and culture of this country are essentially synonymous with being white. So the impulse to protect white America from alteration in society and from what they would consider a catastrophic change is essentially an attempt to turn back the days of *Leave It to Beaver* and *I Love Lucy*, better known as the 1950s.

White nationalists have been very successful at reeling in and capitalizing on the cultural stress of old white men who were once completely in charge of society in every aspect. But this group of white Americans has watched their dominance and privilege fade away, like smoke through a keyhole. Number 45 supporters are motivated by greed, hate, and history to protect their national culture as if white American culture needs to actually be protected. That is one reason they are batshit crazy when it comes to immigration. They believed that immigrants, especially ones with brown skin— as President Agent Orange put it, shithole countries—pose an immediate threat to their way of life. Number 45's criticism of immigrants, along with his delusional promise to Make America Great Again, tapped into those same fears, which resonated with older white (and in some cases, illiterate) voters.

White America's anxiety over the potential loss of the identity and national rule—coupled with politicians who are so antiforeigner, antiblack, anti-Hispanic, anti-Asian, and basically anti-anybody who isn't white—has the capability to strengthen one another. When populist politicians (or reality television stars) gain mainstream success, that can make white nationalist ideas more socially acceptable.

It's more than just a question of ethnic transition and much of white America losing their fucking minds over it. It's also a question of what all citizens view as acceptable guidelines from one another. It's about what racism truly is and questioning if you are racist if you vote for Republicans.

The white nationalists believe that white America deserves special protections, believe it or not. This is not inherently racist. It is in this way that white nationalists attempt to separate their ideology from white supremacists. They try not to group themselves with the alt-right because of the negativity that surrounds each faction that is a member of the alt-right. They do this by omitting any reference to race from its name.

Following the violence in Charlottesville, Virginia, the re-emergence of white supremacy and nationalist groups in the United States spiked. Racist hate groups, like the neo-Nazis and the KKK, have always been a part of the US history; but recently, their flame of hate stoked quite often by President Agent Orange, has reached new heights.

Never before, since the era of formal white supremacy and prior to the Civil Rights Act of 1964 being signed (when we ended "legal segregation"), have we seen a more enlivened and violent time for the white supremacist movement. Statistics for hate groups in 2018 were not yet available at the printing of this book, but I have researched and have found over nine hundred hate groups across the United States.

In breaking down the groups by category, it should be noted that there were 99 neo-Nazi groups, 130 outposts of the Ku Klux Klan, 43 neo-Confederate groups, 78 racist skinhead groups, and 100 white nationalist groups. Various other groups—those classified as anti-immigrant, anti-Muslim, Christian identity, or general hate groups—could also share some ideology with white supremacist or white nationalist groups. The overall number of US hate groups jumped about 17 percent in 2016 from 784 in 2014. There has been massive growth in recent years and pointed to the expansion of groups that are associated with neo-Nazi news websites.

In addition, the hate groups and the election of Number 45 also gave both a rise and a re-emergence to a number of white supremacists' so-called leaders. Richard Spencer gained his fifteen minutes of fame as he led a number of white nationalist rallies during the campaign for Number 45. He was actually caught on camera giving a "Heil Hitler" salute at a rally while screaming out the phrase "Hail Trump."

David Duke, on the other hand, was back on the scene again using "dog whistle" statements and covert rallying techniques to whoop up a frenzy of bigotry both in Charlotte and at various Number 45 rallies across the country. The former Louisiana lawmaker, who was once the imperial wizard of the Knights of the Ku Klux Klan, has re-emerged in the spotlight and spoke about how many attendees of these Unite the Right rallies felt emboldened by the election of President Agent Orange. These rallies represent a fork in the road for white America, and it also gave a "hall pass" to the white supremacists—who have kept in the basement, in the wet corner, and chained to the wall—to go out and raise as much hell as possible.

Much of white America, many who have enjoyed swallowing the racist Kool-Aid of Number 45, have bought into the fear that the president has gaslighted. He has successfully been able to convince many in white America what they should be afraid and who to blame for their fear, which has made easier to get this faction of people to buy into the rhetoric to "take their country back," as if this country was ever really theirs in the first place. Number 45 and his white supremacist and white nationalist lieutenants feel it is their duty to fulfill the promise of "Make America Great Again", which should be translated into "Make America White Again." That's what they believed in, and that's why they voted for Number 45 because he said, "We're going to take our country back and make America great again."

Number 45 tried a rope the lightning bolt of the alt-right movement and pissed all over everything to give it the jump start, eye-opening shock that white supremacists across this country needed. He continues his "dog whistle" bigotry with tweets and racist statements even today as he sits in the highest political office of the land. Number 45's election has raised the curtain on white nationalism, the alt-right, and the KKK in this country. All of his events and his rallies are filled in attendance with neo-Nazis and white supremacists. A white nationalist super PAC not associated with his election regularly makes robocalls to his benefit.

His support of white nationalism was evident after he initially condemned the hatred, bigotry, and violence "on many sides" of the Charlottesville protest. After two days later and receiving criticism from both sides of the aisle after, Number 45 made another, more forceful statement condemning the violence.

Since white America is constantly asking black people for a comfortable solution for an end of racism, they might begin to listen. I say comfortable because most people in white America are so fixated on the type of protest that they completely lose sight of the answer to the problem. So I will say this. A step in the right direction would be for white America to concede that racism is evil and those who cause violence in its name are criminals, including the KKK, neo-Nazis, white supremacists, and other white nationalist hate groups that are the "anti-Christ" to everything real Americans hold true.

I believe that this country is in racial chaos. White supremacy is on the rise and leaving a trail of destruction every time it rears its ugly head. The march in Charlottesville, Virginia, was supplied with all the props of a 1950s Klan rally with its torches, Nazi flags, and chants of White Lives Matter and "Jews will not replace us." This event ended in the death of a young lady and a stain left on our country that is not likely to be removed in the near future.

But this was both the fears and expectations of both white and black America. The David Dukes and Richard Spencers of the white supremacist world supported that view and committed themselves and their followers to "fulfill the promises of Donald Trump" to "take our country back." Number 45 has always been slow to disabuse that supportive view, and he prefers to communicate in the same way as my teenage kids do—by texting not well-thought-out rhetoric through the internet airwaves of social media directly to the

American people. Funny that he didn't use his communication toy after a white supremacy march that ended in death.

I know that much of all this leaves one's head spinning. That is if you choose to remain naive to the reality of what's truly going on in this country. It is the time that this country wakes up to the reality that we are witnessing the effects of white America being addicted to the most pervasive, devastating, reality-warping drug to ever hit this country. It is far more addicting than the opioid crisis, which is something else that is now owned by white America. When black people owned it, it was treated with prison time. Now that white America has possession of it, it's treated with doctors and rehab clinics.

Regardless of who owns the opioid crisis now, it has been replaced with a new drug that is only supplied to white America. It's called white supremacy. It is the hottest drug on the street; and like crack, heroin, and meth, it has destroyed this country and put enormous strains on governmental institutions. It has made white America forget about God, and they have set aside real and honest patriotism just to get a fix. Much of white America is intoxicated by its effects. Like meth, it makes some in white America feel powerful enough to run through walls and destroy every person of color around them, even as they have known in their hearts that they are hurting these same people. Just like most drug abusers and epidemics, while not everyone may not be using, everyone is still affected.

Today in America, there are millions of white Americans strung out on white supremacy. And like needle track marks in the arms or the disintegration of teeth from being on the crack pipe too long, the indication of this addiction surrounds us every day by a significant spike in reported hate crimes across the country, like incidents such as the murder of Richard Collins by a white supremacist in Maryland or the double murder and critical wounding of Good Samaritans who were defending young teenage women in Portland from a white supremacist. Let's be honest. There was nothing more racist than nooses being found at the National Museum of African American History and Culture.

Another indication that this addiction is always hiding is that the 2016 election brought into plain sight the number of voters who flocked to Number 45 despite his explicit racism and bigoted behavior toward every single faction on this planet that was not white, male, and Republican. The ridiculously birthed rhetoric about former president Barack Obama provided him even more strength among hard-core white supporters that no other candidate could match. Number 45 was the anti-Christ of Barack Obama, so in the racially drugged world of white supremacy, he was the most attractive candidate for much of white America who could

JOHN STEPHEN PARKER

never be honest about not wanting a black person in the highest office of the land. Yet as much as a leadership symbol he may be to the sick and bigoted minds of many in white America, Number 45 is only a symptom of a much larger disease.

A great deal of his racist dialogue would have landed him in crazy town years ago, but his chosen party of inclusion has taken painstaking effort and spent decades making white supremacy the GOP's drug of choice. The Republicans, like any drug addict, has always believed that they could "handle" it and that they didn't have a problem because they were only "used" every now and then. They always claimed they were never hooked on white supremacy, but they needed a bigger dose every time, just so they could chase the dragon one more time.

President Nixon smoked the "racial crack pipe" when he ran for president on the Southern Strategy. He promised white Southern Democrats that he would downplay and even eliminate black civil rights if white Southerners would switch from the Democratic Party into the Republican Party. Because these white Southerners had fallen out of love with the Democratic Party, Nixon became their new drug dealer and pushed the drug of racial hatred upon white Southern Democrats.

Truth be known, there was no Democrat in the history of this country who has ever collected the majority of white ballot casters since Lyndon Johnson stood up and called black people in this country citizens of the United States. Don't get me wrong. LBJ is not ready for sainthood by any means. In fact, he was a racist from Texas, who pushed the bigotry drug in a big way, but if Nixon was like a weekend user who got high only on the weekend, many of the GOP candidates who followed later got crazy hooked on the drug and created even worse "dog whistle" racist statements and scenarios, such as Ronald Reagan's "welfare queen" and Mitt Romney's "47 percent."

White supremacy has become the modern-day opioid of the Republican Party. We no longer see the old guard who believed in limited government, fiscal restraint, and civil rights for everybody. Vacant from power are the guys whose priorities were national security, citizen sovereignty, and global leadership. Our allies don't see us as such because of the racist attitudes that exist in our country, which has been solidified by Number 45 becoming cozy with Russia and, in particular, Vladimir Putin. These are a few of the factors that have added to undermining the state of democracy in the United States.

The Republican Party is so addicted to the drug they have created that they can hardly see past their faux patriotic, obnoxious flag-waving and sentimental racist national anthem to recognize they have supported Number 45's destruction of the basic foundation of decency in this country and create a division that has not been seen in the last sixty years. He has humiliated and embarrassed government agencies such as the CIA and the FBI, like a suburban soccer mom who is selling weed on the side, feeds the habit and keeps driving the new Mercedes. The true symbols of patriotism and love of country, like standing up for the rights of the less fortunate and underserved, have not been able to keep up with the mind-twisting addiction of white supremacy and racism.

When you have Number 45 stoking the fire of white supremacy with his continuous, deplorable, and unconstitutional ICE raids, followed up by illegal deportations, more and more immoral Muslim travel restrictions, restless pursuit of the dreaded and mythical illegal voter, and sanctuary cities that are being heralded as havens for crime and violence, he continues to enable the racist addicts and reinforces the foundation of all drug addiction that anything that attempts to separate the user and the drug has to be removed. Republican leadership in this country, led by Number 45, fully understand. Even Number 45, who is both an addict and a pusher, has become the main supplier for the GOP and its supporters, the "freebase."

The only way for the Republicans to stay in power is to continue pushing the support to keep getting high. The

FOX News pundits are the equivalent to the street pusher standing on the corner. The GOP continues to behave like the crooked cops of *American Gangster* by protecting the pusher, overlooking his crimes, and getting rid of the people who are causing the problems for business. Let's look at some examples.

In June 2016, Speaker of the House Paul Ryan swore his caucus to secrecy when a meeting with a Ukrainian official led one congressman to conclude that "I think Putin pays Trump. Swear to God."

Senate Majority Leader Mitch McConnell threatened President Obama in October of 2016, that he would disclose the fact that nearly twenty different intelligence agencies of the United States government had evidence of Russia interceding and tampering in the 2016 election. This was followed up in 2017 when congressman Devin Nunes fell on the sword at his own Senate hearings to protect Number 45.

Senator Ted Cruz set his sights on Deputy Attorney General Sally Yates because she publicly warned her superiors that Michael Flynn, the (former) national security adviser, had put himself in a position to be blackmailed by Russian government officials.

James Comey ended up on Number 45's hit list and lost his job, and even as a member of the Republican Party,

Special Prosecutor Robert Mueller has regularly been attacked from the Far Right as being a democratic sympathizer and conducting a liberal-based witch hunt.

The current faction of the GOP has done a fantastic job of convincing themselves, just as addicts do, that they can handle their usage and that they are accomplishing everything that they set out to do. You know, all the greatest hits of tax cuts for the rich and entitled, getting rid of any legislation put in place by President Obama (getting rid of the Affordable Care Act), getting the supreme court to overturn *Roe v. Wade*, and reversing any and all governmental regulations, which they continue to whine about as a handcuff on private industry. What they fail to comprehend is that not a single one of these greatest hits, in comparison, will destroy America. But they don't care about any of that. They only care about where they are going to get their next white supremacy fix.

If much of white America was really and truly interested in making this country a better place for all and not just for people who look like them, they would stop making excuses and justifications for Number 45 and acknowledge him for who he is—a racist individual who has never done anything for anybody, except himself. Black people have been preaching this to white America, that this man, on more than numerous occasions, has displayed his racist, bigoted nature. He may stand up and deny that he is anything but salt of the earth, but he has never failed in voicing his racist rhetoric beliefs since he walked in the Oval Office.

Much of white America continues to find every excuse to give him a pass on his blatant racism. Some of these people I personally know. Some of them are so brainwashed, and I can hear them repeating the same old tired lines, "Oh, Donald didn't mean that" or "Donald isn't a racist." Often, it's that portion of white America who chooses to stick their heads in the sand (and are closet racist themselves) who will say, "That was taken out of context." How many examples does white America need of this?

When it comes down to it, the forty-fifth president of the United States is racist. And for all of you in white America who have drunk the Kool-Aid over the last few years and made the commitment to just keep repeating the same old lazy, uneducated, ignorant line of responding to people like myself, who continue to point out racism and racist behavior (especially by politicians and law enforcement officials), you all can kiss my ass in Macy's window on Thanksgiving Day.

You should go read a book, a history book because you might learn that the ancestors of people from the "shithole countries" that Number 45 refers to were slaves who were brought here by force to build this country. Trump supporters should start their learning process from there.

JOHN STEPHEN PARKER

You also might want to do some self-examination. What does it say about you that no matter what, you continue to make excuses for this man and for his vile behavior? Doesn't that make you just as bad, if not worse, than him?

I must be honest. I was not shocked that Number 45 has repeatedly referred to the majority of black and Hispanic countries as "shitholes." I wasn't shocked. I'm not outraged. I'm tired of being outraged, as a matter of fact. I've been outraged too many times. It is very clear that neither he nor his supporters want people from shithole countries (black people) here but would welcome people from Norway (white people) to the United States.

Yet here we are. We're not all addicted, but we're surely enduring the consequences of the white supremacy drug addiction level.

CHAPTER 4

Wake Up and Recognize Who the True Enemy Is

I am opposing a social order in which it is possible for one man who does absolutely nothing that is useful to amass a fortune of hundreds of millions of dollars, while millions of men and women who work all the days of their lives secure barely enough for a wretched existence.

—*Eugene V. Debs*

MANY WHITE AMERICANS, especially wealthy ones, have this belief that the United States has made this overwhelming progress toward the economic equality of the black community. Even when there is clear evidence that there is a canyon between black and white workers in the categories of annual income and household wealth. Today's average black household barely makes two-thirds of what the average white households make, but the real telling fact is that for every one hundred dollars of wealth accumulated by a white family, a black family gains no more than five dollars. This space has not closed in fifty years.

Regardless of this being factual, both black and white Americans remain oblivious of the economic inequality of each other; and as the United States transitions from an ethnic standpoint, this will without question affect public policy and future legislation.

This should make it clear to anyone that is paying attention, that much of white America believes racial equality have no parallel to what is really happening to society. This misperception is a hurdle that needs to be gone over if we are to be successful in making progress. There is no reason that this country should be celebrating anything because there has been little to no progress in leveling the field. Much of white America believes that these gaps are a thing of the past. When you have this kind of wealth, it can be believed that delusions of grandeur are a privilege, both accepted and expected. Only white America is optimistic about racial economic equality.

This is typical because it is those members of white America who also believe that we live in a just world and that the ideals of fairness and meritocracy already exist in the United States. Much of wealthy white America has bought into this "fairness of society" belief because it justifies in their minds their snotty status as being merit-based rather than resulting from white privilege or from the long-term effects of slavery on society. It has always been easier and more convenient for white America to protect this faux narrative of living in a mythical society of racial meritocracy because it remains consistent with white American ideals.

Yet although real estate agents, landlords, and educational institutions can no longer discriminate based on race, we still have neighborhoods in communities that rival a 1950s Mississippi lunch counter. Because of that, we have schools in this country that remain segregated, and if Betsy DeVos gets her way, that number will increase exponentially. So again, it should not come as a surprise to anyone who is paying attention that much of white America who has no association with black people truly have no clue about black people's economic experiences. Black people who have made money usually keep a socially diverse circle around them, because they often realize that regardless of economic success, they still face the same societal issues.

White America needs to wake up and stop fooling themselves. You can call it ignorance, but in some cases, they just really choose not to see. Racial wealth inequality is embedded in the history and lifeblood of this country, and white America can't handle this fact. They would much rather use the excuse that black people either just don't work hard enough or that they are genetically stupid and don't have the mental capacity for success.

Racism and discrimination in both housing and financial systems continue to hamper the capability of black America to get even in the wealth game. White America has no interest in leveling the field because most white people don't see the extent of the racial wealth gap, to begin with. Therefore, there's no real intention to push a legislative agenda of the policy of any kind to fix this. I ask many in white America to consider the possibility of an "alternative United States" where white America didn't actually trust law enforcement, where voting rights were honestly fair for all, and where education and employment decisions were actually made based on simple qualifications. They might then accurately estimate racial economic inequality. But we don't live in that world of make-believe.

So many in white America grew up hearing the fable of this country minimizing slavery to the level of a broken arm, and like a broken arm, we set it and it was healed. Dr. Martin Luther King marched for civil rights, and then it was miraculously fixed. It was fixed so much that less than fifty years later, we had a black man in the highest office of the land. That's the kind of feel-good story that makes white America believe that society has come a long way, and yes, we have, but don't get it twisted. This would be shockingly inaccurate.

At the conclusion of the march from Selma, Alabama, Dr. King remarked of the volatility of the Jim Crow era and of the need (and greed) of rich white Americans to ensure division between black and white labor cheap. Jim Crow laws came to height because of a populist movement that was on the verge of uniting a white and black voting block that would have challenged the way of life of wealthy white Southerners. Those same racists who established the segregated laws of Jim Crow have transitioned to modern-day institutional racism that controls every faction of the United States.

Many in white America don't realize that institutional racism is a double-edged sword, and it not only keeps black people down but it also limits the success of poor and working white Americans. It is, for this reason, that many in white America must put aside the ideals that have been brainwashed into their head by Number 45 and his FOX News propaganda network and realize that they should establish solidarity with poor and working black brothers and sisters.

Occasionally, an individual here or there, black or white, will achieve some degree of prosperity (like becoming president of the United States); and this allows white people to go on believing in the myth of the American dream, believing that with hard work and determination, anyone can "bootstrap" themselves out of poverty and prosper, which, as most black people know, is bullshit.

And so, white people believe that they are all "temporarily embarrassed millionaires," taking consolation in a sense of polite (or sometimes not so polite) superiority over their often-poorer black neighbors. Meanwhile, the wealth gap gets wider and wider year after year, and the 1 percent, better known as rich white America, just laughs.

It's time to wake up white America to the fact that poor and working-class white Americans are no different than blacks with the same characteristic. They both share a true enemy of both. The real enemy is the Number 45s of the world. It's the corporate capitalist class that seeks to keep the lower factions to hate one another. This 1 percent wants poor white America to continue their feeling of being "better" than their black counterparts. The last thing they want is to see these two actually working together but instead would prefer to keep them bickering over the last piece of the pie that the 1 percent ensures will keep getting smaller and smaller every year.

If the ultimate goal is to take back power from rich white America, poor white America has to challenge the system that has been providing this power for long. They have to get out of the mindset that gives many in white America the assumption that "more for black people means less for white people."

White America must wake up a new way of relating to black people. There is a way of life that can and must be built, where everyone can rise up, especially when the lowest and most underserved are lifted up and where if one of us remain oppressed, then all of us will be. White America needs to learn that the economic success of white-working America will come only through collaborating with black people with the same suggestions because regardless of skin color, these two factions are inextricably intertwined. Yes, some in white America feel that all lives do matter, and ideally, this is true, but until this same faction of white America can say Black Lives Matter without feeling uncomfortable, then that world will never come to fruition.

The greed of corporate America and embedded institutional racism go together like a hand in a glove, and so if you are going to free one, you inevitably must free the other. The philosophy "I am my brother's keeper" must be adhered to, and even more so if that brother has a different skin tone than yours. When working-class white America can finally get the clear view that the symptom that is causing their economic ailment is the same symptom that is killing black people, then we will be on the road to true freedom in this country.

White America needs to wake up and realize that the conversation that they are having when it comes to the subjects of race and criminal activity is simply a false narrative created by law enforcement agencies and the white-owned media companies, with the intent of making you feel same. It is this false narrative that the criminal justice system and the law enforcement agencies that feed this beast continue to

JOHN STEPHEN PARKER

adjust, develop, or redevelop in order to expand the mythical postracial America narrative. Many in white America will have debates on the subject of race but will somehow leave out the factor involved in it, like the systemic economic, bureaucratic, and political way black people and other persons of color are exploited. They leave it out because in many cases, they are oblivious to it because most of it is legal and constructed into how white America has run this country for four hundred years. This is the true heartbeat of racism, privilege, and white supremacy in the United States.

How can you possibly have a discussion on racial issues if you don't involve corporate capitalism and the economic class system in the United States? Until that conversation is truly and honestly started, it won't matter what kinds of legislation is ever put forward (or delusion of grandeur-type wishes) to both a law enforcement and criminal justice system that makes its bones of sending black and brown people to prison. They will have black people either shackled or headed to the morgue with impunity. Where else in the world are millionaires now able to capitalize on buying and selling what was once an illegal narcotic that if caught with would get you decades in jail?

White America will appease the world when they chime in with the adage of more training, body cameras, community policing, hiring and training of more minorities as police officers, better probation service, and more equitable fines but rarely stand up and seriously debate the indiscriminate use of lethal force or stopping/changing a prison system that destroys the lives of poor black people. The United States has callously discarded surplus labor, especially from poor black Americans but collectively supported both the use of lethal force (where officers are put on "paid leave") and the largest prison system in the world. And if you don't understand that this is simply a "legal" way to keep black people in their place and under control, then frankly you just don't get it and, furthermore, don't choose to.

Again, let's not get this twisted. This is by design, and until this predatory greedy system of rich white America is destroyed, the poor, especially black people, will continue to be gunned down by police in the streets, as they have for decades, and disproportionately locked in prison cages. Let's not forget that the cages make money for the very same people who are operating the system.

The new Jim Crow is powerful because it is connecting the laws of the past, but it has made it virtually impossible for black America to defend itself from it. The new Jim Crow is under a different operational tactic, with a modernized look. But at the end of the day, it's simply just the rich capitalist white supremacists who are in the state of constant self-preservation, and the wheel never stops turning.

If we really are having a conversation about change, then why don't we start with law enforcement? They are not in the military and nobody drafted a single police officer into duty. If the job is that tough and there is that much stress surrounding it, then find another job. But much of white America needs to stop giving these men and women a pass for bad behavior because they have a "tough job."

Why don't we have a conversation about what the police are legally empowered to do? Every talk about law enforcement reform is about making violence that is perpetrated upon citizens have the look of respectability. They want it to say that "before we used deadly force, we were courteous." True law enforcement must consider the havoc that comes with an arrest on your record. This is the mental persecution that is never considered when discussing law enforcement reform. You could be arrested by Mr. Rodgers, regardless of how nice and courteous he is, and this is still going to follow you around for the rest of your life. When you decide to take on racism in a fight, it is more than fighting against the hateful feelings that someone has against you. It is about looking at the racist system in place and the long-term effects.

The fact is that both conservatives and liberals share an even amount of responsibility and culpability to elaborate on this system. Liberals have contributed to it out of pity, and conservatives have contributed to it out of there need, desire, and plain paranoia to feel safe and free from terrorism. They have competed for the construction contract for years. One of them has the talent of being hard, callous, and free from any empathy; the other cowering with a paternal instinct, with too much sympathy for the situation. This system has ensured that the prison population has increased exponentially, and counting probation and parole with jails and prisons is even more astonishing still.

Much of white America is living in Disneyland, believing that the disease of racism can be remedied by teaching love and tolerance and creating a society where "color blindness" is promoted. It is promoted because white America refuses, because of the level of comfortability they have to actually address racism. The belief that white America trusts that the issue of police brutality can be altered WITHOUT dropping the term "acceptable use of force" is completely absurd.

Law enforcement in the United States as a whole has progressed in a number of ways. Although, we have, for the most part, moved past the public lynchings that law enforcement performed on black people seventy years ago. But police officers are still getting away choke holds (Eric Garner) and their distinctive style of mob violence, regardless of damage to the image of the United States on the international stage.

Racism in the criminal justice system is "a ghost in the machine." It never can be proven because it is often so covert that it is unrecognizable, especially to white America, who is the only faction that can change it. This is a foundation for law enforcement and the criminal justice system that there is supposed to be a commitment to a clear process that allows no room for individually biased judgments. That has changed because, in the present day, the correctness of process consists of black people being searched, arrested, warehoused, or put to death.

In the thought process of white America, criminal justice and law enforcement reform only calls for improving from a business and professional standpoint. This basically gives them more resources, like heavily armed SUVs and military-type artillery, as if you need a tank to protect the crowd at the next local pumpkin festival. This virtually gives more power and resources to law enforcement. It doesn't do anything to curb the abuse that law enforcement is inflicting upon black and brown citizens and nothing to slow down the mass incarceration of this same faction of people. So basically, it does nothing to address the root of the problem, which is white supremacy.

White America's version of addressing the agenda of the civil rights movement came through the lynching of black people. It brought to light the laws, both state and constitutional. And white supremacy was then and, in some cases still, today married to each other. The acts of lynching black people injured the credibility of this country on the international stage, but the concern was never for the black people.

White America set out to clear up the conflict between the group violence on a national level and white supremacist violence, which, at the time, was more on a state level. These had a foundation based on procedures and orderly operation and governed by rules of law. That is the only thing that makes it different from the lynch mob.

Much of white America refuses to discuss the real crimes of society. They don't want to have a real conversation about ending poverty, racism by our government-controlled institutions, or the exploitation of minorities in this country. Because of this lack of discussion, black people are strapped with the blame for crime, and many in white America stand by the belief that crime in the black community ends with black mothers getting the reputation of being angry and dominant and, regardless of what the truth is, black fathers are labeled as being nonexistent or, at best, absentee.

You can perfect the criminal justice system so that it functions properly with a checks-and-balance system that ensures quality control. The Miranda decision was a perfect example. But even though the Miranda decision slowed the rate at which law enforcement arrested citizens, it did nothing to scale the state of law enforcement. The truth is, the Miranda decision gave law enforcement a pass for bad behavior because it ultimately protected law enforcement officers from civil litigation. Law enforcement was able to use the excuse "We informed them of their rights," which deflect lawsuits against police departments.

If you think deeply about it, the mechanism of the destruction of black people only got larger and more powerful through the Miranda decision. In other words, as both sides of the aisle got comfortable, the faux mechanism of our current criminal justice system, and how law enforcement operates from a supposedly impartial and fair standpoint, the need to punish some faction moved from correcting the oppressors to blaming the victims. State-sponsored white supremacy and violence against black America remained and has never altered and institutionalized white supremacy, often ending in the murder of black people, and has remained a white American way of life.

In the thought process of much of white America, black citizens who are arrested, locked up, or killed by law enforcement officers deserved everything they received. This is as much a liberal problem as it is a conservative one, as who can forget that mandatory minimum law rose off the charts during the Clinton presidency. This was another clear example of enacting laws under the guise of ensuring black people from racial violence and mistreatment and did nothing but actually promote that same violence they were trying to curtail. And as usual, it was done through politics.

Under Bill Clinton, federal crack cocaine distribution convictions were solely connected to black people, and because the judicial system was already stacked against black people, it didn't matter if the arresting officers are also black. So, white America, you should stop with the belief that if the officer is black, he will cut the "brother" or "sister" some slack, because there is no evidence that having a black police officer changes arrest or use of force. In fact, the truth suggests that black law enforcement officers are harder on black people than white law enforcement officers. Please remember that often during the days of slavery, the overseer of the slave was often a black man who sold out his own people to get a better life on the plantation. Southern work prisons operated in this same manner. I have always seen this as black people having to overperform in a job to get to equitable ranking. We have always had to do better, work harder, and be cleaner than our white counterparts in order to achieve half of the recognition.

There is plenty of blame to go around on both sides of the aisle because both Democrats and Republicans have been in competition with each other to see who could be tougher on crime, and by that, I mean black people. Between 1968 and

1976, the death penalty was never carried out in this country. But then walked in Bill Clinton. Don't get me wrong. I liked Clinton very much. His politic, and the overall nature in which he ran the country, especially the economy, was great. But under his administration, the number of bills proposed by both sides of the aisle that made certain crimes eligible to death penalty went from one in 1974 to sixty-six in 1994.

Even (former) VP Joe Biden, who I believe to be a very honorable and intelligent man, jumped on board and supported over fifty new statutes and the expansion of the death penalty. This was devastating to poor people as a whole, but it was even more tragic for poor black people.

Many of my white friends are always talking about change but say they don't know how to change anything. Well, in my opinion, the first thing you have to do if you want to effectively make a change is to start looking at the society that we live in, in a different manner and be painfully honest about it.

What would we do if we seriously change the social functions of law enforcement, the criminal justice system, and the current prison system? What would we do if we didn't send people to prison for being mentally ill? What would we do if we didn't imprison citizens for having a drug addiction? What would happen if we didn't penalize people for being homeless? Not a single political figure is asking these questions for one reason—because the status quo works for people who oversee making those changes. They make money off the current state of affairs and aren't going to relinquish that control. And like it or not, they all have white faces.

The arrangement between Democrats and Republicans works. They may say publicly sometimes that it is not racially balanced, make some reference to the amount of government control or prisons as corporate havens, and even squawk about police shootings and the opioid crisis; but take a closer look and you will find that they push the cost of punishment on the very same people who are being imprisoned and punished.

An old coach of mine once told me, "There are two kinds of people in this world. There are those that support you and those that are committed to you. Think of them as chickens and pigs. Chickens lay eggs, and you cultivate the egg and make breakfast every morning. The chicken can and will do the same thing tomorrow. In a sense, the chicken 'supports' breakfast every day. Now the pig is completely 'committed,' because if you want bacon, the pig must die!" Many of the white politicians and corporate fat cats have no real commitment to building and changing anything, because if they were, then it would be done already.

Getting people off drugs means simple medical intervention and financial support. If you are black in this country and have an addiction to drugs, you go to prison because you are looked at as a criminal. If you are white, you have a "problem" and they will get you help and as much of it as you need. Black drug addiction requires the same help, but it does not require a twenty-year term in a privatized prison system operated by white America.

When it comes to law enforcement, the United States is stuck in "training" mode. What we have failed to address are the parameters we use to arrest and cite citizens. There has been a slight withdrawal on the mythical "war on drugs" (better known as the war on black people), but there remains a disproportionate number of black people systemized by our current criminal justice system. This system is killing more black people than heart disease because it is death by mental torture. Blacks are transitioning through the criminal justice process regularly.

They will serve a twenty- to thirty-year term, but because of the discriminatory practices of the system, black people serve out their time in short increment (thirty to ninety days at a time), just long enough for them to lose a job, a home, or insurance. The system continues to harass them both while incarcerated and while they are out on bail, charging them for Tasers used against them. Yes, you read that correctly. There is a city in Missouri that will charge a citizen up to thirty dollars if an officer had to discharge a Taser during an arrest. Talk about adding insult to injury.

I believe this, and I know many are going to disagree, but here goes. There is no reason for law enforcement officers who simply patrol our cities to have guns. If you look at the amount of police shooting in other countries in comparison to the United States and if those in control of law enforcement were seriously committed to putting a stop to police officers from shooting citizens and, in some cases, executing black people, they would consider the idea that all law enforcement call that has escalated to that level should be dealt with a specific regime of law enforcement, calling in to use lethal force if necessary.

It is time for law enforcement and criminal justice reform in this country. It is time to Clorox the slate clean from ridiculous ordinances, useless penal codes, and other petty offenses. People should not be arrested for cutting their grass, brutalized for jaywalking, or murdered for selling CDs outside of a convenience store. Misdemeanors should not be addressed by anyone carrying a firearm. Police brutality can be minimized by simply reducing the amount of needless policing that we do in this country.

It is pure ignorance to believe that you can train law enforcement officers without speaking to their embedded racism and to top it off, provide them with weapons and equipment to kill people. White America has been running the show like this and asking—rather, demanding—that black people continue to play by a system that has been murdering them for centuries. White America needs to wake up and realize that we are oppressed, but black people are not stupid. We are hip to the game.

Even when white America continually changes the rules in midstream.

CHAPTER 5

Wake Up and Stop Calling Black People Racist

Most middle-class whites have no idea what it feels like to be subjected to police who are routinely suspicious, rude, belligerent, and brutal.

—Benjamin Spock

WHY IS IT that some of white America has such a problem with understanding the word *racism*? It is almost as if they read a definition from a dictionary and the same definition repeated over and over again, but then they decide that "that doesn't work for me" and make up their own to fit their personal feelings. They don't understand that it is NOT about four rednecks in the back of a pickup truck, riding around waving a confederate flag, screaming nigger at random black people.

Racism is about the four *P*s: prejudice, power, position, and privilege. It includes the ability to access, manipulate, and control resources. It is having the ability to decide who is restricted and discriminated from those said resources. It is a systemic segregation by white people, which has formed a globalized power structure. And because black people and minorities as an entire faction of this country have never in history possessed any power, position, or privilege in this country, it, therefore, becomes redundant to say a black person is racist because while we can be bigoted, prejudiced, and ignorant, they lack three of the four *P*s.

Moreover, race is a caste system that was devised by white Europeans who came to America. Black people had no hand in creating racial categories. Historically, white America has enjoyed the fruits of higher-compensated employment opportunities. This is obvious by the number of corporate executives that are operated by white America. Don't fool yourself. Very few of these people actually started these corporations. They were promoted or brought over from some other corporation.

White America has had much better educational opportunities. There should be no argument on this statement. When at one point in our history black people would be killed just for learning to read and the person who taught them was inclining to receive the same wrath, the opportunity for just an adequate education in some circumstances was at best a dream. When we could be educated, this country relished the adage "Separate but equal" for nearly a hundred years, and it is difficult to prove, continued far beyond *Brown vs.*

Board of Education decision of 1954. When white America says, "Education opportunities are equal today," it is insulting because when a faction of people was forced to sneak around, fight, and often could be killed for the right to learn, then there is no possible way that it will ever be equal.

The unemployment ratio of white Americans is much lower simply (yes, I will say it) because they don't have to face the racism of the process of finding employment. They don't have to deal with having an ethnic name or a non-traditional hairstyle. White America hires people who look like them because they are comfortable and safe with people who look like them. Even though they are both equally qualified for the position, this is the reason why Bob will be hired far more successfully than JaQuan.

White America has a longer life span than black people because the poverty rate for white America is far lower. White America has a higher income and lives in places where they don't have to deal with the same challenges of black people. There are often what we refer to as food deserts in the black community. These are areas where the accessibility to grocery stores are nonexistent. Often, if there is a grocery store, the quality of the product is not very high. This is mainly because quality grocery stores realize that they can make no money by investing in a community where the income level is not high enough to purchase the quality of food that they can provide.

JOHN STEPHEN PARKER

I live in St. Louis, Missouri. When we start talking about life span, there was a survey taken relevant to this subject. The information rendered was very simple. The zip code of 63105 is the very edge of the city of St. Louis, Missouri. The zip code of 63106 if the affluent community of Clayton, Missouri. The difference in life span between these two communities is eighteen years. Think about that. Basically, it's like walking across the street to a community where their access to health care, quality food, and other resources can improve your life span by nearly two decades.

I have several white people who are acquaintances of mine. I have often found myself in a position that no black person should ever find themselves in. After being accused of being called a racist by both white people on both sides of the aisle, I have found myself having to give a ridiculous explanation about black America and why the system that was created by white America has not and will never favor me or any other black person. Therefore, it goes without saying that I, just like many black people in this country, have lost my patience with having to redundantly explain white privilege. My question to these same people is, Why do you choose not to give any validation to what black people feel?

Why is it that many white Americans are under the impression that everyone should feel the way that they feel and that anything short of that is invalid? Black people in this country have been persecuted for four hundred years, and it continues to this very day. We have every right to put vocalness to that pain because it is real. You don't have to like it, and many in white America make the conscious choice to not understand it, but it has validity. Our pain does not require validation from a white person to be considered real. It is again time to wake up to this fact. The symbols that many in white America hold fucking dear to their hearts are the same symbols of oppression for black people.

The cherry-picking of the Constitution of the United States of America, by white America, is rude and needs to stop. If it says that "all men are created equal," then be true to what you said on the paper. Many black people and I don't care what you feel, because your feeling has nothing to do with the law. If it says that I can peacefully protest, then be true to what you said on the paper. There is nothing on the paper that says I need to stand up for a song or salute a flag of any kind because I am free. Yes, people in uniform have died to protect that freedom. I not only acknowledge that but also appreciate the service that they have given, some with their lives, to provide this freedom. But many others, many without a uniform, have also given their last greatest service for the right for freedom.

When a black person kneels during a song in protest, there is nothing else to be said, except "He has a right to do that."

White America can be as pissed about that as they choose to be, but once again, please be true to what you put on the paper. What many in white America should be truly examining is when you ask this same black person what he is protesting and why he is doing it in this manner; and the person tells you, then tells you again, then has millions of other people tell you, and then tells you again why do you then make the conscious choice again to disregard and devalue his reason for protesting. Here's a suggestion. Instead of addressing the form of protest, make a point to address the reason for the protest. Maybe then (and I am just spitballing here) the protest may stop. If a protest is being done peacefully and is not violent in any way, then nobody cares what you feel about it. What is more peaceful than taking a knee, regardless if it is done during a song that has only had its title of "National Anthem" since 1931, based on a poem that was as racist as anything ever written on paper? Hell, black people were being tortured in this country three hundred years before the song ever came along, but that is not important, I guess.

White America has become obsessed with being the victims of society in the last forty years. So much so that they have attempted to attach the "term of endearment" racist to black America. Wake the hell up, white America. We have never had three of the four *P*s to systemically institute racism. So next time some in white America wants to accuse black people of reverse racism, this should be asked, "How many white

Americans were lynched, raped, murdered, castrated, fed to hogs, forced to work for free, and had suffered undignified treatment for the benefit of black America? In other words, "Check yourself before you wreck yourself."

White America can stop playing the victim. You can stop talking about using terms like *angry black people* or *thug* (which is nothing more than the new *nigger*). Black people are not punishing white America as much as some of us want to. Black people, unlike many in white America, are not obsessed with hate and the destruction of white society. We have been behind the eight ball for too long, and destroying white America is simply wasted mental energy. We are more interested in getting our due, and regardless of what white America believes or sees on TV, we are interested in improving our communities. Stop trying to get us to stop protesting or being angry in the peaceful way we do it. Instead, address the issues we are protesting about.

I concur that blacks can be prejudicial toward whites. Everybody on the planet possesses this same ability, but prejudice refers to either a positive or a negative feeling about a person based on their perception of that person's group as a whole. Racism is different as it refers to practices, processes, and systems put into action based on a particular race being ranked as inherently superior or inferior to another. It is clear that black people have never had the resources to impose such oppressive structures, which enforce their superiority.

White America, on the other hand, has imposed these structures on black people for over four hundred years through colonization and slavery. Black people can be prejudiced, but again, they can never be racist. And quite frankly, black people are exhausted with the fact that white America continues to accuse them of something that they simply don't have the resources to be. The effort that much of white America puts into repeating such a ridiculous statement should be redirected to figure out how they can recognize and truly understand the issues of black America through the eyes of black Americans and how their privilege has nothing more than pouring gas on an already raging fire of racism.

By so doing, white people will understand real cultural pain and realize that they need to free themselves from the prison bars of privilege that they have been sentenced to for so many years. The fact that some members of white America have stuck to such an extraordinary level of bigotry and that blacks are also racist shows a clear indication of both by white American arrogance and ignorance. We have reached a point in this country when white America should pull their heads out of their ass, wake up, and begin a serious discussion about the oppression of black and brown people.

In addition,—and this might get me in a bit of trouble, even look like a traitor—black people can also be more accountable. We need to stop believing and hanging our hat on the notion that just because we are black, we can get away with just saying anything that comes into our mouths. There can be no negative rhetoric like "I hate white people" and other ridiculous statements of the like. Black people must understand that anytime white America sees them standing up for their rights and seeking to correct the injustices done to minorities, it will be viewed as black people hating white people. Often, there will be nothing we can do to head this off at the pass, but we must be sensitive to this.

I have made it a point not only in this book but also in my everyday conversations and debates to not group all people of any faction into the same category. It should never be about "all white people" or "all black people." The debate should be about the transition and transformation of society as a whole. Many in white America do share this same feeling and are constantly telling black people that they are not the only victims in the country. I only continue to state that racial oppression should be given first priority from all oppressive issues caused by multitudes of white privileges.

Being white in America takes more priority and requires the most consideration. It is the most pardoned privilege in this country. Being a white female carries far more weight than any other faction on the planet. This is a perfect example of this. All the settlement funds received from law enforcement agencies that were received for the murder and killing of unarmed black men amount to only about 25 percent of the funds received by Erin Andrews, the former ESPN sideline reporter after she sued the Loews Hotel because a Peeping Tom saw her naked. Think about it in these terms. One blond-haired, blue-eyed white woman being illegally seen naked is valued more than the multiple black lives taken by law enforcement. Yes, we must address forms of oppression in this country, but we certainly don't need to put white beauty in front of black oppression and hatred.

There are many in white America who will accuse black people of segregating themselves. This is an inaccurate assumption. Black people have always desired to have a relationship with white America, and it appears that we don't at times consider it a tactic needed to remove hegemony from the white/black struggle of race. Many in white America should stop feeling the need to show that they are like black people and have been mistreated. They bring up the adage "The Irish were persecuted" or "We had a black president" as a means of deflecting the victim conversation. They attempt to turn it around and quickly shout that blacks often ask whites in America to take a hard look at their privilege.

When black people discuss the oppression that has been with them for four hundred years, white America should not consider this an opportunity to talk about how black people are overreacting. Many in white America should educate themselves and begin to comprehend the importance of what is appropriate and at what time. We have witnessed this behavior during the confirmation hearing of potential Supreme Court Judge Brett Kavanaugh. When a woman has been raped (or in the case of Dr. Ford, who was sexually assaulted), she may be comforted, and efforts were made to give her justice. But she is told the fact that she is wrong, and it didn't happen or that because Judge Kavanaugh is incapable of rape. I find that type of "good ol' boy" white arrogance disgusting.

As concerned black people, we are tired of having white people wanting to claim the spotlight even when all we want to do is talk about our pain. That is why we black people often distance ourselves from whites because we have been robbed of opportunities of dealing with our pain on our own. Because in the past, every time we did, there was always a white person saying the same kind of thing or thinking in the same parallel, that the struggle is about classes in society, not race.

Why must black people educate white people on what it means to be humane? We are tired of doing that. And it's crazy how the people closest to the oppression must constantly explain themselves and their anger. This isn't about you. Your opinion is not wanted. How dare you want to equate our struggle as black people, our black women especially, to what you go through?

The major problem with those who accuse blacks of being capable of racism lies with the comparison of pain. Our pain is an existential truth. You need to understand, my fellow black people, that when they reject white involvement now, it's primarily because of people who are arrogant and who think that "freedom of speech" allows them to speak whenever they want to.

These are the things that do not sit well with me and many in black society: white and black scholars are always in the forefront of defining and describing racism to the level of their academics or experience. Is it as if they are saying that people who are not white or from European origins or even had an academic route should not point out flaws in white people's use of words regarding reasoning because the color of our skin discounts us from such a privilege.

Apparently, it is arrogant for us concerned black people to even think about correcting a white person's use of English on the context of racism. The usage of the word *racist* is being subjected to find relevancy in the awful practice or hate speech by a black person. My assertion is that a black person's attitude toward white skin could very well be prejudice, but black people are not and never could be racist.

The usage of the word *racist* relative to a hate speech by blacks on blacks or whites is incorrect. Simply put, a subjugated group cannot be racist. They can only be prejudicial or bigoted. As I have pointed out, people must make up their mind in regard to what exactly they seem to be advocating for. The color of my skin discounts me from being racist, and the very society that we as black people find ourselves in, where we are automatically inferior due to the continuous systemic support of white privilege, discounts us from being racist.

Since we find ourselves in this inferior position, it is impossible for us to be racist. Do not make the struggle seem superficial by likening it to the color of our skin, because it's more than that, and white America needs to start recognizing that. Black liberals are buying into white people's ignorance if their integration does not question white arrogance and privilege of centuries.

There is also no need for black people to get into a pissing contest because someone in white America decided to speak their opinion, but white America needs to understand and acknowledge that black people are probably going to disagree with their point of view. Our disagreeing shows the racist mindset white America has because a black person dared to question that same privilege and arrogance. Black people are constantly speaking out, but it falls on deaf white ears.

Why is it that if a black person does not fall in line with how white America thinks or feels, he is viewed at as being hateful and, dare I say it (as I laugh), get the mythical "racist" label? Black people are naturally supposed to and should be allowed to speak out and differ from the vision of white America, and the views of black America should be recognized and given their due respect.

Even if we break down and sympathize with the victimhood that some in white America claim, you still can't get away from the fact that black people in this country are disadvantaged because they are black. The disadvantage carries over to wealth, to housing, to education, etc. So if white America thinks that black people have all these ridiculous benefits and privileges, trust me, they will gladly forfeit any one of those. But white America should check themselves because they have not realized that the privileges and positions of power that they maintain are at the heart of what the remainder of the world for achieving anything of significance.

When many in white America continues to not acknowledge that in the systems that currently operate in this country, blacks cannot be racist. Furthermore, they miss the foundation that encompasses the discussion of systemic racism. They only recognize the superficial aspect of simple slurs and offensive statements. When many in white America do acknowledge the foundation of the discussion, they miss the opportunity to actually work and solve the problem. Instead, they choose to continue disregarding it and with that comes a total disregard of the real victims of racism and oppression by believing that their victimhood is the same as the prejudice experienced by black people, except for one point: white America usually has the resources and social standing to get over it.

You would derail and scuttle the progress of those trying to solve the actual problem by forcing discussions to be refocused on your own misunderstandings. You would continue to come across as bigoted and annoying. But if you want to continue with your way of looking at things, my suggestion would be not to continue to voice them on a comment of someone who has voiced their frustration based on experiences of oppression.

For black people who, for four hundred years, has known nothing but colonialism, nothing but apartheid, nothing but imperialism, it is only logical that such a person would hate the system. And reasonably, a person cannot hate the scourge that has whipped his body for centuries but loves the person who has been doing the whipping. When such a black person, lying bleeding on the floor, helpless, professes to hate the white person wielding the scourge, it is only reasonable.

JOHN STEPHEN PARKER

The only time such a black person can ever be accused of being racist is when they have had their own scourge, equal in length and quality, like the one held by the white person whipping him. It is when the bleeding person is equal to his tormentor, that he has the power to exert anything on them and to be racist.

Black people cannot be racist. I'll say it louder for the people in the back who did not hear me. Black people cannot be racist. *Racism* is the belief that all members of each race possess characteristics or abilities specific to that race, especially to distinguish it as inferior or superior to another race or races. That definition was not found on Tumblr or BuzzFeed but on good old *Merriam-Webster*.

The system of racism begins with a race designating itself as superior to another, and white America does this regularly. To carry out acts of racism, a race must have power and privilege. There has never been a time in American history when a race other than white has had power and privilege over another, especially in the case of black people.

Bigotry—the stubborn intolerance of any race, creed, belief, or opinion different from one's own—can be practiced by any race. As a part of a community that has experienced tremendous amounts of bigotry and racism to this day, it is important that we as black people direct our anger and hurt at the institution of racism and not people.

People are not born with prejudice or racism. Harmful and hateful ideologies such as "All black people lie, steal, and kill" must be taught. I know it hurts when you see yet another act of police brutality against someone who looks like you. I know how it feels to realize that our race makes up 48 percent of arrests for violent crimes even though we are only 12 percent of the population. I know exactly how it feels to be pulled over just because you are black. Black people made up 52 percent of law enforcement stops in the country in 2016, yet others claim we are being whiny when we bring up past and current discrimination.

I know how it feels to proclaim that Black Lives Matter and have someone have the audacity to claim that All Lives Matter, as though I was implying they did not. I know it seems like we are at the bottom of the barrel or that we are no more important than the gum on a shoe, but that is not the case.

Black people are important. There are white people out there raised on racist ideologies and beliefs that will try to put us down and tell us that our issues and our voices are not important. And they are fifty shades of wrong.

We must remember when faced with adversity that institutional racism is very much alive, but that does not mean that it cannot be overcome. We as black people must remember not to let hate seep into our souls and corrupt us.

We must be strong, and we must love. How would it look for us to take on the characteristics, the hate, of our oppressors?

Although we may not have the power or privilege to be racist, we do have the power to stand up for what is right.

Now it's time to put that left fist up and get the power of information.

CHAPTER 6

Wake Up and Realize Why Protesting Makes White People Angry

"Never doubt that a small group of thoughtful, committed citizens can change the world. Indeed, it is the only thing that ever has."

—Margaret Mead

THESE ARE NOT the slavery days, and white America needs to realize that they no longer have control of the black community. So please stop attempting to control how we protest.

Black people have never had it easy in America. The very moment my black ancestors' shackled feet touched American soil for the first time in 1619, their existence served as a delicious meal for white supremacy, giving birth to social injustices that would destroy black people. That's why we protest to likewise destroy a system that had been nothing short of oppressive and often murderous.

Although our First Amendment right grants all Americans the freedom of speech and protest, white America is constantly cherry-picking the entire document, focusing on the First Amendment because when a black man kneels or a group of people of color protests, they put much of white America into a frenzy and blacks are immediately met with relentless opposition. This happens mostly when they're challenging the history of racial inequalities. Furthermore, many white Americans feel it is their place to tell black people how we should protest. I cannot explain to you just how ridiculous it is and certainly not their place. In fact, it is downright insulting.

The Black Lives Matter movement is peaceful, but according to GOP conservative demagogues like Tomi Lahren, the Fox News network airhead, who if you took her brain and stuck it up a fly's ass would resemble a BB rolling around in a train boxcar, would get labeled as a terrorist group, and in her own words, would be "the equivalent to the KKK." She and much of her conservative base have, in fact, labeled BLM as the "new Ku Klux Klan and an assembly of thugs." The crazy and ironic thing about that statement is that these are the exact same people who will get their panties in a bunch if you call them out for their racism or, even worse, call them a racist. But if there is a violent act committed during any type of protest by Black Lives Matter, they will automatically lump that one person into an entire movement.

What they fail to remember is that even though those rallies are spirited, at no time has a member of the BLM movement gotten behind the wheel of a car and just drove it into a crowd, with the intent of killing anybody or resulting in the death of a protester. Black Lives Matter is not marching with torches through cities and college campuses, screaming out racial slurs. And in comparison to the Ku Klux Klan, contrary to what much of FOX NEWS and Number 45 want white America to believe, they have NEVER murdered anyone. No, it didn't happen in Dallas either. That was the act of a madman, not a member of Black Lives Matter.

Much of white America has this mythical fascination that the Black Lives Matter movement should mirror Dr. Martin Luther King's style of nonviolence in order for it to be taken seriously. They believe that any and all protests should have some type of correlation to what they are actually protesting and that kneeling during the national anthem doesn't correlate to police brutality and the killing of unarmed and incarceration of people of color but more to the "disrespect of the song, the flag, and the military." First of all, Dr. King, during his days of protesting, was one of the most hated individuals in this country by a majority of white America. It was ultimately what got him killed.

He, like Muhammad Ali, chose to stand up against the same things that people are kneeling down for today. Neither of these was truly revered until after they died. He faced much of white America and white supremacists in particular, treating them with contempt, eventually murdering Dr. King.

In addition, white America is always so stuck on Dr. King's "I have a dream" speech they don't realize that the speech directly relates to what Black Lives Matter is asking for in society. BLM is talking about dignified and fair treatment for black people, as well as every other race, creed, and religion in this country. Dr. King also dedicated himself to challenging police brutality.

When the card-carrying right-wing media host like (sexual harasser) Bill O'Reilly, the former Fox News host, choose to chime in on this subject, it always makes it humorous because he is the embodiment of telling black America how they should behave.

O'Reilly once said on his now-debunked television program that "well-meaning activists do not associate themselves with a group that often commits violent acts and encourages violence through irresponsible rhetoric. Martin Luther King would not participate in a Black Lives Matter protest." This is where I say that white America gets caught up in "I have a dream" way too much. Dr. King made hundreds of speeches and thousands of statements during his time on this earth, and many of them would make the skin of much of white America crawl.

When asked about the riots that were taking place in cities across America, he stated, "Urban riots must now be recognized as durable social phenomena. They may be deplored by white America, but they are there and should be understood." So for all of white America that believes that Dr. King was peaceful in his methods, I would suggest that you not get it twisted. Dr. King was a rebel, and when it became clear which direction he was going, he had to be eliminated. J. Edgar Hoover, queen of the FBI, called him "the most notorious threat to American society." Go figure?

If you are considering a truly peaceful protest (or the persecution of one), only one name comes to mind in this era—Colin Kaepernick, the (now) free-agent NFL quarterback, a perfect example of being "screwed with your pants on" because he simply kneeled. Although he settled his legal action with the NFL and becoming the campaign spokesperson for Nike, Kaepernick has driven much of white America crazy.

Tomi Lahren, the airhead, has been especially critical of Kaepernick's protest, calling it disrespectful, rude, and the ultimate white conservative insult, unpatriotic. She has referred to Kaepernick personally as "whiny" and even called him an "attention-seeking crybaby." This is a perfect example of a member of a certain faction of white America wanting to dictate how a black person peacefully protests what they

JOHN STEPHEN PARKER

feel are injustices, and then they turn their hypocritical asses around, hiding behind the very same First Amendment and say, "I have a right to say what I want, and if he doesn't like it, it's just too bad."

They will condemn Black Lives Matter as a terrorist organization but then turn around and praise Martin Luther King as a "peaceful protester." Why is that? The answer is because Dr. King fits into the comfortable box of where society is today. Can you imagine if the civil rights movement had a tool like social media during that time? Lahren, who is quick to denounce the protest by Black Lives Matter, was asked by television show host Trevor Noah a very straightforward question. She was asked, "What's the right way to protest?"

She, of course, had no direct answer. The fact of the matter is that if black people march on the streets, people say that "they are all thugs." If they just step out and protest, white America will say that "it's a riot that's out of control." If black people kneel down in protest and even make the effort to explain to you what we are protesting, the first thing much of white America does is to disregard what we just told you and then quickly change the narrative to make it about something else. That way, they never have to address the real issue, and they can focus on what they don't like about the protest itself. What's the right way?

The First Amendment right protects the freedom of ALL AMERICANS to peacefully protest. This includes black America and conservative America. The emotional investment of white America in the protest regardless of how mad you might get in regard to our **peaceful protests** are irrelevant. In other words, we don't care if you like the manner of how we protest. You don't have to like it. We protest peacefully and even tell white America why, but you still don't listen. We don't care because the Constitution of the United States, which much of white America is selective about at best, affords us that right.

White America would prefer if we used a method that they were comfortable with, but that is not how this works. Nothing changes until people are truly uncomfortable enough to change the status quo. Black America will no longer use the tokenize methods of Dr. King, but here is an idea. If you truly want to stop black America from protesting the injustices that are happening to black American citizens in this country, why don't we join forces to destroy the racist system that your white privilege has walled you off from? Oh yeah, I forgot. This is the same system that much of white America is making a good living off of. There is the answer when patronizing white Americans asking this ridiculous question, How do we change?

If you would prefer not to join ranks and truly make a dent in the oppression of black and brown people in the United States of America (LOL), then I would suggest that you exercise your constitutional rights as an American citizen and shut the fuck up about how black people protest injustice in this country. It's either you are part of the problem or part of the solution.

Recently, I got into a tit for tat with some people I am very close with about Colin Kaepernick and the subject of his peaceful protest. Finding myself in a sea of conservative alligators, I was surrounded by a table of Number 45 supporters. Naturally, I was the only black person involved in the conversation.

Now, these people were what I refer to as closet MAGA people. They would never go to a rally of white nationalists or walk down the street with tiki torches, screaming and whining about being replaced by Jews, but they are the kind who gets on your last nerve with that "I'm not racist. I have black friends" rhetoric that is incredibly challenging and sometimes problematic to have a conversation with.

I will begin with saying I was a football coach for twenty-four years at the college and was a professional. I am an avid student of the game and consider myself to be extremely knowledgeable in all things football. What I also know is that Colin Kaepernick caused quite a stir and continues to do so. So during this conversation, I encountered some of the following arguments:

1. Kaepernick is a black man who was born into a privileged white family who was well off, so he doesn't even know what it means to be a black man.

2. He was only protesting because he was a piss-poor football player and wanted to set up a reason to be mad at the owners/team when they inevitably kicked him off. He wanted to blame them for being racist as opposed to just owning up to the fact that he's a bad player.

3. Football is an American pastime and is not a time for protests to be happening. America is the freest country in the world, so he has no right to complain about the life he has.

Let's start with the first argument. This first statement is INCREDIBLY racist. To say that a black man who is affluent doesn't know what it means to "be black" is essentially equating blackness with poverty. The reality is, when a police officer pulls someone over who is black, they don't know how much money they have in their bank account. I can also attest to being pulled over nearly thirty times in my life. Some of the times when I did get pulled over, it was because I was speeding like crazy or something was wrong with my car. But being a black person with money doesn't erase the fact that black people are two and a half times more likely to be killed by police and are more incarcerated than any other ethnicity.

For the second argument, now when I brought up the fact that twelve players on Kaepernick's old team took a knee during the national anthem, it was completely ignored, even when four of those players were white. I wish I would have gotten a response to that because I think it would have made for some interesting dialogue. If Kaepernick was protesting just because he was a "bad player," what were the excuses of the two hundred other players in the league?

This part of the conversation mostly focused on his playing skills and how poor they were, which led to his "whiny baby" attitude. Again, I am pretty knowledgeable about football. But I wonder, if he was one of the greatest players of all time, would his protest have been seen less intrusive or unpatriotic? My guess is, probably not.

This argument suggests that someone has to have incredible talents in order to be heard, listened to, and respected. Never believe that a small group of like-minded individuals can't change the world because, in fact, it is the only thing that ever has. White America is always ranting and raving about the right to speak freely, but in this situation, the tune changes to fit the feelings of white America, and it translates to "only certain people are allowed to practice it." Constitutional rights are not based on skills, education, or talent. Every single citizen of this country has not only the right but also the responsibility to speak up about the injustices they are experiencing in the United States.

The third argument is that football is an American pastime and has no place for politics. Conservatives have been using this argument since the dawn of sports. It has been used numerous times during Olympic years. Who does not remember John Carlos and Tommie Smith standing on the podium in Mexico, both men wear one leather glove and raise a fist in the air during the national anthem? A white conservative will scream to "keep politics out of sports," but I disagree. People should use whatever platform they have to speak out about injustice, and if it makes people uncomfortable, so be it.

I have listened to countless stories of white America complaining about the way black people protest. We block traffic on streets and highways. We cut into white America's entertainment venues. Black people cost you money because we close malls with our relentless marching and protesting in public areas. There are so many objections to the black America protests I can no longer count them. What many in white America who choose to use these arguments/excuses don't seem to realize is that when they make the very same statement in complaining, they are actually making the point that they don't truly give a shit and has no intention of being bothered by the issues that face black America "until we protest in a manner that they see fit." This faction doesn't care about black America's challenge and struggles. "Your oppression has nothing to do with me" runs through their mind, and they look the other way because they have no intention of facing something that doesn't directly impact them.

When white America attempts to dictate when, where, and how black people show any type of resistance to the racist systems of oppression, they are a major part of the problem. White America believes in telling a high-profile athlete that they can't utilize their professional platform, a platform that most Americans, regardless of color, don't have access to and use a few seconds to open the eyes of America to an issue in our country that affects all Americans because many in white America view it as so disrespectful and is doing nothing more than perpetuating the cycle of oppression and prejudice. In addition, when this faction of white America behaves in this manner, you are also restricting the options of how to peacefully protest.

Colin Kaepernick's peaceful protest was limited to a few seconds, peaceful and silent, and it didn't involve or include anybody else unless they made a choice to participate. Also, contrary to what you hear on FOX News, it never disrupted the flow of the game because it never occurred while the game was actually being played. White America made a choice to pay attention to something that made them uncomfortable but has totally disregarded the reason for the protest. They could have simply turned around and never engage with it at all, which would be how much of white America has approached every other problem that black people deal with. So if you don't like how black people protest. If you don't like it when we stand, sit, kneel, march, speak, or remain silent, then please do tell us what proper protesting looks like.

Lastly, America is supposed to be a "free" country, at least that is what a bunch of slave owners put on a document I read once. And yet issues with people being mistreated based on skin color, religion, hair, education, lifestyle, and even clothing people wear continue to remain. Although there are often too many persecutions for expressing ourselves as individuals, there is also no guarantee that it won't occur.

If we are stifled from using our professional platforms for speaking out, then when would we ever have a better opportunity? Because right now, in this country, it seems that if black America decides to peacefully protest any injustices, it is viewed as being unpatriotic and un-American, which is a bit hypocritical, seeing as this country is "so damn free." Let me tell you. When I drive down the street and I pass a police officer and look back in my mirror to see if he has turned around to come after me or when I walk into a store and, all of a sudden, I have store security following me around or when I am walking down the street and I see a white woman cross the street so that she does not have to walk past me, trust me when I tell you that I'm not feeling all that free.

So when black America chooses to speak up about it and we are suddenly deemed as criminals of the state, what are we supposed to do? Furthermore, if we speak out, much of white America responds with some tired-ass line, "Well, if you don't like it here, then go back to Africa," or white America will tell us how much worse it is in other countries that we should be happy with the oppression we receive here because it could be worse. How exactly are black people supposed to fight in this country when so much of white America responds with "It could be worse, so black people should be grateful" or "If black people don't like it, then they should leave OUR country"?

Conversations such as these usually end with black people being labeled as un-American. But isn't it un-American to be pulled over just for being black or to be harassed for barbecuing in the park, sitting in Starbucks, having a little black kid selling water, babysitting, or doing the vast number of other things that much of white America call the police because black people are doing it? This always leads to white

America re-establishing control of the narrative because of the feel that the conversation "isn't going anywhere," which isn't accurate. It's just not going down a path that they have always been able to control. This ending to the conversation is what angers black America when it comes to protesting.

I'm not sure why there were so many people surprised when Number 45 barked out that NFL team owners fire players who sit out the national anthem before games. Didn't surprise me one bit. These are the actions of a racist president. The league, in cahoots with Number 45, though they remedied the issue by making sure Kaepernick never played again, but the trickle-down of resistance to other players in the league, both black and white, sent much of "patriotic" white America over the cliff. How the hell could these people be so disrespectful to a 250-year-old cloth logo and/or a bad Francis Scott Key poem turned bar song in 1931?

Let's just keep it very real. Taking a knee during the song is disrespectful not to the song or to the flag but to white America, in general, because much of this faction feels as though they and people who look like them are the only factions of people in this country who have ever given up anything for this country. They are the only faction that has served in the military, fought, lived, and died for the United States of America. It is not so much that white America can't understand Kaepernick's point of view or what he is protesting, because he and the others have been very clear when asked. It is that any other point of view, other than this faction of white America, is irrelevant, nonexistent, and pretty much unimportant.

Why do you think this faction of white America hates the term *white people*? It is simply because they consider it a pejorative. So when black America is protesting against the brutality of law enforcement, the unequal education system, and the redlining housing practices that still occur today, we have to be "politically correct" and not make it all about race, even if it completely has a race-based foundation. White America wants black people to call racism a social issue. White America hates the phrase *white supremacy* because it makes them uncomfortable to hear the truth, so they come up with some term, *structural inequality*, and use it like gravy to cover up the fact that you have some mystery meat on your plate.

The term *white people* reminds white America of basic history. It reminds them how their ancestors kidnapped, beat, raped, lynched, and murdered people of color, which now is slowly being revised in history books so that it looked like an instructional time in history where white Europeans had to "civilize" black people and not as an animalistic actuality that it was. So now what does white America do when they hear a sentence that starts with "white people"? They quickly buck up and respond with a flurry of rationalization that usually starts with "Not all white people."

And these guidelines for "respectable" protesting probably grow in their minds, because they also want black America to not only stop lumping white people together but also limit the amount of "blackness" you put into a protest.

Too much of white America, the mention of race creates a division in their head and makes them uncomfortable because they can no longer hide behind the argument that every color has problems. Well, when did white America have to be concerned about Number 45 deporting their children, vilifying their religion, or referring to their mothers as bitches? So no! White America does not have the same struggles.

We all paid attention when the entire country mourned when one white woman was killed in Charlottesville, but what was lost was the fact that these same types of white supremacists have terrorized black people for more than four centuries, and other communities of black people continue to suffer from the vigilante actions of first "paid leave" and then "acquitted" police officers. Yet white America still has an issue with the term *Black Lives Matter*.

The fact is that most white Americans can handle black America protesting, but only as long as it is out of sight, which would make it out of mind. Their patronizing view is that even

JOHN STEPHEN PARKER

black America has a (limited or cherry-picked) constitutional right to feel mad if one of their kids, neighbor, or another black person is shot, choked, beaten, or discriminated against. Just as long as it does not inconvenience their life, slow down their weekend trip out of town or to the mall to pick up the latest Lulu lemon gear, or slow down their next run for the seven-dollar cup of joe, and heaven forbid, they can't get home fast enough to watch the next rerun of *Friends* (the only show I know that can get away without having a black cast member on a show set in New York City).

Much of white America doesn't feel like they have to take into consideration the disproportionate, continual murder of unarmed black Americans because it would interfere with trying to get those half-price cargo shorts at the Old Navy. That's just downright communist (or socialist, Marxist, etc.). This same faction feels like black America should feel free to protest all the inequality of institutions in this country as long as they don't do it prior to a Yankee game, a Celtics game, any soccer game, a Taylor Swift concert, or any country music entertainers' performance. No member of white America wants to think about the harassment, lynching, or murder of a black American while Jason Aldean is singing about some brokenhearted girl on stage. And the list of places is endless (political rallies, social media, schools, and even at an actual protest). But if black America wants to protest anywhere else, they are free to do so.

In addition, if black America does actually locate a sufficient place to stand up for their rights as American citizens, white America wants us to mind our *P*s and *Q*s and bear in mind that there are things that are way more important to them than the actual Constitution of the United States. If black America is to protest, we have to be sure not to disrespect the following items:

1. The American flag

2. The Confederate flag (representation of treason against the US)

3. Any monuments, especially those that memorializes one of the most oppressive times in our nation's history

4. Names on the building, especially those memorializing the biggest oppressors in history (i.e., Washington, Jefferson, Jackson, perhaps we insert name here)

5. Any stained-glass windows belonging to the Catholic Church

6. Cats or dogs, because much of white America values pets more than black Americans

7. Fifty-year-old bad poems with racist third verses

8. Freedom of speech (as long as you say what white America wants to hear)

9. Bathrooms

10. Children (not all children, just the "white" ones)

11. The Founding Fathers (regardless of the fact that they were all slave owners)

12. The military

13. First responders, blue lives (police officers, not Smurfs)

14. Religious freedom (except for Islam)

15. Starbucks

Speaking of the military, white America has an orgasmic rush of lust when it comes to the armed forces. There are literally thousands of videos on YouTube that show law enforcement officers shooting and killing unarmed black Americans, and the only response is "What did they do to provoke the officer?" They can watch Philando Castile be murdered in front of his girlfriend and daughter by a police officer on film after telling the officer he had a weapon and a permit to carry the weapon (in an open carry state) and have no response at all but cry like a damn baby when they see a dog licking a soldier's face after getting off the plane from

Afghanistan. In fact, if you wrap a puppy in an American flag and put it on top of a pumpkin-spice gift certificate to Starbucks and tell a white woman you're giving it to a soldier, she will probably make love to you right there on the spot.

Here is the reality. Never in the history of the United States has there ever occurred a movement for the equality of people of color that white America supported. Name one, whether it be the abolitionist, the antilynching, the Black Power, or the civil rights movement. Today we have Black Lives Matter, which has been compared to the Ku Klux Klan by right-wing conservatives, even with the fact that Black Lives Matter has never raped, lynched, or murdered a single person. And yet white America has never gotten behind any movement where the foundation was the equality of all people.

Black America has been searching for validation from white America for centuries, and I believe that with the creation of the Black Lives Matter movement, we have finally come to the realization that this search is more of a fool's errand. Based on the history of this country and the mindset of white America, the only way to stand up for your right if you are black in this country is to not stand up for your rights.

Protesting is a rite of passage in the United States, going back to when a bunch of white American thugs decided they didn't like the tax placed on one of their favorite drinks, so they threw the drink into the Boston Harbor. Of course, when white America is reminded of this, it is looked at as an apples and oranges comparison mainly because those guys were white.

A protest is supposed to bring about a conversation where the people protesting have an opportunity to educate others on what the actual protesters are experiencing and hopefully gain some solidarity with those who are being made uncomfortable by the protest.

But if in the act of protesting those being disrupted still choose to not listen to the reason for the protest, or even worse, choose to create their own narrative of why the protest is occurring, which leads to automatically shutting down the people who are protesting because you don't agree with the method, then what is the point of protesting at all? This is what is happening in society today. Much of white America continues to regularly either change or end the discussion because they don't like the subject matter. By doing so, they continue the acts of oppression because they continue to view the plight of black America as not being worthy of their time, and with that comes a lack of assistance.

There are factions of white America that are constantly asking black people for solutions to racism in this country. I can offer a suggestion. If white America, regardless of political affiliation, would listen to black people without the intent of responding but more with the intent of respecting and understanding, it would probably be a real step toward cohesion. We don't have to agree, but we have to be respectful of each other's culture.

Listen with the intent of gathering as much information as possible and not just the information that you want to hear or that makes you feel comfortable. Next, white America needs to provide black people space to disagree with you, to protest, and to speak out without seeking retribution against them. Who knows, there might be a day in the future when white America will want to stand up or kneel down in protest for a cause that is important to them (the local Starbucks closing, Seinfeld not coming back on the air, the World Cup going to Mexico instead of the US, etc.). I am sure that at this point in time, you will want some solidarity and people of color to support your efforts.

So let black America protest the way they see fit. We will keep it peaceful, and we will try not to slow up the line at Starbucks.

CHAPTER 7

Wake Up from the Mass Delusion

"For me, it is far better to grasp the Universe as it really is than to persist in delusion, however satisfying and reassuring."

—*Carl Sagan*

IN 1962, 85 percent of white American told Gallup that the black children of America had as good a chance as the white kids of getting a good education. The next year, in another Gallup survey, almost half of white America said that black people in America had just as good a chance of getting a job as white people.

Looking back at those statements, we can see that white America was suffering from delusions of grandeur; not to mention, this gave you a clear indication of the racist thought process of white America at that time. In 1963, nearly half of white America who was surveyed said that if a black person was invited to their home for dinner, they would be uncomfortable. The one constant that has always existed in this country is the complacency of white America. The history of white people's attitudes toward race has always been one of self-deception.

White America is always telling their black counterparts how much things have changed in the world. Hell, much of white America even believes that blacks are treated fairly by the police. How ridiculous is that? So the fact that four out of five white people believe that black children have the same opportunity of getting an adequate education as their white counterparts is almost comical.

Many in white America, many with good hearts and who mean well, fail to recognize that there is a real problem. Instead, they choose to see the accomplishment of one black man becoming president of the United States or a professional athlete receiving a big contract because of their athletic talents or the thing that the issue of racism and discrimination has been resolved. It is because of this thought process that the freight train of racism just keeps rolling down the tracks of society.

Now society has progressed in a number of ways, and I would be remiss. Although it is less prominent today, eighty years ago, the vast majority of white America bought into the rules that black and brown people should be kept out of the living spaces of white America. They have also gotten to the level of excellence in "otherizing" people of color, and they have even enlisted the law enforcement in this task because

JOHN STEPHEN PARKER

they are hired to keep black people in black neighborhoods and keep these same members of black America out of white spaces.

Just so I don't have people labeling me as racist (LOL), I will also say that often, black America sees the world through rose-colored glasses. One of the delusions of some black Americans is the "rub a lamp" belief of black kids having the same educational opportunities or the same job opportunities. But one thing that we have never been misguided about in the history of this country is that the concerns of black people have always been stifled. Based on that, it would be safe to assume that fifty years from now, white America will do a retrospect and get to a bottom line that the racial injustices that have occurred in today's society are "not that bad" and white people were totally oblivious to these issues.

White America, in general, wants black people and, for that matter, anybody who is not a member of white America to assimilate into white American culture while they still choose to not look at us but as a group often labeled as thugs (the new nigger). They want us to be sure that we remain "patriotic" to this country while there has never been any consistency in the treatment of black Americans. This is never truer than the fact that the doctor who treated the seven law enforcement officers after the shooting in Dallas was a black man. But this same doctor who trained to save the lives of everybody, regardless of color, is the same man who was pulled out of his car and placed spread-eagled on the hood during a "routine" traffic stop. Thank God that Dr. Brian Williams, a trauma surgeon, doesn't hold a grudge.

Most of white America has no clue about that happening to black people. Instead, they will turn around and complain about the myth of reverse discrimination and how bad the white man has it now. How fucking stupid does that sound? They often attempt to flip it around in order to play the victim, but failed blacks are more likely to be suspended from preschool, to be persecuted for drug use, to receive longer sentences, to be discriminated against in housing, and to be denied a job interview. Black people don't want to hear about reverse discrimination.

It doesn't mean that black people can't be prejudicial about people, but when a certain faction of people have persecuted and oppressed pretty much every other faction that exist in the world, we refuse to let white America get away with playing the victim card.

Something that is regularly overlooked in the United States is an education system that has been failing black and brown citizens of this country since it was created. Often, we spend so much time on the latest incident of a white law enforcement officer killing another unarmed black citizen that we forget about the fact that we send the most underserved factions to the crappiest educational institutions.

At the same time, funding gets redirected to schools where the vast number of students have white faces. Yes, it is important that we do not put blinders on because systemic racism affects every institution in this country, but white America must wake up from the dreams and delusions of "everyone being created equal" and realize that black lives have not mattered nearly as much as the convenience of white America.

We can take straw polls, but polls are no substitute for the actuality of true society. A poll is going to tell how people feel about something, but it won't tell you if something is actually happening. The evidence of if racism is at an extreme in the United States is all around us every day. You can see it in the murders of black citizens by law enforcement to the Charleston massacre to the neo-Nazi and white nationalists marching in Virginia. The availability of division in this country can be found in every news media outlet.

White America should get a clue and realize that the black community requires no reporting of racial disparage by its white-owned media companies. We already know and have known for decades that the treatment by law enforcement and the criminal justice is unequal in our communities, that a lopsided ratio of black Americans is locked up in prison, and that, economically, there is no balance between white and black people in this country. It is no different today than it was in 2008, and white people know it. White Americans continue to be largely shielded from these realities or plainly didn't care.

The "age of Obama" refers to the belief of naive white Americans that the election of the first black president would usher the end of racism when all it did was stoke the fire of racism in this country. Is there a wonder why the first black president of the United States had the largest amount of Secret Service detail in the history of the organization? A large portion of white America never got on board with the new president's handling of race relations. Many of this same group continue to make the claim that Barack Obama was the cause of division in this country. They continue to this day to create a narrative of Obama not supporting law enforcement, not supporting the military, and being blamed for the racial uprisings in the various cities across the country. This is the clear indication that the first black president was never welcomed in the highest office of the land. A quarter of white America believed the Obama administration favored blacks over whites, which was ridiculous.

President Obama took office in 2008, already behind the eight ball, so to speak. He was a black man and the first to hold that office, and even though much of white America wanted to say that racism was now over, the fact is that the election had no effect at all on the situation. In fact, the incidents of racism increased significantly all the way until he left office. Oh yeah, it then escalated off the charts when Number 45 took office because not every redneck racist in the country now had support to let their bigoted attitudes run free.

The truth is that President Obama stayed away from racial issues until he had no choice. Until August 9, 2014, when Michael Brown Jr. was murdered in the street by then-officer Darren Wilson of the Ferguson (Missouri) Police Department. I understand that being the first black in any area of employment, you are forced to carry the weight of an entire people. This also means that you need to be very careful of the cards you choose to play in this card game. The race card was not a card to be played, but on August 9, 2014, he was forced to place race at the forefront of the conversation.

Being sympathetic to the president's situation, and with all due respect to the man who ascended to the highest office in this country, this is also what slows the conversation about race relations with those members of white America who need to have the most conversation. It stifles the "wake-up" time of white America to the reality of real racism in this country.

Having the tough discussions and heated conversations about race are the only way to getting to the root of the problem. Avoiding this conversation only makes it worse, and the healing never gets started. Even if the conversation is completely unproductive and is a source of discomfort for generally all involved, it still needs to be had because it is the prequel for building a bridge of understanding, which can lead to much stronger race relations. There is never a victory without sacrifice.

Many white people live in the mythical world where they believe that to be an American is such a wonderful thing and that they should truly be honored to live in this country. The issue that most people of color have with that feeling is the description of someone being American intrinsically means that you are a white person, and with the deplorable people who began showing their true colors since 2016 and the election of Number 45, this faction is bound and determined to keep it that way.

America is a melting pot of people that was created under the dictatorship of another country. You have an unlimited amount of different white cultures that all came from somewhere and ended up here. But then some white guy got a great idea that we need other human beings to do their work, help amass their wealth, and literally build this country. So they made the decision to go to Africa where my ancestors were captured, kidnapped, separated from their family and culture, and taken from their home country in chains. They were transported in the hulls of slave ships in a manner that resembled farm animals.

There they were bought and sold off like machinery, and their freedom and dignity as a human being was stolen away. And a fact that white America conveniently forgets is that they were bought and sold by leaders with the last names of Washington, Jefferson, Madison, and others. White America calls these guys our Founding Fathers. I guess they were since they were the early founders of slavery, oppression, segregation, discrimination, rape, lynching, and of course, murder.

As time moved forward, these slaves were emancipated. I say "emancipated" because they were never free. Over time, they went from being niggers to being colored, then moving up to be Negroes. These same Negroes soon became black, and because white America felt that black was way too powerful, they created a term that would be much more comfortable to white America. They changed it to African Americans. Don't get it twisted. There are many in white America who would love to see us as "niggers" again. I run into many of them on a daily basis. If you have white skin, you are simply referred to as Americans. How racist is that?

White America is under the belief that they built this country, but if you are familiar with the true history and not what was written in the grade school history book, you know that white-skinned people built almost nothing in this country. In fact, white America had very little to do with the actual construction of America. If anyone needs to take their country back, it is the native people who lived here and had their land and sovereignty stolen from the United States government.

The truth is, black people built this country, and much of white America built family fortunes off it. Slavery was the cash cow of the original thirteen colonies. Billions of dollars were accumulated up until the Civil War. Wake up, white America. Why in God's name would your ancestors want that way of life to disappear? America was created on the foundation of genocide, murder, rape, theft, segregated and discriminatory policies, lawful racism in the form of slavery, and then legalized Jim Crow segregation.

As much as white America wants to not have this discussion, they must know that we are not that far from that racist past. All you have to do is take a serious look at what's going on in society. As we all watched the protests and violence, the likes of David Duke with other white men, talking about "Jews not replacing us" and "taking their country back" and being emboldened because of their like-minded president.

Regardless of your feeling on the issue, we should all be deeply concerned about race relations in this country. Racism is no different than any other disease in this country. It is what divides us, and because we were not paying attention,

JOHN STEPHEN PARKER

it became the diversion that a foreign government needed to invade our election process. While we were paying attention to white American law enforcement murdering unarmed black citizens, a foreign government put one of their puppets into the highest office of the land.

We have all witnessed the hypocrisy in the words of both the elected and corporate leader. They will sit and be vocal about racism, but often the offices that these people work in resemble a white university fraternity house. They don't practice diversity in their own areas. It is easy to recognize the racism problem of the alt-right radical white supremacists who practice out in the open all over the country. As I stated in my book *From Sheets to Suits*, the problem is, the rest of white America who fails to understand the issue of racism and, furthermore, believe it has nothing to do with them and doesn't affect their world.

White America needs to wake up and begin being honest with the rest of the world and with themselves. They need to stop sticking their heads in the sand because it will never get better until they address the problem and come face-to-face with the truth. America is at a critical crossroads.

White America must begin to ask themselves who they are and how far they have come when it comes to race relations. Then find the guts to deal with the issues that have plagued this country for over four hundred years. I know that there are many white Americans who have bought into Number 45's bullshit. He has convinced them only of what they think is wrong and who they should blame for it. White America has lost jobs and wages, and yes, they are poor. There is not a person in the black community who doesn't understand that, but white America needs to realize that there are many in black America who are in the same boat and, more often than not, in a worse situation because the proverbial boat is smaller and full of holes.

Hate by white America has infested every aspect of society. It has invaded social media. Hate is ingrained in our educational institutions. It has penetrated communities, corporate cultures, and our political leadership. Hate is even infiltrating our churches. The most segregated hour in the week is 11:00 a.m. on a Sunday morning. What happened in Virginia should have been a wake-up call for white America.

It's time for white America to stop asking black people for help and to pull the damn truck up the hill themselves. Much of white America has a drug problem. It's called racism. And just like any drug problem, if it's going to get corrected, it should start just like an addiction program: the first step to solving any drug problem is first admitting that you have one.

Black people already know there is a problem, but the problem is for white America to fix it. Stop asking us to fix it. Because you don't listen when we give you the answer.

JOHN STEPHEN PARKER

CHAPTER 8

Wake Up and Realize that Police Brutality is Real Thanks to Social Media

"I can't bring myself to watch yet another video, not because I don't care, but because we're all just a few videos away from becoming completely desensitized. The public execution of Black folks will never be normal."

—*Andrena Sawyer*

IF IT WAS up to me and I had a few million dollars, I would start a publishing company that focused on social issues like law enforcement killing unarmed black men. I would make sure that the pictures of every single black man and black woman who was on the receiving end of a gun from a trigger-happy police officer were on the cover of every single issue of every single publication that I printed. The number of publications I would need would be high because the number of killings has exceeded an amount of normalcy if there is such a number. I would use those covers to symbolize the next victim and those who died without any publicity.

It's too bad I don't have that kind of wealth. I would probably be significantly more outspoken about what's happening in society. There are days that, unlike most adults my age or older, I am so grateful to social media, because if it was not for this platform, the acts of harassment, abuse, and police brutality and the much-needed conversations about racial issues may have never come to light. Technology has given us ways to put that information into the world, and because smartphones are being improved upon regularly, those platforms will also continue to improve. I am currently on an iPhone X. With any luck, my son and daughter will pick up my torch on their iPhone XXV and continue to "stay woke" because the future of this country, of everybody, depends on it.

Advances in technology have made it virtually impossible for white America to keep up their mythical belief that black people are misreading situations or overreacting to what we know is the unwarranted murder of unarmed black people. Not only does it happen, but it's also been happening for a very long time. Technology even put law enforcement in a position where they can no longer lie and are being held accountable for their actions. The only problem with the body cameras is that it's still connected to other technology in the vehicle. So yes, law enforcement can still create a loophole to be able to kill black people.

Many in white America still believe in the Officer Friendly concept of law enforcement. You remember Officer Friendly, right? He was the police officer in the reading books we had in first grade. He was the guy you could always turn to and ask questions of when we needed information or help. In today's society, much of white America is still in love with the fantasy of Officer Friendly, and never in a million years would this same faction of white America believe that law enforcement would lie on a police report, coerce testimonies of witnesses and cover up crimes committed by other officers.

And because they have this fantasy of *Mayberry RFD* in their mind, they have a wall in their mind when it comes to the concept of black people protesting the fact that these things occur regularly in the black community. We live in a society that actually has very backward thinking. You would think that at this point in time, in the world we live in, where white America still trusts in a criminal justice system they feel gets it right 95 percent, when the fact is, the justice system in the United States rarely gets it right, unless you have enough money for them to get it right. If they got it right, they would shine a light on the ridiculously backward ratio of black Americans dying at the hands of law enforcement. Again, thank God for technology and social media. How else would we get the message out?

Contrary to popular belief, I do not hate the police or any law enforcement agency. In fact, I have a great deal of respect for most people who wear a law enforcement uniform. I have relatives who are members of law enforcement agencies throughout this country. My father was a police officer and my brother also, but I am not so indoctrinated into the world of law enforcement and understand the strained relationship that has developed between the police and the various black communities they are sworn to protect. Again, the police deal with black people from a simple philosophy. They are there to keep black people in their communities and to keep black people out of the communities of white America. It is oppressive, and it's been going on for a long time, centuries actually.

So when yet another unarmed black man was killed by another white American law enforcement officer who, like many of his brother officers, while strapped with a 9mm Glock pistol, continues to spit out that ridiculous claim of "fearing for his life," even when we witness the video that contradicts this claim, makes it clear just how jacked up the judicial system is. And even if you are able to get the police officer indicted and charged with murder (while they are on paid administrative leave) or even voluntary manslaughter, which is a rarity at best, they are usually bonded out of jail often by the police benevolence fund and, as happens more than not, are eventually exonerated and returned to their position.

When the judicial system finally decides to a self-overhaul, we will all be relieved. But until that time, the only real solace that we can hope to find is in the beauty of technology, because if not for technology and the fact that anybody running around with a smartphone is now a film director, rogue law enforcement officers would get away with even more than they already do. If not for technology, there would not be footage of a man running away from an officer while getting shot in the back or a young kid being shot sixteen times in Chicago one police officer while other a few of his brother officers stood there and watched.

In 2017, black people were murdered at a rate more than twice than white people, and while smartphones are great at recording the evil doings and social media is a great platform to keep the conversation ongoing, neither one of these mediums is enough to deliver an indictment, let alone a conviction. Even when you are filmed choking a guy out while he is screaming "I can't breathe," a smartphone or Facebook will not get you indicted for murder.

In a perfect world, all lives do matter, but that is make-believe based on what is happening in society. It has no relevance when it comes to the plague of harassment, brutality, and violence that has occurred upon black people in America.

The ironic thing is, the judicial system is so fixated on laws affecting criminal behavior that it forgets (conveniently) to hold law enforcement accountable in the same way.

Some would insert here that classes and more training are the way to alter the behavior that many law enforcement officers have toward black Americans. One thing is indisputable. This country has never seen a more difficult time for both citizens of color and for law enforcement officials alike, but that doesn't excuse away bad behavior.

White America does not put police brutality on a viable list of things that can actually cause death, but it is a very real circumstance for black Americans and other persons of color. That is obvious. If you are one of white America who doesn't understand that (or one of the rare ones who might actually be reading this book), I can only remind you of a young man named Jordan Edward, the unarmed black Texas high school kid killed by the police. And as is custom, right after this young man was killed, you hear the standard narrative of how tough the job of the police is or if he hadn't resisted, which is always followed by an attack on the character of the dead person. The other is, "Well if he hadn't been doing something, it would not have happened."

Exactly, what was Jordan doing? He was at a party. He was fifteen. Was the vehicle he was inside of in drive or in reverse? And all while many in white America are asking the insulting and demeaning questions of a dead fifteen-year-old kid, black people, including his family, are swinging in the wind like laundry on an old clothesline, because we know the answer. And the only thing we continue to hear are justifications that hold no water at all and insincere condolences.

We have gotten to a point where white America needs to wake up and stop asking questions when they already possess the answers. It's time to focus on the real reason for police brutality, and it's the same reason that it has always been. It's the one polarizing reason that when it rears its ugly head from the MAGA hat that it's usually wearing, you hear the ass of the person just pucker up because it makes white America as uncomfortable as a long-tailed cat in a room full of rocking chairs. It's called RACISM.

Black Americans dying at the hands of law enforcement are only the tip of the sword, but it has brought attention to the broader issues surrounding the reputation management of law enforcement. Clearly, much of white America has not reached a point in this country where they are prepared to address this element of racism in the United States and how issues such as this have led to greater inequality in the areas of health care, education, and employment.

When people talk about police brutality, what exactly are they talking about? Much of white America thinks it is simply about black people being pulled over by the police because of a violation of traffic law and then the person not complying with the request of Officer Friendly. The phenomenon of police brutality goes way past overzealous law enforcement officers throwing a guy on the ground or senselessly beating people without cause or warrant. Police brutality includes the psychological effects of assaulting an individual and the effects that follow. Police brutality can occur regardless of the actual intent of the officer.

What white America doesn't want to discuss is the fact that police brutality has long-term health consequences for black people and people of color who are often the more victimized. Many black Americans and other people of color live in communities with subpar health conditions because of their living conditions, and police brutality is just an additional factor that aid to their poor health conditions. But much of white America never pays attention to black people who are unarmed, being killed, and murdered, if you may, because of direct interaction with a law enforcement officer. That is unless there is a video that clearly shows the behavior of the officer and his full violation of the civil rights of the victim. White America will pay more attention because this is the beginning of the "rationalization period."

Black people and people of color continue to be murdered by law enforcement officers every single day. This is even with protest happening across this country in massive numbers.

It is similar to a large number of mass shootings happening in the country (by middle-aged white men, something else that white America never wants to have a discussion about). This happens because our society is one that likes to scream at the umpire after the pitch has gone by. Our society would rather react to a circumstance that hits them in the face as opposed to preparing for the situation, even after it has occurred numerous times.

When unarmed black people are murdered at the hands of law enforcement officers, we talk about "more training," but it doesn't fix the problem. Just like when mentally ill white men sit in hotel windows; walk into theaters, grocery stores, or churches; and decided who they want to shoot and kill, one or many, we send condolences and prayers. But we have a forty-eight-hour debate on changing the gun laws in this country. Once again, the pitch has gone by, and we are left yelling at the umpire.

White America will look for alternatives to the issues instead of addressing them directly. So they mask the problems with conversations about police officers wearing body cameras and the justification of the video with statements like "We need to see the full footage before we render our determinations." Then they will settle the case out of court for a few million dollars, and it will all go away until the next young black soul is murdered as if money makes all problems disappear. The only thing that has disappeared is a family member and who may have been a productive member of a community. By addressing the foundations of police brutality, we can have a positive effect and possibly prevent another young person of color from losing their lives at the hands of law enforcement.

White America and this country, in general, have to be held accountable for the historical treatment of its own citizens in order to progress with the reality of the present. Black people being murdered by white America is not some moment that all of a sudden requires a media alert. It's just that in the last thirty years, the use of video has made it more prominent. Although the video has been made more easily accessible, dating back to Rodney King being beaten by six Los Angeles police officers, the history of black people being beaten, raped, lynched, and murdered by white America goes back four hundred years; and in today's society, police brutality is no different. In fact, it is the same category as lynching.

I always tell white America that when speaking about racism, they should "get comfortable being uncomfortable," but no matter how uncomfortable white America is about it, the illegal behavior of police brutality, when it comes victimizing black people, is a branching problem from the tree of racism. Black people get confused by it also because often we want to keep it on the level of the law enforcement agency, but that is only the surface issue. The real problem is truly deeper-seeded.

Racism utilizes police brutality as an added way to oppress people of color. It affords opportunities for black and brown people because of their race. Think of the education system in this country. Some students, mostly the marginalized ones, get little to no assistance in education, while the students with a more privileged life receive much more beneficial assistance. This ranks right up there with the adage "The rich get richer, and the poor get poorer."

Police brutality is a factor in the school-to-prison pipeline. Law enforcement agencies are a tool of a criminal justice system that contributes to this same pipeline. And if you don't think that it is also psychological brutality, there is an atmosphere that has been created where a black kid is more likely to be shot by the police than his white friends. The black kid knows that if he is walking down the street with a hoodie on, he will be arrested, charged, and sent to jail long before his white counterpart for a very long time for the same crime.

White America needs to wake up and come to an understanding that black people and other persons of color have made the decision to raise hell now. We are in the streets disrupting your daily commute. We are in the mall so your shopping experience is miserable. We are speaking up after holding our tongues for decades and voicing our frustration. This is no different than the civil rights era of the '50s and '60s in that the grievances are the same now as they were then.

In my home town area of Ferguson, Missouri, where residents suffered through decades of misconduct so egregious that most of white America could scarcely conceive of what was going on, the black community was policed by an entity that is the walking definition of police brutality. In all reality, black people didn't need to wait for a DOJ report to tell them what was going on. They were living it every day, and the evidence was overwhelming. But much of white America, including many in Ferguson, made a conscious choice to not look at it and saw it in a light that kept them in a comfortable mindset.

I am proud to say that I am a pot-stirring shit disturber, and even though my father was a police officer, I have commented on police misconduct for many years, and I feel I have a responsibility to shine a light on national racial scandals in their own rights. Abuses such as a black grandmother's bones that were broken or a black pregnant woman who was violently thrown to the ground by a racist white law enforcement officer, which ended with the woman losing her baby, and the ungodly amount of settlement money that has been paid to numerous victims because of the brutal and vicious behavior of law enforcement, most of this doesn't even hit the radar screen of white America.

I do believe that protests should remain always peaceful, but I have a true understanding of why they turn to violence and destruction. And as much as much of white America doesn't understand, I not only comprehend but I also advocate protesting when a law enforcement officer murders a person of color. I don't give a damn what the circumstances are and let them run as many investigations through as many law enforcement agencies as they want. The more the better.

They made a great stink out of the apartheid condition black people were living in Ferguson after Michael Brown Jr. was killed. But even a black presence doesn't necessarily change things. Baltimore had a black mayor and still had one of the most corrupt police departments in the country. There are so many good reasons for black people to be outraged. If you do your research as I did, it won't be hard to find these reasons, unless you don't want to. Let's start with what makes the world go around. Let's start with money.

The average amount of money paid out to the victims or their families of police brutality is nearly six million dollars. That was what was paid in 2011 and 2017. But that doesn't hold a candle to the fact that on average, over one hundred citizens of this country have won court judgments or settlements because of some form of police brutality and/

or the violation of civil rights by law enforcement officers. But only a small percentage of those same cases ever reach the indictment stage.

If you're imagining that they were all black men in their twenties, don't get it twisted. One of those citizens was a fifteen-year-old black boy illegally riding a dirt bike. There was also a black pregnant accountant who was only twenty-six and a fifty-five-year-old woman whose only crime was selling raffle tickets at her place of worship. But nothing tops an eighty-seven-year-old black grandmother who was trying to help her grandson who showed up to her door already shot by the police. Those cases detail only a few of the thousands of black people who have been brutalized and even killed during questionable arrests. Some black people have even been beaten while handcuffed, and others were thrown to the pavement. A guy in Ferguson was charged with destruction of property for bleeding on a police officer's uniform after he was beaten.

When pondering the fact that these cities paid out $5.7 million in brutality settlements over four years, consider that the payout, in this case, was a mere $95,000. There is so much I haven't included (example), and I've just trawled through the archives of newspapers for a three-year period. They cover most police-involved deaths, but no newspaper covers more than a minuscule subset of use-of-force incidents. Again, don't get it twisted. Investigations such as these are only the tip of the misconduct "iceberg" among police officers.

The period covered in these investigations came immediately after the FBI caught fifty-one Baltimore police officers in a scheme that resulted in at least twelve extortion convictions, such as Abdul Salaam, thirty-six, who was beaten after a traffic stop by two Baltimore police officers who covered it up. Salaam never even got a response to his complaint filed with internal affairs. Those same two officers were involved in another incident that involved the death of a suspect while in police custody. But nothing happened to Freddie Gray?

These don't even get into the real dirt the law enforcement officers are involved in, like drug trafficking, prostitution, fake workman's compensation claims, and murder for hire. Who killed Tupac Shakur? Well, he was being protected by off-duty LAPD, but nobody knows anything, huh?

I can talk about this forever, but I don't want to discuss some cop "whoring out his spouse" and then my only response is, "I've seen a lot worse than that." Law enforcement in this country has become a clusterfuck of a profession, and the citizens of this country, especially those living in underserved communities, deserve better. Look no farther than my home city of St. Louis, Missouri.

So it should be no surprise to much of white America when people march in the streets after law enforcement murders another black man. They should be having discussions on police brutality in stadiums across this country because black people, people of color, and even some very concerned white Americans find this whole phenomenon troubling, to say the least. We attempt to do the right thing and follow the legislative process of contacting elected official to express concerns, but nothing ever changes. We seem to ask the same question, When are you going to do something to stop this? But it always falls on deaf ears.

A young black man's family reports that he was brutally beaten by police during a shoplifting arrest, and police are even videotaped in the act, but nothing ever changes. This is a problem that has been described as a social epidemic and even a disease at times. But what's the cure?

Law enforcement receives a great deal of laxity to conduct their responsibilities because everybody says the same thing: "They have a tough job." They get carte blanche to beat up people and even kill under certain circumstances. But when it is clear that an officer has stepped way over the line (wherever that line is), they are rarely held accountable. Nobody hears about stories of a black person being pulled over by the police and the officers claimed that he was "clenching his buttocks" in a suspicious fashion. This led to an arrest, search warrant issued, cavity search, anal probe, and colonoscopy to determine if the drugs were up his ass. Yes, this really happened, and no, they didn't find any drugs. Can't it be any more humiliating? Also, not a single officer was ever charged, written up, or questioned about the incident.

The other thing that goes completely unnoticed is that when law enforcement engages in brutality, it is ultimately losing the confidence of the very same community they have been sworn to protect. People who witness crimes will never come forward and report them to the authorities or cooperate with law enforcement if there is no mutual trust and respect within that community. I don't care what color or race you are.

And I have to address to a faction of this country that blindly supports law enforcement and the unlimited privilege they have since Number 45 has publicly supported law enforcement personnel in their use of brutality during the detaining and arresting of a suspect by suggesting they receive "head injuries." What kind of a world leader suggest things such as this? I guess that is how he Makes America Great Again.

Much of white America, many of whom are supporters of Number 45, need to wake up to the realization that anybody suspected of a crime, regardless of race, are still "innocent unless proven guilty." That is the law, but often, law enforcement forgets that this same rule of law also applies to black people.

Brutality and inhumane behavior go against the laws of man, but after you stick the word *police* in front of the word *brutality*, you get a totally different animal. If you are being beaten or brutalized, you would want to call law enforcement to stop it. But when it's the very people whom you trust to stop it and enforce the law, which is not only condoning but also conducting the act of brutalization upon a citizen, then how are you supposed to react? Fight back and you could lose your life. File a complaint and you lose your reputation, job, friends, etc. No matter what happens, you are behind the eight ball on this. Police brutality is a disease. It is a tributary river that has flowed from the lake of the history of slavery in this country, from a time when just being black or brown was almost an automatic death sentence.

I can remember police officers beating black and brown people since I was a kid. White America needs to wake up and realize that when you beat up black people, it's not just that one individual. You are inflicting pain and suffering on an entire race of people. When you brutalize people, you instill a sense of fear in that community. Many law enforcement officers get it twisted because they think that by instilling fear into a community, you will automatically gain respect, and that is crazy. Much of white America has no concept of

JOHN STEPHEN PARKER

this because law enforcement doesn't behave in this manner in their communities. They are focused on the "Officer Friendly" myth that "the police are your friends, and if you have a problem, you should call them."

Because of how black people have been treated historically by law enforcement, we will make the (safe) assumption that all law enforcement officials are bad until we see different. White America would call this stereotyping or grouping all law enforcement officials together. Black people simply refer to it in one word: survival.

Now I am not going to say that white Americans aren't victims of police brutality. In fact, we have witnessed some very rare abuse in communities where no black people live. Don't worry. I wasn't robbing anybody in the neighborhood if you were wondering why I was there.

You watch white people in these communities get all shocked and shaken when it's happening to them or their kids. But if these same white law enforcement officers were killing white people's dogs like they're killing black men, women, and children, white women, mothers, would have burned police stations down all over America by now. And these same people get pissed at black people for marching when they know deep down they would never tolerate this behavior.

When you perform your civic duty, vote, and pay your taxes, the same taxes that pay the salary of these law enforcement officers, you shouldn't have to guess if your child is going to make it back home after running a basic errand.

Police brutality is more than just the physical part of law enforcement stepping over the line during an arrest. It is also the degrading and dehumanization that happens during the arrest. I have been pulled out of my car by racist white officers, where they have called me a monkey, sambo, and of course, they love to be able to call you nigger anytime they please. This is the real brutality because if you respond to any of this, you have now opened yourself up to even more brutality that they will undoubtedly find a way to justify.

As was written in the Constitution, it continues with law enforcement in this country. It has been validated time after time that the lives of black and brown people have little value, that our very existence isn't even human. White America is inherently naive to the realization of this systemic and institutionalized problem. The entire law enforcement and the criminal justice system is in need of a system-wide overhaul. Law enforcement has operated like this for centuries, and I applaud the young people who are doing what is needed to bring about a change in the system. These young people both have the stamina and ability to maintain a wave of transition. They are shifting the consciousness of this country that will

JOHN STEPHEN PARKER

most likely wake up white America and finally get them comfortable being uncomfortable. God bless Black Lives Matter.

This change cannot just be about BLM. Like the civil rights movement of the 1960s, movements can get hijacked. Real change is not a sprint but more of a marathon. Young people are often impatient with progress at a slow pace. It took decades for black people to be able to sit at a lunch counter, to drink from a water fountain, to swim in a public pool, and to even exercise their constitutional right of casting a vote. Imagine how long it will take for the tide to change in just being treated humane by law enforcement.

It will start in our own backyards. It will first take black people focusing on our communities. It will mean that we will need to actually come together. We will need to stop the violent acts and heinous crimes we commit upon one another. We need to stop the behavior that white America stereotypes us with—the type of behavior that is perpetuated and exploited by the white-owned media companies—which make their bones off every violence that we perpetrate upon one another.

In the world we live in, the police are used against black people for two very prominent reasons: the first is to be sure that we stay in our own neighborhoods, and the second is to be sure that we stay out of white ones. This is brutality that goes unrecognized, and it is rooted in white supremacy and a privileged mindset.

Law enforcement, in general, has no respect for black people and people of color because if they did, they would think twice before killing us, and the judicial system wouldn't keep making excuses and justifying this behavior. The only thing that law enforcement looks down on more than black and brown people are smart black and brown people. Smart black people challenge the authority of law enforcement by our simple existence.

Black people should come together and devise a unified plan that would affect the commerce of white America, and I'm not talking about protesting in a mall. I am talking about something that cuts off significant cash flow to the country. It needs to be something that gets white America to finally nod their heads.

And make no bones about it. When white America wakes up and decides to nod their head in the right direction, it will all stop.

JOHN STEPHEN PARKER

CHAPTER 9

Wake Up and Understand that Justice Means "Just Us"

"If you are neutral in situations of injustice, you have chosen the side of the oppressor. If an elephant has its foot on the tail of a mouse and you say that you are neutral, the mouse will not appreciate your neutrality."

—*Desmond Tutu*

B LACK PEOPLE HAVE ceased to be amazed by anything that happens within both our judicial and criminal justice system. We are arrested and incarcerated at a rate five times higher than white America. These stats have been validated by academics, voluntary sector organizations, and community activists alike; and yet nothing has ever been done to address it. In fact, some would believe the system is proactively working to keep the system in place. One term that has led to the large numbers of black incarceration is a *joint enterprise*. This term is applied in cases involving groups of black people where one person might be involved in a crime, but they will all be *jointly* implicated. This process has significantly added to the number of black men locked up over the past two decades.

When discrimination is truly and blatantly obvious that it is an unavoidable subject, white America will then turn to a process that makes them feel good and gives black people the illusion that they are "involved" in the decision-making process. That will put together a group of "community leaders" from the minority community, usually lead by a black preacher, to direct some advisory board. This is what happened after Michael Brown Jr. was killed in Ferguson, Missouri.

Former Governor Jay Nixon, who at the time was a "lame duck" in office, decided to put together an advisory board. He called it the "Ferguson Commission." The intent was to study the reason that lead up to the killing, at least that was the way it was promoted. It was led by a black preacher. SHOCKER! This gave the impression that the governor of Missouri actually cared about the black citizens of his state. He had to give out that impression because he wanted the black citizens of Ferguson to forget that he stood up at a podium one afternoon in November before former St. Louis County Prosecutor Bob McCulloch performed his dog and pony "no true bill" show.

Jay Nixon stood at that podium and stated, "We will protect this town," which turned out to be a lie because as there were nearly seven hundred National Guard soldiers placed all over the St. Louis area, the governor never ordered them to protect Ferguson. In fact, he couldn't even be reached. Twenty-one buildings were set ablaze that evening.

So to clear his own conscious mind, he created the Ferguson Commission. It was a publicity magnet. I attended a number of those committee meetings. They were lively, expressive, and very vibrant; and they did give everyone (except me) the impression that this group of individuals was going to affect real change. But it was all smoke and mirrors because this commission lacked the one thing you must have if you are truly going to effect change. This commission had no power, and when the report was finally published, the only thing that could be done with it was to wipe your ass with it. However, the report did indicate the unfairness among racial lines and, whether intentional or not, how it was conveniently filed away when the arguments of black people are oppressed or not. If white America had lived some of the experiences of black people who—across class, age, and gender—can give examples of the very serious injustices they have faced in their encounters with the criminal justice system, there would be no need to suppress this information.

Overall, this commission was a joke. Many other black people and I have heard time and time again about initiatives that would transform these racist systems into ones that are equal to all citizens. Clearly, this has never happened, and black people have reached a point in our society where revolution is at the doorstep of white America. Any and all suggestions by white America are going to fall on deaf ears because why would we accept suggestions from another faction, especially from one whose many members have fought for the very right to oppress people of color? **"The revolution will not be televised."**

We are tired of the high rates of stop and search. It's the racist taunts, the humiliating and unnecessary strip searches, and the assaults and brutality that because of technology and social media, we are now able to witness. We are tired of the excuse we have made for decades. It shouldn't matter if a black kid was a good kid. It shouldn't matter that he got great grades in school. It shouldn't matter that he was well-liked by his peers, his teachers, and his friends at his high school.

The epic stories of black people being harassed and killed by law enforcement officers for no other reason than sitting in a car or during a traffic stop or just walking down the street, minding their own business, highlight a deep-seated truth that is devastating black people in America—the truth that even if you behave correctly and do things properly, you are still not safe, and even if you will be treated fairly by law enforcement, you can still lose your life.

Society today, as a whole, likes to discuss fairness. The reference is made on every subject from politics to the economy and even immigration. But there is nothing fair about the treatment of black people or people of color in the United States. The stories of tragedies continue to be told to the world. For much of white America who believes that racism has diminished and that we are all equal, these stories remind them that black people have not achieved a fair and just relationship with law enforcement in this country. And as much as the criminal justice system works to protect white America, this same system continues to fail your black counterparts.

The outlook is not great for any improvement of either law enforcement or the criminal justice system as long as Number 45 is in office. In fact, I fear that he may be harming both to a point that it is irreparable. Number 45 constantly supports the myth that law enforcement is made up of good people putting themselves in harm's way to protect us. In some ways, this is accurate, but he tries to align them in terms of a military-type agency, which they are not. He praises these people and often screams about the need to make it easier for the cops to do their jobs, which can be done by eliminating restrictions on conduct.

This man is a racist a leader as they come as, even to this day, no shame in continuing to publicly convict the Central

Park Five despite the fact that DNA evidence exonerated those young men without any question. The young men went to prison and served time after being wrongly convicted. Number 45 put himself in the role of the "law and order" POTUS, which made no sense (or perfect sense), because his redneck, ignorant, and toothless supporters, after all, are just as likely to say that they know someone who has been incarcerated also.

Everybody sees how both law enforcement and the justice system operate, and it is all about money. The majority of America, regardless of color, believes that if you have the financial resources, you have a better chance of avoiding prison than if you are poor. While the majority of white America still runs with the belief that race has nothing to do with how law enforcement treats black people, mostly young people, both black and white, know that law enforcement harassing black people is a problem. And the criminal justice system is extremely unfair to people of color. These same young people know that justice is not blind, as it should be, but much of white America continues to push the myth of the justice system treating people of all races equally.

What white America needs to understand when black people are talking about criminal justice reform is that it does not mean that they are against law enforcement as a whole. That would lead to anarchy. We are only saying there should be equal treatment for all. We black people are not against the police, but we no longer tolerate police officers harassing us, beating us, and murdering us and our families.

For over four hundred years, black people in this country have lived and died battling against the deeply rooted foundation of white power, white privilege, and the segregated judicial system. When Jim Crow came to town, this same racist judicial system pushed ridiculous claims about evidence that attempted to state that based on the physical features of black people, we were less intelligent and, of course, the same stereotype we hear today, that black people are more prone to criminal activity. This "evidence" further fueled the national hysteria about a growing black population and offered justification for criminalizing black men.

If you simply take a look at the number of black people who are incarcerated, it should be difficult to understand that there is a plague that has come over the country, which was unleashed by the judicial system. This plague, like the many in history, is destroying black people who live in certain neighborhoods. Although incarceration is just one piece of the pie, it is certainly the most damaging.

If white America was truly interested in achieving equality in the judicial system, they would step up and be more vocal. They would demand that legislators in positions effect change to put a stop to the discriminatory treatment of black people.

White America has not yet come to understand that black people are only thirteen percent of the population of this country and that we have no power and are in no real position to get changes made. Ultimately, it is white America that must challenge individuals, communities, cities, states, and the entire nation to be accountable for what the justice system does to all people.

Don't get it confused. Black people and people of color continue to be under attack in this country. Between the vocal young people who walk the streets in protest of law enforcement killing another unarmed young black kid to professional athletes of all colors taking a knee during a song to protest the same, black people are speaking up on issues around law enforcement and the inequities of the system. We realize that this discriminatory behavior is not limited to law enforcement, as there is a battle going in the areas of health care, housing, and education as well.

Most reports that appear in the public often get shortchanged. The reason for this is very simple. We live in a world where the foundation has to be sound and secure. That foundation is shaken if white America is not comfortable with their everyday routines. Factors in that foundation are their everyday things, like baseball, fast food, and in some cases, Fox News. They don't want that they're disrupted by a protest over civil rights violations and complaints about law

JOHN STEPHEN PARKER

enforcement stepping over the line. White America manages to avoid discussions along these lines, but rest assured that to black people, these issues are of the utmost importance. Black people are not dumb, stupid, or naive to the facts and true reality that until white America wakes up, decides to step up to the plate, and deals with these realities that this racist system is completely illegitimate, invalid, and unfair and until the system is rectified, it will always impede any real progress toward a truly post-racial society.

The first step in this rectification process would again be to stop asking black people what can be done to change all this because white America has never listened to black people on anything. White America might simply try giving control to black people because we already know what the issues were and should not be defined by or tended to be based on the guidelines of white culture. This would be a starting point toward some progress, which should be the end goal.

In the meantime, as black people, we are used to progressing at a snail's pace; and since this is the case, we should be investing in our own community. We could put our own sweat equity into supporting the volunteer organizations and other individuals who are neck-deep fighting injustices. There are a number of different aspects of criminal justice that can be addressed, and they all help give people an opportunity of those individuals who have been affected by this racist operation. If given the opportunity to control the situation, black people can have the wherewithal to make a difference.

Because of the injustices that black people have been through for centuries, the conversations and discussions on the criminalization of black America have moved into the area of the family unit and just how the system is also destroying the black family. The criminalization of black people also continues the cycles of poverty and oppression in our society. Black children are being put into the system at an earlier age and at a greater rate than white children.

White America needs to wake up and realize that it has become abundantly clear that for us black people to survive and thrive, we must call out this unjust criminal system, protest the regular injustices that occur, and take a stand for ourselves. The American dream has never included black people and, in fact, kept us from being able to raise our families in a correct manner. White America needs to realize that if you don't include us in your dream, then we will be forced to create our own. White America is either going to open the front door, let us in, and welcome us to the table willingly or be prepared for us to kick in the damn the door, by any means necessary, and take our own seats (and probably a few of yours also) at the table.

Contrary to the beliefs of white America, black people are the real experts in their communities and the operation

JOHN STEPHEN PARKER

of them. White America truly has no real connections to the life experiences of black people in this country. White America is told every single day that having a prison system in this country is essential for the protection and security of your family. What that translates to is that "we need prisons because we need a place to keep the scary black and brown people out of our neighborhoods."

What they refuse to recognize is that the policing and imprisoning of black people actually creates a grave situation, and because of this, it puts the future existence of black people in question. I question if this isn't a terminal illness for the black community. Black people have ceased living in fear. We will continue to protest and call out white America (including Number 45 and any other who should come to the office after he has destroyed it) and the policies and legislation that is being pushed, which would bring more problems to the black community. Black people have been to the puppet show, and they have seen the strings. We have stopped being our toughest critics because now more than ever, the black community is under attack by much of white America.

Black people realize that we have come to a time in history, again, where simply being able to walk outside and live our normal lives are being threatened. Regardless of what white America has never opened their eyes to, black people are resilient as a community, and we welcome any challenge to that resiliency.

It's no longer time to be on the defensive. It's time to stand strong and proud because it's clear that our justice system isn't now and, in all reality, has never been looking out for us.

It truly does me "just us."

JOHN STEPHEN PARKER

CHAPTER 10

Wake Up. President Obama Changed Nothing. Racism Lives

"I wish I could say that racism and prejudice were only distant memories. We must dissent from the indifference. We must dissent from the apathy. We must dissent from the fear, the hatred and the mistrust . . . We must dissent because America can do better because America has no choice but to do better."

—*Thurgood Marshall*

IN HIS 2014 grand jury testimony over the shooting of eighteen-year-old Michael Brown in Ferguson, Missouri, Police Officer Darren Wilson described Brown less like a human being than a possessed animal. "He looked up at me and had the most intense aggressive face. The only way I can describe it, it looks like a demon. That's how angry he looked."

The image he conjured of Brown, even after he shot him six times, including once in his eye and once in the top of his head, was of a man both physically superhuman and emotionally subhuman. "He was almost bulking up to run through the shots like it was making him mad that I'm shooting him. And the fact that he had was looking straight through me like I wasn't even there. I wasn't even anything in his way."

The manner in which white America has looked at black people—and in particular, black men—have long been an object of fear, excessively and promiscuously sexual, insufficiently cerebral or dumb, physically imposing, and as usual, inherently and instinctively criminal. If white America was truly intuitive of black America, they would realize that these assumptions came from their own creation. White America enslaved us, broke up our families, humiliated, brutalized, raped, and lynched us for years. In today's society, white America puts more money toward keeping black people locked up than on education. This is a situation that was created by white America, so I am at a loss as to why many of them are so fearful. Maybe it's the idea of black people reaching their human potential and, with that, karma coming back around.

I am sure Barack Obama hoped his presidency would change the world more than it did. I am sure he hoped that when he was sworn in as the forty-fourth president of the United States, he wanted it to be the moment in our history where racism and discrimination would completely disappear from our society. I am sure he told his beautiful wife, Michelle, that the day he took the oath of office, the world would look at black people differently, and millions of kids, especially black kids, across this country will look at themselves differently.

When the world looked at black men during those eight years, for the first time in history, it got a different look. The powerful man was black, but there was much more. He was a great father to two wonderful young ladies. They saw a faithful husband. He was intelligent, measured, and even-tempered. That is also a far contrast to the childish person who followed him into the same office.

But white America is easily mesmerized by nostalgia and is stuck in that belief that good always conquers evil. They believe that because a black man was elected to the highest office in the land, the racial climate of the country was over and a spine of inclusiveness was finally here. But such was never the case, and in fact, the election of President Obama sparked an increase of racism and discrimination that was only surpassed when Number 45 was elected.

White America may have the view of black men that is inclusive of fear, excessively and promiscuously sexual, insufficiently cerebral or dumb, physically imposing, and inherently and instinctively criminal; but I would like to know any position in this country where a black man could stand up in front of the world at a podium with five children from three different women. If you want to know what white male privilege looks like, then look no further than the podium on the inauguration day of Number 45, because there isn't a black man on the face of the earth that could be elected with the history of Number 45.

There are standard emotions that much of white America believes is uncontrollable in black people. The stereotypical ones that are drilled into the mind of white America every single night on the evening news and on primetime shows are the rage, anger, promiscuity, and the like. The problem was that again, much of white America has had this instilled like a belief that Columbus discovered America. They made the assumption that Barack Obama would behave like this in pressurized situations. Contrary to the stereotype, he rarely displayed any fiery emotion at all. In fact, I believe he was a black man who was aware of his place and position and made the choice to hold his "blackness" back at more times. I think this hurt him, especially in the eyes of many black Americans, because it came across as being a little to calm and serene. This was the case even when people would publicly attack him. Many didn't feel like he was asshole enough to get things done for the average American, and in a sense, he failed in representing those who had little to no representation.

Black people have always wanted to feel like there was a leader who was specifically fighting for the needs or causes that most affected them. It would have perpetuated the stereotype that many in white America have if Obama would have just gone "gangsta" on their ass. This would have appeared to be more consistent with the standard black personality. Instead, my man was dignified and calculating all the time. He made sure that he calculated what a black male in public office could or couldn't do.

Obama was the guy who was not going to show his ass in public. When black people were being killed by law enforcement, he was smooth, like cream cheese on a bagel, even though you knew that this man, coming from Chicago, was ready to catch a case on somebody. He let this out a little bit after Michael Brown Jr. was killed, but even then, he kept it calm and cool. He brought a sense of tranquility that no other president has.

You would have thought that during his second term he would have turned a little more "ghetto" and become the white American stereotypical "angry black man," because even if you rise to sit in the highest office of the country, you can never get away from it. But Barack Obama remained like butter—smooth and playing the role. Even if you become president of the United States, you still can't escape these stereotype expectations. But I have to keep it real also, and as much as I despise Number 45, all of America needs to realize that Obama was "gangsta" in that he was responsible for killing more people around the world than Frank Lucas killed in *American Gangster* because he did it through drone strikes.

While Obama was in the chair, white America was forced to view black people differently, whether they wanted to or not. They saw what real, honest truth is to be black in America through the thoughts and actions of a strong, powerful, compassionate black man; and for eight years, that made them give consideration to how they viewed other black men. The stereotypes didn't disappear, but much of white America woke up and realized that the stereotypes have no factual basis.

Okay, I will give white America a few points because it is accurate that blacks are less inclined to tie the knot (marriage) and black men are less likely to live with their girlfriends (or boyfriends). But white America needs to continue to awaken and know that when the children of black men are under five, they receive a great deal of quality time with their fathers. We feed them, wash them, and diaper them. We get them dressed; we do our daughter's hair. That last one can be an epic in the process.

We do read books to our children. Both my son and daughter got stories from me. We transport them to activities. I cannot tell you how many ballet, hip-hop, lyrical, and many more dance classes I have attended. We are better than any other racial group, whether we live with them or not, and the

JOHN STEPHEN PARKER

fact is, we are more likely to be single than any other racial group. So President Obama was not that big of a role model for being a father and how black men should live their lives because we were already doing it. But that narrative, put in place by white-owned media companies, needs to remain in place, in order to make white America feel more comfortable.

It aggravated me and many black people I know when President Obama talked about the negative stereotypes surrounding black fathers or "baby daddies" when he spoke on Father's Day in 2008. He ran to the white American stereotype and talked about how many black fathers have shucked their responsibilities. He made reference to us "behaving boys and not like men." He basically blamed the downfall of the black family on the behavior of some black men and call our community "weak" because of it.

It is quite the contrary. We are fully aware and also aware that our responsibilities do not cease at conception. We know that raising a child is far different than making one. It takes a great deal of intestinal fortitude to raise a child, and you better have serious guts because there is nothing easy about it. But the thing that bothered me most is that Obama would never give that speech to white America when it is clear that they need to hear it at least, if not more.

White America needs to wake up and conclude that law enforcement and the judicial system operates on two different standards. You have one standard for white America, which pays attention to details of crimes and actively looks for loopholes to keep from sending members of this faction to prison often for committing some of the most heinous crimes you can imagine or, as we have seen, often when crimes are committed right before our eyes, such as the killing of unarmed black people.

You have a completely different standard for black people and other persons of color. This can be verified by the number of black people who are arrested, charged, tried, and incarcerated for the same exact crimes as their counterparts and others with much harsher sentences. Black people don't use drugs any more than anybody else and certainly less than much of white America, but because of the rules of the game—a game that was set up by white America mind you—we will be crucified for the same things that much of white America receives a slap on the wrist for.

For instance, the time of sentencing for possession of powder cocaine, as opposed to possession of crack cocaine, is astounding because there is a "mandatory minimum" guideline. Powder cocaine can get you probation, but crack gets you a minimum of ten years in prison. Knowing that, crack cocaine in a fixture in the low-income black community makes this sentencing guideline automatically racist. President Obama felt the same way and reformed the guideline,

JOHN STEPHEN PARKER

in addition to progressing toward lighter sentencing for nonviolent drug offenders. This made strides on the degree to which black men were able to contribute to their families, communities, and society as a whole, just like the convicts of white America.

After having a black president in the United States, does white America actually see different? That can be answered by simply looking at Number 45's time in office and the race-baiting he has perpetuated. With all the unarmed black people killed by law enforcement in this country on a regular basis, do you think that any one of those officers who pulled the multiple triggers and ended those lives consider for one moment that they might be killing a future leader of this country?

There is a faction of this country (white America) that is quick to label black people as unpatriotic and not caring for this country. Colin Kaepernick got tagged with this accusation when elected to silently protest police brutality against black and brown people. Black people love this country even though, for most of history, it has never loved them back. For my whole life, my parents, my grandparents, and for most black people, this system has never worked for us. But we still play the game in a system that disrespects us black people on a daily basis.

We have tried to do our best to live and play by the rules even though we knew the same rules and standards would never work out in our favor. We often live in neighborhoods that white America doesn't even think about driving through. We send our kids to schools with books so beat up that white America would not attempt to read them. We work jobs (when white America hires us) that many in white America wouldn't consider in their nightmares.

Black people in the United States have been waking up every day believing that our lives would change, even though everything around us says it never will. Truth be told, if you ask most black people, they will tell you that no matter who won the 2016 election, there were no expectations of things getting better in the black community, but they still voted because our ancestors fought and died for that right. Therefore, that is what you're supposed to do.

Yes, I am pissed that Hillary Clinton was not elected, but not because she was a woman, but because she was the most qualified of the two. I wake up every day now with the fear that the world we live in will be destroyed by nuclear war, so yes, I am terrified about what Number 45 will do. I am even more terrified of what could happen if his successor, Mike Pence, should ever become president. I would be remanded to the back of the bus again in a matter of days.

But not unlike every black person in this country, I'm used to things not going my way. It's too bad that white America, living under the umbrella of white privilege, has never experienced that, and it's blowing their minds. But excuse me if I get a little offended because I didn't see all this outrage when everything was happening to black people refusing to give up seats on a bus or sitting at lunch counters or trying to buy a house on the "other side" of town.

Black people love this country as much, if not more than white people do. Hell, we built this country, and white America should never ever forget that. The presidency of Barack Obama changed nothing in this country, and white America can stop using that as a fallback argument when questioned about racism in the United States. That was the accomplishment of one man, not an entire faction of people.

Nothing has changed. Excessive force used by law enforcement is still resulting in the murders of unarmed black men again and again. And afterward, nothing happens again and again and again.

How do we fix the problem? White America, when they have their moments of empathy, always present that question to black people. Again, they always start with the popular black preacher of the moment (the Rev. Dr. [insert name here]). They do this to try and deflect the fact that they created the game, but once everything appeared to become even, it was time to change the game. Therefore, white American fronts, as if they want an open dialect about the real issues of racism.

The truth is, white America has always known how to fix it because people, both white and black, have been telling white America what to do, how to begin, and where to start for centuries because none of the racism, brutality, harassment, murder, and whatever else has happened over the last several years is new. Read your history, and you will find that the system is not broken. This is exactly the system that was created.

As much protesting as has been done, and let's face it, there has been a ton of it. The realization is that people protesting cannot change anything. Just ask the families of the dead, unarmed black men. So I'm tired of being tired or being outraged. I'm tired of the same old responses and stereotypical accusations about a victim. We follow the same course moving the video around social media. These videos end up having millions of viewers but somehow never make it to the desk of the CEO of XYZ (white-owned) media company. The protests and demonstrations begin with black people disrupting white America's norm whose day at the mall just got ruined by a group of "loudmouthed, uppity niggers."

Occasionally, we will see an indictment of a law enforcement officer or two but rarely ever a conviction. It's as if they all wear Teflon or something and can never be scared. They are protected by the coating of a judicial system that overlooks bad behavior of law enforcement. They are protected by a shroud that believes because they have a tough job, they should get a pass. They are protected by a narrative that white America must sustain because they cannot imagine waking up in a world where the majority of people with Caucasian faces didn't trust law enforcement in this country. Even worse is that they would be forced to agree with black people; the police in this country are a tool or even a weapon for racism to continue.

We repeatedly hear of investigations and inquiries, which are regularly followed up with thoughts and prayers, but satisfaction will only come the bereaved when accountability is put in front of protection. In this country, black people are forced to settle for demotions or suspensions (with pay) when we lose a loved one by the hands of law enforcement. When you suspend someone with pay, you are virtually giving them a paid vacation and send them away (until things settle down). This is like a bad version of the movie *Groundhog Day*. It constantly repeats itself because you have a next incident or a new video that will come to light. Usually, it will provide more evidence of bad procedure and horrible behavior, and before it starts again, it will end with white America always asking black people, "What kind of solutions can WE come up with so this doesn't happen again?"

Richard Pryor was a great comedian. Like all great comedians, much of his material came from real-life experiences, like fights with his many wives or being raised by his grandmother. But he always had a routine that was in reference to how police officers treated black people. He once made jokes about the difference in treatment between blacks and whites. We all laughed at the time, never realizing just how true it was. The routine played up the fact that the relationship between law enforcement and most of white America is generally one of respect, courtesy, and politeness. Most of white America doesn't fear to lose their lives during a traffic stop.

That is a very real thought for every black person that is ever detained by the police for any reason. Pryor would joke that when the police would stop him and request his driver's license, he would immediately scream, "I AM REACHING INTO MY POCKET FOR MY LICENSE." His reasoning for this was very simple: "Because I don't want to be no motherfucking accident!" Truth, however shocking as it is, has some humor in it; but for black people, this is a constant truth, no laughing matter, and painfully real in today's society.

Number 45 and all his "*Make America Great (White) Again*" rhetoric keeps much of white America under the delusion that when a police officer kills an unarmed young black kid, it can be classified as fake news. If you are able to open your minds for education, you take an opportunity and read the nonfiction pieces called *Jackson, 1964*. These publications go back and discuss the trials of getting black people registered to cast their ballots and discuss race relations in the United States. One particular passage talks about police brutality that happened against people of color in Seattle in 1975.

The bottom line and reality in this county is very clear and has been for black people for four hundred years. I have advanced degrees, but it only takes a kindergarten education to see that in the United States, the life of one white citizen is far more valuable than the lives of millions of black ones.

Regardless of the pace and convergence of Black Lives Matter protests and the little legislation that is proposed to continually ban the various forms of racism, much of white America and their racist president keep up their constant barrage to keep their fellow supporters convinced that transformation is at hand, and it will be bad for the country.

I am not as pessimistic as I sound because I do believe that we have transformed this country in the last one hundred years because we, good people in this country, have transformed ourselves along the way. The United States is a million times better than it was one hundred years ago, but it's also a million times that same point from where we should be. Everybody, both black and white, can agree with that. But even though we are aware of the progress that has been, we are still witnessing harassment, brutality, and murder of black people. We even have black security guards who break up a fight in establishments getting killed by the same law enforcement that they support. Does that mean black people can't even go to work without fear of being killed?

White America can be outraged as much as they want to be, but when will you show some sincere empathy for the situation? Let's remember this also. White America created the game. Black people are only trying to play by the rules that you people laid down. It takes imagination to empathize with someone else's situation, and based on simple history, white America sucks at that. In fact, one might say that the most dangerous place for black people is in the minds of white America.

Let me say this also. The fact of the matter is—and I have no problem saying any of this because by now you know me and know that I am that guy, so I am just going to put it out there plain and simple.

If you support Number 45, you are a white supremacist. You might be in the closet, but you have stuck your head out now, so just own up to it. And you are more than just the massive amount of white supremacy that you end up participating in, in an inherently white supremacist system. It doesn't mean that you are a mean person. Quite the contrary. You are often respectful, but at the end of the day, you know

JOHN STEPHEN PARKER

what side of the fence you are on. I would just prefer that you just freaking own it.

Now some of you may be asking, "John, are you really willing to call, openly call, some white people white supremacists?" And to that, my answer is HELL YES. This may seem like a bold statement to some, but honestly, I can't understand why.

Human beings can quite easily fall in line with violent hatred and oppression. Just looking at history, you will find that to be true. Do you think that the Nazis came to power against the will of the German government or with the support of the German people? Do you think that slavery was upheld purely by the few who were rich enough to own slaves or by an entire society that even built an army to defend it? And no, none of this can be excused away as "that was just the way it was at the time."

Society does not have a few "bad years," but we should stop placing the blame on the "the times we were living in." This country—more specifically, white America—needs to be held accountable because these horrific systems of abuse, oppression, murder, and even genocide were upheld by everyday white America. That simply means that EVERYDAY PEOPLE are capable of some pretty, HORRIBLE shit.

The same people who claim to praise God, attend church, support the military, pay their taxes, and volunteer for charities are many of the same people who uphold the oppression of others. It has been done before; don't fool yourself, because it is being done now all around us. So yes, much of the white population in the United States is actively working to uphold white supremacy in this country, and like it or not, yes, Number 45's presidency is a violently white supremacist one.

So I'm not sorry to say this, but your grandma who supports Number 45 is a white supremacist. Your buddy (regardless of if you hang out with him regularly or not) who supports Number 45 is a white supremacist. It doesn't mean you can't exchange political views, but at the end of the day, I know which side your bread is buttered. That's what happens when you actively support white supremacy.

And yes, the whole "Make America Great Again" movement is a call to white supremacy because you simply need to ask the question, When was America greater than it is now? Was it the '60s? the '50s? the '40s? How you answer that question depends on how old and white you are.

Most of white America my age can only answer that because they were mid-sixties babies, but go back to any time before 1964, and my very existence would have been looked at as being lower than animal stock in many states. Hell, two decades after I was born, interracial marriage language was finally removed from many state constitutions, so for me, I have between 2000 and now to draw from.

Every period of time in the history of the United States, prior to this one, was less safe, more segregated, far less diverse, and less free for black people and other persons of color. So if you plan on Making America Great (White) Again and you are referencing any time in the past, you're truly asking for a return of white supremacy. Just own it so everybody knows what lane you are in.

Truth is, Number 45's anti-immigration rhetoric is racist as fuck. I'm not saying that if you believe in tighter immigration rules, you are immediately a white supremacist (although you might just be). I believe in immigration laws. But if you go about it by insinuating that the Mexicans crossing the border are rapists and if your proxies are warnings of "taco trucks on every corner," then you are trying to tap into a white supremacist narrative of the black and brown haters and you are sure as hell dog-whistling that white culture in the United States is under attack.

Number 45's Islamophobic rhetoric is racist as fuck, and before you slap me with the "Islam isn't a race" crap, let me please remind you to sit the fuck down and shut up. I know Islam isn't a race, but Number 45's Islamophobia sure as hell is racist.

If Number 45 and his followers didn't think of SCARY BROWN PEOPLE when they thought of Islam, Islamophobia wouldn't exist. If Islamophobia wasn't racist in nature, we'd treat all problems within other religious communities not affiliated with scary brown people the same way we treat Islam. If Islamophobia wasn't racist, we'd be trying to "liberate" Mormon women currently being punished for their own rapes at BYU.

If Islamophobia wasn't racist, we wouldn't have conservative politicians fighting against raising the statute of limitations on child sex abuse so that Catholic priests could finally face justice for their crimes. If Islamophobia wasn't racist, we would have declared war on Christian fundamentalism after the Oklahoma City bombing and the multiple deadly Planned Parenthood bombing and gun attacks by, excuse me, WHITE MEN over the past ten years.

If Islamophobia wasn't racist, Number 45 would be seeking immigration bans on people from ALL countries that produce terrorists (which is basically every country), not just brown ones. But because Islamophobia IS racist, Number 45 has been able to stir up white supremacist hatred and fear of the brown "other" and turn it into support from his supporters.

This is just a sample of the white supremacy that has seeped into every corner of society through the window of Number 45's presidency. It's not everything, but it's enough.

It's enough to overshadow any possible positive you could entertain in supporting his presidency.

So if you support Number 45, you are supporting all the above, and yes, you are supporting white supremacy. If you support Number 45 for other reasons, you are STILL supporting all the above, and you are supporting white supremacy. If you believe that you are actively against white supremacy and yet you will support Number 45, you are lying to yourself.

People are being hurt right now by the racism that Number 45 is peddling by the bravado that the legitimization of his presidency is giving to white supremacists. What in the world could Number 45 possibly be offering you that would cause you to overlook all the above?

And I'm not saying you should have voted for Hillary Clinton in order to not be a white supremacist. I'm not saying that there aren't some Clinton supporters who are white supremacists. You could have been a supporter of any candidate or a die-hard anarchist and still be a white supremacist. But if you are a Number 45 supporter (in my best Maury Povich impression), you ARE a white supremacist. You looked at a campaign built on open, gleeful, hate-filled white supremacy; and you said, "Sign me up!"

I don't hate anyone, but I am not willing to coddle people anymore either. As I went to the midterm polls in the fall of 2018, I realized that I am past the point where I'm willing to create a safe space for many of white America to be able to elect white supremacy into law without calling out what you and people like you are: an unabashed, willful proponent of white supremacy. And these people need to stop trying to mask it in any other costume.

There is no middle ground to be found here. There is no compromise between equality and white supremacy. And there is no gentler way of confronting racism when my basic humanity as a black man is not enough to sway these people against electing a regime that is built on the hatred and fear of people who look like me. And if you are one of these people, please don't get it twisted. Those of us directly harmed by the hate that some of you elect into office will not forget that you traded away our safety and humanity for empty promises of "winning" and "greatness."

Life is a big damn circle. What goes around comes around. I am not into revenge. It is a "dish that is best served cold." But I am all about the reckoning. A reckoning is simply about evening the score.

JOHN STEPHEN PARKER

CHAPTER 11

Wake Up to the Differences and Be Okay With It

"It is not our differences that divide us. It is our inability to recognize, accept, and celebrate those differences."
—*Audre Lorde*

WE HAVE SEEN a resurgence of racism and division overtones in the United States. You have thought that since the election of the country's first black president, we would have taken further steps to eliminate the issue, and yet we still are unable to have the hard discussions necessary to move the country forward.

There is little disagreement that there are significant differences in the way white America and black America look at racial discrimination and the future toward a more harmonious transition. As black Americans, we are treated unfairly on the various level in society. It doesn't matter if you are trying to get car insurance to achieving the American dream of homeownership by securing a load to the way we are handled by law enforcement. For many black people in the

United States, racial equality is the one illusion that seems to be just that—an illusion.

There is not a black person in this country who does not feel they are treated unfairly in many instances, and if we are ever to achieve true equality to white America, there will need to be a legislative change. There are also a few black people that truly believe that it will ever change. And if you can believe this, there is actually a small fraction of black people (Number 45 supporters, if you can even comprehend that) say the country has already made the necessary changes. I have no idea what planet these people are from, but clearly not here.

About half of white America believe the country has made progress but also feel that there is work to be done in order for black people to truly reach a level of equality with white America. But only a few of those actually feel it will ever happen.

I once had a conversation with a white man who took issue with the word *nigger* being considered unspeakable. Let's call him Bob. Bob's problem is with the strong reaction many black people have to this word, especially when directed at them as an insult by white people. Now I know this sounds ridiculous, but there are people in white America who truly don't understand why black people don't like being called a *nigge*r. Go figure?

JOHN STEPHEN PARKER

Nigger is a term that brings a polarization to any situation for a black person because it is an insult like no other, rooted in the history of racism in this country. Bob attempted to justify the use of it as an equivalent to call an Italian person, a Wop. Furthermore, he went on in his infinite wisdom to explain that black people should "get past" the belief of facts that racism still exists in the United States.

The most dangerous thing about Bob is that he is far from being by himself in this belief. Almost two-thirds of white America believe that the United States has moved past racism and that it truly doesn't exist in this country anymore. That is even considering the ratio of killings by law enforcement between blacks and whites, and the fact that the number of incarcerated black people is so out whack. Black Americans as a whole disagree that this is the case. This alone makes the case of importance to open up and maintain a constant dialogue of prejudice and racism. Many in white America fail to understand that the two are very different and that racism still has a strong foundation in this country.

The Wop stereotype and the humor that surrounds the term continue to give life to the stereotype. This is considered a form of prejudice. *Prejudice* is defined as "a preconceived opinion that is not based on reason or actual experience," or to make it clearer, it is a prejudgment that is assumed but not actually experienced. The funny thing about prejudice is that often, it can have both positive and negative connotation.

Often a prejudice will come naturally that will cultivate racist endings, but this is not true for all forms of prejudice. This is one reason that it is important to understand the difference between prejudice and racism. Bob told me that as an Italian, he actually experienced some real shit in his life because of the type of prejudice that focused on Italian people. But there is a big difference between being laughed at and made fun of because you may eat a ton of pasta or because you may have an uncle in the mob and being called a nigger.

Referring to an Italian person as a Wop could very well irritate or even aggravate a person, but I have never heard of it escalating past that irritation. The reason being is, in this country, that person is still a white American and will most likely not be denied resources to establish themselves in society. These would be things that black people in this country have fought and died for and continue to fight and still occasionally die for. The basic resources are available to most of white America, such as a college education, the freedom to live in any neighborhood, employment, and the right not to be killed by the police. As I spoke about in the previous chapter, prejudice like this comes in the form of humor where a minority is usually the butt of the routine. If prejudice were a weather anomaly, it would be considered a

JOHN STEPHEN PARKER

thunderstorm, whereas racism is a category 5 hurricane that has impacted our society on a permanent basis.

Nigger is a word with a dark history and has been used by white America since the first African enslavement ships landed on the east coast of the United States. It is all-encompassing that not only perpetuate the prejudices that come with it, such as the ridiculous belief that black people are more animalistic and naturally progress toward criminal behavior. It also promotes the belief that we have some hyper sex drive (which I personally believe to be an asset) and, my favorite, that we are lazy slugs that have no work ethic at all. The word *nigger* and the prejudices that are accompanied by it are no comparison to an Italian person being called a Wop.

Nigger has and is always used to make black people out to be less than human. The Constitution of the United States, in its original manuscript, classified me as "three-fifths of a man," which meant I was not a man at all and that I did not deserve the same rights and privileges as members of white America. The Constitution of the United States, a document that much of white America seems to enjoy cherry-picking to suit their needs for the moment, was not only prejudicial but at the very least was also written on the foundation of racism.

Racism is the establishment and reproduction of systems of control and domination using race as the establishing factor. In other words, racism establishes an unequal power based on race. It is for this reason that the word *nigger* is more than a red flag signal for prejudice. It is more of the calling card of the people who created the system and lets black people, for the last four hundred years, understand that they are a subclass of a human being in a country controlled by white people.

When you hear the word *nigger*, you are painfully reminded of this fact, but worse is when that certain faction of white America hears it. It reinforces the stereotype in their minds that black people are dangerous criminals who are lazy and deceitful and are only interested in fucking and making as many children as possible only to never take care of them. In those minds, we are truly the "black plague" on society.

When black people hear the word *nigger*, it has a different reminder. Our memory is brought back to the issues of harassment, brutality, arrest, and murder by law enforcement officers. We are reminded of how many black people are incarcerated. We are reminded of the fact that we can't get a good-paying job because we may not have an acceptable name or that our hairstyles may be a problem, even though we are more than capable for the position.

It brings to mind the fact that the white-owned media companies don't give a shit about crimes against us and our communities and that the police care even less, because unless they can keep their advertisers happy with heinous stories of the mythical black-on-black crime that is supposedly killing our neighborhoods, it's truly irrelevant what is going on against us. The word reminds us that white America is more committed to exposing crimes against white women but fails largely in talking about the lack of economic investment in our cities. *Nigger* is a racist word that reminds us of all the other problems that result from systemic racism.

The topic question that all my white would-be allies can't seem to get out of their head is, Who is allowed to actually use the word *nigger*? It is a sensitive deal and obviously not a subject that I take lightly. I don't believe that we as black people will agree who has permission to use it. I can promise you that none of those individuals have white skin. Yes, I do agree that it's unfair for black people to continue referring to one another in a term that has been a pain in our very existence. I am sure white America does not understand how black people can get away with the use of *cracker* in reference to white people, but I can simple and only say this: this is our only one and that by no means evens the score for four hundred years of oppression and murder. So it's not fair, but you need to wake up and GET OVER IT!

I do understand where they a coming from though. In the world of rap music, the term *nigga* is used a great deal. However, why is it when we say it, it becomes automatically acceptable, but when a white kid singing the same song says the same word, not only does he feel awkward but the eyebrows of every single black person in earshot also rises up in the corner, like Mr. Spock getting ready to repeat the word *fascinating*?

My only solitude for white Americans who are in this position and feel like they are on notice while listening to the latest mind-numbing rap song that refers to "bitches and hoes" (and hiding behind the belief that these lyrics are like this because we are a product of our environment) is that you might feel picked on, but this is not the black community's way of karma. And I am not dictating to white America that they can't say the word, although I would not recommend it. And I'm not giving black people a pass for using it, because based on history, I personally feel that the word and all forms of it should be abolished from usage in society. The United Nations has stated that black people are entitled to reparations, but I am not willing to trade straight-up cash so that I can use the word *nigger*. I will hold out for the financial reparations the government owes us.

When the word *nigger* is spoken, everybody tends to think of the South. In the words of Eddie Murphy in the movie *48 Hrs.*, "Not a very popular place for the brothers." From a historical standpoint, this was the most overtly racist region of the country; therefore, I won't spend a great deal of time here. But when you think of the old South, can you imagine the slave master on the plantation yelling at one of his slaves? What word is he yelling at the human being after every single crack of the whip against that man's bare back?

Yes, he repeatedly calls him a nigger.

Pump your brakes now, because I am not throwing down some line of guilt on white America, but I do hope it makes you feel uncomfortable. White America wants to often forget about slavery because it makes them feel uncomfortable or guilty. But guilt is not a helpful reaction. I'm just making a simple point that there is a big difference between black people calling white America crackers and white America referring to black people, ANY BLACK PEOPLE, as *niggers*. And if you don't believe that, then all you need to do is play back the slavery scenario you just read. In fact, the reason the slave owner was ever strapped with the title of "*Cracker*" was that it referred to what white people did with whips, cracking them on the bodies of livestock and slaves. *Cracker* was the word that black people referred to in speaking about their oppressor. But there was never a time in the history of this country when the word *cracker*, in reference to white America, was spat while being castrated, got their foot cut off for trying to gain freedom or had their fingers amputated for learning to read.

Cracker has never been heard by a member of white America before being lynched. That's because, in the history of this country, there was never a moment when black people, as a whole, made a decision that white America was inferior and subhuman and deserved to be murdered just because they were crackers.

I believe that the context of usage does matter, but the context has to be looked at through the historical time periods of slavery and Jim Crow. White America needs to wake up and realize that they cannot simply ignore these facts. White America cannot just remove centuries of history and forget that this history plays a role in modern-day racism and race relations in the United States today.

So now that we understand from a historical perspective why the word *nigger* is such a polarizing word in comparison to *Cracker*, it should be easier to put it into a reference in today's standards.

The current power dynamics between white America and black people and other persons of color are far from equal. Slavery and Jim Crow have all but formally disappeared, but they have the substitutes of police brutality, mass incarceration, voter suppression, and situations like the Flint, Michigan, water crisis that have taken their place. Regardless of all the technological breakthroughs that our society has made, the second-class treatment and racial oppression of black people in our society have never missed a beat.

White America hates the fact that the oppression I speak of goes along with white privilege. All of white America, regardless of if they care or not, reap the rewards from being white in the United States. Those benefits range from dealing with law enforcement to employment to health care and various other institutions. I am not saying white America does not experience oppression in their own individual right. Quite the contrary, because I am sure they do. But they can live normal lives without the overall fear because of their race. That obviously gives white America a privilege that is not extended to black people. In the history of this country, black people have never had that kind of power or privilege in the United States.

So when white people use the word *nigger* (yes, even with an *a* in place of the *er*), it is coming from a foundation of power and privilege because the word is historically linked with oppression—the type of oppression that white America has never experienced.

Hearing or seeing *nigger* spoken in a crowd or written in an email or on the stall in a public bathroom has virtually no effect on the majority of white America. But it has the ability to screw up the entire day for a black person. It brings us back in history when my ancestors were viewed lower than livestock. Nigger doesn't put white America in anguish. Racial oppression is not a part of white society (no matter how much ridiculous banter you hear about reverse racism). A complete irony of this is that many of these same very privilege members of white America who would just take over the opportunity to say *nigger* or *nigga* choke and spit before they would utter the phrase, Black Lives Matter.

They will walk away from an opportunity to speak out about the harassment and brutality committed against black people every day in this country. They will remain silent while law enforcement officers shoot an unarmed kid in the street sixteen times while his "brother" officers sit there and watch him do it, but they would give their left nut to be able to sing along with a rap song that talks about "nigger this and nigger that." They won't join with the same black people they always claim they want to support but would die to say the word *nigger* and not become a pariah. They don't have to fight alongside black people because they don't want to, because their day-to-day life isn't as impacted by racial injustice. That's where that power dynamic sometimes hurts the most.

Privilege and power provide white America the opportunity to "have it their way" because they get to be selective about where and when they can possibly "have my back." When they are down, you hear them belting out YG's song "My Nigga." But then like a 2:00 a.m. booty call or when another cop is standing over an unarmed black kid's corpse, they will support that cop when he spouts the same tired-ass line "I felt my life was in danger."

Black people don't have and have never had the power that comes with privilege. We don't because racism targets us while sparing our white counterparts. This is not our game. The most that black people can do is chuckle when we hear about white America not seasoning food and not being able to carry a damn beat, even if it has a handle on it. These are petty jokes and a far cry from racism.

Racism may be mean, but meanness does not always equate to true racism. The difference lies in who has the power and privilege, which, in this case, is still white America. If a black person calls a member of white America a cracker, they can pick up their ball and go home if they want to because they still have the power and privilege to control the game. But they do not have the right to scream racism or, in this case, reverse racism. It makes the black person an asshole and, at most, a bully. That's still very aggravating, but don't get it twisted, because it is still a far, far cry from racism.

I'm not even going to go into the ridiculous myth of reverse racism because discrimination against any faction of white America is a fantasy and a ridiculous concept. I have scanned social media pages and gotten in a discussion where some privileged white girl got called a honky once in her life. The only thing that ensues afterward is black people, along with a few supportive white social justice leaders, supplying links, which are never read by the white people on the thread who have gotten their feelings hurt. Reverse racism is nothing more than white America feeling threatened because the world that they have had control of for centuries is finally changing ever so slightly. And in a decade or two, they will no longer be the majority. Apartheid, here we come.

Now we all know that there is a faction of white America that will never change. They are dug in like gopher and will never change. There will be another faction that will claim to not understand, and there will be others who don't care at all because they don't believe it will ever affect their immediate environment. Therefore, they will keep their heads stuck in the proverbial sand.

White America will try and make the argument that context matters when a white person says the word *nigger*. Maybe they are only using the *a* rather than the *er*, maybe their two black friends don't mind if they say it, or maybe they just want to sing along to their favorite songs. But because we are stuck with the past of this country—a country that has never been held accountable for the treatment of black people—when white America uses the word *nigger*, any context is really irrelevant.

It doesn't matter in what context the word *nigger* is used, it is painful to the black people around you. And even if any

JOHN STEPHEN PARKER

member of white America is in a private setting, it may not hurt anyone's feelings in direct earshot, but speaking the word *nigger* is still and will always be a form of their privilege and power.

As a society, both white America and black people together must be sure that they keep their eyes on the prize and have the backs of people who are fighting for inequality. We should be focusing on the privileges of white America. Any other direction defeats our real work toward true social justice and equality for all. I understand that discussions on race are sometimes uncomfortable. They should be difficult. The history of this country is not truly about greatness but more about genocide, murder, rape, and annihilation of people. And white America, in general, should genuinely be embarrassed by their history.

White America, having their shit put on front street and called out on their abuse of privilege and power, should feel embarrassed. But like being disciplined as a kid, it provides an opportunity to learn something new, see another perspective, and become a better ally if they so choose to be.

So before white America begins bitching and moaning about how they feel attacked and discriminated against, they should first think about how they might be making themselves the focus of a discussion at the expense of progress for all people of color. At the end of the day, if white America is truly about solutions and really about social change, then they should wake up and learn to listen. They should wake up and understand how their actions support or oppress others. And if those actions are oppressive, then they have to learn how to make changes.

Finally, for the love of God, Black Lives Matter, Martin Luther King Jr., and "Franks RedHot Sauce" on everything, please wake up and give up this strange desire to want to say the word *nigger*. It just makes you sound ignorant!

CHAPTER 12

Wake Up, Start Understanding Black Culture, and Stop Shooting Black People

"No one is born hating another person because of the color of his skin or his background or his religion. People learn to hate, and if they can learn to hate, they can be taught to love, for love comes more naturally to the human heart than its opposite."

—*Nelson Mandela*

THE PAST DECADE in the United States is full of both relevant and irrelevant conversations about race and racism. Most of these conversations stem from the killing of black people by law enforcement officers, which is usually followed up by no indictments and certainly (if it ever makes it to a courtroom) an assured acquittal of all charges. It is my sincere belief that up to this point, the deaths of Michael Brown Jr., Walter Scott, Eric Garner, Tamir Rice, Trayvon Martin, Eric Harris, and hundreds of other black people by the hands of a law enforcement officer has been in total vain.

The conversations are not without tension, and much of white America is holding their ground, with their heads in the sand, and continuing the blind rhetoric of race not being a consideration in these deaths. They also run along with the narrative of "The victims were engaged in criminal activity, so they got what was coming to them."

Meanwhile, black people still believe that law enforcement continues to hold individual biases because of race and, with malice, seek out black people and other persons of color to detain, harass, arrest, incarcerate, or even worse, murder. If you really want to know what the truly scary part of this is, consider this: this method of oppression and violence directed at black people and the fact that nothing ever comes of it or it has never changed is that neither one of these accurately conveys the total situation. Yes, I believe that racial bias is a major factor in this phenomenon, but that hardly completes the story.

There is no shortage of visual evidence all over social media with footage of black people being detained by white law enforcement officers. In most of the cases, the black people who were stopped admitted that they may have violated some driving law, but they never disrespected the officer, and the traffic stop simply ran its normal course. There are two factors with those videos. One is that it is the ridiculousness and reality of the need of black people to film every single interaction with law enforcement out of fear for safety. Second is the validation that whites give to the social media audiences that not all police officers are racists. These types of video footage, accompanied by the amount of validation that they receive, are a clear indication that most of white America doesn't know the difference between personal prejudice and systemic racism.

This goes way beyond the debate of whether law enforcement is inherently filled with racists or not. This is more about the examination of the system and how it operates. It is naive to look at anything in a singular form or in terms of personal experience. Much of white America looks at these interactions between law enforcement and black people from a personal experience standpoint, which makes it easy to not see racism.

We had a black president (and again, God, how I wish white America would stop using that as a barometer for equality), black artists are all over the radio, and *12 Years a Slave* won Best Picture. With these accomplishments, BY INDIVIDUALS, many in white America believe that racism is over (LOL). God knows I wish it could be that simple, but that simplistic thought process is nonexistent. The truth is that racism is truly difficult to see and even more difficult to point out, prove, or prevent.

I talk about the killings of Michael Brown Jr., Trayvon Martin, and a large number of other black Americans by white law enforcement officers at great length, but I want people to understand that these individuals didn't lose their lives strictly because they were black. Police Officer Darren Wilson, while in Ferguson, Missouri, may have very well been a card-carrying member of some white supremacist hate group. I not sure if that would be accurate to say or not, but I don't think that anyone will disagree with the fact that he was a true indication of how discombobulated the law enforcement and judicial system really is.

I also don't believe I would find anyone to disagree with the belief that citizens being brutalized and murdered by law enforcement officials who have sworn an oath to protect and serve the public (and who pay their salaries through taxes and are never held accountable for their behavior and actions) is reprehensible. But when the person's skin color is the deciding factor on whether these officers are actually held accountable or not screams of one simple word (white America gets a sick feeling in their stomach when they hear it). The word is *racism*.

Much of white America disregards the factual belief that police officers are more successful in getting away with excessive force and police brutality if the person they are brutalizing is black, which is why police brutality is more than not directed toward black people and other persons of color. How is it that we are only thirteen percent of the population but nearly fifty percent of the prison population in the United States? This is the ideal representation of racism in this country. The United States is a place where black people and persons of color have a bulls-eye on their backs. They are constantly in the sights of systems that are foundationally racist.

The white-owned media companies paint the picture of us as animals every day, even though we are walking into buildings and shooting them up. And we are the first people whom white America wants to lock up. This racist system feeds off the belief that if we create as much disruption, keeping the narrative going and stacking the odds in our favor, the system will always benefit white America first. Everybody else will get what is left, which won't be much.

Society as a whole gets distracted by social media and come to the ridiculous conclusions and assumptions that every law enforcement officer in the United States is racist or that the civil rights movement put an end to racism or that white America will be wiped off the planet in five years. As much as I think social media is important, nothing you read there is ever true or simple. I believe that society as a whole is better than it was a century ago without question. We have softened and are more compassionate now, but we have also brought along the same biased and racist beliefs that were here fifty years ago.

White America IS less racist now than sixty years ago because society made it "uncool" over time. But we have seen it rear its ugly head again, which means there is a long way to go and a lot to do. Discrimination is still very prevalent in every aspect of society, and it needs to be repaired and abolished. Racism isn't over yet, but I am very optimistic that one day it will be. But I am realistic, and I know it won't happen in my lifetime. And I know I spoke on this briefly in the last chapter, but I will say it again because I have not stressed this enough. Reverse racism isn't real. No, really. It is a myth.

Reverse racism is a fantasyland where white America goes when black people call them on their bullshit racism and discrimination. They also take a visit where black people create areas (clubs, bars, television stations, etc.) for themselves that white America is not feeling all "warm and fuzzy" about (think BET). White America runs to this mythical land in their minds in order to validate to themselves that black people are only whining because clearly, they have it pretty good or "See, black people, aren't the only people that are singled out."

White America has gotten confused with the actual meaning of *racism*. They are confusing it with the other factors like prejudice, bigotry, ignorance, and hate that are part of the racist system of operation. As I have said before, white America will experience prejudicial behavior from black people because guess what? We can be just as stupid as any other human being on the planet. Stupidity does not have a racist boundary, but racism is far more complex.

Now before you cry and send me a bunch of nasty messages on social media about how reverse racist this article is, pump your damn brakes. Listen. Some people simplify racism as one group not liking another and think *racist* and *prejudiced* are interchangeable. But they are not because racism is a concept system that operates on both individual people and institutional procedure.

At the foundation, racism in the United States is a system in which white America benefits off the oppression of black people and other persons of color, regardless if it's on purpose or not. Contrary to what much of white America insists on, the fact is, we don't live in a country where black people have equal power, status, and opportunity. I know what the argument is, and yes, white people have experienced atrocities. But when we discuss the history of the United States of America, white America was never held in bondage. They were never colonized or faced discrimination, segregation, and murder to the extent of black people, especially when white America has been in charge of every factor just named. White America has never been told where and where not they could live, rarely faced employment discrimination, and as I have beat to death already, are rarely involved in incidents of police brutality or incarceration at the level that black people do. Do they have the ability and often face the same poverty as black people? Yes, they do, but again, not on the same scale, not even close.

That is the reality of racism.

The reverse racism argument reveals a racists' need to refuse the belief that they have privilege in society. They would rather deflect with rhetoric that black people "get special treatment" instead of facing the realities of how black people deal with racism. Many people smarter than me have said how the reverse racism thought process is crazy talk, but perhaps another way is to discuss one of the issues that get called out as reverse racism.

I am not a fan of affirmative action. It is in place because, throughout the history of the United States, white America has failed to simply do the right thing. But one thing white America needs to understand and be clear about is that it takes **no job opportunities** or **education scholarships** away from any faction of white America. Affirmative action has been a source of discomfort to white America for decades now, especially from an education standpoint. Much of white America believes the white students are purposely rejected for college admissions because those same colleges are forced to admit "less qualified" black students.

Nobody pulled affirmative action out of their ass, and white America has a short memory because there was a time, and it continues today, where black people were not even allowed to attend a college or university. So was there a need for the system to address the history of underrepresentation of black people academically? Without question, there was.

But here is the reality: affirmative action doesn't work for people or any people of color. It only ensures that the proportion of equality is reached. White students are still the majority of receptors of scholarship money and maintain a huge majority of the population of mainstream universities. Affirmative action doesn't take anything away from anyone. It only levels the playing field. And if white America can take credit for black culture (music, art, invention), is it so farfetched to say that white culture can be appropriated for black people too?

I was overheard explaining to a friend of mine why it can create problems for white women when they wear black hairstyles. Man, oh man, did I receive some looks from some angry white people because of that. One white woman asked me, "Well, what about black women straightening their hair or dyeing their hair blond?"

First of all, there are, contrary to the history books in white mainstream America (gasp), black people in the world with naturally blond hair and blue eyes. I know that is difficult for the Jennifer Aniston clones out there to believe, but that is both true and beside the point. The need to flip the script and get defensive when it comes to what is appropriate is ridiculous because it attempts to eliminate the context of history from the discussion.

When black people are conforming to the beauty standards and guidelines of white America, we are only trying to fit in. It is pure survival mode for us. If we do things like wear our hair naturally or dress based on our culture, we can be ostracized; and it can cost us our jobs, education, and lifestyle altogether. How many stories do we have to account for black women being asked to change their hairstyles for someone's office setting?

So for the record, contrary to the feelings of much of white America, not all aspects of modern civilization are the possession of white culture, and anyone who thinks they are has been smoking the racist joint way too long. Furthermore, things like Black History Month, BET, and *Black Girls Rock!* are not reverse racist against white people. They're not examples of a double standard in which White History Month, the White Entertainment Channel, and White Girls Rock would be considered offensive.

JOHN STEPHEN PARKER

But for the trolls out there who are still screaming "Why isn't there a White History Month?" let me say this to you. All history is white history because that is all that has been drilled into our society for over four hundred years, and it is filled with lie after lie after lie. Most black children in the United States will learn they are descended from African slaves before they learn they are descended from African kings. White America has kept this narrative up out of a necessity to control.

Number 45 had a problem with the show *Black-ish* and actually referred to the situation comedy as being racist. He stated, "Can you imagine the furor of a show *Whiteish*! Racism at the highest level?" Yes, you idiot, it would be a racist show with a fascist title. The difference is that *Black-ish* is one of the few black family sitcoms on TV, which is produced and written by a black person. It playfully picks apart racial stereotypes but also includes everybody in the conversation. The White House under Number 45's administration is racism at its highest level.

Consider this. Reverse racism, if it existed, could actually be a good thing for society. If it did really exist, we would be living in a society where all racial groups have an equal amount of power. But contrary to the thought process of much of white America, that is just not the case. So to those who cry reverse racism when a show like *Black-ish* is on the air, please just stop being ridiculous.

Wake up and remember that the network that it is on is still owned and operated by white America.

CHAPTER 13

Wake Up and Tell the Truth about the History of America

In those days I imagined racism as a tumor that could be isolated and removed from the body of America, not as a pervasive system both native and essential to that body. From that perspective, it seemed possible that the success of one man really could alter history, or even end it.

—Ta-Nehisi Coates

I N THE UNITED States, every time a law enforcement officer takes the life of an unarmed black person, the black community responds with first, a protest that always transitions into a spectacle that white America always views as a violent riot. Admittedly, these protests have at times escalated into an act of public nuisance, but the reason they are happening is that black people are flat-out tired. We are tired and fed up with long patterns of police abuse, harassment, and violence toward our communities with no accountability. We are exhausted with systemic racism and the mass incarceration of people of color. But one thing that we are tired of and we don't really talk about it much, but it is a big deal—we are tired of white America lying about history.

The reasons why black people protest or riot for the faction of white America who thinks we are animals anyway is not difficult to comprehend. It truly is not rocket science. The Kerner Commission put it down on paperback in 1968. Black people in this country protest to respond to the violence toward the black community by law enforcement. We understand that much of white America fails to understand and that there is a percentage of that faction that is in complete denial of the fact that black people are killed by the law enforcement, for no reason, every year.

White people develop both a selected and temporary loss of memory and recount when it comes to the history of this country, especially when the conversation turns to the heinous crimes that were committed against black people. Patriotic white America, with all their obnoxious flag waving and the MAGA racist beliefs, forget about the millions of black people who died while enslaved and were killed for wanting their constitutional rights. This country has been referred to as the United States of Amnesia because white people only tend to remember only their accomplishments and want to forget their atrocities. White America has no idea that they are cheating themselves out of a true context.

JOHN STEPHEN PARKER

If white America is to understand the phenomenon of brutality by law enforcement and the violence that is regularly inflicted by police officers upon people of color, they must not continue to blind themselves to their own history, no matter how heinous that history may be. There has been a standard of jealousy that white America has held against the success and prosperity of black people. White America has a rich history of public persecution of black people in the United States. For those members of white America who don't believe me and still want to know their history, do your research on a town in north Florida called Rosewood or examine the destruction of Black Wall Street in 1921. These are the stories that are not written in the history books of white America because they do not want to be reminded of the atrocities that they have committed against mankind.

When black people are angry and protest, white America is almost certain to describe their demonstration as a riot. White America tends to never be interested in the reasons and foundation for the demonstration. The actual comprehension of the problem, even when the protester tells society why the demonstration is taking place, is that there is quickly a deflection led by the white-owned media companies and is replaced with ridiculous claims that the uprisings are happening because of absent black fathers, out-of-wedlock children, and lifestyle of poverty and violence. Both the media and much of white America will label black people as the vermin of society. This is the basis of racialization and dehumanization.

Somehow white America, combined with the narrative of the white-owned media companies, almost never publicly acknowledge that the angry response black people have is because of the cruel and repeated demonstrations of brutality and killing of black people by law enforcement. If they would consider this, they might understand these demonstrations to be logical, reasonable, and clearly within the guidelines of the Constitution of the United States and the spiritual foundation of the American political tradition.

White privilege is a foundational belief in this country. This privilege has made the dominance of white America as normal as breathing. White privilege has directed every stitch of history. In today's society, it is the narrative message that is put out by the media, and it is reproduced in terms such as *black pathology* and *thugs*. These terms are thrown out by the white media during a demonstration like nightclub leaflets on a street corner in Las Vegas. This privilege feeds the beast of white supremacy and continues to service underserved advantages in the white-dominated political, social, and economic systems of this country. And with control comes the spoils, because then you can control how history remembers.

The history of slavery in this country has been mistold and missold so many times on so many levels that it has become a crime of humanity. It may very well be time for some sort of truth commission to be put in place in order to deal with America's original sin. But could a truth commission work for the United States? It would certainly help the United States face the truth about its past atrocities and racial injustices committed against black people.

Truth commissions are put in place to examine the context of atrocities and then follow the historical path leading up to its effects on modern-day society. They also allow other races and cultures to give a different and often a more truthful version of the story. This allows for an accurate examination of history and results of gross violations of human rights of black people and other persons of color.

Let's not fool ourselves. These commissions would have no legal power whatsoever. They would have no power of subpoena or any ability to prosecute citizens. However, these commissions would be able to take a more analytical view of the past in this country and how those injustices impact our current world. One other thing it would provide is an open forum. When there is a discussion of history, often it is an uncomfortable one. These commissions would secure a safe environment for people to have uncomfortable conversations about their experiences and their personal perspectives about history, especially where the topic of slavery is discussed.

Because these commissions would be diverse, they would also bring a diversity of perspective and skill. This is an important characteristic. Though it is important to have commissioners with a legal background, I believe it would be crucial to have people with a broad range of skills from an expansive amount of disciplines.

We have an abundance of dedications and commemorations with regard to recognizing the history of civil rights. These methods of remembrance, such as the National Museum of African History and Culture, present various markers from the boycotts in Alabama to the assassinations of Medgar Evers and Martin Luther King. These dedications help us to realize the importance of this period in the history of our country, and we should never disregard the progress we have made. But they also remind us that the United States of America has a long way to go.

When we don't acknowledge the true nature of history, we dishonor the legacy of the entire civil rights movement, as well as suggest that the work of this nation is somehow complete. This acknowledgment also provides white America an opportunity to tell the truth, which is the true barometer by which we gauge the progress toward racial equality in the United States.

Sixty years ago, this country was a mirror of South African apartheid. How you might ask? Because there was an entire region of the country where if you were black, you weren't even considered a person, let alone a citizen of the United States. But we have seen a transition. The racial climate of extreme hatred and bigotry began to fade. The sun went down on the Jim Crow era, and laws were changed. The Voting Rights Act passed, and black people were finally able to exercise their constitutional rights as citizens. For much of white America, this has been a painful process, but there is no "R" on the drivetrain of America. It only has a "D" because it keeps driving forward.

But in the society that we live in currently and with the election of Number 45, one might consider that the goals established during the civil rights movement have been disregarded, that the country is actually going backward. How do we know this? Well, look at a few clues such as discrimination and segregation re-emerging in our educations system. The progressive legislation that was essential under Barack Obama is being reversed, and much of that legislation is removing the ability of black citizens of the United States to cast their votes. Others are losing their rights because of the flawed criminal justice and judicial systems that subject them to incarceration, because once you're labeled a felon, the old forms of discrimination (employment discrimination, housing discrimination, denial of the right to vote, denial of educational opportunity, denial of food stamps and other public benefits, and exclusion from jury service) are suddenly legal. Furthermore, the economic wealth gap between white America and black people continues to widen every day for all white America who believes that black people have better advantages today than ever. Don't let the smooth taste fool you. There is no difference in the unemployment gap that existed in 1963.

This country is regressing to a period where there was significantly more segregation and much less integration. There was a time when a white man would never face legal recourse for criminal action against a person of color. But what have we all witnessed in the last several years? White police officers killing unarmed black people and never being held accountable.

As a white criminal in white America, the level of respect that is recognized today is still higher than a black person in the old South. As much as white America believes we have reached this post-racial society, the realization of the world we live in is clear. We have never transitioned out of the archaic racial caste system we live in, in the United States. You can wash off, clean out, and eat from a garbage can; but it still remains a garbage can.

I am not as pessimistic as I may sound. I know that we have had a great deal of racial progress. Yes, there was a black man elected to the highest office of the land, which is funny because when I was a kid, I wanted to be president of the

United States. But I was told by my kindergarten teacher, "John, you should probably rethink that because we will never have a Negro as president." Imagine my disappointment when, as a little kid, you are told you can't be something.

Not only did we have a black attorney general but the position was also held by a black woman. Imagine what J. Edgar Hoover must be doing while rolling over in his grave, although as the director of the FBI, he was a bit of a woman also.

We see more and more interracial relationships in society. I myself have been married to a white woman. This was something illegal in many states (and still is) and could have resulted in my murder. Finally, the areas that surround our major metropolitan cities are becoming more diverse, regardless of the fact that much of white America hates it (Chesterfield, Missouri).

If both the civil rights and Black Lives Matter movements were simply about the ascension of black faces to positions of power, we would all be able to call it a day. But it wasn't. It was about equality, and the problem is not that we still have a great deal of progress to be made or that progress is too slow. It's that we are headed, especially with Number 45 in charge, in the wrong way. And this is not a rare occurrence or some anomaly. This is not the first time this has happened.

After the supposed abolition of slavery, there was a brief period during Reconstruction when black people made amazing progress in society, only you have it destroyed by the all-out racism of the South. They solidified that onslaught of this time with the birth of Jim Crow. White America is always good for giving the narrative that black America gets hit with the occasional setback. White America looks at this as an "accident," but accidents are uncontrollable. What happens to black people is not accidental. It is done on purpose and with malice in the heart.

The period after Reconstruction is the reason we have things happening in society today. That part of our history went on for a little less than a hundred years, and it took nearly an act of God to bring it to a halt. In the minds of black people today, this is considered blasphemy.

Much of white America will never speak the accuracy of racism in this country. A thought that occasionally keeps me up at night is what the future will look like. When looking at both the history of the country and the subsequent progress or lack thereof, there really isn't much to get excited about. Since the birth of this nation, how white America has dealt with race and, more specifically, how they have dealt with race as it pertains to black people had been a difficult task to understand. Even in today's society, it is a taboo subject and makes most of white America's stomachs queasy to think about.

JOHN STEPHEN PARKER

I mean, let's face it. The assumption is to be that black people in this country would always bow down to white America. Even after we have reached such milestones in history—such as the Voting Rights Act, the Civil Rights Act, putting a black man in the highest office of the land, Denzel and Hallie winning the best actor and actress award, and of course, Beyoncé Knowles being born—we find that the conversation on race in America has not been altered in any significant way. And I am sad to say that I will be long gone from this earth before it does.

Everybody remembers when one of those singing reality show contestants was in a southern restaurant and one of the other restaurant workers and staff at a restaurant in Atlanta recognized him and simply referred to him as a "white boy." He lost his mind and broke out the reverse racism card quickly on Facebook. It was then picked up by the media, and of course, this got a great deal of support from that faction of white America. He said, "If I said that about a black artist, I would have been boycotted. They would have destroyed my [already purchased] albums and nobody buying any new ones. I would be hung in effigy everywhere."

It's this type of white "victimization" thinking that is the most commonplace false equivalency in white America. Much of white America believes as long as they talk about race and racism, it will absolve them of their history and the heinous acts that were perpetrated by their ancestral family. Bear in mind that many of these family members are still around and still committing the same acts. They believe that they have no connection to the effects, like black citizens being blocked from home ownership. This is a problem that to this day has had no reckoning. The atrocities of white America's history remain unchecked, unevaluated, and nobody has been held accountable.

I saw the video footage of four black teenagers who kidnapped and assaulted a mentally ill white man. Many saw the same footage as I did, even the part where they were yelling expletives about Number 45. I was glad to see these young black men arrested and charged with a hate crime because I do not accept or condone this type of behavior. But before the arrest and indictments went down, FOX News couldn't wait to use this as a beacon to rile up conservative right-wing America. And this same faction started their same old tired rhetoric of claiming that Black Lives Matter was to blame because the teens yelled, "Fuck white people." They felt that the incident should have been looked at as a hate crime.

Officials eventually concluded that the Black Lives Matter movement had no responsibility for the situation. But—and I am again not saying I condone this heinous act by these young black men because I don't—we need not

JOHN STEPHEN PARKER

forget that it took a quarter of a century for the Chicago Police Department to admit to torturing black people into giving false confessions.

Trying to compare racism and acts of violence is apples and oranges, but an underrepresented faction should never be forced to prove racism in a situation. White America has held the higher ground in the oppression of persons of color and that relinquishing of power is not coming soon. The problem they face now is fatigue of the victims who no longer feel an etiquette or responsibility to keep their mouths shut. White America better wake up, and before they get bent out of shape over some stupid black kids yelling "Fuck white people," they should check themselves and not get it twisted. They are still the ruling class in the United States. They created a system that benefits them and, since its creation, has disenfranchised black people.

Now I have gotten my social media hammering by many in white America on this subject, as I well expected to. I have to say that I went to school with white people who have—with a passion, I might add—shared their displeasure with me and about me to the world. They say unsubstantiated and unreasonable things. "This is bullshit, Parker. Why can't I say *nigger* if it's fine to make fun of white people?" one post read. The fact that the education system in the United States, as well as our society, has not addressed this word and why it should be removed from the English language and has often promoted its usage is a clear indication of why I have very little optimism for race relations in this country. White America not wanting to speak the accuracy of this country and not telling the truth about its history is not something new. This is where we live. This is the United States of Amnesia. It was built on lies, deceit, slavery, genocide, rape, and murder.

When Dylann Roof walked into a church in Charleston, South Carolina, and murdered those people—faith leaders, politicians, media pundits, most of whom are white—they broke out those same tired-ass questions, "How could this happen at a church? How could this happen in America?" Questions like this are a true indication of white America's amnesia with their own history. They suffer from this amnesia because they are so busy beating the shit out of one another with the baseball bats of the narrative propaganda of patriotism, freedom, justice, and mythical equality. The truth is that what happened in Charleston, South Carolina, was just as American as apple pie.

And it continues to happen because much of white America is afraid of real justice. Many in white America are terrified that this empire, which has been constructed on a foundation of greed, might all come tumbling down because black people are tired. They are tired of fighting for rights to

JOHN STEPHEN PARKER

be real citizens in a country they built, cultivated, lived, and died for—the same land where white America has generated wealth on their backs.

If white America is for real about moving society forward, they cannot and should not hide from the historical truth of this country. That history is painful, but for whom? The telling of these truths is not nearly as painful for white America as it was for black people to perish in the creation of the society they reap the benefits of. The great force of history comes from the fact that black people carry it within us and are unconsciously controlled by it in many ways, and history is literally present in all that we do. White America as a whole remains in hiding history because it tells the truth of their achievements. It also tells the truth of the unfair advantages they have received through heinous crimes against mankind.

On the flipside of that, black people stay hidden in the darkness out of the habit of history also, because we have been taught that it was unacceptable to make white America uncomfortable. So many of us continue talking about freedom, justice, and equality but often do very little to fight for the real thing.

The events of the early 1800s are a true resemblance to today's society because although we have built beautiful cities and advanced technology, we still have the scars of our racial past that rear their ugly head. Until this country and white America's truth is held accountable and the deep-seated wounds are uncovered and justice, not tolerance, becomes the order of the day, we will never succeed as a country and truly be "united" in these states.

Another reason we continue to fail is that we don't look at our system of government and what it truly is. We do not live in a democracy in the United States, meaning the citizens of this country can make no laws, which is what a true democracy is. We live in a republic. That means we elect people who make laws for us. I don't care what side of the aisle you are on, what race you are, or what religion. Every single politician at his core has the same foundation narrative, which you can't get elected without. They all spout the same ridiculously repeated rhetoric "America is a good and moral nation. America is ordained by God for a special purpose." This is such bullshit because any violence in white America's history, current or future, has always the work of isolated (white) individuals, but not the acts of "true" Americans (unless the perpetrators are black, brown, or Muslim).

If white America truly valued its real history, it would not be so difficult to connect a kid walking into a church and killing black people with the same guys who are on statues that they are raising hell out being taken down. If those memorials to hatred have to stay in place, then you should tell the truth about them and not how you want it to fit the mythical ideology of this country. Please supplement the Southern racist penchant for glorifying a cause that was possessed of no nobility with a large ingredient of murder toward black people.

Can we change? I would say yes, we could, but not without white America waking up with a true willingness to deal with the truth of American theology, politics, and economics. Stop with all the white American self-congratulations and move toward a little more self-reflection.

It might start by putting these names on a memorial somewhere: Cynthia Marie Graham Hurd, Susie Jackson, Ethel Lee Lance, Dewayne Middleton-Doctor, Clementa C. Pinckney, Tywanza Sanders, Daniel Simmons, Sharonda Coleman-Singleton, and Myra Thompson.

This country, not wanting to talk about its real and truthful history, is not an anomaly. This is the United States of **Amnesia**.

CHAPTER 14

Wake Up and Start Talking about Racism Openly

"Racism does not have a good track record. It's been tried out for a long time and you'd think by now we'd want to put an end to it instead of putting it under new management."

—*Thomas Sowell*

I AM OFTEN in conflict when I start talking about racism. It is a subject that is difficult to validate when many of the people who are in charge of the system itself are the same people you are trying to prove its existence. How can I, as a black man, talk about racism in a constructive way with a white America who constantly turns a blind eye and never speaks openly about it?

I have seen enough racism to be well versed when I see it, and I probably always will possess this talent. Furthermore, anybody that knows John Parker knows that I pull no punches and I am open (and some would say "asshole" enough) to saying the uncomfortable thing in an uncomfortable way. I believe that you never ease the Band-Aid from the wound. I believe you just rip it off, live with the momentary pain, and move on.

I believe that it is time for this country to rip the bandage off its terrible seeping wound and look inside. I realize that in doing this, I risk losing people who are very close to me, but the time has come for people to stop being afraid of being misinterpreted or misunderstood. The time for political correctness is over. Let's truly take off the gloves and give that portion of white America that is comfortable in their safe little lives with their comfortable little narrative and give them a moment of pause. These feelings that many black people and I in the United States experience have led me down the road of realization that white America really needs to face the music.

White America has never spoken about racism from a foundation of honesty. There is an underlying sense of pride to have held the type of power for over five centuries. But there is also a faction of white America that holds a sense of shame and outrage when it looks at the atrocities committed against black people by their ancestors. This pain has been passed down through generations, and they have expanded into feelings of intense fear, self-loathing, and self-hatred. The phenomenon of racism is like an ugly growth that has become resistant to any and all disinfectants that society can use to clean it away. It's a disgusting, ugly, awful stain on the face of a society that has refused to address it, and it has gotten out of control.

The United States is responsible for some of the most horrible atrocities and human genocide tragedies in the history of the world. This country was started with first killing the people whom it rightly belonged to. I mean, how can you discover a world where there are already people living? Columbus never discovered anything. At the very least, he was lost and rescued by the indigenous people of the West Indies. He brought along with him, disease and criminal activity. This was only the beginning, as what Columbus started grew into the future capture, enslavement, torture, rape, lynching, and murder of black people.

Centuries after Christopher Columbus started this demise, black people in today's society are still the bulls-eye of the target of white America. And just like rings on a target, the success of their aim is based on how successful they are at institutionalized murder, discrimination, police brutality, incarceration, and government-controlled poverty.

Much of white America is always saying racism has run its course in this country, but this could not be further from the truth. Were they blinded by the light of the tiki torches in Virginia? They may say it has run its course, but that's not true. Racism is no longer rednecks riding around in pickup trucks, drinking beer, and yelling *nigger* out the window. Well, it's not only that. The manners in which racism takes form have simply changed.

It would be great if white America could momentarily step out of their privilege and become a black person. They should experience real racism for a month or two. Real racism, not that fake reverse shit that they whine about. I mean, the kind that keeps you from getting a home loan, a decent insurance rate, or even good service at a restaurant. They might then have a true understanding of the effects a lifetime of racism does.

This country often pleads a white American case for civil rights because it comes from white America. What white America really needs is a broader peak of insight into the black American experience. They might then see how limited they are by the ignorance that begets a white America with the belief that they possibly understand racism.

Black people at least invite white America to experience firsthand black people and then include them in an open dialogue, because the experience itself is a mixed bag. There are moments of insight and intelligent discussion, and there are moments that unabashedly reinforce racial stereotypes. The black family generally views their experiences as a validation of their existing perceptions about racism in the United States. None of this is news to us, and of course, as black people, we already understand the ways racism takes form firsthand.

When the white family takes on the black appearance, lots of cringe-worthy racist antics ensue. A white American mom might wear some African cultural attire to church and follow it up by requesting to touch a black woman's hair at the beauty salon. White America is constantly glorifying black culture but is ignorant of basic rules, like for instance, most black women who are truly about themselves and their appearance do not play when it comes to their hair. And attempting to touch it, even if you are her man and in a relationship with her, is a big no-no. The point is that white America really doesn't understand anything genuine about black culture, and when their own racism hits them square in the face, they become frustrated and, for some reason, feel attacked even though they had offended the black person.

It's in these moments that you could actually learn something, but the black person who is legitimately offended will cease any conversation. My personal belief is that white America has acquired this type of racist behaviors and assumptions through some type of natural osmosis. This would explain why much of white America that behaves in this manner get all shocked and shaken when you call them a racist.

JOHN STEPHEN PARKER

The manner in which we utilize the word *racism* gives a definition of negativity and ugliness, and for the most part, I believe nobody wants to be tagged with that, but white America needs to begin to have an open and honest conversation about racism in America and how they view it. Only then will they be able to develop a true understanding of it and how it affects our society. That is the only true way to grow our society out of its constraints. Racism comes in a few forms. Much of it is out in the open and leave little to questions, but much of it is also inside of a person's subconscious. This is the type that requires a great deal of discussion in order to transform.

So can white America do better? I think the portion of white America that is overly terrified of black people is simply basing that fear on ridiculous assumptions that come from a much deeper level. It is this feeling of terror that make much of white America not see a person in front of them, because they have been brainwashed to only see a black person. When this happens, their imagination automatically kicks in, and the most dangerous place for a black person to be is in the imagination of white America. The person stopping at your house to ask for directions or for simple help, like using a phone, is the same person in the imagination of white America who is going to steal your car, break into your home, or rape your daughter. A friendly gesture from a black person while walking down the street or getting in an elevator translates into "I have a gun, and I going to kill you" in the mind of much of white America.

How many stories do we have to hear about black people being shot at or even killed for simply knocking residential front doors? In fact, every twenty-eight hours, an unarmed black person is allegedly killed by a law enforcement agency, a security guard, or by some neighborhood vigilante who "feared for their life" because a black man was walking down their street. This is something all of white America should wake up and find deeply concerning. We as Americans need to be discussing the change.

White America needs to wake up and understand that when a black person, especially an unarmed one, is gunned down by a law enforcement agency, a security guard, or by some neighborhood vigilante, it is because of racism, not because they "fit the description" or were "acting suspiciously." White America is quick to jump on the All Lives Matter bandwagon, but even the majority of this same faction fails to stand up when these incidents are delayed in investigating, covered up, or explained away. This is murder, the taking of another human life, and white America needs to finally WAKE UP and deal with their own racism and truly own it so that as a nation, we can finally make this ugly problem go away.

JOHN STEPHEN PARKER

Getting a true picture of racism is not about some ridiculous Halloween costume of blackface and an Afro, only to see how someone may treat you if you pretend to be black. And finding a solution will never come from easing into a situation. White America is always talking about diversity in corporate America and how difficult it is. They say, "We might lose people if we move face-to-face with diversity programs." If you were to have a diverse company, then make it diverse. PERIOD. If someone doesn't like their job and the QUALIFIED people they are working with, then show them the door. It is time to cut through the politically correct bullshit and start doing things the right way. Much of that requires simple honesty.

Solving the problem of racism in this country will not happen with black people protesting. It will have to come and, quite frankly, need to come from white America waking up and simply being honest with their behaviors and attitudes. White America truly has no idea what racism feels like. They need to be honest and have open discussions with black people of what being racist, in all its forms, feels like. So these forums, like *Witnessing Whiteness*, that basically are meetings for WHITE PEOPLE ONLY to talk about racism but do not feel comfortable if there is a black person in the room are just another convenient way that white America gets to be comfortable about their own racism.

Events like the white man's "tiki torch" march have eaten away at the foundation of what this country is supposed to stand for. The ideas of life, liberty, and the pursuit of happiness have all but become a faded memory, even a mythical place only to be seen through a looking glass. Events such as those do nothing more than make us keenly aware that racism in the United States of America is alive, well, and living in the hearts of much of white America and that we are continually failing at improving this country's social health.

Racism does need to be dealt with, but it should not be done in such a convenient manner for white America. You can have a constructive, meaningful dialogue, but the level of comfort for the faction of this country that has been behind the wheel of the racism vehicle for four hundred years should be limited. Racism must be addressed in all manners that affect society. That includes our everyday institutions and not just when an unarmed black person being killed by white law enforcement stirs up racial hatred in our nation. Racial hatred by white America has created basic everyday issues, but it has become such an established institution in this country that it has stifled our ability to achieve any long-term solutions. After four hundred years of this, with all the progress this country has made, you would think we would be able to lick a basic problem.

Black people have been rubbing the lamp, hoping that the post-racial America genie would come out and grant us our three wishes. We did get one granted with the election of Barack Obama to the office of president of the United States, but the wish of putting the racial hatred of the past one hundred years behind us has never materialized. And the wish of all people, regardless of race, to live in harmony with one another does not even appear like a mirage. It is not in the cards, but black people never seem to give up on it. We walk through the desert of racism every day, and when we see a glimpse of what we believed to be the oasis of a post-racial United States, it ends up being a pool of more sand, in the form of another unarmed black person being killed and a law enforcement officer getting paid leave.

Life-altering events in places like my home of Ferguson, Missouri, only supports much of white America's racial hatred of black people. It also reinforces the belief of black people that we are not living in a postracial society and that there are no guaranteed rights to black people to the benefits of our so-called democracy. This country has been talking a good game for decades, but conversations and hard discussions about a racial reconciliation never happen until the next shooting of a black person occurs. It is a sorry-ass cycle.

We need to be honest about another thing. The requirement for white America to have an uncomfortable conversation has not come to fruition for a number of reasons. First, any time white America has a discussion about race or racism, they do get uncomfortable; and because they have control of the situation, they will automatically shy away from any constructive yet uncomfortable dialogue.

Second, much of white America is like a drug addict. They have a problem, but they will never admit to it. How many times have we heard "the first step in fixing a problem is to admit that you have one"? White America remains in denial, or they think they can "handle" their problem and "kick it" whenever they feel like it.

Thirdly—and this is probably the most concerning—is that much of white America doesn't even believe that racism is a problem in our society when it clearly infects nearly every single avenue of our society in ways we don't even realize. And while all those MAGA supporters continue sucking on the patriotic, American flag–wrapped cock of this country while listening to a song written by a slavery supporter, they avoid the clear fact that racism and racial hatred is real and continues to be the true foundation of the "land of the free and home of the brave." What this country continues to stand for is oppression, and we have the nerve to masquerade as a country that supposedly leads the free world and preaches, like some fraudulent television evangelist, about democracy across the globe. What a lie.

JOHN STEPHEN PARKER

Has white America forgotten the dream of life, liberty, and the pursuit of happiness? Have they disregarded the true message of democracy? It's time for white America to wake up and be accountable. This country has been divided long enough, and we can no longer afford to be one white and one black. But the reality of the world is this. Black people do not possess the power, position, and privilege to be racist or to end racism. White America must open dialogues with the truth. White America's accountability of its crimes against the humanity of both black and indigenous people must be met in order to move our society forward. There has been enough wrongdoing, social injustice, and oppression.

I care deeply about fighting racism and improving race relations in America, but I know that when the issue of race is raised, many of my white friends resist putting racism at the center of conversations. I have been lucky enough to have some very open conversations about race with some of my white friends, but most of them simply acknowledge that racism exists and then move on to what they feel are more pressing issues of society. There have even been several times where I have been in a strong and heated debate with a white person, in which they cut it short when the topic of institutional racism or white supremacy reared its head.

I had a discussion once with a group of white people about the election of Number 45, which is nothing short of being a radioactive subject. We were all talking, and strangely enough, we agreed that he is a horrible president and, all the more so, a horrible person. But when I argued that it was a shame that more candidates didn't make racism and racial inequality a bigger part of their individual political platforms, you would have thought I said 9/11 should be made a holiday.

I asked why race and racism don't get its due in presidential debates. Man, did I become an instant pariah at that point? One woman answers with "I don't know why, but there are many important issues to discuss, so I guess it doesn't really sit high on the priority list." After which, she quickly moved into talking about her new car and her weekend plans and if the issue of race and racism was the equivalent of wiping a runny nose or another region of your body after going number 2.

I am a liberal person, and I speak out about both racial and social injustice. But I'm an intellectual debater and am always interested in a way to keep another Michael Brown Jr., Trayvon Martin, or Alton Sterling from being killed by law enforcement. I love discussing the difference in how white America and black people view subjects like racism, police brutality, and the Black Lives Matter movement. I am also intelligent enough to understand that not all people, regardless of color, are going to agree with me or even be as in-depth on these subjects as I am. But I find it infuriating that much of white America, especially the ones who love to focus on politics, fail to address the topic of race and racism with any real seriousness.

It's not new because as a black man in the United States, the refusal of my white counterparts to have a discussion about racism is not new, but I understand the frustration of hard-core social activists who are constantly working to improve race relations and progress social change when much of white America still refuses the conversation, even after another unarmed black person is killed. The concerns of black people are readily dismissed by white America because they often refuse to even try to understand the hurdles that black people from disadvantaged backgrounds have to jump over to achieve any sort of level in this country. This refusal supports the foundational racism and bigotry that has kept our society as a whole stuck in neutral.

I understand that discussing racism is not comfortable or easy, but it is a fact of life in the United States. When white America continues stepping over the uncomfortable conversation, they purposely put a halt to the progress that others are making in attempting to make the country a better place to live for everybody. We are constantly hearing the "Make America Great Again" rhetoric, but if we truly believe that, then the focus should be on building a society that is more inclusive. In order to do that, white America needs to understand the side of people of color, listening actively to the lived experiences of black people.

Because of learning and often false history, it is difficult for many members of white America to understand racism as a system. Instead, it leads to many going on the dense and deflecting. I have tried to say "many" or "much" when I speak of white America because I know it does not apply to every white person. But many in white America live, play, love, work, and die in a permanently segregated atmosphere; and they never see this as shortchanging themselves. Think about that. The idea of losing absolutely nothing by never interacting with a person of a different race? There are many members of white America who would be absolutely content if this happened because they feel there is no value of interacting, being in the presence, or listening to the perspectives of black people. This is the type of white supremacy and white privilege that exist in this country today.

Many in white America view the idea of racism as a bias of simply mean people; and if they don't have mean thoughts, don't tell racist jokes, are nice to black people, and even have a few black friends, then there is no way they can be considered racist. They believe in the simplicity of if a person is a racist, then they must be a bad person and if a person is not racist, then they must be a good person. Oh, how I wish it could be that simple.

JOHN STEPHEN PARKER

Yes, racism does happen by acts, but in the larger picture, racism is systemic, and most of white America has no idea that they regularly participate in it. And because they often see only some individual events, they fail to address the entire system that creates the event itself. Racism being right or wrong is what makes white America deflect from the subject because they fail to ever look at the system and never truly come to understand how implicit bias operates. White Americans have learned over time to view one another on an individual case by case. But they have also been taught to look at black people as a group. This individual thought process gives them the privilege to deny that racism is a constructed cog of this country.

For instance, they don't have to discuss how their wealth has grown over centuries and how, in today's society, they reap the benefits of that said wealth. They have the privilege of separating themselves as individuals from the history of their ancestors, which is why much of white America gets pissed when they are "accused" of racism. They say things like "I never owned a slave or lynched anybody" because as individuals, they consider themselves to be separated and different than their history.

Because this faction controls nearly every aspect of this country, they are acceptable to racism, whether it be overt or covert. They don't have to build up a tolerance for racism because they are comfortable. If an event arises, like the killing of an unarmed black person, this same faction of white America responds by blaming the person who triggered their discomfort, which in most cases is usually a black person. They then respond to their discomfort with the event with the usual responses of either retaliation or just an outright refusal to continue engagement in a conversation about it. Essentially, they just cop out.

Racism is oppressive to black people, and there is no getting around that, but since society is focused on the comfort of white America, this pretty well seals the agreement that racism will never truly be addressed except in superficial ways. Most of white America has no true understanding of racism because history has never taught them to conceptualize about it in a complex manner and also to think of what benefits them if they don't have to think about it. But they will argue with a black person in a heartbeat if the subject of institutional racism, affirmative actions, or white privilege arises. White America, in general, will not even acknowledge the informed perspectives of black people, as opposed to listening with humility to experiences what they are truly unfamiliar with. Then they would attempt to seek more information with the end goal of understanding.

For four hundred years, in the eyes of white America, race has been something attached to only black people. White America has never, in the history of this country, ever had to pull the truck up the hill in terms of race. They have been able to glide through life without the societal burden of racialization. Most of white America is under the belief that race is for us to think about or that race is a "black problem." Black people can talk about race. Everybody knows that when we do, white America usually dismisses us, accuses us as with playing "the race card," or my favorite is, says, "John Parker is just an angry person and hates white people." This type of dismissal simply stops white America from developing the dialogue, discussion, and in many cases, stamina to address the issue of race and racial injustice.

White America is always on the receiving end of the white societal narrative that they are better and more important than black people. It is in the lies of history textbooks used in our schools. It is a constant in the misrepresentations and fraudulent perspectives. The media companies that are all white-owned promoted it every single day. The ill-prepared teachers, fake so-called role models, and everyday propaganda of this being a "very good place to live with great schools where all or most of the kids look like them." It is driven by situation programs on television where all the little cliques are all white people. I mean, the shows like *Friends* or *Seinfeld* are a joke in themselves. How do you have two situation comedies based in New York and not have one black person in the fucking cast? Movies are even worse, especially movies about Christ or anything set in the Middle East because during that time in history, there were no white Europeans living in that region. How could white America avoid internalizing the message of white superiority when it is so obvious in mainstream culture?

It is reasons like this that white America has a difficult time listening to or comprehending the perspectives of black people, and the only way to bridge the gap is for this faction to hold themselves accountable, open a dialogue with humility as the foundation, and just listen. White America must bring themselves to tolerate their own discomfort. They must wake up to an honest assessment and open their minds to a serious discussion of their mythical white supremacy and privilege. They have begun to look at themselves as having little to no understanding of race.

White America must tune themselves to the racial realities of black people, which can only be done by listening to the experiences of black people and not being guided by the narrative propaganda of media. They must also address the racism embedded in their institutions.

As a black man, I have developed a much deeper and more complex understanding of how society works. I now challenge much more racism in my daily life, and I have developed and cherished fulfilling cross-racial friendships. I do not expect racism to end in my lifetime, and I know that white America will always possess racist patterns. Much of white America is probably assured that they do less harm to black people than they truly do and certainly less than what has been done in history. But I urge white America to wake up and take a step. Let go of your feeling of white supremacy and strive for basic humility.

JOHN STEPHEN PARKER

CHAPTER 15

Wake Up! We Aren't Forgiving and Stop Asking Us for Solutions

"Be the one who nurtures and builds. Be the one who has an understanding and a forgiving heart one who looks for the best in people. Leave people better than you found them".

—*Marvin J. Ashton*

I HAVE THE ability and heart to forgive people. I believe this, above all else, is most important. It is essential, especially if you happen to be a religious individual. If you have the capability to forgive, I believe that you are truly blessed because not everybody has this capability. It's like giving the person who did you wrong a free "get out of jail" card.

I have two strikes against me as both black and Catholic. My mother was always insistent on having religion in our lives, but the intellectual understanding and reasoning behind a lot of religion have faded in me. There are a ton of people out there who are constantly drinking the Kool-Aid of religion, but my faith is not something that I ever reasonably looked at with real conviction because I question many things. The questioning of biblical occurrence has always been a mainstay of my life and remains today.

I believe my ability to forgive is one of my ways of attempting to stay right with God. I am not a preacher, so I am not getting in the weeds on the subject. I certainly don't go to confession nearly as much as I should (or never), but when I do, I know I am talking to God through his middleman.

Forgiveness doesn't require you to change, only that you acknowledge the sins you have committed. So if that is accurate, consider how many times black people have been asked and, frankly, are expected to simply and always forgive law enforcement and the institutions of this country for the systemic racism they promote.

Furthermore, when we don't forgive immediately, it raises the old white American fear that black people will one day seek revenge for the past oppressional treatment by white America. Let's just be honest. White America is terrified of black people who one day would seek revenge for their historical treatment, and there is nothing on the planet scarier to them than an angry black person who might seek justice, although we are not the ones shooting up schools, movie theaters, or concerts from hotel windows?

JOHN STEPHEN PARKER

When much of white America sees a black person in pain or agony, you can hear a mouse fart a hundred miles away because white America goes into stealth mode and goes silent. When a white kid walked into a black church and killed nine members, the families of those who were killed almost immediately began the forgiveness rhetoric. But I have to be honest because all that forgiving pissed me off. I never tell people whom or whom not to worship, and because I am Christian, I understand the requirement to forgive people who have wronged you. But my hypocrisy has limitations with the way this went down, and the way Dylann Roof took the lives of those people, the forgiving bug disappeared.

Why is it that as one of the oppressed factions in this country, black people are not only expected to forgive white America but also told to "forget it" or "get over it." We are asked to do it all the time. Forgive and get over slavery. Get over Jim Crow oppression. Get over the racism that still is alive, well, and living in today's society. Get over the assault, rape, lynching, and murder on black people all throughout history and still happening today. I think of all the crimes against humanity that white America has yet to be held accountable for, which white America actually demands forgiveness from black people.

Therefore, many black people and I refuse to ride that train because although forgiving is asked of you by God, forgetting to me is never in the cards. Forgetting is why white America suffers from a concussion of history, and it has given them the privilege of not having to understand the reason why things happen and why society is the way it is. Reconciliation will never come with accountability because there never been a commitment to transition, grow, and change. Much of white America contends that there is no reason to change or they are oblivious to any wrongdoings. In other words, "if it isn't broke, don't fix it."

Forgiveness has become the norm for black people in this country. Black families who have lost loved ones at the hands of law enforcement are expected to have funerals that equate to a circus and then turn the other check as the officer gets paid leave while on administrative hiatus. Every white-owned media company asked the same question of every single family of an unarmed young black man who was gunned down by law enforcement: "Do you forgive the officer who killed your son?"

Black churches across this country have also played a part in perpetrating this unwavering of forgiveness by promoting a belief that black people can find "divine justice" if they forgive. This was the foundation of Dr. Martin Luther King's nonviolent demonstrations during the civil rights movement. He believed that if you were able to forgive your oppressor, it would aid white America in transitioning out of the racist culture they were living in for four hundred years. But regardless of your religious stance, the standard assumption is that black people are never supposed to let go of their composure and truly express their grief or rage, not even when your loved one is choked to death on camera on a New York City street by a law enforcement officer using an illegal chokehold.

This is yet another burden for black America.

The double standards of white America never cease to amaze me because, after the attacks of September 11, 2001, I don't remember any discussion of forgiving al-Qaeda or Osama bin Laden. This country quickly and concisely declared war, but I have no recollection of the words *love*, *peace*, or *forgiveness* when ISIS was chopping off the heads of people.

Does anyone truly expect the Jewish community to forgive and forget Nazi Germany for the murder of six million people and the anti-Semitic acts of terrorism that continue to this day? But black people who have been the victims of every known inhumane act known to man are held to an impossibly higher standard and are expected to forgive their oppressors without any questions. This rush to forgive, without going through the grieving process or allowing the judicial system to move forward with addressing these crimes, in addition to the required black empathy is an issue.

White America does not address black agony until the flag of forgiveness for the white perpetrators has been flown loud and proud. If black people show emotion or rage, it is deemed as inappropriate. It is then exploited more by the media as they interview an emotional family member and play up their ability to handle the tragedy with compassion and love because white America is terrified of a black person who may be so pissed that they decide to extend some retribution of their own. When black people forgive, white America receives an automatic atonement and the privilege to rationalize the racist violent acts that are perpetrated against black people. Black redemption of the heinous racist acts of white America has always taken precedence over being held accountable for the act itself. It reduces black suffering and grief to an almost meaningless level.

White America needs to understand and not mistake the forgiveness of black people as absolving themselves for its historical treatment of black people. I believe that because black people have been long conditioned to forgive, it has been made more difficult to make both the judicial and social changes that need to be made. I would actually elaborate; that is, if we continue to turn the other cheek, we are asking for the cycle of abuse and harassment to continue. It is a form of survival that is the equivalent to novocaine to the clarity of black people. It has actually become the norm because black people live under the constant terror of, unapologetically

JOHN STEPHEN PARKER

simple as it may be, being black in the United States. We are constantly both forgiving and reconciling with the very people who keep murdering us in a desperate method to prevent more harm to come to black people. Somehow, black America has come to believe that this forgiveness and reconciliation will translate to white America and we will finally find acceptance.

Even though white America is constantly putting black people on public blast about absent fathers and a black culture that is riddled in crime, illegitimate children, and little accomplishments, these acts of forgiveness might remind white America that black people, who are this country's most historically tortured and oppressed faction of people, are truly good people. This might even get us past white America's historical belief that we are indecent, inhuman savages, although that is probably impossible. White America cannot say the same thing about their whiteness because they have relished in their superiority. White America has a natural expectation of forgiveness for its crimes and heinous acts against humanity, and white America is not trained to comprehend forgiveness from black people as anything more than a sign of no backbone.

Let's keep it real. If white America really truly believed, with conviction, that the lives of black people in the United States honestly mattered, they would push back the forgiveness card that they are always so quick to accept from us, because by accepting our forgiveness and forgoing their own accounts of action, they show that our forgiveness has little to no value at all.

Black people have a right to express their own range of emotions and all outrage. We have a right to be heard, and accountability is of the utmost importance. If someone has hurt you, then they should earn forgiveness. That goes for white America also. If white America wants the forgiveness of black people, then they should hold themselves accountable for their actions and earn our forgiveness. Black people practice legitimate self-preservation on a regular basis, while white America continues to reap the spoils of history.

Black lives won't ever matter to white America, and we will never cease to get off the merry-go-round of racial violence and hatred if white America continues with the importance of white supremacy and racial salvation as the number 1 priority.

Please don't get it twisted, because I am not asking black people to forgive Dylann Roof or anybody else who has perpetrated crimes against black people, nor am I suggesting being violent by settling a score. I am saying that it is time for white America to finally be accountable to society because it is the only way to show evidence that black lives do in fact matter. But in order for this to come to fruition, white

JOHN STEPHEN PARKER

America needs to visit society's confessional and finally make a good and honest confession.

I also have to ponder why that question of forgiveness by black people has to always be asked of us. Forgiving someone is truly a choice. It is personal, and I don't believe it should be given because racism is not the act of one person. Racism is a systemic problem. We constantly sit back and watch the white-owned media companies in the United States stick some sort of forgiving into the discussion, and by doing so, we allow them to devalue the racism in those discussions like it is a personal preference of some kind. It's like if we talk about forgiveness, we will get away from the actions of racism that have plagued us for over four hundred years. Every time a cop gets acquitted for killing an unarmed black person, mainstream media will shoulder shrug and say, "So what? Didn't you people forgive the man? If you have done that, then God is his only judge from now on."

White America needs to stop putting the responsibility of forgiveness on black people. We are less than 13 percent of the population, with little to no power to do anything significant when it comes to this. The burden of repairing and replacing this inhumane system should fall completely on white America. White America, for the most part, controls legislation in this country. Now mind you, it is also a legislative system that stands on the foundation of white supremacy and privilege but, nonetheless, under white American control. I believe that until white America addresses this problem of AMERICA, black people should refrain from forgiving any acts of violence by white America. I am dead serious, and I know that is going to rub many of my white friends and counterparts the wrong way, but until this accountability has been met, black people should stay away from the conversation of reconciliation. Basically, that means this. White America needs to stop asking black people to forgive and fix the problems that they have created.

Reports of police brutality in the black community are as commonplace as a cold, and many black people are feeling frustrated. But at the same time, they are also realizing that the killing of unarmed black people has finally, after centuries, if it is happening, become part of a national discussion. We remain confused because over and over, we hear the same tired line, even with video evidence, "There must be more to the story." Much of white America is still under the myth that black people are the problem. "If you people would just comply, nothing will happen." This leads to the same old deflective-type adage that "police officers have a difficult job too" as if they were drafted into the position. There are others who infuriate black people also. Here are just a few:

"White people get shot too."

"If he wasn't a thug, it would not have happened. He got what he deserved."

"If he would not have been wearing a hoodie, they would not have mistaken him."

"Why did he run away if he wasn't guilty?"

"Why do you people have to always make everything about race? You always have to place the race card."

"You are always complaining about cops killing black people, but what about black-on-black crime?"

And of course, my all-time favorite, All Lives Matter.

I myself feel like a piñata who has been beaten for days by kids trying to get candy out of it. I am just numb and too unfeeling to be frustrated anymore about these heinous acts. I am exhausted from reading damn near every week on web articles, Facebook, and other blogs filled with comment after comment from black people, trying to bob and weave around the boxing ring of white supremacy and privilege. Why do black people even continue to put in the work? Why are we giving up precious time out of our everyday lives and getting carpal tunnel in the process, attempting to explain to some "backstreet boy" the fact that All Lives Matter is a fucked-up way of saying black lives don't really mean shit?

We are sick of explaining to white America because that is all we have been doing for decades, and we have spelled it out so much we feel like white America should take a simple "hooked on phonics" course. Your revered "men in blue" police forces are full of violent, inhumane murderers who abuse their power when dealing with black people, and it has regularly cost us our dignity, our freedom, and our lives. Black people have been back and forth over the statistics. And we have testified in courts of law, courts of public opinion, and in religious places all over the country.

We know that police brutality is a new thing to the white community and has only come on to your radar screen in the last decade because the white-owned media companies have chosen to see tragedy and sensationalism to its white American viewership. But black people have been talking about this subject for decades on end. But with all the media coverage, ridiculous deflections, and abundant information that gets regurgitated on a regular basis, it still blows me away that when the phrase "black lives matter" is spoken, it still requires some dissertation-type conversation. I am still here, against my better judgment, trying to explain it even now.

You have to explain it too much of white America who is always so defensive in such a manner as "You wouldn't go to a breast cancer rally screaming 'All cancers matter,' would ya?" Would white America please stop behaving like this? This country needs to stop behaving and treating that certain faction of white America as if they have never gotten an education of any kind. We all filled out the same bubbles on those ridiculous standardized examinations. At some time, we need to assume that they "got it," but they just don't give a damn. White America is big on putting validity on the statement of All Lives Matter, but if they are so dead set against Black Lives Matter, how do they validate the term Blue Lives Matter because then they would consider Blue Lives Matter to be just as offensive as Black Lives Matter? But they don't. There are actually no blue people in this world.

They embrace the term Blue Lives Matter, but they raise holy hell if you substitute one color as unearned special treatment. They will support the class protection of law enforcement officers, which is a joke because both morally and technically, they already possess this protection. I don't know of any in this country where committing a heinous crime against a law enforcement officer would bring down the wrath of God on your head. No protest needed. They will find a criminal or some random black man to pin it on. It's amazing how fast investigation proceeds and are wrapped up when it involves a crime against a cop, and often, they are not concerned with an indictment, trial, or guilty verdict when it comes to the murder of a law enforcement officer. Many times, they aren't even charged.

If law enforcement kills an unarmed black man, there is an automatic knee jerk to scrutinize the victim's background, medical records, education transcripts, and birth records; but does anyone ever put a dead law enforcement officer through the same scrutinized process? Believe it or not, white America, there are more than a few "dirty cops." But in the United States, white America has this ridiculously delusional admiration of police officers. Clearly, we go out of our way, as a society and as a system, to do everything possible to ensure the lives of law enforcement officers.

But imagine this. Consider what would happen if white America woke up tomorrow and, as a collective majority in this country, were completely distrustful of law enforcement in this country. Armageddon. Cats and dogs sleeping together. OMG!

Also, contemplate this. Consider this a theory because it would be hard to prove, but maybe white America may not be as concerned with "backing the blue" unequivocally and certainly not in comparison to as much as they are in keeping the status-quo narrative "It never happened" when it comes to racist behavior of law enforcement officers. White America would never in a million years believe that law enforcement would purposely kill black people for "shits and grins." It could be, and I'm just slinging crap against the wall here to see what sticks, but could much of white America simply be "full of shit"?

So this is why I throw out the idea to black people to just simply stop. Stop with the appeasement. Stop with the engagement and certainly stop with the endless and mindless conversations about race and race relations in this country. Let white America continue with their tiki torch rallies, their doublespeak newspaper comment sections, and certainly the support of their homophobic, xenophobic, racist, bigoted leadership poisoning the White House. Let's stop buying into the pointless arguments and debates of white America, because of as much effort as we have and continue to put into changing this country in favor of equality, it is exactly the same efforts that they put in avoiding the subject. The only reason much of white America even listens to the stories of hate and violence toward black people is that of their own personal contempt for us.

Our suffering means little to nothing in the grand scheme and is usually addressed with a condescending attitude at best. Our passion as black people has fallen on deaf ears for most of our lives. That is a shame because we may not be the best at getting our point across but it nearly always originates from a place of frustration and fear, which is a far cry from our white counterparts, because when white America debates issues on race, it usually originates from a place of total indifference, meaning their experience is the only one that has validity, and ours, meaning black people's, is irrelevant.

The well-meaning faction of white America, those with good hearts, even have a tendency to place themselves at the eye of the hurricane in the discussion. I do believe there are many white people in the United States who are not racist or who do not hate black people. I am sure there is a faction of white America who doesn't unequivocally support law enforcement and run around screaming Blue Lives Matter with some blind allegiance, but that is because they don't truly have anything to lose.

The landscape of society is changing over from one that was based on white supremacy to one of multiculturalism, so I understand why much of white America is pissed. White America has had a rule on everything for centuries, never ever considered that they would not ever be in control of and never really had to think about race. But the script has been flipped, and white America is finally getting the long-awaited wake-up call that it has had coming for centuries. This bastion of glory, this "land of the free and home of the brave" that was founded on murder and genocide, is finally starting to get an honest look at the cracks in the armor, and much of white America is running for the cover of darkness, like roaches in an old house.

JOHN STEPHEN PARKER

Black people should let them run. We should bask as we listen to them bitch and gripe about how the color of this country is becoming more multi instead of all eggshell. We should sit back and laugh as they debate reverse racism because some qualified black man got a job where their best friend was working and overlooked them. We should observe as they express their displeasure when some black person follows them around a department store because they don't look like they "belong" there. How nice it must be to have the option of simply logging off your computer. We need to let them cry, and black people need to learn how to just sit back and enjoy it when law enforcement pulls them over because they are driving an expensive car in a black neighborhood. But instead of getting good and drunk like we should while enjoying these things, too many are fighting with white America about why nothing we do should be considered racist. We need to take a win when we can get one.

Colin Kaepernick made a call to silently but powerfully kneel in protest of the injustice, and it has provided us a true inner scope. And it has proven a real point. White America is way more concerned about how black people protest injustice and a lot less concerned about why we are protesting. When someone tells you exactly why they are doing something and you make a choice to ignore the reason because you don't like or agree with the method of protest, then you truly had no regard for the reason in the first place. So let's step away from the idea that "if they would just be nicer, we would be more receptive."

We, black people, don't need white America to be happy, supportive, or comfortable with the way we protest, so we will keep on blocking traffic on public highways when white law enforcement officers get paid leave after shooting another unarmed black person. One of these days, we will unite and transfer black dollars to black banks because we will no longer need or want to keep battling white America for the American dream, which has been a nightmare for us.

White America does not need to be spoon-fed like a baby on how to show allegiance to black people, and we certainly should not have to validate those who feel like we do. They can learn what they need to learn on their own on how to show support to a black culture that regularly has to battle racism, and they can do it without the "that a boy" that black people are always so quick to give. Black people need to stop checking up on members of white America to see if they are actually doing what they say. That should not be our responsibility, and if that means that we need to stop associating ourselves with white America that "talks the talk, but doesn't walk the walk," then oh well.

The thing that is so aggravating when you are having a conversation about racial issues with white America is many of them fail to comprehend what you are trying to get across, so it is difficult to decide when you should just give up. They never seem to understand the resolution, and white America walks away from the discussion, perplexed because they still claim to not know exactly what black people are "complaining" about or what they are seeking as a resolution.

One of the things we want white America to understand is that white privilege is a real thing and not some illusion made up by black people. It's something that white America didn't earn. It is a benefit gained simply because they are white. It's the favoritism of the white race above any other race achieved by a system based solely on dominance, and it comes in a variety of forms. White America has the freedom to behave in pretty much any manner they choose without it being attributed to the stereotype of their culture, and they are never asked to or looked upon as the representative of their race. They retain the individuality and are never singled out as a race when it comes to situations such as car insurance, home loans, tax returns, and certainly not when it comes to confrontations with law enforcement. Privileges such as these automatically support white America, and never have they had to earn any of them. The fact that these privileges are just in part of what contributes to the uncertainty among white America because they truly have no clue how to address them, even if they wanted to.

So for those of you members of white America who are always so ignorantly perplexed and are constantly asking what black people want and don't want while you are gazing at your next protest without much interest, I will simply give you a few things. If you are feeling guilty about how you or your white American counterparts treat black people in this country, do something about it, but don't lay your guilt on black people. That guilt does nothing to help black people and is truly a waste of our time.

You created the situation. You fix it. You have created the education system that does little to nothing for inner-city black kids. You created a criminal justice system that incarcerates black people more times than it incarcerates whites. You created the poverty that has enveloped nearly every major city in this country. Your guilt means nothing and is nothing more than a ploy to transition your culpability of the situation. And during this transition, you find it easier to just simply wash your hands of the situation and go back to your everyday privileged lives. It's a cop-out and looked at by black people as cowardly.

White America, in general, has no clue about their privilege; and when they get into discussions about the subject, on the ones that I have been involved in, they tend to shy away in a deflective manner, mostly because most of white America doesn't believe that they possess any privilege whatsoever. They spout statements like "I have worked for everything I have, and nobody has ever given me anything." They believe they are well educated on racism and privilege because they have never used the word *nigger* or feel like they have never treated or oppressed any person of color. This is their privilege. They have the privilege of denial, and every single time you hit white America in the face with it, they automatically go to the denial reflex, which is always followed up with playing defense and then blaming black people for the problems in their world.

The only thing that is even more frustrating is when members of white America chooses to own their privilege but then try to separate themselves from other members of the faction who are racist. Then you get "I get that I am privileged, but I am not nearly as racist as that guy is." White America accepting the fact that they are privileged and accepting the fact that they are a problem is exactly what the issue is, and instead of fixing a society that they created, white America wants to fix black people. At the end of the day, we don't need white America to fix us. We want white America to fix the problems that they have created and stop putting racism around the neck of black people, like some albatross. We did not bring this shit on ourselves.

But also at the same time, we need to climb ourselves out of the stereotypical how that white America has dropped us in of being lazy, illiterate criminals who never want to better ourselves and truly get away from this handle that white America has strapped us with for centuries. Much of white America, in general, has washed its hands from the culpability of slavery because, in their eyes, it happened "a long time ago."

But the fact is that although no member of present-day white America has owned a slave, this is where we are in society, and this mess was created by your ancestors, so wake the fuck up, because yes, that responsibility has been passed on to you and your current-day status. White America needs to wake up and take ownership of the oppression/privilege narrative and start being the solution instead of continuing to not only be part of the problem but also be the damn problem as a whole.

We want you to get over yourselves and stop asking us for solutions to your fucking problem because you aren't listening to us anyway. We have been providing solutions for decades, and for the most part, they have all fallen on deaf ears. White America is so blind to racism and privilege that they don't even understand the fact that even though they control nearly every aspect and institution in this country, this subject is one of the few that we are the experts on. We have been fighting, arguing, and begging white America to close their mouths and listen. White America needs to listen with the idea of

JOHN STEPHEN PARKER

truly understanding first and responding second when black people explain these subjects to them.

Black people have been thinking about racism and white privilege and having a conversation about their significance way before it was on the radar screen of white America. Mainly because this very same privilege has given you the convenience of disregarding it every day of your life. You have the privilege of not seeing race. You have the privilege of believing in your mythical "postracial society." This is something that we can't even laugh about because we continuously watch people that look like us destroyed by a system that you created for your benefit.

White America needs to wake up and take a hard look at their privilege and how a system that they have created has kept people of color in a category of meaningless faction. I wake up every day concerned about being black in America. I am constantly aware of my surroundings whether I am in a restaurant, in a concert, in a shopping mall, in a business meeting, or simply driving in a neighborhood where I know there are not many people who look like me live. I am aware that I am almost always one of the few black people nearly everywhere I go, and this is an awareness of which many black people and I are incapable of escaping.

What black people want from white America is for them to pull their head out of their ass and finally acknowledge that this a very real thing. It will never stop until you, as the faction in power, make a conscious decision to actually stop it. When you decide to put the issue of racism and white privilege to the forefront of society's problems and stop hiding behind the veil of this being black people's problem, we might then be able to fix this.

White America, you should all get together and talk among yourselves. You should all be uncomfortable and in pain until it doesn't hurt anymore. That which doesn't kill us always makes us stronger.

Just ask black people.

CHAPTER 16

Wake up to the Myth of Black-On-Black Crime

"Black-on-black crime" is jargon, violence on language, which vanishes the men who engineered the covenants, who fixed the loans, who planned the projects, who built the streets and sold red ink by the barrel.

—Ta-Nehisi Coates

WHEN I DECIDED to sit down and write this book, it was mainly because nearly every conversation I had with some ignorant member of white America, I was interrupted with the same ridiculous statements. Because of being asked about solutions to racism, I found that many of the conversations I had with members of white America would always contain a rebuttal of some kind. So for example, if you talked to a person about social justice organizations like Black Lives Matter fighting against police brutality, the knee-jerk reaction from that white person was always the favorite phrase "What about black-on-black crime?"

I am very well versed on the fact that white America never wants to discuss any culpability in the downfall of society because they feel accused and then feel forced to defend themselves. Often, much of white America feels like black people dump all the problems of this country in their front yard. Trust me when I tell you, although white America has created much, if not all, that is wrong, that's not what black people are trying to do. But I have to ask, What is white America's fixation with a black-on-black crime?

White America hangs on this like a dog with a bone in its mouth, as if black people aren't aware of violence in their communities. Contrary to what white America comes up with at the local Elks Club meetings, black people do not sit around eating chitlin and watermelon, doing the running man, and clanging mason jar together that is filled with grape Kool-Aid when a black person is the victim of a heinous crime committed by another black person. It hits us in the face, more so because usually, our community is very close-knit and everybody knows everybody. But here is the thing. This may come as a shock to the Number 45 followers out there, **but there is no such thing as black-on-black crime**. I will concede that black people do commit crimes against other black people. I will even concede that white people commit violence against other white people more than we do, but not by much.

JOHN STEPHEN PARKER

Almost every day, an advocate of conservativism or some member of the alt-right post something on social media on how lazy, crime-inclined black people are ruining this country. The foundation of this rhetoric is based on the statistic that 86 percent of black people who are murdered are murdered by other blacks. I would be bothered by that statistic if I didn't know that the same 2017 FBI report says that 86 percent of white victims of murder were killed by white people. Shocker! The concept of white people killing white people—again, dog and cats living together.

Black people do kill black people. I know what you're thinking. "Yes, but black people do so disproportionately." You're right, even though white people commit most violent crimes. But what that really means is that because of the raw numbers, if the truth were presented with the choice of stopping white-on-white crime or black-on-black crime, the fact is that stopping white-on-white crime would pay far greater dividends.

These stats are exactly the same because, frankly, people commit heinous crimes against people in their own communities. So it is not surprising that most people who are victims of violent crimes are victimized by someone in their own neighborhood. So for all the pundits out there who insist on jumping on this ridiculous bandwagon narrative, believe me when I tell you that there is no such thing as black-on-black crime. **It is just a crime**.

The fact of the matter is that crime is the follower of poverty, so if white America is so dead set on talking about crime in the black community, they should really just be asking why there are so many more black people living in poverty than those in white America. I told someone the other day that you have the so-called black-on-black crime going on in your front yard. It is the same as grass growing. If you have two blades of grass fighting for the same resources in the soil to grow, one will get pushed out of the way, so that the other can thrive. And when it comes to poverty-stricken areas, it is no different, because human nature kicks in and survival skills move to the forefront. Those survival skills will force you to fight and even kill for what one needs to stay alive. If black-on-black crime is a real thing, then it is going on in your front yard. It is one blade of grass fighting with another blade of grass over the living resources needed to grow.

Black people labored for free to construct this country. Our knowledge is the foundation for mathematics, astronomy, and science known in the western hemisphere. For some reason, white Europeans and, specifically, white America was able to create a stereotype that labeled us as being genetically lazier and dumber. Because of this stereotype, a system of racism was constructed, and that system has led to the shortchanging

JOHN STEPHEN PARKER

of black people in the form of systemic discrimination in financing, unequal employment, disparities in home lending, and segregation in education. White America has the privilege of believing that this country has been fair, but we need to remind this country that every law, opportunity, and constitutional right was not truly available to black people until fifty years ago. And yet you wonder why we will kill one another simply to get what should have been rightfully ours.

I wonder why it is always easy for much of this country to jump on the bandwagon of black-on-black crime when they examine any aspect of race and race relations. Many in white America have labeled Black Lives Matter a terrorist group when all they seek to do is stop the violence being committed by law enforcement against black people, but when you bring up Black Lives Matter to much of white America, their go-to is "What about black-on-black crime?" What does Black Lives Matter have to do with black-on-black crime?

The word *lives* is clearly a source of discomfort to this faction of white America because it gains their complete attention. White America, in general, has never been concerned with black lives. But because it bothers you some much, let me assist you in pondering these thoughts.

When you shop at Dollar Tree, you don't actually find a tree that has one-dollar bills growing on it. There is a certain pun that goes along with titles and statements. Captain

America, regardless of him being from white America, is not actually the captain of America. And yes, there is no such thing as military intelligence.

White America needs to understand that, as a whole, black people are not fans and supporters of crime. We have truly been concerned and have been attempting to stop violence in our own community for decades. We have been at this significantly longer than white America give us credit for; and we have addressed in songs, verses, marches, sit-ins, and protests in a broad range of form. The Black Lives Matter movement is in no comparison to a large number of parents, grandparents, aunts, uncles, and cousins who have been fighting to stop crime in black neighborhoods for decades. But white America never really thinks about it from this standpoint because they have been brainwashed by the narrative that is constantly being perpetuated by the power, position, and privilege they possess.

In the mind of much of white America, we need to have an annual report available that shows every time we stood up in our own community and did something productive to show we want crime to stop in our own neighborhoods as if we should keep a ledger of good deeds. The reason white America does see us doing these things is that they have the privilege of not really caring anyway because as long as we keep it in our community, there is no reason for them to get involved.

JOHN STEPHEN PARKER

So we black people have chosen to oblige white America and keep our good deeds to ourselves. In other words, we don't want white America "all up in our cornflakes when they aren't really bringing any milk."

So we would appreciate it if you would stop running to the broken record of "what about black-on-black crime?" and in return, we will keep the "olive branch" of conversations about race extended. Blacks would like to see a united world and would be more than open to bringing our culture to society in a way that we can all learn, because the first thing we would do is teach much of white America how to actually season food and refrain from putting unnecessary shit, like raisins, into potato salad. More importantly, we would like for you to learn how black people still have the foundation of singing, dancing, and entertaining people, both white and black, even after knowing at one time in history that you would beat us, lynch us, and even murder us if we didn't entertain you well enough.

White America has to face some serious first-world problems in the last decade. You have been perplexed by crazy white men's obsession with mass shootings, Number 45 being afraid of two thousand poor people walking thousands of miles for freedom, Kanye West speaking, which Kardashian is going to help a sports franchise win a championship, and a black woman becoming a member of the royal family. You know, real world shit. Black people are more than willing to assist you in trying to figure these things out, but we feel (sarcastically) that white people killing white people should be high on the priority list, and you people should address that because black people are terrified by this phenomenon. When conversations are raised about the brutality of law enforcement upon black people, stop trying to connect it to black people committing crimes against other black people.

Crime in the black community is a major concern, but it doesn't hold a candle to systemic racism. Law enforcement in the United States has killed nearly five hundred unarmed blacks since 2014. That number isn't in the same ballpark as the number of cross-racial killings of whites by blacks.

In nearly every instance, when a black person is murdered by a police officer, there is no immediate accountability for the action, but there is an instant reflection, "What about black-on-black crime?" The right and alt-right in this country run to it fast now than when they were ready to lynch our first black president. It is where they run to when one of their white cops shoots a black kid. Even while the families of the victims are visibly and publicly upset, they still flock to it like flies to shit. This only translates that white America would love to have a conversation about race, racial issues, and being black in America; but first, you people need to do something about black-on-black crime. This has even enveloped some prominent black celebrities who I feel have sold out their own race and heritage. I believe that the go-to argument of black-on-black crime is virtually on life support. It was wrong thirty years ago that black leaders included it in every single speech given and completely avoided the conversation of poverty associated with trickle-down government policies.

But the fact is that white America refuses and is fighting with tooth and nail to understand that the concept was a fallacy, to begin with. The entire concept perpetuates a racist ignorance and not only goes against all common sense but attempts to remove accountability for a racist system created by white America. There is no such thing as a black-on-black crime, just as there is no such thing as a white-on-white crime (or "let's just insert a random color or race here" crime). It is all just crime, and in the black community, the basis of it is simply just poverty.

Crime happens anywhere there is a large population. White America looks at community crime patterns like an old girlfriend who doesn't understand that you don't want her anymore, but they never want to talk about the deep symptoms of why it's happening. People usually live among their own kind of people, so most black people will live where blacks live. And the same goes for most races. It's only human to associate with people who are the same as you. Even the most diverse cities—in particular, my home town of St. Louis—are the most segregated. White America always talks of a big diversity game, but communities in the United States appear to have grown more politically and economically homogeneous in recent decades. Interestingly, a larger margin of black people preferred living in racially diverse communities than whites. This should tell white America clearly that we have no problem associating with people that don't look like us. It is you that would prefer to not have us around. And because we have this segregation in communities, white America keeps the black-on-black-crime assumptions.

But you white Americans are interesting because even though you are in control of every aspect of this country, you will get pissed if blacks want to have something that doesn't involve you, because if we have a "black club," it ruins your dream of a post-racial America where you remain in control. It's not all about white America all the time. Sometimes it's about income, resources, and just about a need to be around other black people.

What America doesn't seem to understand (but is oh not so happy about) is that often we want to move to a white neighborhood not because we want to but because we need to. There is little opportunity to move on up in most black communities in comparison to those where white people live. But the fact of the matter is, most black people can't just pack and leave the "hood," and we certainly aren't welcome in just any neighborhood in this country. So we are subjected to majority-black neighborhoods, many that have seen much better days and have been infested with the effects of low income, poverty, unemployment, and oh yeah, crime.

But crime is there not for the reasons that white America always runs to, like the assumption that black people are just simply prone to criminal activity. It is simply because of poverty. The most dangerous cities in the United States have a black population concentrated in urban centers, just like St. Louis, and white America also has to recognize that these very same urban centers have the highest poverty rates in the country. So it should not come as some shock to white America that black people in these areas have identified crime as the biggest concern in their neighborhoods.

But even with that being the case and contrary to the racist beliefs from much of white America, murder rates in the black community have dropped steadily over the past decade. But honestly, none of this has to do with race. As long as you have criminals, you are going to have crime. Those crimes will be perpetrated simply based on proximity and opportunity. Because of that fact, you realize that most crimes are committed in your own neighborhood and, unfortunately, usually by some whom you are familiar with.

White America will never acknowledge this, but based on statistics, the three most dangerous states are Alaska, Nevada, and New Mexico. And if they need something else to deflect from, I will add this fact: the most dangerous states are all states where there is a white population over 70 percent. The CDC is not able to put this statistic out there because Congress will take away their funding. Six out of ten dangerous states are places where you can openly carry a gun. I wonder why we have so many assaults and murders in those places. Maybe we SHOULD be having a conversation about white-on-white crime because white America will refer to black people as self-destructive, even when we are nothing of the sorts. But the fact they address the content is ridiculous from the start. Deflecting to black-on-black crime is and has always been white America's way to disregard black people's appeal that our lives matter. This is not only insensitive but also inherently racist.

It is a racially charged term that white America has categorized as a "special" crime. If I was wrong about that, then white-on-white crime would be as much of a household term. By associating race in the term, white America automatically associates crime to a race of people, and it is unjust and unfair because of the fruit of the poisonous narrative that already existed in this country.

Wake up white America, please! Black-on-black crime is a myth because it promotes to the world that black people are

JOHN STEPHEN PARKER

not normal and inherently prone to killing one another as if we are cannibals. This is part of the narrative to continue to dehumanize black people—the same narrative possessed by your ancestors. It has provided white America to destroy anyone who was not like them, going all the way back to the indigenous who were living here when you first arrived. Mind you, I said *arrived*, not *discovered*. Use some common damn sense and stop trying to sell this to your ignorant faction. You know, the ones who elected Number 45 to the office. Blacks are no more prone to killing one another than whites are to killing other whites because no race is inherently prone to destroying itself.

Instead of promoting the racist narrative, make an attempt to look at why things are truly the way they are. Why have black people been forced to fight for social justice, economic equality, and jurisprudence? Then own your own history by being accountable for the actions of your ancestors. Ask yourself the question, What part has racism and the racist acts of white American racism played in the destruction of black people? The list will resemble the phone book.

Although crimes perpetrated by blacks against other blacks do occur, white America needs to realize that we had some very good instructors of history, and the majority of that instruction came from someone with a white face. The foundation of black anger and violence was born from the white American's oppressive and dominating class that snuffed out the self-worth of black people four hundred years ago. You left us with low self-esteem, hopelessness, and despair to achieve our own financial status and a great deal of fake validation. White America created this anger within an oppressed body of people, so now you are simply reaping the seeds of oppression and domination that you have sown for four centuries, and the chickens are coming home to roost in a most detrimental and visually self-destructive way. You white Americans need to open your eyes and realize that you are directly responsible for the loss of hope in the black community.

We black people are caught between a rock and a hard place because we are neither immigrants nor indigenous. White people brought us here not of our own free will. We didn't arrive all smiley, full of hope, and ready to drink from the cup of "liberty to pursue happiness." We began in chains. We were tortured. We were raped, lynched, castrated, and murdered; and white America needs to understand that every black person in this country suffers to this very day the direct consequences of this history.

Wake up, white America, and realize that black-on-black crime is a myth. Stop using this as a deflection for your lack of accountability. It will take an accountable white America, greater than what we've seen in the past, to act upon that destructive path if this country ever reconciles and heals people who have been greatly disgraced, assaulted, and offended.

JOHN STEPHEN PARKER

CHAPTER 17

Wake Up and Know that Black Lives Do Matter

"I am angry. It is illegal for me to be angry. Remember: Don't get angry. It is illegal to be a black man and be angry. Right. Got it. I will remember this next time."
—*Kara Lee Corthron*

BLACK LIVES MATTER. All Lives Matter. These two phrases symbolize the separation in this country. This is memorialized by the deaths of Michael Brown Jr., Eric Garner, and the countless other unarmed black people who have lost their lives by the hands of law enforcement. Do we actually need to discuss (among ourselves obviously) why one life matters and one doesn't? Black people will proudly protest that Black Lives Matter, and it will continue to fall on deaf ears because white America will continue to disregard us as simply human beings.

In the current racial climate in this country, white America is steadfast to reduce black people to a group of racist titles ranging from "suspect" and "thug" to "criminal" and "felon." This type of categorization is the foundation for the dehumanization of black people in general, because once you get labeled with any of those, white America ignites the privilege and they no longer have to treat black people with any type of human dignity, regardless if they have millions of dollars or if they have broken the law.

Black lives matter because black people are human beings. Much of white America may want us to "go back to Africa," but this faction would be living in dreamland if they were delusional enough to believe that this country can succeed without black people succeed as human beings. Since Europeans arrived in this country and enslaved us, black people have been on the battlefield to simply be recognized as human beings.

If white America would ever be honest with themselves, they would admit that black people have been the foundation for their world. We have been the basis of white America's creativity, self-direction, and spirituality. Since the ending of the civil rights movement, white America has reduced black people to individuals with nothing more than "rights," which, other than that, they have no regard for us. And the truth is that in this depersonalized, individualistic white American society that we live in, black people don't really give a damn about the betterment of white America. Much of white America has done little more than piss all over the

JOHN STEPHEN PARKER

aspirations of black people, so the whites should not be getting all shocked and shaken because black people are standing up to this oppressive society and screaming about our lives having value.

White America must wake up and truly realize that the only way to have long-term peace in this society, there must be a realization of basic human decency, meaning we must first understand what it means to be human. When black people fight for black life without having a moral basis from white America, we may as well be pissing in the wind. When white America spouts the phrase All Lives Matter, we need to recognize that they are simply being inadvertently racist, and they need to be called on it. When black people call them on it, they will get both upset and defensive, but then we should seek to educate them on the meaning of what you meant by calling them an inadvertent racist.

White America believes that All Lives Matter and the black lives shouldn't matter any more than anybody else's because all lives matter anyway. They are not incorrect (in a perfect world), but the issues of concern are the things that white America hates to talk about and usually goes without having any light shined on them. The BLM movement is simply bringing to light to white America that based on very public incidents, our lives have been shown to have less value than those with white skin, especially when it comes to dealing with both the judicial and criminal justice system.

Attempting to get this point across to white America is where the difficulty comes in because white America has absolutely no clue and no interest in the Grand Canyon–type division that exists in the United States, and this division is a shape-shifter that takes on a number of different forms. White America has the privilege of not having to pay attention to the treatment they receive in comparison to that of any other racial group. This privilege extends to everyday occurrences from how the new media covers any crime involving a person of color to the products that are sold to the public in drugstores.

White America will automatically deflect, defend, and/or disagree with any theory whatsoever that our "cleaner than the driven snow" government would do such a thing as being biased toward black people, but they would be unequivocally incorrect in that belief, and there is plenty of literature out there that proves this fact. If they would actually take the time and do some research, white America might begin to get an idea of what is really going on and what the true picture really is.

Let's just spitball here again and go with some simple common sense. Most of white America, the faction that is spouting All Lives Matter, we can pretty much agree that this faction probably lives in a neighborhood that is all or mostly all white. It is also probably likely that they have no black people in their social circle or that their frequent settings don't have any either. Why do you think it is ONLY white America spouting All Lives Matter? Because it's all they see in most of their social settings (like Chesterfield, Missouri).

If the members of this faction lived among more black people or persons of color in general and were able to witness the treatment of black people by law enforcement, they would probably get why the term All Lives Matter is so blatantly racist. White America is unaware that they are the ones who can't see the forest for the trees.

Before I go any further, please understand, I'm not judging white people for where they live or who they socialize with. That's their choice. Admittedly, I led with the salty title of this book. I've been doing things like this that get under the skin of white America for a long time because nobody can seem to get through to white America. I come from St. Louis, Missouri.

The members of white America I witness spouting the company line All Lives Matter are people, in some cases I know personally, who have good hearts and mean well. These people get up and go to work every day and take good care of their loved ones. They are not evil in any way and would give you the shirt off their backs if you needed it. I am making an appeal to people like this, especially in my home city of St. Louis, to begin to open their minds to the potential of inclusion and to open their hearts to the possibility of togetherness with pride and dignity. It is time to move beyond fear or pride and think about the big picture. If you are a good person, then it is time that the rubber actually met the road.

Now for that faction of white America that thinks John Parker hates law enforcement, I do not, and I will never defend the murders of citizens in this country, regardless of race or profession. Killing police officers is not the answer, nor is killing anybody else. I am against murder and injustice across the board. What I am simply pointing out now is how white America has had the privilege of sitting back on the beach while black people have been forced to swim in the ocean of sharks, and for the most part, we have been nothing more than chum. In fact, in most cases throughout history, we were bitten, left for dead, and healed ourselves while white America was getting a tan.

Let me put it this way. I don't watch soccer; in fact, I hate it, so why should anybody with any common sense pay any attention to anything I might have to say about the sport of soccer? I'm allowed to have an opinion, sure, but isn't, say, a professional soccer player or coach's opinion more valuable than mine would be? If you were to be placed in a room with a professional soccer player and myself, who is going to listened to and his perspective of the game before they think of mine? I, too, would be able to learn more about soccer by listening to someone with extreme knowledge of the game.

So if you look at it from this simple perspective, white America should be doing a whole lot less talking and a ton more listening if they are to learn about racism, and you not only look ignorant, but it is truly rude and inconsiderate the argue with black people about racism. We live it every single day, so we are experts on the subject. Also, from this perspective, it appears that the Black Lives Matter movement is saying the same thing. Wake up, white America, and stop talking. Maybe just listen for a while. You are correct when you say all lives matter equally, but the fact is that this country and white America who is always cherry-picking the Constitution, to begin with, are just not staying true to what you put on the paper.

When white America says All Lives Matter, the only thing they are doing is diverting attention away from a momentum of change that is trying its best to move this country forward where what they continue to spout that is counteractive can actually come to fruition. White America continues to spread the toxicity of racism by using that phase, and by doing so, they are continuing to keep up the wall that makes it more difficult for the people who are attempting to change our society. Their message is "We don't need change" when the rest of the world can clearly see that a change is much needed.

If they really wanted to, white America could cease being ignorant and racist in an instant. It would be a no-brainer, and it could be done effortlessly. The only thing it would require is a desire to want to learn and be educated, which is not a bad thing. I learned and grew up a better person just by simply listening to other points of view. It would require white America to check their ego and privilege at the door and gain both some courage and humility and realize, acknowledge, and be accountable for the inhumane way black people have been treated. They truly have no idea a large amount of growth they could experience by simply relinquishing this control that they have had on society for centuries.

But it has always been easier for much of white America, the Republican Party, and its supporters in the (FOX) news media to ride the narrative that the Black Lives Matter movement is evil and is here to destroy the country when this movement has only come into play in response to the normalcy of law enforcement killing unarmed black people. We have all heard the rhetoric spewed by racist Republican pundits like former Governor Nikki Haley of South Carolina and Senator Rand Paul of Kentucky. They have both, among others, referred to the Black Lives Matter movement in the same inflammatory category as the Ku Klux Klan by maintaining that the movement is filled with a hateful antiwhite expression that has no place in "their country."

Former Governor Mike Huckabee of Arkansas jumped on the bandwagon and said that "if Dr. Martin Luther King Jr. were he alive today, he would be 'appalled' by the movement's focus on the skin color of the unarmed people who are disproportionately killed in encounters with the police." This argument truly acknowledges a real ignorance of history in general and of the civil rights movement. There was a time when Dr. King was the most hated man in the country, not to mention, Huckabee clearly hasn't listened to all of Dr. King's speeches. He is stuck on "I have a dream" because if he was to listen to many of the other speeches that Dr. King gave, they would make his skin crawl with anger.

The civil rights movement was about bringing to an end the violence against black people. It was incidents that mirror the nine people being murdered at the Emanuel African Methodist Episcopal Church in Charleston, South Carolina, that were the basis of what the civil rights movement was fighting against—the end of the state to simply be able to murder black people at will. It forced the government of this country and white America, in general, to wake up to what was really going on, which was black people being murdered with extreme prejudice for expressing constitutional rights like voting. The civil rights movement wanted support from white America, but it never coddled them by softening the message or the language of the message. It regularly described the death and destruction that black people were enduring simply because they were black.

The movement documented and publicized incidents where black people experienced horrible deaths after being turned away from hospitals, where only white patients were allowed. It spoke publicly about the number of lynchings and torturous treatment black people received before they were killed by a faction within white America. Much of this torture occurred enormous crowds of white American who had, in some cases, bought tickets and paid admission to enjoy the sight of such torture.

When those nine black people were murdered in that church, it brought back to memory the four little girls killed in Birmingham, Alabama. The public shock over the bombing pushed Congress to pass the Civil Rights Act. Those little girls, just like the nine church members, were killed for one reason and one reason only: they were killed simply because they were black. They were killed by a member of that faction of white America who is obsessed with ridding the country and the world of black people and people of color in general.

Much like these young people involved in the Black Lives Matter movement, the same type of young activists of the '50s and '60s served themselves up to ridicule, except one of the past that ran the risk of death on a daily basis in an area of the country. They saw firsthand the brutal effect of the Jim

JOHN STEPHEN PARKER

Crow law, and they rose up to meet it. They were successful in places like the Edmund Pettus Bridge in Selma. It was public incidents such as these that forced Congress to step up and ensure black people full citizenship. This led to more legislation being passed, such as the Voting Rights Act. Like the fight that is still happening today, there has never been a moment when we lose sight, which has always been to ensure rights for black people.

Today's Black Lives Matter movement has the intent of waking up white America to the fact that black people have died at the hands of law enforcement. This fabric has been woven into American society, and it needs to change. These young people who repeatedly yell this old familiar phrase is making the very same point that civil rights activists made sixty years ago. Please don't get it twisted because they are NOT saying that black lives are more valuable than those of their white counterparts. They are only trying desperately to convey the fact that black citizens' lives and well-being are not valued, have not mattered, and continue to be discounted.

White America somehow remains to be ignorant and, by privilege, unaware of this history. This ignorance is why they are uncomfortable with the message of the movement. Politicians, however, are a bit slicker about their ignorance. It is a bit more selective, which is why they want to remove the racial content from the issue altogether because they would rather pull a shroud over the very revealing truth about this country, and they work like hell to get that certain faction of white America to do their dirty work. I realize that most of white America is never going to agree, nor do I care if they do or don't. I am not a stupid person. I'm sure a lot of people won't, and that is completely okay. I respect your opinions, and you should respect mine too.

Black Lives Matter was born out of mourning and was followed up with rent-a-cop George Zimmerman's acquittal for murder. But the origination of both the hashtag and the message behind it was after (then) Officer Darren Wilson shot an unarmed black kid named Michael Brown Jr.

In August of 2014, Ferguson was right out of a '60s civil rights march in Alabama, complete with a protest that was met with tear gas and building being set aflame. This was followed up by a New York City police officer choking the life out of Eric Garner on a sidewalk. Most of America has no idea that on the anniversary day of Brown's killing in August of 2014, an unarmed young black man named Christian Taylor was killed by police.

Who mourns for him? I mean, we might have never known anything about Taylor because nobody was paying attention to the fact that unarmed black people were being killed at the hands of law enforcement. In fact, if you can believe this, most of white America, according to a poll, describe themselves believing that "the treatment of black citizens was more than adequate." The Black Lives Matter movement has shown that poll to be inadequate in many respects. The movement has worked to bring light to this situation.

Black Lives Matter has brought to the forefront, a socially unacceptable problem in this country. It has people, as they refer to it, woke and keenly aware of the white privilege and white supremacy that has kept the good folks of white America silent for centuries. Even during the 2016 presidential campaign, when almost no candidate wanted to talk publicly about the concerns of social justice, the request made by the Black Lives Matter movement for candidates to address legislative policy issues surrounding the judicial and criminal justice systems were brought to task. Yet even today, after hundreds of black people who have been murdered by law enforcement, there are still politicians on both sides of the aisle who has Black Lives Matter as a subversive faction in racial relations in this country.

That someone is like Number 45, who believes that the people fighting racism are no different than the tiki torch walks in Virginia. Remember, "there are some very fine people on both sides." You can't have it both ways when it comes to racism in this country, especially black men, who are seven times more likely to die at the hands of law enforcement than white men.

Uncle Tom, Dr. Ben Carson, has talked about how he "doesn't see color" because he is a doctor, and in the operating room, he can "steer clear" of racial issues. He has said that "the skin doesn't make them who they are. The hair doesn't make them who they are. And it's time for us to move beyond that. Because our strength as a nation comes in our unity. We are the United States of America, not the divided states. And those who want to divide us are trying to divide us, and we shouldn't let them do it."

It is no question who he was talking about. Were those dividers who were carrying the torches in Virginia, protesting for the rights of black people or folks like Dylann Roof? Even after Roof murdered those people in a church no less, Carson followed up his rhetoric by saying that "not everything is about race in this country. But when it is about race, then it just is." The fact is that the members of white America who are in the same mindset as Dylann Roof will never get past race in their lifetime, and while they are here, they will continue to pass it on to a younger generation. Being a black conservative, with the talent of undervaluing racism, Carson was simply telling black people, in general, to just "forget about it and move on."

Carson, like his white conservative allies, continues to find a reason to blame black people for their own peril as if we are the cause for what happens to us at the hands of law enforcement and a never-ending racist criminal and judicial system. Just like most conservatives and much of white America, he believes the real problem falls on the doorstep of the black people who are raising the issue of being murdered by law enforcement. The real problem is on the back of the people who are denied due process, not on white America, regardless of the fact that they possess the keys to the city and make the rules of the game.

White America will behave as if you have personally insulted them when black people refuse to put their trust into a recommendation for a legislative candidate or even for a presidential candidate because not one of white America's recommendations has truly ever worked for the improvement of black people. But they will come up with slick marketing campaigns with catchy slogans like We Stand Together because they hope if they show some good will and fake promises of "unity," it will be able to hoodwink any possibility of black people protesting.

I will be the first to say that often the protest of black people doesn't seem to have a clear point, and much of this is because often, many of the people involved are just mad but not really sure who or what they are mad at. However, the consideration that black people, in general, are not helping themselves by being vocal in challenging white supremacist rule comes from the belief that black people are responsible for making all the changes, which is simply a lie that comes from white privilege. Wake up, white America. Because you hold all the power, the burden of change sits squarely on your shoulders.

Too much of white America is too busy being pissed about the method of protesting because it rubs them the wrong way. They are more concerned about protesters being rude, disrupting their trips to the mall, lengthening their daily commute to and from their jobs, or setting their sights on the wrong people because "I am not racist. I have black friends." Hey, white people, protests are designed to make you feel uncomfortable and to annoy the shit out of you. That's why they call them protest, and sorry that it's an inconvenience to your trip to Starbucks, but you are not exempt.

It is hard to understand how, with as many unarmed black people who have been killed by law enforcement and more violence in cities across America, we still have conservatives. And some of them are even black (which I truly don't get) still preaching to the country that organizations such as Black Lives Matter and other black activist groups who are attempting to bring remedy to this appalling situation are the reason that we have a racial problem in the United States and that white America would appreciate it if you could protest injustice "more quietly."

Wake up, white America. There is an immediate problem in this country with black people being murdered by law enforcement before any sort of due process has happened. It's almost as if law enforcement has the mandate to disregard the judicial system handling its part. Let's just get to the sentencing part. Then to add insult to injury, we give these same officers a paid three-week vacation with no consequences, as if they have received a bonus for killing another black person. Read that last sentence again because it is the basis of what black people are upset about. Because black people have been witnesses to these stories far too many times.

It's the same one that starts with an unarmed black person being confronted by law enforcement either while driving, walking, standing, talking, etc. The standard harassment for conduct ensues, such as barbecuing in the park, selling loosies on the street, or hocking mix CDs in front of a convenience store. You know, the standard dastardly crimes we black people commit. Somehow, this escalates, and we are killed by the officer. The officer receives his three-week paid vacation, while the prosecuting attorney who is usually a great "friend" to law enforcement (Bob McCullough) conducts a sham of an investigation. At some point, the officer will testify before the grand jury about what he says happened, but since the black victim is dead, there is no contradiction to the officer's story; therefore, no consequences will be handed down. It is legalized execution without so much as a fine for bad behavior.

This is a real problem in a country is when law enforcement officers are given carte blanche to hand down justice. There is a real problem when white America decides to have the backs of these monsters who see black people as some sort of virus that should just be wiped out. So they take it upon themselves to skip the work of both the judicial system and the criminal justice system and dispense "street justice." This sends a clear message that black people have no value and are completely undeserving of their constitutional rights. Let's remember that that original document only measured me as three-fifths of a man, and in the minds of many in the law enforcement community, black people still just don't matter enough.

This is why organizations such as Black Lives Matter are protesting, fighting, and bringing awareness to this important issue. And the issue, mind you, is not at the forefront of the thought process of much of white America because right now, in white America, black lives don't seem to matter. We are expendable and disposable like razors. We are what goes into the hot dog after all the meat has been carved. We are considered the leftovers that go into building a country, even though we are the ones who actually built it. When a black person is executed by a law enforcement officer, especially when there are no consequences realized, it sends the message that we don't really matter. Wake up, white America, because **the lives of black people do matter.**

JOHN STEPHEN PARKER

We are not saying that no other lives have value, and white America needs to stop using this as their fallback. Talking about black lives mattering in society does not take away the fact that all life should matter. When we discuss human treatment and behavior toward people, especially an underserved group, we are not taking the dignity and humanity away from any other group. This country will only move forward helping those who are oppressed. The Black Lives Matter movement brings light to issues that would stop the racial progress of the United States. It is not a "terrorist organization" like the "Uncle Tom" Sherriff from Wisconsin, who was "shuffling" for white America, called it.

Much of white America will only use the phrase All Lives Matter when they hear a black person say, Black Lives Matter. It is simply an opposition phrase used to make sure that white America conveys the message that "we are still in control," which simply makes it an irrelevant statement. Again, nobody supporting the Black Lives Matter movement has ever made the statement or belief that all lives don't matter because anyone with common sense and a heart knows they all matter.

White America has, for centuries, had the privilege of dictating us black people how we should progress toward achieving our own liberation, except to black people, White America has been the actual roadblock to that happening because they are the ones who have always been telling us what we could and could not do or where we could and could not go or what we could and could not be. So, white America, the time has come when that is ending. Your privilege of racial ignorance and arrogance is over. We will no longer let you tell us where we can go, what we can do, or what we can be; and we are certainly not going to allow you to tell us how to protest or to be sure that it fits into your schedule and doesn't inconvenience your daily way of life.

White America, your job is not to direct our social justice movements or to tell us how to achieve our own liberation. Your job is to be accountable for our depth of hurt and anger. Your job is to recognize the injustice that occurs to us on a daily basis. Your job is not to tell us what you are going to do for us. Your job is to ask us what we need you to do to help us. This country has revolved around the privilege of white America for centuries, and it is time for you to stop making it all about you. Get in the passenger seat, close your mouth, don't touch a black man's radio, and enjoy our ride. And since we built the damn car, you should feel honored that we allowed you to even ride in it. That should be the role of white America.

So realize this. When white America spews out the phrases All Lives Matter and Blue Lives Matter, you need to check yourself and understand the insensitivity of those racist and hate-filled statements. White America has never been at risk of being murdered by law enforcement because of your very existence. You are not the ones being murdered without a trial. You were not slaves who are working for free, building this country, and providing a foundation of wealth for another group of people for nearly 400 years. You were not restricted under Jim Crow from voting, going to an adequate school, using an indoor toilet, trying on shoes in a store, drinking from a water fountain, sitting at a lunch counter, and experiencing a great deal of other (legal at the time) state-sponsored racism for 150 years.

You do not need to be free from any bondage, so there is no reason why you need to now spout why your lives matter. You control history, so your lives have always mattered. You have never had the fear of domestic terrorism and hatred supported by law enforcement because of the color of your skin.

So when you shout out the competitive response of All Lives Matter in response to black people saying Black Lives Matter, you do nothing more than perpetuate white America's privileged superiority and devalue black people. It should also be remembered that because of the oppressive and racist history of the United States, it was solely white America who had their foot on the neck of black people. It is insulting to attempt to stifle the voice of the very people you oppressed and clearly puts you on the side of racism.

It's time, white America. Wake up and realize that it's not all about you. You are not victims. I understand that your fear is that we might someday come into real power and begin treating you like you have historically treated us. That fear is not without legitimacy, but black people do not have a history of killing white America. Therefore, you don't need protection from black people. You don't need saving from black people. And you don't need to fight back with slick competitive phrases, actions, or laws. White America has always been the perpetrator of racism and violence. You do not get to play the victim card now because you are scared.

Black people make up about just over 12 percent of the population of this country, but we are nearly half the prison population. We are incarcerated six times more than white America. We get longer sentences for the same crimes as white America does, even when our rap sheets aren't nearly as long. We don't commit crimes at higher rates than white America. The main reason for our incarceration is drug use, and white America has a much bigger problem with it than we do. This is an injustice. This is institutionalized racism, and white America is responsible for this.

Racism is not knowing or being aware of race. Racism is the active, passive systemic segregation and discrimination against a group of people based on their ethnicity or skin

JOHN STEPHEN PARKER

color. It usually happens with a majority (white America) against a minority (black people).

It is not racist to say Black Lives Matter, but in the context of what is happening to this country, the phrase All Lives Matter is. White America needs to wake up to its culture of oppression of black people and its history of murder, rape, and genocide. White people can no longer live in this society free from its own heinous past. You are not and has never been the oppressed.

Black people own that, and you can never take the title from us.

CHAPTER 18

Wake Up and Understand that Thug is the New Nigger

To those who would call me a thug or worse because I show passion on a football field—don't judge a person's character by what they do between the lines. Judge a man by what he does off the field, what he does for his community, what he does for his family.

—Richard Sherman

I T IS HARD when white America went through the transition of using *nigger* and moved into the more Fox News acceptable term *thug*. But my guess is that social media and the media, in general, made some conscious decision that it would be acceptable mainly to their viewers that they must keep the "black people are bad" narrative going for them and for their advertisers who feel the same. Today's usage of the term *thug* doesn't have anything to do with whether you have committed a crime at all. The only true prerequisite to having the label is that you just be black because it gets tagged to professional black people all the time. You can be a Stanford graduate with a master's degree who has competed in professional athletics on the highest stage and has no criminal history at all. Thug. You can be the first black president of the United States. Thug. You can even be other young black children being discussed by that same black president and the mayor of your own city. THUG!

Hell, I have even been tagged with it once or twice.

Being politically correct in our society has become an art, so it goes without saying that the development of terms and the usage of words has become, at the very least, an interesting phenomenon. Many in white America can no longer run around calling black people niggers because it is socially unacceptable, and they are always concerned about being labeled racist when deep down that's who they truly are. In order for racism to go underground, words like *nigger* had to be replaced with words that white America can use in a more neutral manner, knowing full well exactly who those words and phrases are truly reserved for.

The end goal for this faction of white America is to be able to covertly connect these words and phrases with the racial group it was intended for, and in this case, "*thug*" is associated with black people—in particular, black men. It was to be sure that this association would trigger a deeper remembrance of what may be a shrouded hatred and could deliver a much more racial impact on the audience.

Thug is an example of the metamorphosis of the lure of racism, and white America has taken the bait. It has really gotten a great deal of prominence during the various protests of social injustice, and white conservative politicians alike have been riding the horse of the so-called respectability politics with this term like Zorro.

We all watch the various responses to protest around the country and how the word was always worked into both the question and the answer. Whenever a black community stands up to the evils of injustice, it doesn't matter if we are marching in the street or kneeling down on the sideline. The canvas controlled by white America is broad-stroked with the painting that we are thugs. Calling black people protesters would be too difficult or has too many syllables or something. So black people marching, or kneeling is grouped in with the vultures who steal, loot and burn buildings because it is easier for white America to think of us all being the same. I mean, many of them already think we all look alike, so we must all be the same. We all become thugs, regardless of our activities.

But when white America flips over and burns cars, breaks windows, and vandalizes cities after, say, an NBA championship or a Super Bowl victory, the narrative is totally different. White America engaging in the same activity is simply blowing off steam while celebrating, but black people doing the same things and behaving, in the same manner, are

JOHN STEPHEN PARKER

labeled as thugs. The reality is, the term *thug* exists almost to the exclusion of white America, even when the behavior is identical.

Codes to imply a racial stereotype is not a shocker in this country. Black people have been tagged with a number of them. Black women have been referred to as welfare queens, and black men always get the tag of being angry when we decide to stand up and tell the truth about this country. Even the former president of the United States couldn't avoid being labeled as the "angry black man" whenever he spoke out against injustice. A thug is only a different form of these labels, but it has achieved some serious notoriety in recent years—a little too much notoriety, if you ask me—and the sad thing is that black people have played a significant part in this notoriety.

We all know that the white media plays into it because it keeps the racial narrative going, but the black community also plays into the thug narrative by allowing our young black men to wear this term as some ridiculous badge of honor, as if it is some "red badge of courage," even when they are far from the persona of behavior that could really be considered thuggish. It becomes even more concerning when respectable black people play into the fake meaning of the term that is usually perpetrated by the white media. This was never more prominent than when Barack Obama used the term from the podium of the White House while discussing Ferguson. In doing so, he aided in the solidification of the application of the term to black people.

The real problem of this solidification is that it runs deeper in a broad number of institutions in this country and, in particular, the criminal justice and judicial systems of the United States. These are already racist systems where black people are considered guilty until proven innocent and therefore get passed over when it comes to the wheels of justice turning in the correct manner.

It is time for black people to get in the driver's seat of their own destiny and reclaim their own control of their own future. Yes, white America will be heavily involved because this is basically their mess anyway. One suggestion is, address the word *thug* the exact same way you would address the word *nigger*. Just don't let it come out of your mouth anymore. If someone is engaging in criminal behavior, this is what it is. It should not have a race or color connected to it. It is time to get rid of code words for criminals. *Thug, nigger,* and *hoodlum* racially charge and portray a stereotype that is inaccurate, and this is not something to delay. This needs to be addressed quickly.

Thug has become the buzz term for white America, used when speaking about the criminal and potentially criminal behavior of black people—in particular, black men. This is not a new word, but *thug* has become the new *nigger*. Black people have been debating this with white America and discussing the denigration of black people because of their use. If you ask me, *"thug"* is not the newest form of *nigger* because *nigger* was blatant and oppressive to black people in general. The word *thug* is more sinister. It is more covert. It is much worse than the word *nigger*. To fully comprehend that, white America needs to fully understand the meaning of the word *nigger*.

When you hear the word *nigger*, you think of the dehumanization of black people. White America needs to come to terms with and be held accountable to the fact that for nearly four hundred years, black people were simply considered property. Nothing more than field and farming equipment, much like cattle or mules. When you associate the word *nigger* with slavery, you get the full picture of the level of oppression connected to the word. In this association, white America should realize that black people were regularly traded on the auction block like a stock commodity. Even worse, the same as you would breed cattle or horses, we were bred by slave owners in order to continue this animalistic practice.

Although we were enslaved for nearly four hundred years, when black people ceased to be slaves and stopped believing in what has been referred to as the slave mentality, *nigger* stopped being a word that could enslave us. *Nigger* is a symbol not of blackness but of white hatred toward black people. When we hear the word *nigger*, black people are reminded of the hatred and disdain that white America holds for black people. It also helps us to realize that if white America could go back to that bygone era of being able to murder us on a regular basis and have that murder governed by the laws of the state.

When the era of civil rights began running on all eight cylinders, nigger was the fire hose that was turned on us in Birmingham. *Nigger* was the hot coffee poured on us while we attempted to sit at a lunch counter. *Nigger* was the knife stuck in your back when you wanted to sit in the front of a bus but were forced to ride in the back. *Nigger* was the baseball bat beating you received when you drank out of the wrong drinking fountain or tried to use a "white only" public bathroom. *Nigger* was the lynching you received when you attempted to exercise your constitutional rights at the ballot box.

Nigger is an education process for black people because when we hear the word, we are educated about the individual who has dared to revert back in history to a time that should be archived somewhere, because of the heinous oppression and violence that has always been attached to the word.

Racism during slavery was at best a terroristic experience for black people, but if there is a difference in that time of history in comparison to today, it is the openness of racism. Today, black people don't often recognize racism because it is very covert and operating in the shadows of society. White America was losing its ability to keep us under their thumb through the use of physical violence. White America—and in particular, white men—began feeling the pressure from black men in every aspect of society, including competition for their most precious commodity: your beautiful white women.

In order to combat this competition, white America had to create and validate the narrative of black men who, regardless of success, are still savages at the core. They created the narrative of the "black brute." It is the persona that black people—and in particular, black men—have the mindset of a child, with no discipline or self-control. It is the persona that we are violent animals that have basic needs to survive. Those needs would be food and sex, and we will do anything for those two needs to be satisfied.

Black men have been murdered or castrated or both because of a simple accusation of raping white women. We have been killed because some white person said that we THOUGHT about raping white women. Take a look at the story of Emmett Till, the young black boy who was murdered in a most horrible way because he allegedly whistled at a white woman. This narrative was like a virus in the South and consumed the life and liberty of thousands of innocent black men.

Because of this "black brute" narrative, the state basically sanctioned murder and violence against black men. It was all one big faux narrative, and there were few verifiable claims of black men raping white women, but just the idea of it happening inflamed white America. Those unsubstantiated claims against black men don't have any comparisons to the actual and verifiable cases of white men raping both white and black women. In fact, the idea that black people are accustomed to violence and are prone to killing one another doesn't compare to how many white men are killing one another.

Laws on self-defense have nothing to do with black people. When legislation such as stand your ground gets passed, it has absolutely nothing to do with giving black people the ability to protect and defend themselves against people who are trying to harm them. When Philando Castile was shot and killed by a law enforcement officer in Minneapolis after telling the officer he was armed, carrying a license for the weapon, in an open carry state with his girlfriend and daughter in the vehicle, the one organization that you never heard a peep out of was the National Rifle Association.

The NRA, with their ads featuring Moses (actor Charlton Heston), is always preaching about the Second Amendment.

They are constantly spouting off about the need for the everyday person to be able to defend themselves and against all the deadly Mexican gangs that have supposedly infiltrated this country and are hiding underneath your bed, waiting to strike. When Philando was murdered by a police officer during a routine traffic stop, you never heard a fucking thing from the NRA. They don't defend the right of black people killed by law enforcement. There is never a conversation about black people, some of which are the most impacted by gun violence. The NRA could care less about the rights of black gun owners. If this country really wants to get a logical and ethical gun law, it would be very easy. Just tell every black person in this country, over the age of twenty-one years old, to go to their local sheriff's office and apply for a carry and conceal license. I bet you would get gun laws in this country overnight.

Again, let's remember that the same legislation and lawmakers who approve stand your ground in this era are the same type of lawmakers who said it was OK to own human beings. The language and titles at the time have changed, but the narrative is still the same. You don't hear the word *nigger* as much. Now you hear it the same when you hear the word *thug*, and not only does it validate violence against black people but it also negates our ability to gain access to the basic services of survival. *Thug* stifles our right to be protected by law enforcement because the word automatically makes us a target of bad policing.

Thugs limit our ability to lock down gainful employment because white America is naturally scared of us. Thugs cut us off from being able to learn or gain an adequate education. How many times have we heard, "Those thugs don't want to learn." As long as the narrative of black people is "dangerous thugs," white America will continue its reign of white supremacy. This is while they are constantly riding the coattails of black-on-black crime rhetoric.

Thug is a word that gives white America an excuse to blame black people for their own circumstances. It says, "You deserve to be shot, you deserved to be stopped, you deserved to be harassed, and you deserve everything negative that is happening to you." Not only this, but it gives a justification to law enforcement to kill us because white America feels we are a danger to good (white) people everywhere. If we were in the Old West, *thug* would be associated with the bandit who is always wearing black. It is covertly racist because it actually takes race away from the visual of the public. It's not like nigger because it brings legitimacy to a racist person and it makes a hero out of a vigilante. It turns the murder of hoodie-wearing black men into acts of "necessity."

Every time black people march, they are thugs. Every time a professional athlete decides to use his or her platform as an opportunity to speak out, they are automatically ungrateful thugs. Richard Sherman, a multiyear All-Pro football player in the NFL, came out publicly when he stated, "The black activists on the ground of various cities so often reminds us the word *thug* has become little more than a socially acceptable version of the rightly outlawed word *nigger*."

I am a very professional person, and yet because I have protested the killing of young black men by law enforcement, I have also been labeled a thug. When white America decides to act a plum damn fool after their favorite basketball team wins a championship, they set fire to cars and buildings and break windows, but you never hear the word *thug* associated with any of that behavior. It is the same behavior as black people who are on the streets, protesting against inhumane treatment. Not only do we get the term thrown at us but it is also supported by law enforcement in riot gear, shooting bullets and firing tear gas into the crowd,

Can we spell and smell hypocrisy?

It's not only one person being called a thug because black people have been forced to, as an individual, be representatives of the entire black race. It was once said that "a riot is the language of the unheard." When the "unheard" are black people, black people are condemned, and we are all either directly or indirectly held responsible. One of the reasons for this is the media coverage that black people receive in this country. The media is used to be sure that the narrative stays in place. I remember in 2014, in the days following the killing of Michael Brown Jr. in Ferguson, the media companies were oh too happy to cover the nighttime activities in the community. Much of that activity involved protesters being teargassed, beaten, and assaulted by law enforcement. It was a scene that supported the belief of much of white America that we are not civilized people. It also helped to perpetuate many dangerous stereotypes that are part of the chemistry invalidating discriminatory law enforcement, harassment, and violence against black people, all of which are associated with a racist criminal justice system.

How is it that young white kids can get a pass on their mistakes, many of which happen into their early adult lives, but an adolescent black kid is a very dangerous factor and needs to be governed much harsher? So harsh that if he is playing in the park by himself, the law enforcement is in so much fear that they shoot the kid from the window of the squad car.

The media lays down the foundation for the opinions in this country. We watched the media go on the campus and report on the termination of former Penn State's football coach Joe Paterno, a firing that I was not in favor of, having known Coach Paterno for several years. But when the media goes on that same campus to cover a protest surrounding the kneeling down of athletes during the national anthem, the media narrative is totally different. By different, I mean it smells of censorship and a one-sided view supporting white nationalism shrouded in a flag of patriotism. We should all have the desire to change the narrative of the media and demand more from our so-called journalists to stop. They need to cease with the language that speaks to the criminalization of black people. Stop with the use of the word *thug*. Language that criminalizes black people is the same as the language used for covert discrimination and violence, and it's the language that has added a racist undertone to the word *thug*.

So instead of the word *thug* and the narrative that goes along with it, let me address why language matters as a vehicle for racism and face this facet of white supremacy instead of the usage of the word *thug*. Here is the thing. Black people need to pay close attention because language racism becomes more pervasive. There are more and more codes being used by members of white America than ever before because it has become necessary for racism to go underground.

I have been referred to as *angry*. And although the word is usually used to describe an emotion, much of white America is quick to tie it to the history and experience of black people. I have them automatically and, without warning, become the "angry black man." I have assumed all the stereotypes associated with the title. It is also white America's method of trying to get black people to shut up.

White America needs to wake up and realize that black people are not stupid. We are the "hip to the game" that you are attempting to play. Your language of white supremacy is still as it was two hundred years ago. It still has the same purpose, and we will not stand for it. So when you go down that road and think that you can get away with it or try and pull some okeydoke, truly you are playing yourselves. We know that you can't say, *nigger*, so you will insert the word *thug*, and if not that, you'll find something else, like *angry*. Just because you changed the wrapper doesn't mean the candy changed.

These words hurt us, and you should be surprised when black people push back against them. We are not responsible for the vocabulary of white America, and we will call you out and fight when we feel you are attempting to dehumanize through language.

The word *thug* is only the beginning. You are no longer dealing with our grandfathers.

We are different.

CHAPTER 19

Wake Up. Don't Hate the Player. Hate the Game that You Created

"On a given day, a given circumstance, you think you have a limit. And you then go for this limit and you touch this limit, and you think, "Okay, this is the limit." And so, you touch this limit, something happens, and you suddenly can go a little bit further. With your mind power, your determination, your instinct, and the experience as well, you can fly very high."

—Ayrton Senna

COLOR BLINDNESS, WHEN it comes to race, is a socially constructed delusion of white America; and it has been associated with real, murderous, and genocidal consequences. This is not some new revelation. There are libraries full of books that will support the heinous construction of race by white Europeans.

These books validate the way white Europeans created the caste system, and for lack of a better term, for *white people* by essentially setting up this caste system based on economics and assuring slaves were simply cut out. White America was created by law. That way they would have complete social control of the emerging politics and policies of this, at that time, very young country. But there is a downfall to this also, as the history of racism has forced natural suffrage on society because it associated human beings with colors. It associated Africans with the color black, just as it associated indigenous people with the color red, and Asian people with the color yellow. White America created this division to ensure the total rule of this land.

The racial incident in Charlottesville and Number 45's support of Nazi flag wavers and white nationalists brought the politics of the United States to the forefront of the global stage. People have varying views of his base constituents, but there is no doubt that from a racial standpoint, Number 45's presidency has brought white supremacy back on the social scene. It is not spoken of in the same manner it was during a time when unless you were a white man in this country, your rights as an American citizen were limited at best.

Number 45 called them "very fine people," as they shouted obscenities at people who were there to stand up to their hatred and bigotry. Frankly, I am tired of listening to people defend Number 45 and not simply admit that the man is a true and real racist. His history tells his whole story, and it is amazing that much of white America still refuses to hold this man accountable for his racist rhetoric. And let's not fool ourselves though because racist individuals in Charlottesville and tiki torch-bearing fools on the campus spouting "Jews will not replace us" all got there, walking orders from Number 45 and his (then) band of racist lieutenants. These people claim to "love" America, and yet they will stand with an America flag, the sacred shroud of white America, that they regularly hide behind, directly next to a Nazi flag, while screaming USA ad nauseam. This was a show of racial hatred that had not been seen in quite some time.

White America believes in most cases that this country has gotten past racism. This is mostly because racism does often affect the majority of people in the United States. But racism has never gone away; it has never been dealt with in a manner to permanently relieve this country of the burden of the disease. White America has never been held accountable for its murderous racist history. It has never been held accountable for the horrible treatment of its own citizens. White America has kicked this can down the road for a hundred years when it comes to this accountability.

Sure, every time an unarmed young black person is killed by law enforcement, white America will show some brief fake empathy for the situation and give out the same pointless excuses or just simply start asking black people, "What can I do?" This usually comes from the "good" white people who may have good hearts in some cases but are usually only interested if it directly affects them. In fact, I would indirectly put out there that much of white America who also has a few black friends whom they care deeply about are usually the most racist. But inadvertently, hate and prejudice play a small part in racism or white supremacy. It is like the gas on the fire, but it is not what ignites the flame. Ignorance and privilege are the lifeblood of racism and white supremacy, and those two factors are what keeps its heart beating in today's society.

I will keep making this point until I am blue in the face. Much of white America doesn't have a clue as to what the true definition of racism is, and they keep using the term incorrectly. So I will say it again for the members of white America who don't hear so well, who are blinded by emotion, or just for the ones who are just simply experiencing some form of self-imposed ignorance. Racism does not only mean that you dislike another person based on their skin color or ethnic background. Racism is also different than bigotry and is much deeper than a person's ethnicity.

Wake up! Pay attention, please, because you can get it right here and right now. Here it goes. **Racism is the systemic oppression of black people that empowers white supremacy. It is a system structured around oppressing a culture because of their race.** Did you get that? If not, then go back to the beginning of the paragraph, wash, and repeat.

Although there is a large faction of white America that is still fighting historical fact, most have come to terms with the fact that race is a social construct without any scientific bearing. If you read the Bible, which is also the basis of the Ku Klux Klan and their white Christian beliefs, you will never find a mention of race, believe it or not. That's right. Race is never ever mentioned in the Bible. I am sure that every good churchgoing white Christian reading this book is probably screaming blasphemy right now, but it's true.

The issue with the creation of this social order is that much of white America thinks that it just happened naturally and fails to believe that around 1690, white Europeans created the racial caste system that we currently live in because they discussed individuals in terms of race. The phrase *white race* made its first reference in a law book in the Commonwealth of Virginia, and it described the rights and privileges of white servants. This was after slave ships began arriving. There was a time when these indentured poor white Europeans had the exact same right as black Africans. They worked the fields together, but there was a significant difference in that those poor white servants were thought of as people. These black people were considered farm equipment.

Out of fear of these two factions unionizing under a common association, wealthy landowners created a caste system, which gave the poor whites a (mythical) way to work their way out of indentured status. This system was never extended to the enslaved Africans. Through legislation, the term *white race* was given birth. Under this legislation, white servants could acquire "freedom dues." This merit system gave you rights that included a musket, money, and crops when they had "paid their dues" as an indentured servant.

Black servants, on the other hand, were considered property and were not eligible for any freedom. In fact, black people, in general, could be killed for carrying a firearm of any kind. Funny how that is not much different from the times we are living currently. South Carolina was merely a bookend to Virginia as it gave all white men (and I will use the exact wording of the statute) "absolute power and authority over his Negro slave."

This is how white people created white supremacy, and with it came a word that white America hates to here: racism. Being white meant you and only you were able to benefit in any way for the fruits of society. Being white meant that you were above every other race of human being on the planet. All other races were looked as being inferior, though it was not the case for black people. We were considered to be at the level of an ape. We weren't even considered human. Farm animals, in many cases, received better treatment than enslaved black people. This was all because of racism. If you don't have racism, then there is no supremacy of white America.

This made it easy to deal with issues surrounding freedom for black people. So even after Lincoln (supposedly) freed us, white people were still in charge of every aspect of this country, so they passed more and more legislation to ensure that black people would never be on the same citizenship or economic level of white America, mostly out of the fear that if that would ever happen, black people would be in a position to fight back or slaves would then revolt. Southern states had loophole after loophole in their legislation that if blacks violated, they would be returned to the ranks of a slave. Some other Southern states simply said "We don't want you here anymore" and became what was known as sundown towns. This simply meant to have you as out of town by sundown.

Please don't get it twisted either, because the myth was that the North was a place of "paradise," where a black man could prosper, but the fact is, Northern states were just as racist as the South. In fact, many Northern states would refuse black people entrance, or worse off, they would make them post as much as $750 in bond money to enter the state, as a promise not to get into any trouble. Plus, you still had to prove that you were free and not a runaway slave.

Now I know what the deflection argument of ignorant white America always is. They will say that "countries all over the world had slavery. It was not just in the United States. How come nobody ever makes a big hairy deal out of those?" I will agree that slavery has existed in a number of different cultures throughout history, but never in any culture in history was there a system that benefited only those who had white skin and dehumanized every other race. This system didn't exist until the late sixteen hundreds and has dominated the planet since its birth.

This caste system separated human beings by color and inevitably established a group that was destined to serve and a faction that was destined to rule over those serving. This racial caste system gave a true definition of the word *freedom* and took away the birthrights of human beings.

This was the foundation by which the Civil War fought because slave owners believed that the idea of freeing black people, these savages, to live among "fine white folks" was a ridiculous thought. Add this to their undying loyalty to states' rights and the idea that "if I pay my taxes, I should have the right to own slaves if I want to" mentality. The violation of those states' rights, in combination with potentially losing all the free help that they had for decades, is what guided the South into the war.

The problem was that owning a slave was an expensive venture, and it was usually a position held by prominent Southern white citizens. Although a vast majority of whites in the South didn't own slaves, the idea of them being free was considered a threat because there was a possibility of hundreds

JOHN STEPHEN PARKER

of thousands of newly freed people who would be looking for work, and because they were already hard workers, they could be hired for a lower wage than what would be acceptable to whites.

This was the type of control that white America had on black people then, and don't be fooled. That control has never, to this day, been relinquished. With this type of power comes another factor of racism; that is, privilege. Many in white America misunderstand privilege. You always hear the same shit from much of white America. They will spout the same tired line, "I was born with nothing. I had to work three jobs and sacrifice this and that." They believe that just because you had to work hard, you never received the privileges that living in white America has afforded you. Privilege is not about how hard you work. Privilege is about unearned access to benefits. In the case of much of white America, privilege (or rather, your fear of losing privileges) is the main cause and what keeps racism alive, well, and living in the United States today. Take privilege away from white America, and it resembles what black people have been experiencing for over four hundred years. It is called oppression.

That privilege and an entire way of life that had benefited white America for so long was in trouble at the Civil War, and white America became even more territorial with what they had always believed was "theirs." It had become part of their psychological makeup that black people were inferior and, in many cases, not even considered to be human. This anxiety created a need for more rule, and thus, white America began an onslaught of social atrocities against black people. Here are a few examples:

Black Codes and Pig Laws

Loopholes in the Thirteenth Amendment

Jim Crow

Separate but "equal" segregation for public facilities

FHA creation of the white middle class while denying home loans in a black neighborhood

Sixteen states still banned interracial marriage until 1968

Gerrymandering and redlining—silencing black voters

Just to name a few

This anxiety led to even more violence toward black people and gave rise to organizations who thrive on the hatred, fear, and violence toward black people. The leading organization whose foundation was built on this is the Ku Klux Klan.

JOHN STEPHEN PARKER

Even today, self-proclaimed hate-mongers and white supremacists use electronic technology to not only spout their view but also to recruit new members into their culture of hate and violence. Much of white America wants their culture (privilege through the oppression of others) back. This is the meaning behind the Make America Great Again rhetoric spouted by Number 45 supporters. They are adamant that "they have black friends" or "they have no hate for anybody" but are quick to get behind a culture that is based on white supremacy and the inferiority of every other race.

Much of white America is terrorized, so they will put hatred and bigotry in the same category as racism, and they would be wrong to do so. We have watched the escapade of the campaign that lead up to the election of Number 45 in 2016. I watched the true "colors" of many of my white "acquaintances" come to the forefront. When he was calling "all Mexicans rapists" and attacking every single faction of race and gender while playing to the base of ignorance, the other side cheered. They cheered! They cheered in support of hate, of fear, and racism.

In addition, white America—particularly, Christians— always throws up their hand in rage when someone accuses them of being racist. They will fall back on the rhetoric and meaning behind the Bible and that as Christians, "we believe that Christ teaches love not hate." If they really got it, they would also understand that Christianity has been a foundation for hatred. The Ku Klux Klan burns a cross as a sign of their loyalty to Christianity. This would often happen before they would ride and find some poor black souls to terrorize, dehumanize, and murder.

We need to stop being shocked that racism and white supremacy exists in America. In 2019, of course, there is still racism. While we tried to get rid of slavery and slowly granted civil rights to black people a hundred years later, we failed to address the issue of white supremacy. And because of that, racism went covert. It went underground. Racism is not rednecks in pickup trucks, screaming nigger anymore. Racism lives next door to you now. It works in your office every day. It is walking down the street in your neighborhood. It's at the gym, the church, or the corner tavern. It delivers your mail and checks you out at the grocery store. It is in the legislation that marginalizes black people. Wake up, white America. We know where it is.

White America is quick with the label of black people being lazy. Funny thing is, we were not lazy when we were working for free. They will make the statements that we don't want to learn. They ask, "Why do we need to consider your lives when you don't even have any consideration for your own?" Let me say this to that faction of white America asking this ridiculous question. If you think we are only marching

JOHN STEPHEN PARKER

because your racist white-run law enforcement agencies are killing us at will, then you would be mistaken. This is about way more than police brutality.

This is about the fact that white America has never had any accountability whatsoever for its actions. White America has never considered any type of reparations for the rapes committed, lynching committed, castrations performed, and murders of thousands of black people in this country. You have lived on legislation, the equivalent of dog whistle politics and racist-coded language that has kept us segregated and discriminated against.

White America misrepresents history in every way. You believe that the Thirteenth Amendment, the so-called abolishment of slavery, was your victory or more of penance for the bad behavior of your brethren. I wish I had a nickel for every time I heard, "Slavery doesn't exist anymore, but do you know how many white people have lost their lives so that black people could be free?" Black people were already free.

White America enslaved us, forced us to work for free, then murdered us out of fear of equality. I would say to the people spouting this tired line, "Do you know how many black people lost their lives during the middle passage on a slave ship? Do you know how many families were sold and separated? Do you know how many black women were raped by their slave masters? Do you know how many black men had limbs cut off for running away and seeking their freedom? How many were lynched, castrated, and murdered?" And much of white America wants us to give reverence to soldiers who died trying to defeat a system that their relative created? Nope, not me!

Hating black people is not what makes white America a racist society. That makes you a bigot. That makes you an asshole, but not trying or even wanting to try tearing down the system of white supremacy is what makes you a racist. Right is right and wrong is wrong. Nobody is "a little bit pregnant." If you are silent, then you are a part of the problem. White America must no longer be given the "privilege" for ignoring their "privilege." It is time to step up to the plate, take your cuts, be accountable, and take full and outright ownership of the emotions about your privilege. Black people have a right to continually point out the power privilege and position you have, and you don't have the right to get angry about that. White America is in the position to use its power to destroy racism in this country, and they are the only ones with that power.

When I heard about Number 45 vowing to Make America Great Again, I again have to ask the question, When has America been greater than it is currently, and when exactly was America great for black people, gay people, Native Americans, and women, all of whom have been denied equal rights? When has it ever been greater for anybody except white men?

Make America Great Again translates to Make America "White (and Male)" Again. Much of white America is pissed because white male privilege is falling to the wayside, and they want the 1950s back.

What can black people do? Nothing, because in twenty-five five years, the reign of white America will probably be over. And white America is so pissed at this probability that they turn a blind eye to injustices against black people. Black people are killed by the police at twice the rate of white people. Unarmed black people are killed at five times the rate. Yet somehow, it's always our fault. So white America always comes with the standard justifications for these MURDERS. Here are examples:

What if he has a legal weapon, but it's not anywhere in use? **HIS FAULT.**

What if he has no weapon? **HIS FAULT.**

What if he's just a child? **HIS FAULT.**

What if it's a woman mysteriously found hanged in her prison cell with no possible motive for suicide? **HER FAULT.**

What if he's screaming in pain from an injury sustained in the police encounter? **HIS FAULT.**

What if he's complaining about a video that the police are choking him and he dies as a result of those injuries? **HIS FAULT.**

I mean, come on, people! Why do black people have to lose their lives before white America will come down from the patriotic land of "blue people" and simply admit to some culpability of law enforcement?

Do you want more? Then consider this. There are more black people in prison today than were slaves before the Emancipation Proclamation. Black people get harsher prison sentences than white people for the exact same crimes. Black people are segregated into poor communities with underfunded schools. People with black-sounding names are less likely to get a job than white counterparts with the same experience.

And on and on and on.

And still, white America continues to "see no evil, hear no evil, and speak no evil" about a system that black people are forced to live with. Not only does white America refuse to acknowledge it, but they also have the nerve to get pissed when black people bring it up and will actively support it with evidence. This is the textbook definition of racism.

It's 2019. Legal slavery ended more than 150 years ago in this country. The civil rights movement ended more than 60 years ago. So why do we still have systematic racism baked into the fabric of America? Answer: BECAUSE WHITE AMERICA HAS CHOSEN TO HAVE IT REMAIN!

In 1963, the black writer James Baldwin asked the same question. He said:

> *The future of the black community in this country is precisely as bright or as dark as the future of the country. It is entirely up to the white people, and their representatives, it is entirely up to the white people whether they're going to face and deal with and embrace the stranger who they've maligned for so long. What white people must do is try to find out in their own hearts why it was necessary to have the nigger in the first place. I am not a nigger. I am a man. But if you think I'm a nigger, it means you need it . . . You, the white people, invented him, and you must find out why. And the future of the country depends on that.*

Why does white America need racism? Well, in the interim, it's useful. It serves as a function in the white supremacy of society. It services to the status quo. In fact, white America wouldn't have the status quo of white supremacy without racism. White America needs racism to keep their faction of society together. In the United States, the top 1 percent own more than the bottom 90 percent. The richest eighty-five people in this country have as much wealth as the bottom half of the country. The United States, or any country on this earth, that hold such a great amount of wealth—or should I say, wealth inequality—could never survive without a scapegoat, without a population to blame, to shame, or to treat as the "bad people." We are the scapegoat of white America. And the whole system is based on misdirection because the population would not let these rich bastards continue to feed on their riches unless they had a plan that would force the rest of the population to take their eyes off the ball.

Rich white America will distract you from the crooks in the banking industry and the even bigger crooks in the financial firms of Wall Street with images of black people standing in welfare lines. They will move your attention away from education and the fact that public schools and teachers are being underfunded with images of a black kid with tattoos and his pants sagging. This is the "okeydoke" of white America.

We are in this country because white America needed to make a profit, and the only way to do that was with cheap (free) labor. Welcome to slavery. It was a labor-intensive process, and the only way to make a substantial profit of it was immoral thrift.

Why weren't black people treated equally after the Civil War? Rich white America required that cheap labor workforce to remain in place. The future wealth of this country was in the balance. This is where I insist people read the Thirteenth Amendment fully because it only granted freedom to persons of color if they were not convicted of a crime. One of the highest incarceration rates of black people, in the history of this country, occurred within eighteen months after the ratification of the Thirteenth Amendment, on a violation of nothing more than vagrancy. Black people were free but had no place to go, so they were subsequently arrested because they had no place to go.

Moreover, throughout the entire history of this country, the rich have needed something to keep middle-class white America coming to those jobs every day. They hated the labor unions because they were in the business of being "fair" (fair wages, overtime pay, child labor laws, workplace safety, etc.). But providing poor and middle-class white Americans a faction of people they could blame, and kick around made them feel better about their lives and not as willing to complain so much. It went something like this: you may have to work in the factory all day, but at least you aren't one of **THEM BLACK NIGGERS**.

What an amazing swindle!

The late comedian George Carlin said it perfectly when he put it this way:

> You have three types of people in this world. You have rich people. These are the people who do none of the work and make all the profit.
>
> You have the middle class, who do all the work and make little to none of the profit.
>
> Then you have poor people. These people are simply there to scare the living shit out of the middle class because they know that if they hate their jobs and stop coming, this is where they will end up.

Rich white America has convinced poor white America to feel proud to simply be white! Not of their cultural heritage or the struggle of their parents or even their ties to their religion or ethnicity. No. Just to be proud of their skin color. "Okeydoke!" How stupid do you have to be? If intelligent aliens ever crossed light-years of space and time to investigate the intellect of human beings, that one fact would have them rushing back home, shaking their tentacles and multiple heads in disbelief!

Your interests have much more in common with all those people you've been taught to hate. Poor white America should all be banned with all poor black people. We should be joining together and taking an equitable piece of the pie. But instead,

JOHN STEPHEN PARKER

this faction of white America is satisfied with protecting their share of national wealth all because they have white skin.

During the same interview, Baldwin was asked if he thought there was any hope America would change its ways. He said:

> I can't be a pessimist because I'm alive. To be a pessimist means that you have agreed that human life is an academic matter, so I'm forced to be an optimist. I'm forced to believe that we can survive whatever we must survive.

I agree.

It's all up to white America. If white America would wake up, they would find that racism doesn't help you. It brings you down and oppresses you, the same as it has been to black people throughout history.

Rich white America will throw poor white America a bone. They then watch you guard it against black people as if it is so damn valuable. When are you going to wake up? When are you going to stop complaining about the players, put away hate, choose love, and truly focus on the ridiculous game being played? When are you going to join your black brothers and sisters in the struggle and demand what's truly all of ours?

Rich white America may need racism, but everyday white and black people don't.

CHAPTER 20

Wake Up and Realize that you are Privileged because of Racism

Privilege is when you can afford to sit back and criticize others who have to fight for the things you take for granted.
—*DaShanne Stokes*

RACISM IS TRULY a bizarre phenomenon because it is an education process with no real scientific evidence to support it in any way. It will lay claim that because of race, there are varying degrees of intelligence. I was an athlete at one time in my life, and I can remember when black athletes were always stereotyped as not having the intelligence to handle difficult circumstances in sports. The NFL used this excuse for years as a way to keep black men from excelling at the quarterback position. Racism is also the foundation for the belief of a difference in character since according to this doctrine, black people are more prone to violence and criminal activity simply because we are black.

Another baseless factor of racism is the belief that the white race is more superior than any other. I would say that it might be prone to more violence than any other. Throughout the history of the world, pretty much any place that white Europeans landed was followed by disease, rape, murder, and genocide of the indigenous culture. Even in today's society, it is white men who are mainly responsible for the number of mass shootings. So if there are any feelings of superiority, they should be toward a natural violent.

Additionally, this teaching of racism involves a psychological mindset where it is necessary to keep dominating. White America has been able to for centuries because it has maintained control over every single governmental institution in the United States. That means that through legal legislation, they not only control the policies but they also control the language of the said policies. In other words, white America has set the rules of the game and controls where, when, and how the game is not only played but also if they need to change the rules without warning to benefit them. Racism, plain and simple, clearly states, without any real evidence to support it, that black people are inferior to whites.

Today, racism has graduated past rednecks calling us niggers and committing hate crimes like painting a racial slur on someone's home. It comes in the form of covert beliefs, behaviors, and discriminatory practices. It is practiced by individuals in the boardrooms of corporations, in the halls of justice, and in governmental agencies. It is often in a form of subtle discrimination, and that subtleness comes from the privilege only possessed by white America.

Like racism, white privilege holds its own bizarre quality, but it differs in that it is this preference for whiteness that, like a disease, has infected every aspect of the American way of life. White people hate to face this fact, but white privilege provides you with a benefit that is just handed to you. You have never worked and, I mean, really put in the time and effort and had to earn the right to have. And let's be honest, because of this privilege, it has provided white America which advantages that you can't really fathom. I am not saying that white people don't work hard. I believe you do, but I always like to ask this question to random white people only because I like to see the look on their faces as they try and find an answer, How has racism impacted your life?

The challenges that black people face on a daily basis never even show up on the radar screen of white America. The privileges that you receive a pass is right by you every day because they are natural assumptions and occurrences. Consider the following:

- If a white person cuts their finger, they get a flesh-colored Band-Aid.

- If a white person stays in a hotel, the complimentary shampoo generally works with the texture of a white

JOHN STEPHEN PARKER

person's hair because the assumption is that a white person will be staying in the room.

- If a white person buys hair-care products in a store, their shampoos and conditioners are in the aisle and section labeled Hair Care and not in a separate section for Ethnic Products. Not only that, they are out in the open, where often black hair-care products are behind lock and key.

Now I know that most of white America would simply argue that this is nothing more than basic supply and demand, but even if that is true, it is still a white privilege. White people get what black people don't, plain and simple.

White privilege is more than just beauty products because it is also the foundation for a broad number of other advantages that, again, usually go unnoticed by most white people.

For example, because you have white skin, nobody automatically questions how you handle your finances. We have all heard the stereotype "Black people often have credit issues." Why is that? Most black people I know are very fiscally responsible, and my eighty-year-old mother has saved every dime she ever made because that what she was taught to do. This ridiculous stereotype not only affects our buying power but also affects how much we are required to pay for services, which is something else that much of white America doesn't understand. For example, most black people who reside in a predominantly black community will pay 20 to 30 percent more for automobile insurance or receive a higher interest rate on a mortgage. This is a challenge that many in white America never face.

The skin color of white America does not work against when it comes to their style of dress. Many black people, myself included, often dress a bit more stylish. I personally do it because I feel better when I think I look better. But I can't tell you how many times if I come to a business setting or even out with my (white) friends, I am asked, "Why are you dressed up?" As if I am trying to make a statement of some kind. I don't know a single black man who, if he were wearing a suit, has not been asked by some white person, "Where are you preaching at today?" As if all black men wearing a suit must be church ministers.

The one that really gets me is the privilege that white America has when it comes to public speaking skills. You have the advantage of never being questioned on your use of correct English and good diction when you are speaking, but if a black person speaks properly and professionally, we are considered different. Unfortunately, we are often judged by both white America and other black people alike. Much of white America will judge us because they will first make the superiority assumption that, based on the color of my skin, there is no possibility of me being actually educated and capable of carrying on a professional conversation. How many times have we all heard the comment "Oh, he speaks so well" as if I am supposed to sound like Mush-mouth from the old *Cosby Kids* cartoon show or from a "Stepin Fetchit" vaudeville act? White America is under the assumption that most black people have to keep repeating the phrase "you-know-what-im-sayin" at the end of a sentence, which is just not true. Most of us don't but receive a judgment from our own community often because if we behave in a proper and professional manner. We are believed to have very little street credit, or we are referred to as an Uncle Tom. My reply to black people who feel this way is simple: I am fighting the same battle that they are. I am just simply trying to fight it from inside the system. In order to get inside, I have to be professional. You can't change the system if you are outside of it.

Another challenge that white Americans never have to face or an advantage that they have is that others in white America don't make the assumption you got something because of your race. Black people who are hired in the majority of white companies and corporations are nearly always tagged with the "affirmative action" hire. As if we would never achieve enough merit, education, or experience to get a great position at the C level. Let me make this clear. I HATE THE FACT THAT

AFFIRMATIVE ACTION EXISTS. But I understand the need for it, and it's simple. We need it because human beings don't inherently do the right thing. We want comfort. We hire our friends, and we want people around us that we know and who often look like us. In the workplace, who you know is not always the best person for the job.

White America has the advantage of not having to concern themselves with these issues. But man, when you're faced with them and that privilege is challenged, damn, you folks can act a plum fool. How many videos have we seen of white America having their privilege challenged, especially by law enforcement? You automatically go straight to "do you know who I am? I pay my taxes, and I am good friends with the police chief / judge." White America gets indignant if they think anybody is challenging the simple privilege of being white.

Face this also. White privilege has molded how you look at the world and the way the rest of the world looks at you. Consider this fact. Even though most of the information taught to us in school has now been proven to be a lie, black people were taught that the development of civilization was because of white people. The schools that I have attended use standard textbooks, and the only thing you read about were the accomplishments of white America, except in February, which is Black History Month, the shortest month of the year, which always gave us a moment to talk about our greatest hits, which were also the ones that white America was comfortable with. You know, the usual subjects of Martin Luther King, Harriett Tubman, the Underground Railroad, Fredrick Douglas, and the usual cast of black characters. But remember that even Black History Month began with the story of a great and honorable white person "freeing" us. Who didn't have that same tired cutout silhouette picture of Abraham Lincoln on their bulletin board in grade school?

As a black man, I see white America in every aspect of this country, even in aspects that they had nothing to with. After building this country from the ground up, why have black people always been excluded?

There is an old saying that "the victors of war get to write the history of the world." White privilege is a living example of this statement. Because white America has been in control for so long, they have had the privilege of making a determination of what is important and what is not. I look at it as they have had the option of telling the truth and of lying when it suits them. White America has never steered away from this option. As black people have raised the issue of diversifying what exactly is taught in schools, white America, in their most privileged and racist comment, has simply stated, "We are not willing to lower standards for the sake of minority representation." As if telling the actual truth would be a lowering of standards?

The National Black Student Coalition raised these issues in college campuses all over this country several years ago and fought for the curriculum of literature classes to include black writers. They were faced with enormous backlash, with objections such as "You want me to replace Chaucer with the likes of Alice Walker?" Who is in charge of putting a value on authors, and why is the value of a white author like Hemmingway more than, say, the writings of Alice Walker, Morrison, author of *The Color Purple*?

Do I see a light at the end of the tunnel? Yes, I do. I have seen some changes come in the form of more ethnic classes and programs being offered in high school and college campuses, but is it necessary for us to continue to keep this division by months or classes because it might make white America uncomfortable? White America needs to come to terms with the fact that black history is US history.

White privilege is difficult to confront. We know it has given white America a sense of entitlement and created advantages for white America, which has, without any merit, promoted their status on the world stage. What I don't understand is how white America continues to deny the existence of white privilege. You are enveloped with evidence of it all around you, but you stick their heads in the sand to the facts because if you are honest about it, you will see your racial group for what it is.

White America refuses to acknowledge that white privilege augments your lives because you see the world in a white view. All information is processed through a white mindset and then decided upon what is vital and what can be discarded.

White America has been educated to believe that you are "the best of the best" in every category. You have also been educated to believe that you have no responsibility for the lack of equality in today's society because of your past behavior and treatment of black people or because of the racial privilege that you enjoy in today's society. Instead, you continue to show ignorance of what is so obvious. This ignorance has become your hammer by which you continue your mythical reign on the world—and in particular, the United States. With your continued unfairness and discrimination, white America has never had to confront their own white privilege.

Because of all this, white America fails to understand the mess that they have made. The United States was constructed on a foundation of white privilege. You will never admit it. It was built on the domination of black people. White America has been programmed to ignore this fact, which is why they never have come to terms with this fact. Only black people, sadly, have reprogrammed themselves in this way. Our culture has taught white America nothing about their privilege. It has merely reinforced the belief that if it does actually exist, white America has had no responsibility for creating this privilege. Our culture has granted white America "absolution," for lack of a better term, from any culpability.

For those in white America who want to consider that this privilege is a real, living, breathing thing, you must first start by believing black people when we talk about our experiences and not associate them with the fact that most black people are poor. Often, when white America hears of black experience, the first thing that happens is that you get angry and attack us because you believe we are blaming ALL of white America for our problems.

Let me also say that black people are aware that there is a portion of white America that has also had to struggle and has been faced with some unbelievable challenges because of economics or the criminal justice system. We acknowledge that, but please understand that our experiences are not in competition with yours. However, white privilege has always been a factor not because it provided cover from economic downfall but because of the insurance, it provided that you would never have to face the injustices and inhumane behavior that black people had to.

It is time for white America to check your privilege at the door. Black people understand white America better than you understand yourselves. We have had no choice in this because it is a matter of life and death for us. We have been schooled to anticipate all the emotions and fears of white America because your problems eventually come crashing down on us. We also realize that just because we suggest you check your privilege at the door does not ensure that you will heed our suggestion. In fact, we know you won't.

Instead of checking it, you will turn it around into something we are not doing or something negative or translate it into "This is how black people feel about us." This will eventually run off the rails into a conclusion of the problem being "Black people talk about white privilege way too long and in the wrong way."

Maybe someday someone much smarter than me will come up with a plan to convince white America that they have this privilege. It will have the same conclusion. White America will still choose ignorance behind door number 1 as opposed to knowledge behind door number 2.

The difference between the two doors is, number 1 is how the world truly is. The other is how white America imagines it to be.

CHAPTER 21

Wake Up, Period!

A T THE END of his life, Martin Luther King Jr. spoke pointedly about white supremacy:

> *"Somebody told a lie one day,"* he said as the congregation rustled out of frame. *"They couched it in language, they made everything black, ugly and evil. Look in your dictionary and see the synonyms of the word 'black'. It's always something degrading and low and sinister; look at the word 'white'. It's always something pure, high and clean. But I want to get the language right tonight. I want to get the language so right that everybody here will cry out, 'YES I'm black, I'm proud of it, I'm black and beautiful!'"*

Dr. King never referred to black people as "black." He always referred to himself and other black people as "Negroes." White America gets so stuck on the "I have a dream" speech that they don't realize or pay attention to the fact that Dr. Kick gave hundreds of speeches and that most of them would make the skin of white America crawl.

Until the murder of Trayvon Martin, liberal white America preferred to remember Dr. King in much the same light they viewed President Barack Obama—as a magical "Negro" whose prominence mythically ended white supremacy without ever having to name it.

It is true that Dr. King was a man with a dream, and President Obama used to say, "Yes, we can." Both trailblazers in their own right had a belief that liberal white America could come around and escape a society that permeates with the smell of white supremacy. They both believed that they could show "good" white America how they have been complicit in the discriminatory history and operation of this country. Ultimately, as great men as they were and are, they both failed.

White American hates to hear this. Dr. King, at the end of his life, ultimately embraced black power while he was fighting to bring poor white and poor black people together across America for a common cause. And then just like that, he was murdered, and a funny thing has happened on the way to white America waking up—they never have.

White America has a mindset of superiority to everyone—in particular, black people. But in truth, white America is only superior with a weapon, and that is people. Without the dehumanization, discriminations, and undignified treatment of black people, white supremacy cannot exist.

Today, Black Lives Matter and organizations that fight for the rights of underserved communities have awakened the echoes of a misremembered legacy. BLM has shown that black people once again will give their lives so that white America will not have to sacrifice anything personally in the struggle to dismantle systemic racism in America. And at the same time, it has once again given white America the option of being accountable for their history. That's how both white supremacy and white privilege continues to function in this country. Black people move forward only to get knocked backward; all the while, white America never has to take full ownership of the mess they created.

If this country is truly to progress toward justice and equality, white America has to come to terms with and truly understand white supremacy. It is a disease that has been like a plague upon this country since its inception. White supremacy is not a rarity. It is not that four-leaf clover found in a field somewhere. It is a fabric of American society. It is apple pies, hot dogs, and baseball.

Black people fully understand that most members of white America who perpetuate white supremacy are not radical. They are not the people driving their cars into crowds of protesters or walking into churches killing people. I grew up in Ferguson, Missouri, and the majority of people I grew up with were white and can't ever see how they were complicit in white supremacy. I am sure for these members of white America—the ones with good hearts, minds, and souls—it could be traumatizing to come to this realization. But it is true, and it's time they woke up to it.

Let's not confuse white supremacy with white nationalism. The men who walked through Virginia with tiki torches were products of white supremacy. But these individuals were on the extreme spectrum. They were white nationalists, alt-right, Nazis, and Klansman. Wake up, white America, please? You don't have to wear a white hood to be a white supremacist, because it's often much subtler than that. The extremists are obvious, and you can curtail and stifle these individuals and even groups fairly quickly. The larger and more covert proponents of white supremacy fly under the radar, and before you know it, they have infiltrated.

If we are to be all we can be as a nation, we must accept that systemic racism is supported by white supremacy. I am not talking about the ones that we know would be publicly violent with us. I am talking about the ones flying under the radar. When those "good" members of white America begin to not only refuse to be complicit but also call out racism and white American supremacist behavior, we will be on the road to actually change this country. But I am going to ask these same good people to do something else. **Please stop asking black people to fix a problem they did not create.**

White supremacy is a hell of a drug. It's better than alcohol or weed because it has put white America in a position to exploit control and power. White America has been getting "high" for centuries. Like any drug, you can overdose, and clearly, white America has. Will white America ever wake up, come down out of the cloud of their perpetual "high," or will they keep their lips on the cock of superiority and hate until they just eventually suck it dry?

I know I'm not alone in trying to wake up white America to the way that racism destroys this country and, in particular, the lives of black people. There are plenty of members of white America who have no faith in a mythical "postracial America." If you simply listen to the stories from black people who have experienced extreme racism, it would be an immediate wake-up call. From brutality inflicted by law enforcement, incarceration rates, and housing discrimination to economic disparity and job discrimination, many in white America don't know about these incidents, not because they don't care, but mainly because it does not affect their lives. It is time for white America to wake up and see what is truly going on and take the step from oblivious to activist.

Maybe the seed was planted in me by the execution of Trayvon Martin and Michael Brown Jr. I would have thought that watching the videos of Tamir Rice being executed from the squad car or Eric Garner being choked to death on a New York street would have opened the eyes of white America. I would have thought that a light bulb would come on and make them recognize that there is nothing that is okay about this. Maybe they would finally realize that in this day and time, there is a serious problem with the way black people are treated. On August 9, 2014, I knew I would never be the same again. And I am a black man. White America needs to understand that after these events, you don't get a mulligan and there are no do-overs. These are ones you just can't take back.

Do I believe that white America, all of white of America, should have a guilty feeling? You bet your ass I do. But they should also have a broad range of emotions, but guilt is the most prominent because white America's history and lack of accountability have caused all this. But as I am always telling a friend of mine, "Your feelings don't mean shit if you don't do what it takes to rectify the situation."

The first step to rectifying the situation is to sit down, close your damn mouth, open your damn ears, and simply listen. Just sit back, listen, and then listen some more. We will tell you the truth about racism in this country. We have no reason to lie about it. It has killed too many of us. Our feelings about racism are an actual and true racist reality. Then the ball is in your court, and you have to want to participate in the game of educating yourselves. This will start by reading books that may be uncomfortable to read, like this one. Research your own privilege, power, and position and the ways the world has opened doors for you simply because you are white. Then realize that these same doors were and remained closed to black people. Then fucking do something about it. It's like *Alice in Wonderland*. If white America chooses to venture down the rabbit hole and they are truly humans of good, mind, and soul, they should have trouble becoming more and more pissed at every single step they take.

Then simply ask yourself two basic questions:

How did I not notice any of this before?

How is this still the reality we're living in?

So they should fill their internet cart with books by black people. They should want to know, to learn more, to be awake. White America needs to stop getting high and come down from cloud nine.

Once you have awakened, then a whole different set of questions should, again if you are worth your salt, be compounding your thoughts. What should I do with my privilege? How can I help? How do I do my part to make things more equal?

This will be overwhelming, to say the least, which is why most of white America simply gives up. You will feel like you, as one person, could never make an impact on changing this country. Here is the one thing about education. Once you know something, something that truly opened your eyes, you want to tell the world. Here is where you finally get to use social media for what it was truly meant. Post! Post! Post! Don't worry about people disagreeing with you. Just know that you are attempting to change the consciousness of our world.

Warning! Be prepared when the comments begin to start rolling in, and it will be everything from racist memes from family and friends to people actually attacking you personally. A piece of advice to you. Don't be afraid to fight with people you love and care about, especially if they hold racist views. Always continue urging them to see how hurtful their views are.

Remember these helpful hints: Mute. Block. Unfriend. Hide posts. Unfollow. Breathe. Just because you have awakened does not mean that others' alarm clocks have gone off. You will eventually go through social media purge. Racist cousins? Cut them off. That aunt who thinks Obama was an Arab? Cut off. The random person from high school who's always like "How come black people don't protest when a white person gets killed by the police?" Cut off! And might I simply add this? Anyone who supports MAGA or Number 45? You don't have to block, but keep them in sight. If white America would do this, then the consciousness of this country would begin to evolve.

White America must wake up to the realization that racial truths are clear. Law enforcement violence against black people is real, inhuman, and must stop. Law enforcement officers in the United States who kill black people regularly go free. Black people suffer daily racism that white America can never comprehend. The strategy to address racism and white supremacy, however, is simple. It's time for all Americans, beginning with white America, to be part of the solution, not part of the problem, in every aspect of our lives at home and at work. But we face roadblocks of enormous capacity. Everything in this country operates on the basis of money and class, and racism is difficultly intertwined with issues of class because as the beast of capitalism grows out of control, the wages we actually earn continue to go down.

We all face the same dilemma of not knowing how to make real progress. Well, the one way to start is to realize that we are truly all in this together. The things that bide us are much greater than the issues that separate us. White America and black people have far different histories, and there is certainly no argument that can be made to say any different, but in the end, we all want to prosper, both as individuals and as a nation.

I think about what Dr. King wrote in his "Letter from the Birmingham Jail", when white ministers across the country ridiculed him for forcing racial progress in the United States.

King wrote, *"I cannot sit idly by in Atlanta and not be concerned about what happens in Birmingham. Injustice anywhere is a threat to justice everywhere. We are caught in an inescapable network of mutuality, tied in a single garment of destiny."* This is where America—and in particular, white America—must start.

We need to address legislation concerning how law enforcement operates in this country. This is the only way to change the engraved narrative of law enforcement killing black people. In order to progress as a nation, we all must recognize that the effects of the original sin of slavery keep coming back to it. White America must look at themselves and own this sin with both accountability and sadness, but not stifled progress made by it. White America must accept that they carry the largest burden. Accept accountability, but white America must not be allowed to wallow in the guilt of privilege.

This book is a plea for white America to wake up and be accountable. White America, in 2019, is still telling us black people that we must earn our humanity. How is that even possible? Furthermore, we bear all responsibility that for any manner of inhumane treatment we receive must be our own fault. That is truly unbelievable.

To be black is to be face-to-face with the fact that our skin color cuts us off from being safe in society. White America believes in violence against black people to be isolated. After, which will be explained, it will nearly always include shaming the victim in some way. This is always followed up with being excused. When speaking out against the said violence, we are then hit with the deflection of black-on-black crime as if that is more important and we never address it in our own community.

Being black is to be hit in the face every day that everything we contribute to society (art, music, food, clothes, hair, and skin) only exists as unique until white America decides that they like it, then come to claim it as their own, because they have every aspect of society since the dawn of this country.

White America needs to wake up to the fact that in every one of their social circles, there is an extremist who wants to eliminate black people from the face of this planet. Every one of your cliques has a Dylann Roof. It's your friend's quiet kid who doesn't have many friends, who just gets excused as being "quiet." Dylann Roof's family and friends knew he was a disturbed person but thought he would grow out of it. They also knew that he had a problem with black people. His father was aware he had a gun. His friend was aware of his intention to purposely hurt black people. Shit, he talked about it for nearly six months before he went into that church. How many of Roof's white friends could have stopped this from happening?

Instead, they all acted on their privilege to ignore what they heard and saw, and it cost nine people their lives. They were all complicit. White America's denial of white supremacy is more than simple deflection and denial. It is blaming black people for what's happening.

White America expecting black people to do more work to end racism is, in itself, an act of cruel oppression and, if I say so myself, very insulting. How is it that white America can't see what is happening right under their nose? Black people in the United States exist every day of our lives in a state of panic and terror. I for one refuse to allow the death of my son to convince them. I, like many black people, are done being compassionate when unarmed young black people are being murdered by law enforcement and the excuse is because of criminal past or that they had marijuana in their system.

How can white America be acting humanely if we are marching in the streets, screaming Black Lives Matter, and the only thing we're hearing back in a loud and dominant voice is either All Lives Matter or the more hurtful rhetoric Blue Lives Matter? Black people have been strapped with the burdens of white supremacy, white domination, violence, and hatred too long.

It is time for white America to wake up and begin pulling this truck up the hill of society. It is time for white America to hold themselves accountable for a society that they created—a society with an underlying foundation of violence and terrorism, which black people have been dealing with for over four hundred years.

White America needs to stop being so damn concerned about building a wall on our southern border to keep out brown people who are willing to do the jobs that much of white America thumbs their nose at anyway. Try focusing on Xissue of white males buying automatic weapons and shooting up schools, banks, and concerts. If a middle-aged white man shooting up a country music concert isn't viewed as a white-on-white crime, then you should stop referring to a black person killing another black person by the opposite title.

It is the time that "good" white Americans stop being so concerned about hurting the feelings of other white Americans close to them and hurting themselves in the same process as well. Stop making excuses for not doing the uncomfortable work of calling racism what it is and confront it head-on.

The message now is that white American comfort is worth more than black lives.

This message has to change now. WHITE AMERICA, WILL YOU PLEASE SIMPLY WAKE UP?

REFERENCES

http://star.txstate.edu/2016/02/black-people-cannot-be-racist
-and-heres-why/.

https://06880danwoog.com/2017/01/18/teens-what-do-you
-think-of-white-privilege/.

https://thoughtcatalog.com/kovie-biakolo/2015/09/
black-forgiveness-and-racism/.

https://www.phillymag.com/news/2017/08/14/charlottes
ville-white-responsibility/.

https://www.quora.com/How-and-why-did-the-USA-
become-so-rich-and-powerful-Why-arent-countries-from-
Asia-and-Europe-more-advanced-all-together-than-the-
USA-Its-a-fairly-new-country-compared-to-the-countries-
of-Europe-and-Asia.

https://www.theroot.com/open-letter-to-white-people-who-
are-obsessed-with-black-1790856298.

INDEX

U

V

W

Y

Z

Printed and bound by PG in the USA

USA20199GIL

Auto EXAMEN A

livre de l'étudiant

Project Director: MICHAEL BUCKBY
Project Leader: GWEN BERWICK

Language consultants: Danièle Bourdais & Véronique Bussolin

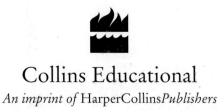

Collins Educational
An imprint of HarperCollins*Publishers*

Table des matières

Introduction

Bonjour et bienvenue à *Auto Examen A*!

Tu as déjà fait beaucoup de progrès en français.

- Tu sais déjà dire beaucoup de choses en français, et tu connais des mots et des expressions utiles dans de nombreuses situations.
- Tu as aussi appris des stratégies utiles pour t'aider à bien apprendre et à bien parler le français.

Bravo!

Les examens

Dans *Auto Examen A* et *B*, tu vas continuer à faire des progrès en français.

Tu vas en particulier te concentrer sur les examens. Nous allons plus particulièrement t'aider à te préparer aux examens, et à obtenir les meilleurs résultats possibles!

Dans chaque étape, tu vas faire des exercices comme à l'examen. Pour t'aider à bien les faire, des examinateurs te donnent des conseils pratiques.

Donc, après *Auto Examen A* et *B*, tu seras prêt(e) pour les examens!

Les voyages

Si tu as la possibilité de visiter un pays où l'on parle français, tu as de la chance! C'est un excellent moyen de faire de grands progrès en français, et de voir comment on vit dans un autre pays. *Auto Examen A* et *B* vont te préparer à faire une visite.

La correspondance

Si tu n'as pas la possibilité de voyager, pas de problème!
Il y a d'autres façons de faire des progrès.

Un(e) correspondant(e)

C'est bien d'écrire et de recevoir des lettres, et on peut
apprendre beaucoup de choses sur un autre pays. Et un(e)
correspondant(e) peut devenir un(e) ami(e) pour la vie!

Une classe-partenaire

Comme tu l'as vu dans *Auto 3*, on peut échanger des lettres, des photos, des
cassettes et d'autres documents avec une classe-partenaire dans un autre pays.
Cela peut être très intéressant, et on peut se faire de nouveaux amis.

Le courrier électronique

Tu aimes l'informatique? Une autre façon de se faire de nouveaux
amis est d'envoyer des messages par courrier électronique. On
peut recevoir des réponses facilement et rapidement.

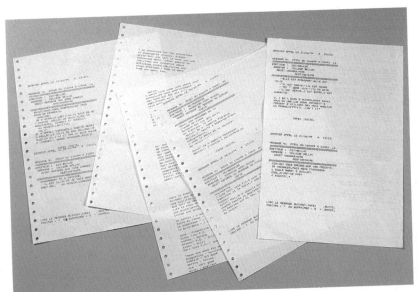

1ère Etape
Résolutions et prédictions

Mes objectifs

**Tout le monde s'intéresse à l'avenir, à ce qui va se passer.
Dans cette étape, tu vas apprendre à parler de l'avenir:**

- **à prendre des résolutions**
- **à parler de ton avenir**
- **à parler de l'avenir du monde en général.**

Au début de l'année, on prend souvent des résolutions. Voici les résolutions de quelques élèves belges au début de leur nouvelle année scolaire:

> Jeanne - Mes résolutions
> J'arriverai au collège à l'heure.
> Je n'oublierai pas mes cahiers.
> Je finirai toujours mes devoirs.
> Je regarderai moins la télé et je sortirai plus.
> J'irai au collège à vélo, je ne prendrai pas le bus.

> Eric
> J'apprendrai à faire un nouveau sport. Je ne mangerai pas de chocolat. Je ferai plus d'efforts en classe.

> Résolutions - Paul
> - Je ferai plus de sport.
> - J'irai à la piscine une fois par semaine.
> - J'apprendrai à jouer de la guitare.
> - J'aiderai mes parents à la maison.

1 ▶ Je comprends et je répète

Lis les résolutions.

a Quelle personne te ressemble le plus? Et le moins?

b Ces trois jeunes ont beaucoup de bonnes intentions – mais est-ce que ça va durer? A ton avis, quelles résolutions vont-ils abandonner? Note-les et compare ta liste avec celle de ton/ta partenaire.

'Je n'oublierai pas mes cahiers.' Tu penses que ça va durer?

Non, ça ne va pas durer.

2 ▶ Je répète

Est-ce que Jeanne, Eric et Paul ont pris des résolutions que toi aussi tu voudrais prendre? Note-les! Il faut en avoir au moins quatre.

Je serai riche et célèbre…

Deux élèves britanniques ont envoyé ce message par courrier électronique à leur classe-partenaire en Belgique:

Chers amis,

En classe, en ce moment, nous parlons de l'avenir.

Et vous, comment voyez-vous l'avenir? Par exemple, imaginez votre vie dans vingt ans. Serez-vous riches? Serez-vous marié(e)s?

Nous vous enverrons bientôt nos prédictions!

Amitiés,

Owen et James

Classe 10JHS

Voici quelques-unes des réponses:

Salut!

Merci pour votre lettre. Moi, je voudrais bien savoir lire l'avenir. C'est un sujet passionnant! Je lis toujours mon horoscope dans le journal. Voici mes prédictions:

Dans vingt ans, je serai riche et je ne travaillerai pas. Je ne serai pas marié: je pense que je resterai célibataire toute ma vie. J'habiterai probablement dans une grande maison à la campagne avec mes six chiens. J'aurai aussi un ou deux appartements en ville. J'aurai une super-belle voiture de sport. Je serai très heureux.

Et voilà! Je suis optimiste, non?

Didier

Bonjour!

Je vous envoie mes prédictions, ou plutôt mes rêves, pour l'avenir!

Dans 20 ans, je ferai un métier intéressant. Je serai une actrice célèbre et très riche. Je serai divorcée, sans doute, mais très heureuse, et j'aurai cinq ou six enfants. J'habiterai New York ou Los Angeles, mais je voyagerai beaucoup en Europe.

Ou bien, pour être plus réaliste...dans 20 ans, j'habiterai probablement toujours en Belgique. Je serai peut-être mariée, avec une fille et un fils. Au choix!

A bientôt

Caroline

1 ▶ *Je comprends*

Tu comprends bien les messages?

a Trouve les prédictions. En général, elles commencent par 'je' ou 'j'.

A l'aide!

Il y a des mots que tu ne comprends pas?

★ Est-ce que le contexte t'aide à les comprendre?

★ Est-ce que les mots ressemblent à des mots anglais?

★ Est-ce qu'ils sont similaires à d'autres mots français, que tu connais déjà?

★ Ou est-ce que tu vas les chercher dans un dictionnaire?

b Trouve dans les lettres deux expressions-clés:

je serai
j'aurai.

Que veulent dire ces expressions? Tu sais les expliquer à ton professeur?

c Quel message trouves-tu le plus intéressant? Pourquoi?

2 ▶ *Je répète*

Votre classe-partenaire vous a envoyé des messages sur cassette.

a Ecoute chaque personne, et répète les prédictions qui sont, à ton avis, réalistes.

b Ensuite, répète les prédictions qui sont plutôt des rêves.

c Recopie toutes les phrases que tu peux utiliser pour parler de ton avenir, par exemple, **je serai riche, j'aurai un appartement. . .**

3 ▶

Comment vois-tu l'avenir?

a Imagine ta vie dans dix ans:

    A Est-ce que tu seras heureux ou heureuse? Riche? Célèbre?
    B Tu seras célibataire ou marié(e), ou même divorcé(e)?
    C Tu auras des enfants? Combien?
    D Où habiteras-tu?

b Maintenant, imagine ta vie dans vingt ans. Elle sera similaire ou différente?

c Pose les questions **A – D** à ton/ta partenaire. Vos prédictions sont similaires ou différentes?

Moi, dans dix ans, je serai probablement toujours célibataire. Je n'aurai pas d'enfants. . .

Comment vois-tu ton avenir?

Tu as trouvé ce sondage dans *Okapi*, un magazine français. Des jeunes de ton âge parlent de l'avenir.

1 ► Je comprends

Si tu ne comprends pas toutes les questions, cherche les mots difficiles dans le dictionnaire.

Pensez-vous vivre un jour l'une de ces situations?			
	Très ou assez probable	Peu ou pas probable du tout	Ne se prononce pas
Avoir un métier passionnant	93%	4%	3%
Etre marié(e)	87%	9%	4%
Vivre une grande passion amoureuse	82%	13%	5%
Etre au chômage	40%	52%	8%
Etre riche	37%	57%	6%
Etre divorcé(e)	27%	59%	14%
Etre célèbre	24%	70%	6%
Faire la guerre	12%	81%	7%
Avoir le sida	11%	79%	10%

9 sur 10 d'entre vous pensent qu'ils auront un métier passionnant, qu'ils se marieront et qu'ils vivront un grand amour.

2 ► J'invente

Réponds toi-même aux questions du sondage:

Très ou assez probable	Peu probable	Je ne sais pas
J'aurai un métier passionnant.	Je serai marié.	Je vivrai une grande passion.

3 ►

Tes amis ont les mêmes idées que les jeunes Français?

a Prépare ta liste de questions:

> Tu penses que tu auras un métier passionnant?

b Pose les questions à tes amis:

> TU PENSES QUE TU SERAS MARIÉ UN JOUR?

> OUI, C'EST PROBABLE.

c Compare les résultats. Est-ce que les jeunes Français sont plus ou moins optimistes que vous?

4 ► J'invente

Tu sais maintenant expliquer comment tu vois ton avenir. Fais une liste de toutes tes prédictions.

> Mes prédictions
> Dans dix ans, je serai journaliste et je travaillerai en France.
> Je visiterai beaucoup de pays et j'écrirai un livre.

5 ►

Demande à ton/ta partenaire de te dire comment il/elle voit son avenir. A ton avis est-il/elle plutôt optimiste ou pessimiste? Qui est le plus optimiste: toi ou ton/ta partenaire?

L'avenir: succès ou catastrophes?

1 ▶ *Je comprends et je répète*

Comment vois-tu l'avenir du monde? Fais ce jeu-test. Compare tes réponses avec celles de ton/ta partenaire.

A l'aide!

Il y a des mots que tu ne comprends pas?

★ Certains mots ressemblent à des mots anglais. Ils sont faciles à deviner.

★ D'autres mots sont aussi faciles à deviner: par exemple, le sida est une abréviation. Le mot anglais a les mêmes lettres, mais dans un ordre différent. Tu sais, d'après le contexte, que le sida est une maladie.

★ Si tu ne peux pas deviner un mot, cherche-le dans un dictionnaire.

Jeu-test: optimiste ou pessimiste?

Pour chaque question, répondez:

A C'est très probable
B C'est probable
C C'est possible
D C'est peu probable

Au 21ème siècle

1 Il y aura une catastrophe nucléaire.

2 On trouvera un vaccin contre le sida.

3 Il y aura plus de pollution.

4 Beaucoup de gens seront au chômage.

5 Les scientifiques trouveront un remède aux maladies comme le cancer.

6 Nous gagnerons la lutte contre la drogue.

7 Il y aura une catastrophe écologique.

8 Les gens seront moins violents.

9 Il n'y aura pas de guerres.

10 Nous ferons des progrès scientifiques.

11 Des gens iront sur Mars.

12 Il y aura beaucoup de famine dans le monde.

Calculez vos points

Pour les questions 1, 3, 4, 7, 12:
A=0 point;
B=1 point;
C=2 points;
D=3 points.

Pour les questions 2, 5, 6, 8, 9, 10, 11:
A=3 points;
B=2 points;
C=1 point;
D=0 point.

Résultats

0-10 points
Oh là là, quel pessimisme! Oui, il y a des problèmes et des risques, mais nous faisons aussi des progrès! Vous devriez avoir plus confiance!

11-24 points
Vous êtes un peu optimiste et un peu pessimiste. Vous êtes peut-être réaliste, ou bien vous n'avez pas sérieusement pensé à l'avenir!

25-36 points
Vous êtes vraiment optimiste! C'est bien de voir la vie en rose, mais il faut être quand même réaliste: pour être sûr d'être heureux dans l'avenir, il faut prendre des mesures maintenant!

Je suis optimiste!

Les élèves belges ont demandé à leurs amis de leur dire comment ils voient l'avenir. Ils ont enregistré les interviews sur cassette.

1 ▶ Je répète

a Ecoute les interviews. Si tu es d'accord avec une prédiction, répète-la.

b Réécoute les interviews. Cette fois, si tu n'es pas d'accord avec une prédiction, répète-la.

2 ▶ J'invente

Concours! Travaillez en groupes:

● les membres du groupe **A** sont 'les optimistes';
● les membres du groupe **B** sont 'les pessimistes'.

Les optimistes doivent noter des prédictions optimistes, et les pessimistes doivent noter des prédictions pessimistes.

Vous gagnerez un point pour chaque phrase correcte. Le groupe avec le plus de points gagnera.

3 ▶

a Relis le jeu-test (page 9) et écris les prédictions. Si tu es d'accord avec une prédiction, recopie-la. Si tu n'es pas d'accord, change-la.

Exemple

Il n'y aura pas de catastrophe nucléaire.

b Si tu peux, écris d'autres prédictions.

4 ▶

Ecoute la cassette. Vanessa, Louis et Brigitte parlent de l'avenir. Est-ce qu'il y a quelqu'un qui est du même avis que toi? Pourquoi?

5 ▶

Tes amis, sont-ils du même avis que toi? Discutez et comparez vos prédictions pour l'avenir.

– Tu es optimiste ou pessimiste?
– Moi, je suis plutôt optimiste.
– Pourquoi?
– Eh bien, à mon avis, nous ferons des progrès scientifiques. . .

A l'aide!

N'oublie pas les expressions que tu connais pour donner ton opinion:

★ **A mon avis**, il y aura moins de racisme.
★ **Je pense que** nous serons plus violents.
★ **Je suis d'accord avec** Paul.
★ **Pas du tout!**
★ **Je ne suis pas d'accord avec** toi!

. . . et pour demander à quelqu'un son opinion:

★ **A ton avis**, est-ce qu'il y aura plus de guerres?
★ **Qu'en penses-tu**, Anna?

A moi, les examens!

1

Ecoute ces trois jeunes Français qui imaginent leur avenir. Pour chaque personne, écris la lettre de l'illustration qui représente son idée de l'avenir.

A

B

C

D

Conseils de l'examinateur

- Avant d'écouter la cassette, prépare-toi! Lis la question pour savoir exactement quelles informations tu cherches.

- Regarde les illustrations. Pense aux mots que les gens peuvent dire. Par exemple, quels mots vont-ils utiliser pour parler de leur famille, ou d'où ils habiteront?

 2

Tu écoutes la radio française. Il y a une discussion: un homme et une femme parlent de l'avenir. Ecoute cet extrait.

a Ils parlent de quels sujets? Recopie et coche (✓) la grille.

	Oui	Non
La science		
Le chômage		
L'environnement		

b Ton frère ne parle pas français. Il veut savoir si la femme est optimiste ou pessimiste, et pourquoi. Réponds-lui en anglais et donne-lui deux raisons.

Conseils de l'examinateur

- Avant d'écouter la cassette, prépare-toi! Lis la question pour savoir exactement quelles informations tu cherches.

- Tu veux savoir si on parle d'un sujet, par exemple, l'environnement. Attention! Tu n'entendras peut-être pas le mot **environnement**, mais est-ce que tu entends d'autres mots sur le même sujet, par exemple le mot **écologique**?

A moi, les examens!

Jeux de rôles

Fais ces jeux de rôles avec un(e) partenaire.

A

Correspondant: **Comment imagines-tu ta vie dans dix ans?**

Candidat: Say you think you will be happy.

Correspondant: **Tu seras toujours célibataire?**

Candidat: Say you will probably be married.

Correspondant: **Tu auras des enfants?**

Candidat: Say you will have a son and a daughter.

B

Correspondant: **Comment vois-tu l'avenir?**

Candidat: Say you are optimistic.

Correspondant: **Pourquoi?**

Candidat: Say that, in your opinion, we will make scientific progress.

Correspondant: **Moi, je suis plutôt pessimiste. Je pense qu'il y aura plus de violence.**

Candidat: Disagree with what your penfriend says and give the opposite opinion.

Conseil de l'examinateur

● Attention aux détails: ne fais pas d'erreurs stupides! Par exemple, si tu es une fille, n'oublie pas de dire 'heureuse', et non 'heureux'.

Conversation

a Prépare-toi pour une conversation au sujet de l'avenir:

★ Prépare deux ou trois questions.

★ Note les raisons pour lesquelles tu es optimiste ou pessimiste.

★ Apprends quelques expressions par cœur.

b Ecoute les conversations entre Tiana et Laurent, et Tiana et Olivier. Qui est le plus intéressant, Laurent ou Olivier? Pourquoi?

★ Olivier donne des réponses intéressantes. Il dit plus que le minimum.

★ Olivier pose des questions à Tiana. C'est une vraie conversation.

c Discute de l'avenir avec quatre membres de ta classe, l'un après l'autre. Le sujet: es-tu plutôt optimiste ou pessimiste, et pourquoi? As-tu trouvé quelqu'un avec les mêmes opinions que toi?

A moi, les examens!

Votre horoscope

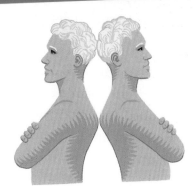

Gémeaux
22 mai – 21 juin

Ce mois-ci, tout va bien en amour! Vénus entre dans votre signe le 6, ce qui est une garantie de succès en amour. Mais des tensions monteront, et il y aura un conflit avec un membre de votre famille. Vous travaillerez beaucoup et vous aurez des succès scolaires.

Sagittaire
23 novembre – 21 décembre

Un mois fait d'amour et de tendresse pour vous. Il y aura quelqu'un de très important dans votre vie. Vous sortirez beaucoup, mais attention – vous risquez de vous fatiguer! Vos relations avec vos parents seront difficiles. Vous n'aurez pas beaucoup de chance. Si vous jouez aux cartes, vous perdrez de l'argent.

Tu lis ces horoscopes dans un magazine français. Tes amis, qui ne parlent pas français, te posent des questions:

★ My birthday is May 25th. Will it be a good month for love? Does it say anything about money or school?

★ I'm Sagittarius. I've not been getting on very well with my parents. Will the situation improve? My love-life is boring – I never meet anybody. Will things get better?

✱ Donne-leur *le maximum d'informations* pour répondre à leurs questions. Réponds en anglais.

Conseils de l'examinateur

● Pour commencer, lis les horoscopes en entier.

● Puis, cherche les réponses. Ne t'inquiète pas si tu ne comprends pas chaque mot! Cherche seulement les informations nécessaires. Pour les trouver rapidement, pense aux mots-clés, par exemple, **amour/amoureux**.

A moi, les examens!

Vous avez demandé à des élèves de votre classe-partenaire de prédire l'avenir.

Vous classez leurs réponses en trois catégories.

Pour chaque message, note le numéro de la catégorie:

1 optimiste;

2 un peu optimiste/un peu pessimiste;

3 pessimiste.

Conseils de l'examinateur

● Pour commencer, lis chaque message assez rapidement.

● Ensuite, lis les messages plus lentement, un message à la fois. Pense à chaque prédiction. Est-elle optimiste ou pessimiste?

Bonjour! Voici mes prédictions pour l'avenir.

A mon avis, il y aura beaucoup plus de pollution à l'avenir, et on verra peut-être une catastrophe écologique. Les machines et les ordinateurs feront tout le travail et le chômage sera un grand problème. Peut-être que moi, je serai au chômage un jour.

Aurélie

A

L'avenir (Jean-Luc)

A mon avis, l'avenir sera meilleur que le présent. Nous ferons des progrès scientifiques et la société sera plus civilisée. Il y aura moins de violence et de racisme.

B

Sandrine - mes prédictions

Je crois que les scientifiques continueront à faire des progrès. Les médecins trouveront des vaccins contre les maladies graves et nos astronautes iront sur d'autres planètes.

En ce qui concerne mon avenir, je pense que je serai un jour une actrice célèbre. J'adorerai mon travail et je serai très heureuse!

D

Moi, pour ma part, je pense que je serai heureuse. J'habiterai une grande maison à la campagne et j'aurai des enfants et plusieurs chiens. Je n'aime pas les grandes villes et je pense que la société sera plus violente à l'avenir. Il y aura un grand problème de drogue et plus de crimes.
Nadège

C

A moi, les examens!

Ta correspondante t'a écrit cette lettre. Lis attentivement la lettre, puis écris ta réponse. Réponds à *toutes* ses questions.

Marseille, le 15 septembre

Salut!

Merci pour ta dernière lettre. J'espère que tes vacances au bord de la mer ont été super! Comme vous, nous sommes rentrés au collège, et le travail a commencé!

En ce moment, mes amis et moi, nous parlons de l'avenir – notre avenir personnel et l'avenir du monde. C'est un sujet passionnant, et je voudrais savoir ton avis. Comment vois-tu ton avenir dans dix ans? Auras-tu des enfants, par exemple? Combien? Où travailleras-tu, à ton avis? Décris-moi ton image de l'avenir pour toi!

En ce qui concerne l'avenir du monde, je ne sais pas si je suis optimiste ou pessimiste. Il y a du pour et du contre pour chaque point de vue. Donne-moi ton opinion – es-tu plutôt optimiste ou plutôt pessimiste, et pourquoi?

Je vais te quitter maintenant. Je sors ce soir pour un match de volley. C'est un match important, donc j'espère que nous le gagnerons! Mais, je ne suis pas très optimiste...

Affectueusement,

Agnès

Conseils de l'examinateur

- Pour commencer sa lettre, Agnès parle de toi: elle mentionne ta dernière lettre. C'est poli. Tu peux faire la même chose. Par exemple, tu peux lui demander si son équipe a gagné le match de volley.

- Tu trouveras souvent dans une lettre des mots et des expressions que tu peux utiliser dans ta réponse. Par exemple, pour présenter tes opinions sur l'avenir du monde, tu peux utiliser la même expression qu'Agnès: **En ce qui concerne l'avenir du monde**. . . .

- N'oublie pas de donner des raisons pour ton optimisme ou ton pessimisme.

Tu comprends maintenant?

Je vérifie

Est-ce que tu sais maintenant parler de l'avenir? Fais ces activités pour voir. Si tu préfères, fais d'abord un peu de révision.

★ **Tu vas faire une enquête pour savoir les opinions des jeunes sur: la société; la nature; la science et la médecine; la vie personnelle. Sont-ils plutôt optimistes ou plutôt pessimistes pour l'avenir? Tu vas envoyer les résultats à ta classe-partenaire en France.**

Activité 1

Tu commences par recopier cette grille:

	optimiste	pessimiste
la société		
la nature		
la science et la médecine		
la vie personnelle		

✳ Activité 2

Puis, tu cherches des informations.

Tu reçois cette lettre de ton correspondant, Antoine. Ecris un '**A**' (pour Antoine) dans la section 'optimiste' ou 'pessimiste' pour les sujets mentionnés dans sa lettre.

> Bourges, le 5 octobre
>
> Salut !
>
> Tu m'as demandé mon opinion sur l'avenir. La voici.
>
> A mon avis, il y aura plus de violence et de chômage à l'avenir, mais je pense qu'on fera des progrès scientifiques : on trouvera peut-être un vaccin contre les maladies graves comme le sida.
>
> Et moi, je pense que je serai assez heureux. J'espère avoir un travail intéressant. Et toi, comment vois-tu l'avenir ?
>
> Amitiés,
>
> Antoine

✳ Activité 3

Trois membres de ta classe-partenaire, Laurence, Damien et Morgane t'ont envoyé une cassette. Ecoute la cassette et écris '**L**', '**D**' et '**M**' dans ta grille pour indiquer leurs opinions.

Activité 4

a Maintenant, interviewe des membres de ta classe. Demande-leur s'ils sont optimistes ou pessimistes pour l'avenir, et pourquoi. Coche (✓) la grille pour noter leurs réponses.

b En plus, prends des notes, pour ne pas oublier les raisons exactes. Elles seront utiles pour ton rapport.

> Pessimistes
> Plus de violence
> Catastrophe nucléaire

Activité 5

Ecris ton rapport:
- Calcule le pourcentage d'optimistes et de pessimistes pour chaque sujet. Recopie la grille avec les pourcentages.
- Ecris un commentaire sur les résultats.

Exemple

> En général, les jeunes interviewés sont plus optimistes que pessimistes. En ce qui concerne la société, ils pensent qu'il y aura moins de racisme et de violence. . .

Tu te rappelles?

■ **Je sais parler de mon avenir:**

Tu penses que tu seras célibataire ou marié(e) dans dix ans?	Do you think you'll be single or married in ten years' time?
Je serai peut-être divorcé(e).	I'll maybe be divorced.
Je serai célèbre!	I'll be famous!
Je n'aurai pas d'enfants.	I won't have any children.
Je pense que je serai heureux (heureuse).	I think I'll be happy.
J'aurai probablement deux enfants: une fille et un fils.	I'll probably have two children: a daughter and a son.
Vous serez riches?	Will you be rich?
Nous ne serons pas très riches.	We won't be very rich.
Vous apprendrez à jouer de la guitare?	Will you learn to play the guitar?

■ **Je sais parler de l'avenir du monde en général:**

Comment vois-tu l'avenir?	How do you see the future?
Je suis optimiste: à mon avis, il y aura moins de violence dans le monde.	I'm an optimist: in my opinion, there will be less violence in the world.
Nous ferons des progrès scientifiques.	We will make scientific progress.
On inventera un vaccin contre le sida.	They will invent a vaccine for Aids.
Les scientifiques trouveront un remède pour les maladies graves comme le cancer.	Scientists will find a cure for serious illnesses like cancer.
Nous gagnerons la lutte contre la drogue.	We'll win the fight against drugs.
Moi, je suis plutôt pessimiste.	I'm more pessimistic.
Je pense qu'il y aura plus de pollution à l'avenir, et probablement une catastrophe écologique.	I think that there will be more pollution in the future, and probably an ecological disaster.
Il y aura plus de guerres et, peut-être, une catastrophe nucléaire.	There will be more wars and, perhaps, a nuclear disaster.
Les gens seront plus violents, et il y aura plus de racisme et beaucoup de chômage.	People will be more violent, and there will be more racism and a lot of unemployment.

Je révise

Utilise ce tableau pour réviser les phrases-clés de cette étape.
Voici une activité:

★ Quelle prédiction est-ce que chaque illustration te suggère?

★ Discute de tes prédictions avec ton/ta partenaire. Etes-vous d'accord?

2ème Etape
Faire du camping

Mes objectifs

**Les vacances en camping △🚐 ou en auberge de jeunesse 🏠,
c'est moins cher que l'hôtel, et on rencontre beaucoup de gens!
Dans cette étape, tu vas tout apprendre sur les vacances:**

■ **dans un camping**

■ **dans une auberge de jeunesse.**

1 ▶ Je comprends

a Imagine! Tu pars en vacances. Tu as choisi la région que tu vas visiter,
mais comment vas-tu choisir un camping? Il est utile d'avoir des
renseignements sur:

A les installations
Est-ce qu'il y a l'électricité, un magasin, etc?

B la situation
Où se trouve le camping? En ville? Près de la mer?

C le classement
Le camping est dans quelle catégorie?
★ une étoile?   ★★ deux étoiles?   ★★★ trois étoiles?   ★★★★ quatre étoiles?

D quand le camping est ouvert
Il est ouvert en été seulement, ou toute l'année?

b Tu comprends tous les mots soulignés? Sinon, vérifie le sens dans le
tableau à la page 31.

2

Voici une liste d'installations. Est-ce que ces symboles t'aident à les identifier?
Vérifie le sens des mots à la page 31.

Installations		
🚿 des douches chaudes		🍷 un bar
🚿 des douches froides		une salle de jeux
des machines à laver		un terrain de jeux
des prises de courant		🏊 une piscine
des plats cuisinés à emporter		une plage
une alimentation		A LOUER 🚲 location de bicyclettes
A LOUER 🚐 location de caravanes		

Camping des Chevrets
Sur la mer
La Guimorais - 35350 St-COULOMB - Tél. 99 89 01 90

Ouvert de fin mars à fin septembre

CAMPINGS
Notre-Dame du Verger ★★★
sur la D 201 - Tél. 99 89 72 84
location mobil-home et caravane - alimentation
accès direct à la plage à 400 m - très calme

Les Genêts ★★ NN Tél. 99 89 76 17
à mi-parcours entre la ville et la plage
eau chaude - électricité - très calme
35260 CANCALE

Camping BEL AIR ★★★
Ombragé - Bar - Salle de jeux
Mer à 800 mètres - Ville à 400 mètres
Équipements de proximité: Club de voile - Plongée - Tennis à 150 mètres
Réservations : **99 89 64 36**

3

Regarde ces publicités pour trois campings.

a Est-ce qu'elles donnent les quatre types de renseignements?

b Quel camping préfères-tu?

4 ▶ *Je répète*

Quelles installations sont importantes pour toi?
Recopie-les dans l'ordre d'importance pour toi.

5

Travaille avec un(e) partenaire, ou en groupe. Vous allez faire du camping en France. Choisissez un des campings sur la Fiche 2.1.

6 ▶ *J'invente*

Invente une publicité plus intéressante pour le Camping des Chevrets. A toi d'inventer les détails!

Vous avez réservé?

1 ▶ Je comprends

Si tu fais une réservation à l'avance, il faut donner ces renseignements:

● le nombre de tentes et de caravanes
● le nombre d'adultes et d'enfants
● les dates de votre séjour.

a Peux-tu trouver ces renseignements dans cette lettre?

b Tu peux aussi demander des renseignements et poser une question.
Exemple

Est-ce que vous avez une piscine?

2 ▶ Je répète

Adapte cette lettre pour la famille Massey.
Regarde l'illustration.

```
                                    21 Dale Avenue
                                    Tywyn
                                    Gwynedd LL36 4XJ
                                    Pays de Galles

                                    le 3 avril

    Monsieur/Madame,
    J'aimerais passer mes vacances d'été dans
    votre camping, avec ma famille.
    Est-ce que je peux réserver un emplacement
    pour une tente, et un emplacement pour une
    caravane et une voiture pour sept nuits, du
    13 au 20 août?  Nous sommes cinq: deux
    adultes et trois enfants.
    Pouvez-vous m'envoyer des renseignements
    sur le camping et les tarifs pour cette
    année?
    Je vous prie d'accepter, Monsieur/Madame,
    l'expression de mes sentiments les
    meilleurs.

                        Peter Williams
```

3 ▶ Je comprends

Si tu ne réserves pas à l'avance, tu risques de trouver le camping complet:
il n'y aura pas de place.
Ecoute ces dialogues. Peux-tu identifier les gens qui arrivent au camping?
Pour qui n'y a-t-il pas de place?

4 ▶ Je répète

Pour t'aider à apprendre ces expressions-clés, recopie-les. Fais deux listes:

● les expressions du gardien de camping
● les expressions du/de la client(e).

Si tu veux, réécoute les dialogues pour t'aider.

Expressions-clés

– Nous avons réservé.

– Quel est le tarif?.

– C'est au nom de Campbell.

– Nous sommes trois: un adulte et deux enfants.

– Avez-vous un emplacement de libre pour une tente?

– Vous avez réservé?

– C'est 28F par personne, 23,50F pour les enfants de moins de sept ans.

– C'est combien par personne et par nuit?

– C'est pour une nuit.

– Vous êtes combien?

– C'est 21F l'emplacement pour une tente; 26F pour une caravane.

– Je regrette, nous sommes complets.

– C'est à quel nom?

– Avez-vous de la place pour une caravane et deux voitures?

 5 ▶ Je répète

C'est toujours une bonne idée de répéter les détails importants, pour être sûr(e) d'avoir bien entendu.

a Ecoute l'exemple sur la cassette.

b A toi, maintenant! Ecoute les dialogues, et répète les détails importants, comme dans l'exemple sur la cassette.

6 ▶ J'invente

Travaille avec un(e) partenaire.

a Inventez des dialogues pour ces illustrations. Utilisez les expressions-clés pour vous aider.

b Imagine! Tu vas en France avec ta famille. Invente un dialogue. Joue le dialogue avec ton/ta partenaire.

Au camping

1 ► Je comprends

a Imagine! Tu as un plan du camping, mais est-ce que tu comprends tous les mots? Voici quelques mots-clés:

Le **bloc sanitaire** est très important. Dans ce bloc tu trouveras les toilettes, les douches, les **lavabos** et les **bacs à vaisselle**.

Attention! Au bloc sanitaire tu verras, peut-être, ces symboles ou ces mots:

EAU POTABLE   Tu peux boire cette eau.

EAU NON POTABLE   Tu ne dois pas boire cette eau.

Il faut savoir aussi où se trouvent les **poubelles**.

Au **dépôt de butane** tu pourras acheter du **gaz** pour faire la cuisine.

La réception d'un camping s'appelle souvent le **bureau d'accueil**.

b Pour quelles installations préfères-tu avoir de l'eau **chaude**:
- les douches?
- les lavabos?
- les toilettes?
- les bacs à vaisselle?

2 ► Je répète

a Peux-tu identifier ces symboles? Recopie les mots qui correspondent à chaque symbole.

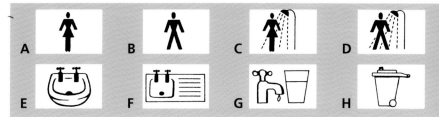

les toilettes pour femmes
les bacs à vaisselle
les douches pour hommes
les poubelles
les toilettes pour hommes
les douches pour femmes
eau potable
les lavabos

b Vérifie tes réponses! Regarde ce plan et écoute le gardien qui explique le bloc sanitaire à un campeur. As-tu bien compris les symboles? A ton avis, les symboles sont-ils clairs?

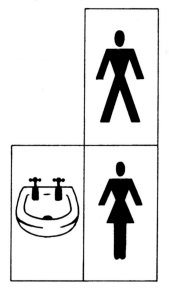

 3

Des campeurs arrivent au bureau d'accueil du Camping de la Plage et posent ces questions au gardien. Pour retrouver ses réponses, regarde cette partie du plan du camping.

Recopie les questions avec les bonnes réponses, puis écoute la cassette pour vérifier.

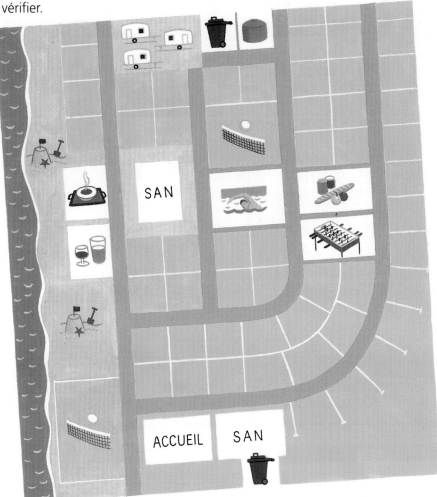

Questions	**Réponses**
– Est-ce qu'il y a une piscine?	– Oui, il y en a deux: un à la plage, à gauche, et l'autre se trouve à côté de la piscine.
– Où se trouve la salle de jeux?	– Non, je regrette, nous n'en avons pas.
– Où est le bloc sanitaire?	– Elle est à côté de l'alimentation.
– Vous avez un terrain de jeux?	– Oui, vous pouvez acheter du gaz près des caravanes, à côté des poubelles.
– Où se trouvent les poubelles, s'il vous plaît?	– Il y en a près des caravanes et ici à droite, derrière les sanitaires.
– Où sont les douches, s'il vous plaît?	– Oui, il y en a une en face de l'alimentation.
– Il y a un bar?	– Il y en a aux blocs sanitaires.
– Avez-vous des machines à laver?	– Il y en a deux: un ici à droite, et l'autre en face de la piscine.
– Il y a un dépôt de butane?	– Oui, il y en a un à la plage.

4 ▶ *J'invente*

Travaille avec un(e) partenaire sur la Fiche 2.3.

Le matériel

1 ► **Je comprends et je répète**

Imagine! Tu vas faire du camping. As-tu le matériel nécessaire ou est-ce qu'il faut l'acheter?

a Regarde ces articles vendus dans un magasin de matériel de camping.
Fais deux listes:

A les choses que tu as déjà
B les choses que tu devras acheter.

A l'aide!

Attention! Cherche dans le dictionnaire si ces mots sont masculins (un) ou féminins (une).

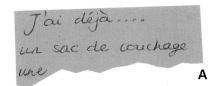

A   B

✳ ** **2 ► **Je comprends**

Ecoute ces deux jeunes Belges, Cécile et Patrick. Ils sont au magasin de matériel de camping et ils discutent du matériel qu'ils ont déjà. Qu'est-ce qu'ils achètent?

3 ► **J'invente**

Tu as une liste de ce que tu dois acheter. Maintenant, tu es au magasin de matériel de camping. Invente un dialogue avec ton/ta partenaire.

A l'auberge de jeunesse

Si tu sais quoi faire pour passer tes vacances dans un camping, tu sauras aussi aller dans une auberge de jeunesse! Beaucoup de mots et d'expressions-clés se ressemblent!

1 ▶ Je comprends

Regarde les renseignements sur deux auberges de jeunesse sur la Fiche 2.4. Ecoute deux jeunes en train d'en choisir une. Quelle auberge est-ce qu'ils choisissent?

2 ▶ J'invente

Imagine! Tu vas en France avec des amis. Vous serez quatre filles et six garçons. Avec un(e) partenaire, choisis une de ces deux auberges de jeunesse. Considérez, par exemple:

- les chambres/dortoirs;
- les installations;
- les activités;
- les horaires.

Je préfère cette auberge-ci. Elle est plus grande.

Oui, mais il n'y a pas de chambres à six lits.

Pour les garçons, on pourra demander deux chambres à trois lits.

3 ▶ Je comprends et je répète

Un groupe de jeunes arrive dans une auberge de jeunesse.

a Lis et écoute la conversation. Quelques expressions-clés sont soulignées. Peux-tu identifier l'auberge? Ont-ils choisi la même auberge que vous?

– Bonjour, <u>avez-vous des places pour cinq garçons et sept filles</u>?
– *Ah oui, voilà. Alors, la chambre des garçons est au premier étage et le dortoir des filles est au deuxième étage.*
– <u>Est-ce qu'on peut louer</u> des sacs de couchage?
– *Vous pouvez louer des draps. Voulez-vous remplir ces fiches, s'il vous plaît?. . . Merci. Il y a des toilettes ici, et il y en a d'autres au premier et au deuxième étages. Dans cette salle-ci, vous avez une télévision.*
– <u>Est-ce qu'il y a</u> une machine à laver?
– *Oui, il y en a trois dans cette salle-là.*
– <u>Quels sont les horaires des repas</u>?
– *Vous avez le petit déjeuner de 8h à 9h, le déjeuner à midi, et le dîner à 19h.*
(à la fin du séjour)
– Bonjour, nous partons ce matin. <u>Est-ce que je peux payer</u> maintenant?
– *Oui. Ça fait donc sept nuits. . . tarif jeunes. . . 3.150F, s'il vous plaît.*

b Lis le dialogue avec un(e) partenaire, puis changez de rôle.

4 ▶ J'invente

Avec un(e) partenaire, invente une conversation similaire, basée sur l'autre auberge de jeunesse.

A moi, les examens!

 Tu es dans un grand magasin en France, et tu entends ces annonces. Il y a des offres spéciales aujourd'hui.

Voici les articles que tu voudrais acheter:

Conseils de l'examinateur

● Prépare-toi à écouter. Regarde les articles que tu veux acheter. Quels sont leurs noms en français? Quand tu écoutes les annonces, est-ce que tu entends ces mots?

● Attention! Si tu entends le nom de quelque chose que tu cherches, écoute attentivement les détails! Est-ce qu'il y a une réduction, ou est-ce qu'on te donne d'autres informations?
Il y a des mots-clés qui peuvent t'aider. Par exemple, s'il y a une réduction, tu entendras des mots comme:
  ★ soldes (*sale*)
  ★ offre spéciale (*special offer*)
  ★ promotion (*special offer*)
  ★ moitié prix (*half price*)
  ★ seulement (*only*).

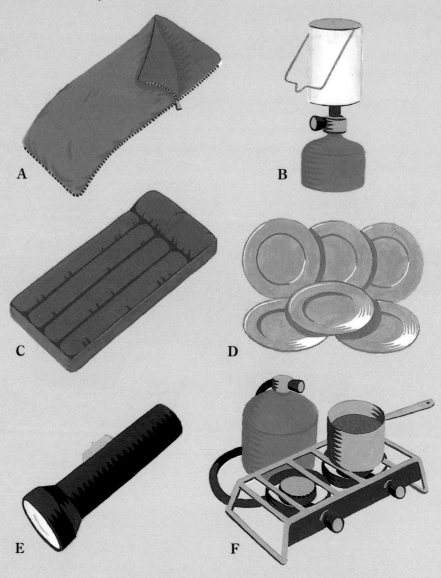

A

B

C

D

E

F

✳ Sur quels articles auras-tu une réduction? Ecris les lettres qui correspondent.

A moi, les examens!

Jeux de rôles

Souvent, un jeu de rôles semble très simple, et puis soudain, il y a un problème!
Qu'est-ce que tu vas dire? Prépare-toi!

a Discute des situations suivantes avec un(e) partenaire. Pensez à ce que vous
pouvez dire dans chaque cas. Ensuite, regardez nos suggestions. Sont-elles
similaires à vos idées?

1 Tu arrives dans une auberge de jeunesse.	2 Tu arrives dans un camping.	3 Tu quittes le camping.
– Bonjour, madame. Vous avez deux places pour ce soir? – *Je regrette, nous sommes complets.*	– Bonjour, monsieur. Vous voulez un emplacement pour ce soir? – *Oui.* – Je regrette, mais nous sommes complets. (Vous avez réservé!)	– Bonjour, nous partons ce matin. Est-ce que je peux payer? – *Oui. Quatre nuits, ça fait donc 236F, s'il vous plaît.* (Vous avez passé seulement trois nuits au camping!)

b Trouve les suggestions qui correspondent aux situations.

Suggestions

A	B	C
– Je crois qu'il y a une erreur. Nous avons passé trois nuits seulement. Nous sommes arrivés mardi. – *Ah, oui. Excusez-moi.*	– Mais j'ai réservé. – *C'est à quel nom?* – C'est au nom de Whittle. – *Attendez... Non, je ne vous trouve pas.* – Ça s'écrit: W-H-I-T-T-L-E. – *Ah, oui. Excusez-moi.*	– Est-ce qu'il y a une autre auberge de jeunesse près d'ici? – *Non, il n'y en a pas.* – Alors, est-ce qu'il y a un camping? – *Oui, il y en a un, près de la plage.*

c Vous avez pensé à d'autres solutions? Discutez de vos idées avec votre
professeur.

d Avec un(e) partenaire, continuez ces dialogues:

1	2	3
– Avez-vous un emplacement pour une tente pour ce soir? – *Je suis désolé. Nous sommes complets...*	– Est-ce que je peux payer? Je pars ce matin. – *Oui. Alors, une personne pour trois nuits, ça fait 160F...*	– Bonjour, j'ai une réservation pour ce soir...

A moi, les examens!

Cette famille veut faire du camping dans le département de la Gironde, en France.
Ils veulent tous des installations différentes.

Conseils de l'examinateur

- Regarde l'illustration de la famille. Quels sont les mots que tu cherches? Souvent, la réponse à une question dépend d'un ou deux mots. Prépare-toi bien à l'examen! Apprends régulièrement les nouveaux mots!

- Lis tout le texte pour chaque camping. Pendant l'examen, tu pourras souligner les mots importants pour t'aider. Ici, n'écris pas sur le livre, mais prends des notes.

Exemple

B: plage. . .

- Regarde les illustrations pour t'aider. Souvent les images peuvent confirmer ta réponse, mais attention! Ne dépends pas uniquement des images, lis attentivement le texte pour être sûr(e)!

✳ Voici quatre campings de la région. Quel est le camping idéal pour toute la famille: **A**, **B**, **C** ou **D**?

13 ★★★★ Airotel **Palace**

Bd. J. Marsan de Montbrun - BP.33
33780 Soulac-Sur-Mer
Gironde - Tél. 56 09 80 22

Entre la forêt de pins et la mer. A 400 m de l'Océan. Alimentation. Libre-service. Restaurant. Tennis. Ombrages. Location bungalows.

A

14 ★★★★ Airotel **Les Viviers**

33950 Lège Cap-Ferret
Principale
Gironde - Tél. 56 60 70 0

Forêt pins. Bord Bassin d'Arcachon. To sports nautiques. Tous commerc Océan à 10 mn. Plage privée. Pêche Mer et Lac. Tennis. Plage naturis Equitation. Sauna Solarium. Locati caravanes. Mobil-home. Réservatio conseillées en juillet-août.

B

15 ★★★★ Airotel **Côte d'Argent**

CAMPING - CARAVANING
33990 Hourtin-Plage -
Gironde
Tél. 56 09 10 25

Océan. Centre commercial. Bar. Restaurant. Plats cuisinés. Terrain ombragé. Pêche. Voile. Animation. Surf. Machines à laver. Location bungalows, caravanes et mobil-homes.

C

12 ★★★★ Airotel **de l'Océan**

CAMPING - CARAVANING
33163 Lacanau-Océan -
Gironde
Tél. 56 03 24 45/56 03 25 6
56 05 41 95

Océan. Centre commercial. Ba Restaurant. Plats cuisinés. Forê Animation. Piscine. Tennis. Machines laver. Location de caravanes et mobil-homes. Plage à 800m.

D

A moi, les examens!

Tu veux passer tes vacances dans une auberge de jeunesse avec des amis. Ecris une lettre de réservation.

Voici les détails:

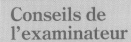

Conseils de l'examinateur

- Avant d'écrire la lettre, fais une liste des choses à dire. Comme ça, tu seras sûr(e) de ne pas oublier de détails, et de ne pas perdre de points. A ne pas oublier:
  - ★ Ecris ton adresse.
  - ★ Ecris aussi la date, par exemple, **le** 20 septembre.
  - ★ Donne les renseignements nécessaires:
    – le nombre de filles et de garçons
    – les dates du séjour.
  - ★ Demande des renseignements.
  - ★ Signe!

- Il faut terminer correctement la lettre. Utilise une phrase comme, 'Je vous prie d'accepter, Monsieur, Madame, l'expression de mes sentiments les meilleurs', avant de signer.

- Quand tu écris une lettre de réservation, c'est une bonne idée de signer et d'écrire ton nom en majuscules. Comme ça, il y aura moins de risques d'erreurs pour la réservation.

Tu comprends maintenant?

Pour savoir si tu es prêt(e) à passer tes vacances dans un camping ou dans une auberge de jeunesse, fais ces activités. Si tu veux, fais d'abord un peu de révision.

★ **Tu veux faire du camping dans le nord-ouest de la France avec un(e) ami(e) (ton/ta partenaire).**

Activité 1

Travaille avec ton/ta partenaire. Décidez des dates de vos vacances. Voulez-vous dormir dans une tente ou dans une caravane?

Activité 2

Quelles sont les installations importantes pour vous dans un camping, et pourquoi? Discutez et décidez quelles sont les cinq installations indispensables pour vous dans un camping. Prenez des notes comme aide-mémoire, pour vous aider à choisir un bon camping.

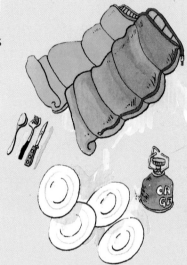

Activité 3

a Faites ensemble une liste des articles nécessaires et du nombre de ces articles.

b Vous allez apporter six choses par personne. Décidez:
  ● de ce que vous allez apporter avec vous, et ce que vous allez acheter en France
  ● de qui va apporter quoi.

Activité 4

Regarde ces publicités. Les campings, ont-ils les installations qu'il vous faut? Lesquelles?

Camping ★★ du Mont-Saint-Michel

– Camping recommandé par les grands guides européens.
– Terrain agréable, reposant, gardé jour et nuit.
– 300 emplacements sur 5 hectares, 2 terrains dont l'un très ombragé.
– Branchements électriques pour caravanes.
– Blocs sanitaires modernes en cabines individuelles avec eau chaude à tous les postes.
– Supermarché, boutiques, bars, plats cuisinés, restaurant 'La Rôtisserie', jeux pour enfants.
– Location de chambres 'Motel Vert' et bungalows-dortoirs.
– Informations touristiques, bureau de change.

Camping International Les Falaises

Ouvert du 1er avril au 1er novembre. Réservation possible.

10 ha de nature sauvage dans le site exceptionnel des 'vaches noires' avec le confort d'un 4 étoiles.

Branchements individuels eau. Tout à l'égout. Electricité. Sanitaires modernes en cabines individuelles. Eau chaude tout poste 24h/24. Grande piscine chauffée. Forfait annuel. Tout compris (hivernage et séjour). Séjour temporaire. Location de caravanes.

Camping-caravaning Le Pas d'Opton

Au bord de la rivière 'La Vie'. Alimentation, plats cuisinés. Bar, soirées dansantes. Piscine (2 bassins). Aires de jeux d'enfants bien équipées. 140 Emplac. 80 à 120 m² délim. par des haies. Site tr. reposant et calme. Domaine le Pas d'Opton ★★★★ NN. Branch. élect. Eau, tt-à-l'égout. Ter. boisé. Pêche, T.V., mach. à laver. Loc. bungalows, mobil-homes. 2km, tennis, équitation. Plage 5 km. Réserv. conseillées.

 Activité 5

Un ami te recommande un autre camping. Tu téléphones à ce camping pour demander des renseignements. Prends des notes:
● Quand est-ce que le camping est ouvert?
● Qu'est-ce qu'il y a comme installations?

Activité 6

Prends une décision avec ton/ta partenaire: quel camping allez-vous choisir?

Activité 7

Ecrivez une lettre de réservation au camping de votre choix.

Tu te rappelles?

■ Je sais demander un emplacement dans un camping/une place dans une auberge de jeunesse

Avez-vous de la place (un emplacement de libre) pour deux tentes (une caravane)?	Do you have room (a free plot) for two tents (a caravan)?
Nous sommes trois: deux adultes et un enfant.	There are three of us: two adults and a child.
C'est combien par personne et par nuit? Quel est le tarif?	How much is it per person and per night? What are your prices?
J'ai réservé trois places au nom de Smith.	I've reserved three places in the name of Smith.
Je peux louer un sac de couchage ou des draps?	Can I hire a sleeping bag or some sheets?
Où est le dortoir des filles?	Where is the girls' dormitory?

■ Je comprends et je sais demander des renseignements

L'auberge de jeunesse est complète (est ouverte toute l'année).	The hostel is full (is open all year round).
A quelle heure ouvre (ferme) l'alimentation (le bureau d'accueil)?	What time does the grocery shop (the reception) open (close)?
Où se trouvent les poubelles, s'il vous plaît?	Where are the rubbish bins, please?
Il y en a deux à côté du dépôt de butane.	There are two next to the gas depot.
Il y a une salle (un terrain) de jeux?	Is there a games room (games ground)?
Quelles sont les installations?	What facilities are there?
Nous avons un bloc sanitaire avec douches chaudes, bacs à vaisselle, lavabos, toilettes et des machines à laver.	We have a toilet block with hot showers, washing-up sinks, wash basins, toilets and washing machines.
C'est un camping trois étoiles, près de la mer (la plage).	It's a three star campsite, near the sea (the beach).
Il y a des prises de courant pour les caravanes.	There are electric points for caravans.
'Plats cuisinés à emporter'	'Hot dishes to take away'
'Location de bicyclettes'	'Bikes for hire'
'Eau potable'/'Eau non potable'	'Drinking water'/'Not drinking water'

■ Je sais parler du matériel nécessaire

J'ai une tasse, une soucoupe, une assiette, un bol et un verre en plastique.	I've got a plastic cup, saucer, plate, bowl and glass.
Il faut acheter un matelas pneumatique, un réchaud à gaz, des allumettes et des couteaux.	We need to buy an airbed, a camping gas stove, some matches and some knives.
Je voudrais cette lampe de poche et ces piles.	I would like this pocket torch and these batteries.
Je prends cette lampe-là.	I'll take that lamp.
J'ai besoin d'une fourchette et d'une cuillère.	I need a fork and a spoon.

■ Je comprends le règlement

Quel est le règlement?	What are the rules?
Il est interdit de faire du bruit entre 22h et 7h.	Making a noise between 10pm and 7am is forbidden.

Je révise

Utilise ce tableau pour réviser les phrases-clés de cette étape. Voici des activités:
★ Trouve les expressions illustrées ici dans le tableau.
★ Dessine des symboles. Ton/Ta partenaire trouve les expressions correspondantes.

A la mode

Mes objectifs

■ Dans cette étape, tu vas apprendre le vocabulaire utile pour acheter des vêtements.

Tu connais déjà les phrases-clés pour faire les courses et acheter des cadeaux. Ça va t'aider à acheter des vêtements!

Quel style préfères-tu?

H une chemise en nylon blanc

G une veste verte

F une cravate rayée

E un imperméable

D un chapeau gris

C un parapluie

B un pantalon noir

A des chaussures

I un mouchoir

J une robe rose

K un manteau marron

N un pull en laine rouge

L un collant

M des bottes

O un blouson en cuir

P une ceinture en plastique

Q un jean

R des chaussettes jaunes

S des baskets

T un chemisier en coton

U un gilet bleu foncé

V une jupe bleu clair

W des sandales

1 ▶ Je comprends et je répète

Regarde les images. A ton avis, quels vêtements et accessoires sont essentiels:

● pour le travail?
● pour le week-end?

Fais une liste des vêtements pour chaque situation.

2 ▶ Je comprends

On a demandé à des jeunes Français ce qu'ils portent le week-end.
Ecoute la cassette. Est-ce qu'ils portent les mêmes vêtements que toi?

3 ▶ Je répète

Aujourd'hui, beaucoup de vêtements sont unisexes, c'est-à-dire, pour
garçons et filles.
Ecoute la cassette.

a La première fois, répète le nom des vêtements qui sont, à ton avis, unisexes.

b La deuxième fois, répète le nom des vêtements pour filles.

c La troisième fois, répète le nom des vêtements pour garçons.

4 ▶

a Fais une liste de six vêtements que tu aimes porter. Peux-tu deviner quels
sont les vêtements sur la liste de ton/ta partenaire?

> *Tu aimes porter un jean?*

b Fais la même chose pour les vêtements que tu n'aimes pas porter.

5 ▶

Tes vêtements reflètent ta personnalité? Fais ce petit test!

Ton caractère et tes vêtements

1 Tu achètes une chemise/un chemisier:
  a rayé(e), en coton
  b en soie noire
  c en nylon gris.

2 Ta nouvelle ceinture est:
  a en cuir naturel
  b en cuir rouge
  c en plastique noir.

3 Pour ton anniversaire, tu voudrais un pull:
  a rayé, en coton
  b en cachemire vert clair
  c en nylon gris foncé.

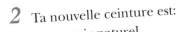

4 Tu vas acheter des chaussettes:
  a en coton bleu foncé
  b en soie rose
  c en laine blanche.

Résultats

Tu as une majorité de **a**: Tu aimes la nature. Tu préfères les vêtements confortables.
Tu as une majorité de **b**: Tu es sophistiqué(e), et tu aimes le luxe. Tu achètes des vêtements chers.
Tu as une majorité de **c**: Tu as l'esprit pratique, et tu ne t'intéresses pas beaucoup aux vêtements.

Dans un grand magasin

Quand tu vas dans un grand magasin, il faut d'abord trouver le bon rayon.
D'habitude, il y a un guide, comme celui-ci:

GALERIES GONCOURT

Sous-sol	Rez-de-chaussée	1er Etage	3e Etage	4e Etage
Boutique sport	Parfumerie	Lingerie dames	Papeterie	Cadeaux
	Bas-collants	Confection hommes	Confection enfants	Disques et librairie
	Accessoires dames		Jouets	Service clientèle
	Chaussures dames	2e Etage		
	Chaussures hommes	Confection dames		

1 ► *Je comprends*

Ecoute quatre clients du magasin Galeries Goncourt qui demandent à des
employés où se trouve le rayon qu'ils cherchent.

Pour chaque client, dessine si l'employé(e) est sympathique et poli(e),

ou si l'employé(e) n'est ni sympathique ni poli(e).

2

Trouve dans les dialogues **A** et **B** deux phrases-clés pour demander où se
trouve quelque chose. Regarde le guide pour vérifier les réponses.

A
– Pardon, madame, où est le rayon des vêtements pour femmes, s'il vous plaît?   – *Vous le trouverez au deuxième étage.*

B
– Pardon, monsieur, où est-ce que je peux trouver les disques?   – *Les disques? Ils sont au sous-sol.*

3 ► *Je répète*

Quand tu poses une question, c'est une bonne idée de répéter la réponse
pour vérifier que tu as bien compris.

a Ecoute la cassette. Imagine que tu accompagnes le client. Répète la
réponse à chaque question.

Exemple
  Client: Pardon, monsieur, où est le rayon des jouets, s'il vous plaît?
  Employé: Il est au troisième étage.
    Toi: Au troisième étage?

b Ecoute une deuxième fois, et regarde le guide du magasin. Répète
seulement les réponses correctes.

4

Avec ton/ta partenaire, lis les dialogues **A** et **B**. Puis, adapte-les pour demander
où sont les autres rayons.

5

Test de mémoire! Partenaire **A** demande où se trouvent certains rayons aux
Galeries Goncourt. Partenaire **B** répond, sans regarder le guide. Changez de
rôle. Qui donne le plus de réponses correctes, **A** ou **B**?

Je peux vous aider?

1 ▶ Je comprends

Pour acheter un vêtement, tu devras connaître des phrases-clés. Vérifie le sens des phrases soulignées à la page 44.

- Je peux vous aider, madame?
- **Non, merci. Je regarde seulement.**

- Je peux vous aider, monsieur?
- **Oui. Je cherche un pull.**
- En laine ou en coton?
- **J'aime bien les pulls en coton. Ils coûtent combien?**
- 260F. Nous les avons en vert foncé, en bleu clair, en jaune et en noir. Voilà.
- **Euh, j'aime bien le vert et le noir. Je peux les essayer?**
- Bien sûr. Vous faites quelle taille?
- **Je fais du 38.**
- Les voilà en 38.
- **Où sont les cabines d'essayage?**
- Elles sont là-bas, à côté des manteaux.

- Alors, ça va?
- **Oui. J'aime mieux le noir. Je le prends.**

2 ▶ Je répète

Entraîne-toi! Ecoute les deux dialogues et répète ce que disent les clients:
- après la cassette
- avec la cassette
- sans la cassette.

3

✳ **a** Ecoute les autres clients sur la cassette. Qu'est-ce qu'ils achètent?

   b Réécoute les dialogues et répète ce que disent les clients.

4 ▶ Je comprends

Si tu veux acheter un vêtement, tu devras savoir demander la taille correcte. Regarde ces tableaux et note la taille et la pointure que tu fais en France.

Tableau de comparaison des tailles

Robes, chemisiers et gilets femmes

F	36	38	40	42	44	46	48
GB	10	12	14	16	18	20	22
USA	8	10	12	14	16	18	20
AUST	12	14	16	18	20	22	24

Costumes hommes

F	42	44	46	48	50	52	54
GB	32	34	36	38	40	42	44
USA	32	34	36	38	40	42	44
AUST	42	44	46	48	50	52	54

Tableau de comparaison des pointures

Chaussures femmes

F	35½	36	36½	37	37½	38	39
GB	3	3½	4	4½	5	5½	6
USA	4	4½	5	5½	6	6½	7½
AUST	4½	5	5½	6	6½	7	7½

Chaussures hommes

F	39	40	41	42	43	44	45
GB	5½	6½	7	8	8½	9½	10½
USA	6	7	7½	8½	9	10	11
AUST	6½	7½	8	9	9½	10½	11½

5 ▶ J'invente

Avec un(e) partenaire, choisis deux illustrations et invente un dialogue pour chacune.

C'est trop grand

Un magasin a préparé un manuel pour former ses employés. Regarde cet extrait. A ton avis, les conseils sont bons?

Vendre des vêtements
Huit problèmes fréquents

Problème:

1 'Elle est trop longue.'

2 'Elle est trop courte.'

3 'Elles sont trop larges.'

4 'Elles sont trop étroites.'

5 'Il est trop grand.'

6 'Il est trop petit.'

7 'C'est un peu trop cher. Avez-vous autre chose dans ce style?'

8 'Ça ne me va pas. Ce n'est pas mon style.'

Stratégie:

Encouragez le/la client(e):

'Mais elle vous va très bien. Les jupes longues/courtes sont très à la mode, en ce moment.'

Ne perdez pas patience. Souriez!:

'Essayez cette paire-ci, monsieur. Celles-ci sont plus étroites/larges.'

Beaucoup de clients ne connaissent pas vraiment leur taille.
Conseillez-les avec tact!:

'Un petit peu trop grand/petit, peut-être. Voulez-vous essayer celui-ci?'

Proposez autre chose, avec tact:

'Vous avez vu celui-ci? Ce jean-ci est très à la mode.'

Proposez autre chose, toujours avec tact:

'Vous aimez celle-ci en laine, madame? Elle est très chic.'

2 ► *Je comprends et je répète*

a Ecoute les vendeurs et les vendeuses sur la cassette. A ton avis, ont-ils bien suivi les conseils du manuel? Sont-ils de bons vendeurs et vendeuses?

b Réécoute la cassette et répète ce que disent les vendeurs et les vendeuses qui sont polis et gentils.

3 ► *Je répète et j'invente*

a Avec un(e) partenaire, lis ce dialogue. C'est le quatrième dialogue de l'activité **2 ►**. Le/La client(e) est difficile. L'employé(e) du magasin doit être très patient(e) et très poli(e)!

Employé(e):	Je peux vous aider?
Client(e):	Oui, est-ce que je peux essayer ce pantalon?
Employé(e):	Oui. Voilà la cabine d'essayage. . . Ça va?
Client(e):	Non, il est trop petit.
Employé(e):	Voulez-vous essayer celui-ci? Il est un peu plus grand. . .
Client(e):	Non, ça ne va pas. Il est trop grand. Avez-vous quelque chose dans le même style?
Employé(e):	Oui, il y a ceux-ci en vert foncé. Ils sont très à la mode.
Client(e):	Je préfère celui-là, en gris. . . Non, il ne me va pas. Ce n'est pas mon style.
Employé(e):	Voulez-vous essayer celui-ci? Il est très à la mode. Ou celui-là? Il est très chic.
Client(e):	J'aime bien celui-là. Il fait combien?
Employé(e):	350F.
Client(e):	Ah non, c'est trop cher!

b Changez le dialogue selon les illustrations. Changez de rôle. Qui joue le rôle de l'employé(e) avec le plus de patience et de politesse, toi ou ton/ta partenaire?

Je peux l'échanger?

Qu'est-ce que tu vas dire s'il y a un problème?
Ne t'inquiète pas. Ce n'est pas difficile!

La fermeture éclair ne marche pas.

C'est déchiré.

Il y a un trou.

1 ▶ Je comprends

Ecoute ces gens. Ils ont tous un problème. Trouve la bonne illustration pour chaque personne.

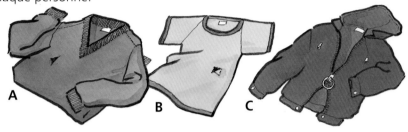

A   B   C

2 ▶

a Fais une liste de stratégies à employer s'il y a un problème. Es-tu d'accord avec toutes les stratégies dans la boîte? Peux-tu en ajouter d'autres?

b Compare ta liste avec celle de ton/ta partenaire.

> **Stratégies**
> ★ Il faut expliquer le problème.
> ★ Il faut être ferme.
> ★ Il n'est pas nécessaire de rester calme.
> ★ Il ne faut pas sourire.
> ★ Il faut demander à être remboursé(e).
> ★ Il ne faut pas être trop poli(e).

3 ▶ Je répète

a Lis et écoute ce dialogue. Vérifie les mots que tu ne comprends pas.

b Lis le dialogue avec un(e) partenaire, puis changez de rôle. Chaque fois, le/la client(e) joue son rôle d'une manière différente: calme et polie; ferme; agressive et fâchée, etc. Quelle est la meilleure façon d'expliquer un problème, à votre avis?

> – Je voudrais me plaindre de ce jean. Je l'ai acheté hier. La fermeture éclair ne marche pas bien.
> – *Je peux voir?*
> – Et je viens de remarquer qu'il est déchiré ici.
> – *Ah, oui, madame.*
> – Et en plus, il y a un trou là!
> – *Oui, vous avez raison.*
> – Vous pouvez me rembourser, s'il vous plaît?
> – *Je regrette, ce n'est pas possible, mais vous pouvez l'échanger contre un autre.*
> – D'accord.

4 ▶ J'invente

Avec un(e) partenaire, invente un sketch similaire. Utilise les stratégies de l'activité **2** ▶. Demande à tes amis de t'observer. Est-ce qu'ils pensent que tu expliques bien ton problème?

A moi, les examens!

✳ 📼 Trois personnes achètent des vêtements dans un magasin. Ils achètent quels vêtements? Note la bonne lettre pour chaque personne.

Conseils de l'examinateur

- Prépare-toi à écouter la cassette! Pense aux noms des vêtements illustrés. Comment peut-on décrire ces vêtements en français?

- Ecoute la cassette attentivement. Pour chaque client, il faut identifier **le vêtement** et **la couleur** du vêtement.

A moi, les examens!

Jeux de rôles

Travaille avec un(e) partenaire. Vous êtes dans un grand magasin. Partenaire **A** est le/la client(e) dans un rayon des vêtements; partenaire **B** est le vendeur/la vendeuse.

A

Vendeur(-euse): **Bonjour, monsieur/mademoiselle, je peux vous aider?**

Client(e): Tell the assistant you are looking for a pair of grey shoes.

Vendeur(-euse): **Nous avons celles-ci, et celles-là.**

Client(e): Say you prefer the light grey ones.

Vendeur(-euse): **Oui, monsieur/mademoiselle. C'est quelle pointure?**

Client(e): Say you are size 39.

Vendeur(-euse): **Voilà, monsieur/mademoiselle. Ça va?**

Client(e): Say they are a bit too wide.

Vendeur(-euse): **C'est dommage.**

B

Vendeur(-euse): **Bonjour, monsieur/mademoiselle, qu'y a-t-il pour votre service?**

Client(e): Ask the assistant if they have any striped jumpers.

Vendeur(-euse): **Voilà, monsieur/mademoiselle, vous faites quelle taille?**

Client(e): Tell the assistant that you only know your English size.

Vendeur(-euse): **Grande/Moyenne/Petite, très bien. Ce pull-over en bleu, peut-être?**

Client(e): Ask where you can try on the jumper.

Vendeur(-euse): **Il y a une cabine là-bas, monsieur/mademoiselle.**

Client(e): Explain to the assistant that the colour does not suit you.

Vendeur(-euse): **Désolé(e), monsieur/mademoiselle, mais c'est tout ce que nous avons en stock.**

Client(e): Ask if there is another shop nearby.

Vendeur(-euse): **Il y a un autre magasin en face, monsieur/mademoiselle.**

Conseil de l'examinateur

● Ne t'inquiète pas quand tu vois des expressions que tu n'as pas rencontrées avant. Prends ton temps, et ne panique pas! Il faut tout simplement réfléchir.

Par exemple, tu n'as pas appris comment dire en français, '**The colour** doesn't suit me', mais tu sais déjà dire, '**It** doesn't suit me': '**Ça** ne me va pas.' Tu peux facilement adapter cette phrase pour dire: '**La couleur** ne me va pas.'

A moi, les examens!

✳ Tu regardes une publicité pour un magasin français avec ton ami, qui ne parle pas français. Réponds à ses questions:

a How much is it for a plain red polo shirt?

b How much are the trousers?

c What colours can you buy the shirt in?

d What materials is the jacket made of?

- Le polo uni ou rayé, en maille piquée 65% polyester, 35% coton pour un entretien et un séchage rapides. Vendu à l'unité.

le polo uni 39,50F

rouge, vert ou jaune

le polo rayé 45,90F

blanc/rouge; blanc/bleu; bleu/rouge/vert

- La veste classique pour l'été, réalisée dans une belle toile 50% polyester, 50% coton. Une poche poitrine, deux poches intérieures. Couture milieu du dos. *Vert foncé, bleu et gris.* **529F**.

- Coupée ample dans une très belle popeline 100% coton, cette chemise vous est proposée en trois couleurs, *blanc, gris et rose.* A partir de **235F**.

- Ligne souple et élégante pour le pantalon à pinces. Réalisé en serge 52% coton, 48% polyester, il a quatre pinces ouvertes vers l'extérieur pour le confort. Très agréable à porter, et à un prix imbattable! *Noir, gris ou bleu foncé.* **195F**.

- Un prix très intéressant pour cette ceinture noire ou marron en très belle croûte de cuir surpiquée. *Boucle métal coloris doré.* **85F**.

Conseils de l'examinateur

- Les illustrations t'aident à savoir de quels vêtements il s'agit.
- Pour la question **a**, utilise le contexte pour t'aider. Tu connais déjà le mot **rayé**, donc tu peux deviner le sens du mot **uni**. L'illustration et la liste des couleurs t'aideront.

A moi, les examens!

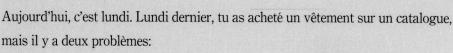

Aujourd'hui, c'est lundi. Lundi dernier, tu as acheté un vêtement sur un catalogue, mais il y a deux problèmes:

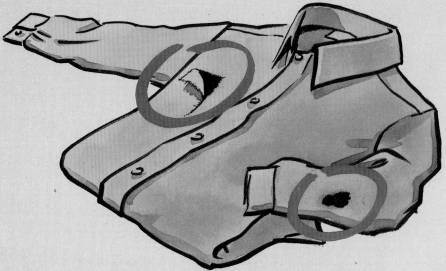

Adapte cette lettre. Donne les renseignements suivants:

★ quand et comment tu as acheté le vêtement

★ les problèmes

★ ta solution préférée.

> 4, avenue de la Défense
> 23000 Guéret
> Creuse
> le 4 octobre
>
> Messieurs,
>
> J'ai acheté ce pantalon dans votre magasin il y a deux jours. Malheureusement, je viens de remarquer que la fermeture éclair ne marche pas. Pourriez-vous me rembourser, s'il vous plaît?
>
> Je vous prie d'accepter, messieurs, l'expression de mes meilleurs sentiments.
>
> *Claude Bouquet*
>
> Claude BOUQUET

Conseils de l'examinateur

● Prépare-toi! Pense aux mots français pour décrire le vêtement que tu as acheté, et aux problèmes.

● Cherche les expressions dans la lettre que tu peux utiliser, par exemple:
J'ai acheté. . . ;
il y a. . . ;
je viens de remarquer que. . . .

Tu comprends maintenant?

Je vérifie

Dans cette étape, tu as appris le vocabulaire pour trouver le bon rayon dans un grand magasin, pour acheter un vêtement et expliquer un problème.
Si tu peux faire tout ça sans problème, fais ce teste. Sinon, révise un peu.

★ **En groupes, vous préparez un épisode d'un feuilleton télévisé, qui se passe dans un grand magasin, Chez Fleury.**

Chez Fleury . . . *pour tout!* **CF**
du lundi au samedi de 9h à 19h
sans interruption

Activité 1

Inventez le guide du magasin. Qu'est-ce qu'il y a comme rayons? Où se trouvent-ils?

Activité 2

A votre étage se trouvent les rayons de vêtements femmes et hommes. Faites le plan de votre étage. Quels vêtements vendez-vous, et comment sont-ils rangés?

Activité 3

Ecoutez la fin du dernier épisode et notez les détails:
- Qui sont les personnages?
- Qu'est-ce qui se passe?

Activité 4

Complétez la conversation du dernier épisode. Est-ce qu'il y a une solution au problème?

Activité 5

Ajoutez la scène suivante. Une femme arrive. Elle n'est pas contente: hier, elle a acheté un vêtement, mais il y a un problème. Imaginez le problème, et décrivez ce qui se passe.

Activité 6

Ecrivez le scénario de votre épisode et apprenez votre rôle.

Activité 7

Jouez votre épisode devant vos amis. Est-ce qu'ils le trouvent intéressant?

Idée!

★ Enregistrez votre épisode sur cassette ou faites-en une vidéo pour une autre classe de votre collège ou pour envoyer à votre classe-partenaire en France.

Tu te rappelles?

■ Je sais trouver un rayon dans un grand magasin

Où est-ce que je peux trouver les chaussures (les parapluies, le rayon des vêtements pour hommes), s'il vous plaît?	Where can I find the shoes (the umbrellas, the menswear department), please?
Au premier étage (au sous-sol, au rez-de-chaussée).	On the first floor (in the basement, on the ground floor).

■ Je sais acheter des vêtements

Je regarde seulement.	I'm just looking.
Je cherche une veste vert foncé ou bleu clair.	I'm looking for a dark green or light blue jacket.
Ces mouchoirs (chaussures) coûtent combien?	How much are these handkerchiefs (shoes)?
Je peux essayer ce chemisier (blouson, imperméable)?	Can I try on this blouse (blouson jacket, raincoat)?
Vous faites quelle taille (pointure)?	What size (shoe size) are you?
Je fais du 38.	I'm a 38.
Où sont les cabines d'essayage?	Where are the changing rooms?
Je peux essayer ces bottes?	Can I try on these boots?
Avez-vous des pulls ou des gilets rouges (roses)?	Do you have red (pink) jumpers or cardigans?
Nous avons ceux-ci en coton et ceux-là en laine (en soie).	We have these cotton ones and these woollen (silk) ones.
J'aime ce manteau (chapeau, collant) marron.	I like this brown coat (hat, pair of tights).
Je le prends. (Je ne les prends pas.)	I'll take it. (I won't take them.)
J'aime cette cravate (jupe) rayée, mais avez-vous quelque chose de moins cher?	I like this striped tie (skirt), but do you have anything cheaper?
Je n'aime pas cette ceinture en plastique (cuir).	I don't like this plastic (leather) belt.
Ces baskets (sandales) sont trop étroites (larges).	These training shoes (sandals) are too narrow (wide).
Ce pantalon ne me va pas. Il est trop long (court).	These trousers don't suit me. They are too long (short).

■ Je sais me plaindre, s'il y a un problème

Hier j'ai acheté ces chaussettes, et je viens de remarquer qu'elles ont un trou. Est-ce que je peux les échanger?	I bought these socks yesterday, and I've just noticed they have a hole. Can I change them?
Je voudrais me plaindre de cette robe. Je l'ai achetée ici, ce matin, mais la fermeture éclair ne marche pas. Pouvez-vous me rembourser?	I'd like to complain about this dress. I bought it here this morning, but the zip doesn't work. Can I have my money back?
Je viens d'acheter cette chemise en nylon, mais elle est déchirée.	I've just bought this nylon shirt, but it's torn.

Je révise

Utilise ce tableau pour réviser les phrases-clés de cette étape. Voici une activité:

★ Recopie les phrases du tableau en trois catégories:

    a ce qu'une femme peut dire quand elle s'achète un vêtement

    b ce qu'un homme peut dire quand il s'achète un vêtement

    c ce qu'un homme ou une femme peut dire.

4ème Etape
Le bon vieux temps!

Mes objectifs

On dit souvent qu'avant c'était mieux, que les gens étaient heureux, qu'il n'y avait pas de problèmes. . . Mais est-ce vrai?

■ Dans cette étape, tu vas apprendre à parler du passé, et des différences entre le passé et le présent.

---

1 ▶ Je comprends

Paul, un jeune Français, a écrit le nom de cinq inventions qui ont changé notre vie. Tu es d'accord avec lui? Il y a d'autres inventions importantes que tu voudrais ajouter à sa liste?

Cinq inventions importantes

a la voiture

Avant la voiture, les gens prenaient le train.

b le téléphone

Avant, les gens étaient obligés d'écrire des lettres. Le téléphone est plus rapide.

c l'avion

Avant l'avion, on devait voyager en bateau pour aller à l'étranger.

d le plastique

Avant, les objets de tous les jours étaient en métal, en bois ou en verre.

e l'imprimerie

Avant, il y avait très peu de livres.

---

2 ▶ Je comprends et je répète

Le hit-parade des inventions! Paul a préparé son 'Top 5' des inventions les plus importantes.

a Avant de l'écouter, prépare ton 'Top 5'. A ton avis, quel est l'ordre d'importance de ces inventions? Recopie-les dans cet ordre.

b Maintenant, écoute la cassette et note l'ordre du 'Top 5' de Paul. Es-tu d'accord avec lui?

Les inventions et le progrès

1 ▶ *Je comprends et je répète*

Pourquoi ces inventions sont-elles importantes?

a Recopie la liste des inventions dans l'ordre de ton 'Top 5'.

b Pour chaque invention, trouve une raison et recopie-la.

Les inventions

le plastique   la voiture   le téléphone   l'avion   l'imprimerie

Pourquoi sont-elles importantes?
Les raisons:

- Avant, les objets étaient en métal ou en verre, et ça coûtait très cher.
- Avant, on copiait les livres à la main.
- Avant, il était difficile de voyager.
- Avant, il y avait très peu de livres.
- Avant, les livres coûtaient très cher.
- Avant, les gens étaient obligés d'écrire des lettres. Le téléphone est plus rapide.

- Avant, on devait voyager en bateau pour aller à l'étranger. Grâce à l'avion, on peut facilement visiter d'autres pays.
- Avant, les voyages étaient plus longs.
- Avant, on ne pouvait pas parler à quelqu'un qui habitait dans une autre ville.
- Avant, beaucoup de gens ne savaient pas lire.
- Avant, les gens prenaient le train. C'était moins pratique.

---

2 ▶ *Je répète*

Tu as copié les inventions dans le même ordre d'importance que ton/ta partenaire? Tu as choisi les mêmes raisons que lui/qu'elle? Comparez vos listes.

3 ▶ *J'invente*

Choisis au moins deux inventions.

a Décris comment c'était avant ces inventions.

b A ton avis, les effets sont-ils positifs ou négatifs?

> 1 les Jeux Vidéo
> Avant les jeux vidéo, les jeunes parlaient plus
> ensemble. On faisait plus de sport. Je pense que
> les effets sont négatifs.

4 ▶

Pour toi, quelle est l'invention la plus importante, et pourquoi? Discute de ta réponse avec ton/ta partenaire.

La technologie et les vêtements

Amila et Jean-Marc s'intéressent à la technologie. Ils ont fait un exposé sur les inventions importantes qui ont influencé la mode.

 1 ▶ *Je comprends*

Regarde leurs illustrations et écoute la cassette. A ton avis, leur exposé est bien présenté?

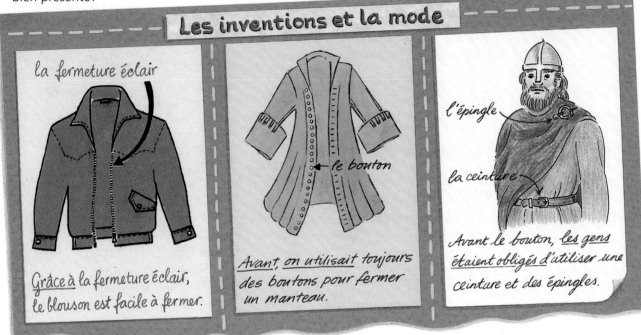

Les inventions et la mode

la fermeture éclair

Grâce à la fermeture éclair, le blouson est facile à fermer.

le bouton

Avant, on utilisait toujours des boutons pour fermer un manteau.

l'épingle

la ceinture

Avant le bouton, les gens étaient obligés d'utiliser une ceinture et des épingles.

2 ▶ *J'invente*

Prépare un exposé similaire sur l'histoire de la chaussure avec:

● des illustrations;
● un commentaire écrit;
● un commentaire oral.

Tu peux adapter le commentaire d'Amila et de Jean-Marc. Par exemple, utilise les expressions soulignées dans leur exposé.
Voici les notes d'Amila et de Jean-Marc.

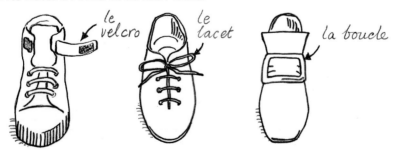

le velcro

le lacet

la boucle

A l'aide!

Avant de commencer, réfléchis: comment bien présenter ton exposé?

★ Tu vas rester assis(e) ou te mettre debout?
★ Tu vas parler fort ou doucement?
★ Tu vas improviser ou préparer des notes avant de parler?
★ Si tu prépares des notes, vas-tu lire tes notes ou essayer de les mémoriser?
★ Tu vas parler d'une voix monotone ou animée?
★ Tu vas présenter tes illustrations en couleur ou en noir et blanc?

Comme tu as changé!

✱ ⌫ **1 ► Je comprends**

On change beaucoup en cinq ans? Nous avons posé ces questions à trois jeunes Français:

● Que faisais-tu le week-end et le soir, il y a cinq ans?
● Qu'est-ce que tu aimais manger et boire?
● Qu'est-ce que tu aimais comme musique?
● Comment étais-tu?

Ecoute Tiana, Christian et Estelle. Note dans ton cahier s'ils ont changé beaucoup (**B**), un peu (**UP**), ou pas du tout (**P**).

2 ► Je répète

Réécoute les interviews et répète les choses que toi tu faisais il y a cinq ans.

3 ► J'invente

Et toi, tu as beaucoup changé?
Réponds à la lettre de Philippe.

a Choisis trois ou quatre aspects, par exemple:

● le week-end   ● ton apparence physique
● le sport   ● ton caractère
● la musique   ● la nourriture.

b Puis, fais deux listes: 'maintenant' et 'il y a cinq ans'. Pour chaque aspect, écris une phrase.

Exemple

Maintenant
Le week-end, je sors avec mes amis et je vais chez mes grands-parents.

Il y a cinq ans
Le week-end, je jouais avec ma sœur et j'allais chez mes grands-parents.

A l'aide!

Est-ce que tu entends des phrases-clés? Exemples:

★ **Il y a** cinq ans. . .
★ **A 11 ans**. . .
★ **A l'âge de 10 ans**. . .
★ **Quand j'avais** 11 **ans**. . .
★ **Quand j'étais plus jeune**. . .
★ **Maintenant**. . .
★ . . .**tandis que maintenant**. . .
★ J'aime **toujours**. . .

Salut!

Tu me demandes si j'ai changé ces cinq dernières années. Oui, je pense que j'ai beaucoup changé.

J'ai changé physiquement: il y a 5 ans, j'étais plus petit et j'avais les cheveux courts.

Comme musique, j'aimais la house et le rap. J'aime toujours le rap, mais je préfère la reggae.

A l'âge de 10 ans, je ne faisais pas beaucoup de sport, tandis que maintenant, je joue au volley.

Et toi, à ton avis, tu as beaucoup changé, ou juste un peu? Comment as-tu changé? En quoi est-ce que tu n'as pas changé?

Ecris-moi bientôt.

Amitiés,

Philippe

A l'aide!

La lettre de Philipe est facile à comprendre, parce qu'elle est divisée en paragraphes. Chaque paragraphe a un sujet différent:

● paragraphe 1 – introduction dans laquelle il dit qu'il a changé
● paragraphes 2 à 4 – explications:
  2 – son apparence
  3 – la musique
  4 – le sport
● paragraphe 5 – il termine avec une question.

c Ecris une réponse en paragraphes, comme dans la lettre de Philippe.

A l'école primaire...

Est-ce que les écoles primaires de ton pays sont similaires aux écoles en France?

Quelques élèves français ont envoyé les questions suivantes à leur classe-partenaire en Ecosse:

- Qu'est-ce que vous faisiez comme matières?
- L'école commençait et finissait à quelle heure?
- Que faisiez-vous pendant la récréation?
- Est-ce que vous appreniez une langue étrangère?
- Que mangiez-vous à midi?

1 ▶ Je comprends

Pour quelles questions peux-tu trouver une réponse dans le message par courrier électronique?

> L'ECOLE PRIMAIRE
>
> NOUS PORTIONS UN UNIFORME: UNE VESTE BLEUE ET UNE JUPE GRISE OU BLEUE POUR LES FILLES, UN PANTALON GRIS OU BLEU POUR LES GARCONS. JE N'AIMAIS PAS PORTER L'UNIFORME!
> NOUS ETIONS A L'ECOLE PENDANT SIX HEURES ET DEMIE: LES COURS COMMENCAIENT A 9H00 ET FINISSAIENT A 3H30.
> A ONZE HEURES IL Y AVAIT LA RECREATION. D'HABITUDE, NOUS JOUIONS DANS LA COUR.
> POUR LE DEJEUNER, NOUS MANGIONS A LA CANTINE OU NOUS APPORTIONS DES SANDWICHES. MOI, J'APPORTAIS TOUJOURS DES SANDWICHES. JE DETESTAIS MANGER A LA CANTINE!

2 ▶ J'invente

Avec un(e) partenaire, fais une liste de dix questions (ou plus!) sur l'école primaire en France pour envoyer à ta classe-partenaire. Vous pouvez utiliser les questions ci-dessus.

3

Maintenant, décris ton école primaire, pour des élèves français. Pour t'aider, tu peux répondre aux questions que tu as inventées pour l'activité **2 ▶**

A l'aide!

★ N'oublie pas la structure de ta réponse à Philippe: un paragraphe pour chaque sujet.

★ Essaie d'écrire une lettre intéressante.

Donne des détails supplémentaires. Par exemple, si, dans ton école, vous portiez un uniforme, décris-le.

Donne ton opinion. Par exemple, est-ce que tu aimais le déjeuner à la cantine? Quelles étaient tes matières préférées?

À moi, les examens!

 1 ▶

Jeu! Ecoute ces gens qui parlent de quatre inventions importantes. Peux-tu identifier les inventions? Pour chaque invention, note la lettre de l'image qui correspond.

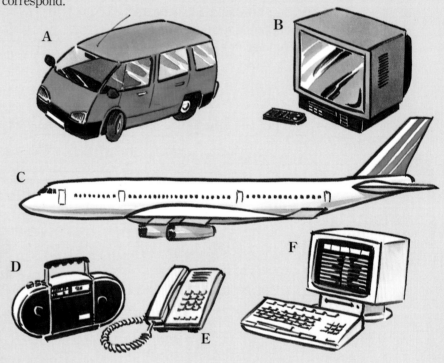

Conseils de l'examinateur

- Prépare-toi! Avant d'écouter la cassette, essaie de faire des prédictions: qu'est-ce qu'on va dire de ces inventions?

- Attention! Il y a **six** images, mais on parle seulement de **quatre** inventions.

 2 ▶

Anna, une jeune Belge de seize ans, a fait cette description d'elle-même. Sur la cassette, elle parle de comment elle était à l'âge de onze ans, il y a cinq ans.

✳ **a** Lis la description et écoute la cassette.

A ton avis, est-ce qu'Anna a changé:

★ beaucoup?

★ un peu?

★ pas du tout?

✳ **b** Donne trois raisons pour expliquer ta réponse.

Conseils de l'examinateur

- Avant d'écouter la cassette, lis la lettre attentivement. Pense aux différents aspects mentionnés dans la lettre: l'apparence physique; le caractère; les passe-temps; la musique.

- Pour chaque catégorie, prends des notes.

- Tire tes conclusions: est-ce qu'Anna a changé?

- Explique ta réponse.
  Exemple
  A mon avis, Anna. . .
  1 Maintenant, elle a les cheveux longs. A onze ans, elle avait. . .

Description de moi-même

Je suis assez grande et j'ai les cheveux longs et roux. Je pense que je suis sympa et je suis heureuse.

J'ai beaucoup de passe-temps. Le soir, je sors avec mes copines. On va au club des jeunes, à la disco ou au cinéma. Je fais beaucoup de sport. J'écoute souvent de la musique. J'aime le jazz et la musique classique.

A moi, les examens!

1

Prépare-toi à parler de toi-même.

Conseils de l'examinateur

- Essaie de penser à l'avance aux questions qu'on peut te poser, par exemple:
  - ★ Tu étais comment, il y a cinq ans?
  - ★ Que faisais-tu en général le week-end?
  - ★ Que faisais-tu en général le soir?
  - ★ Qu'est-ce que tu aimais comme musique?
  - ★ A ton avis, as-tu beaucoup changé?

  Peux-tu trouver d'autres questions sur ce thème?

- Prépare tes réponses à ces questions.

- N'oublie pas de donner des réponses intéressantes.
  Quelle est la réponse la plus intéressante, **A** ou **B**?

  > *Que faisais-tu en général le week-end?*

  A
  > *Du sport.*

  B
  > *En été, je jouais au tennis et en hiver, je faisais de la natation.*

- Si tu peux, donne des informations supplémentaires:

  > *Qu'est-ce que tu aimais comme musique?*

  > *J'aimais le rock et le folk. Je jouais de la guitare. J'aime toujours le rock et je joue dans un groupe avec mes copains.*

- N'oublie pas les expressions utiles quand tu veux comparer:
  Exemples
  Il y a cinq ans, j'avais les cheveux plus longs.
  A 11 ans, j'étais moins calme et moins sérieux.
  A l'âge de 10 ans, je jouais au foot et au basket.
  Je fais toujours beaucoup de sport.
  Quand j'avais 11 ans, je détestais la musique classique, tandis que maintenant, je l'adore.
  Quand j'étais plus jeune, je jouais du piano.

2

A toi! Travaille avec un(e) partenaire.

a Pose des questions à ton/ta partenaire pour savoir s'il/si elle a changé et comment.

b Parle aussi de toi quand tu étais plus jeune, et explique à ton/ta partenaire comment tu as changé.

A moi, les examens!

Quels sont les effets des inventions? Un magazine français a demandé à ses lecteurs de donner leur opinion sur quatre inventions importantes: la télévision, le téléphone, l'ordinateur et la voiture. Voici quelques-unes des réponses:

Lettre 1

A mon avis, le téléphone est une invention très importante. Avant, la communication était plus difficile: maintenant, c'est plus rapide.

L'ordinateur est important, pour le travail. Avant, on devait faire de longs calculs difficiles.

Quant à la télévision, elle a eu un impact énorme sur les loisirs. Avant, il y avait moins de distractions à la maison.

Lettre 2

Pour moi, la télévision a eu un effet négatif sur la vie familiale. Avant, les membres d'une famille jouaient et parlaient ensemble.

Par contre, la voiture a apporté une contribution positive à la famille. Il est maintenant plus facile de sortir en famille le week-end et de partir en vacances.

Grâce au téléphone, il est plus facile de rester en contact les uns avec les autres.

Lettre 3

Moi, personnellement, je trouve que la vie est plus intéressante avec la télévision. Il y a des émissions intéressantes pour tout le monde.

Depuis un an, je travaille avec un ordinateur et j'aime ça. Avant, je travaillais moins vite et je faisais plus d'erreurs.

Quant à la voiture, il y a des avantages mais aussi des inconvénients. A mon avis, la pollution causée par les voitures est catastrophique pour l'environnement.

Lettre 4

Je pense que les inventions ont souvent un côté négatif. Avant la télévision, par exemple, les gens étaient plus sociables. Avant les ordinateurs, il y avait plus de travail. Maintenant, les machines travaillent et les gens sont au chômage. Par contre, je trouve que la voiture a plusieurs avantages. Avec la voiture, il est beaucoup plus facile, plus pratique plus rapide de voyager.

Conseils de l'examinateur

- Lis les lettres une par une.
- Cherche les mots-clés (positifs et négatifs), par exemple, **intéressant** et **problème**. Mais, attention! Est-ce qu'on parle du passé ou de maintenant?

❋ Recopie et complète cette grille. Coche (✓) la grille pour indiquer les opinions des auteurs de ces lettres.

		lettre 1	lettre 2	lettre 3	lettre 4
télévision	pour	✓			
	contre				
	sans opinion				
téléphone	pour	✓			
	contre				
	sans opinion				
ordinateur	pour				
	contre				
	sans opinion				
voiture	pour				
	contre				
	sans opinion				

A moi, les examens!

Les élèves de ta classe-partenaire en France s'intéressent aux inventions.

Ils veulent savoir les opinions des élèves de ta classe, et ils vous ont envoyé le questionnaire suivant.

Répond à leurs questions sur la copie du questionnaire de la Fiche 4.3.

Questionnaire: les inventions

Nous voulons savoir quelles sont les inventions les plus importantes.

Donnez le nom de quatre inventions que vous considérez comme très importantes et expliquez leur importance. Comment ont-elles changé notre vie? Est-ce que ces inventions ont aussi des effets négatifs?

Pour vous aider, nous vous avons donné un exemple.

Invention	Importance	Effets négatifs
le train	Avant le train, si on n'avait pas beaucoup d'argent, il était presque impossible de voyager, tandis que maintenant, beaucoup de gens peuvent voyager facilement.	les trains font beaucoup de bruit.

Conseils de l'examinateur

● Tu dois parler de quatre inventions.

● Pense à cinq ou six inventions qui ont des effets positifs, et, si possible, négatifs. Note tes idées pour expliquer leur importance.

● Pour quelles inventions as-tu des idées intéressantes, que tu peux expliquer en français? Choisis les quatre meilleures.

● Maintenant, écris tes réponses sur le questionnaire.

● N'oublie pas les expressions utiles pour expliquer pourquoi une invention est importante.

Exemples

*Grâce à la télévision, **on peut maintenant...***
*Avant l'invention du téléphone, **on était obligé de...***
*...**tandis que maintenant...***

Tu comprends maintenant?

Je vérifie

★ **Tu vas préparer un exposé sur 'le passé et le présent'. Tu vas parler de deux thèmes:**

- **comment la vie a changé, grâce à certaines inventions;**
- **comment toi, tu as changé.**

Yves, ton correspondant français, t'a envoyé quelques idées, et il t'a demandé de lui envoyer une copie de ton exposé.

Activité 1

✳ **a** Voici les idées d'Yves sur la télévision. Est-ce qu'il est pour ou contre la télé, ou les deux? Pour quelles raisons?

b Prépare des notes sur cinq inventions importantes, et comment elles ont changé notre vie. Réfléchis: est-ce que ces inventions ont eu des effets uniquement positifs, ou est-ce qu'il y a aussi des inconvénients?

> A mon avis, la vie a beaucoup changé, grâce à la télévision. On peut voir des documentaires intéressants et de bons films. Il y a aussi de bonnes émissions scolaires.
> Mais, quand même, je pense qu'avant la télé, les gens étaient plus sociables. Ils inventaient des choses à faire le soir; ils jouaient et discutaient ensemble. Maintenant, les enfants regardent la télé toute la soirée. Ils ne savent pas jouer et ils ne font pas d'exercice.

Activité 2

Ecoute la cassette qu'Yves t'a envoyée. Il explique comment il a changé.

✳ **a** A ton avis, a-t-il beaucoup changé, ou seulement un peu?

✳ **b** Il parle de quels aspects? Fais une liste, par exemple: **apparence physique**, **sport**, etc.

c Et toi, comment as-tu changé? Commence par faire une liste. Vas-tu parler des mêmes choses qu'Yves? Vas-tu aussi parler d'autres choses?

Activité 3

Comment vas-tu présenter ton exposé? A l'oral? A l'écrit? Les deux?

A l'oral

- Prépare des notes écrites.
- Répète ce que tu vas dire à ton/ta partenaire.
- Quand tu seras prêt(e), enregistre-toi sur cassette.
- N'oublie pas de parler distinctement et d'une voix animée.

Pour moi, le téléphone, est une invention très importante.

A l'écrit

- Fais des illustrations ou utilise des photos.
- Si tu tapes ton texte sur ordinateur, tu pourras facilement le changer et corriger tes fautes.

> A mon avis, j'ai beaucoup changé.
> Il y a cinq ans, j'étais petite et j'avais les cheveux longs.

Tu te rappelles?

■ **Je sais parler des inventions, et dire comment elles ont changé notre vie**

L'avion est une invention importante. Avant l'avion, on était obligé de voyager en bateau pour aller à l'étranger.	The aeroplane is an important invention. Before the aeroplane, people had to travel by boat to go abroad.
Avant l'invention de l'imprimerie, il y avait très peu de livres.	Before the invention of the printing press, there were very few books.
Avant le téléphone, les gens devaient écrire des lettres.	Before the telephone, people had to write letters.
Grâce au plastique, les objets de tous les jours coûtent moins cher.	Thanks to plastic, everyday objects are cheaper.

■ **Je sais parler de moi-même, et de comment j'ai changé**

Tu étais comment, il y a cinq ans?	What were you like five years ago?
J'avais les cheveux plus courts.	I had shorter hair.
A onze ans, j'étais moins timide que maintenant.	At eleven I was less shy than now.
A l'âge de dix ans, je ne sortais pas avec mes copains le samedi soir. Je restais à la maison avec ma famille. Nous regardions la télé.	At the age of ten I didn't go out with my friends on a Saturday evening. I stayed at home with my family. We watched TV.
Quand j'avais douze ans, j'adorais les jeux vidéo. Je les aime toujours.	When I was twelve, I loved video games. I still like them.
Quand j'étais plus jeune, je jouais du violon tandis que maintenant, je joue de la clarinette.	When I was younger, I played the violin, whereas now I play the clarinet.
Est-ce que vous portiez un uniforme à l'école primaire?	Did you wear a uniform at primary school?
Non, nous ne portions pas d'uniforme.	No, we didn't wear a uniform.

Je révise

Utilise ce tableau pour réviser les phrases-clés de cette étape. Voici une activité:

★ Regarde ces dessins et trouve dans le tableau les phrases qui correspondent.

5ème Etape
En forme!

Mes objectifs

Es-tu en pleine forme? Tu sais déjà quoi dire si tu es malade, mais sais-tu quoi faire pour ne pas tomber malade?
Dans cette étape, nous allons parler:

- **de nos habitudes**
- **de comment on peut rester en forme.**

1 ▶ **Je comprends**

a Lis cet article. Est-ce que les photos t'aident à le comprendre? N'oublie pas, tu peux chercher les mots que tu ne connais pas dans le dictionnaire.

b Est-ce que ta journée est similaire à celle de Catherine, ou différente?

La journée d'une jeune athlète

Catherine Prignon, seize ans, fait partie d'un club d'athlétisme. Elle s'entraîne régulièrement et aime faire des compétitions. Elle nous parle de sa routine quotidienne.

Pendant la semaine, je me réveille à sept heures et je me lève tout de suite. Le week-end, je ne me lève pas avant sept heures et demie.

Pendant la pause de midi au lycée, je m'entraîne au gymnase. Souvent je joue au basket. Après, je me douche.

2

Cet article est basé sur une interview. Ecoute l'interview. Sur quels de ces sujets est-ce que Catherine donne des informations supplémentaires?

- son régime (ce qu'elle mange)
- son entraînement
- ses vêtements
- ses intérêts
- sa routine quotidienne

✱   **3** ▶ *Je répète*

Voici quelques questions de l'interview. Recopie chaque question et écris la réponse qui correspond.

- Que fais-tu le mercredi après-midi?
- Tu te lèves à quelle heure pendant la semaine?
- Tu te couches à quelle heure?
- Que fais-tu pendant la pause de midi?
- Tu t'habilles comment pour aller au lycée?

 4

Ecoute la cassette. On te donne une heure et un choix de deux activités. Répète seulement l'activité que l'on fait normalement à cette heure-là.

...me lave et je m'habille. Pour aller au lycée, je ...ts un jean et un sweat. Je ne me maquille pas.

Je me brosse les dents après tous les repas. Je prends soin de mes dents, je pense que c'est très important.

Le mercredi après-midi, je m'entraîne. Je fais du jogging. J'ai deux amis qui s'entraînent avec moi. C'est dur, mais on s'amuse bien.

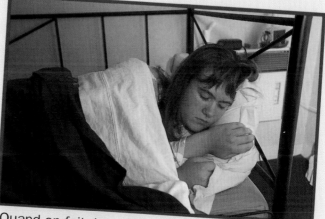

Quand on fait du sport, il faut bien dormir. Je suis stricte: je me couche toujours à dix heures, même quand j'ai envie de me coucher plus tard!

Top santé!

Nous avons interviewé quelques jeunes sur leur style de vie.

 1 ► **Je comprends**

a Pour t'aider à bien comprendre, fais une liste des aspects qu'ils peuvent mentionner: exercice; régime; sommeil. Peux-tu en ajouter d'autres?

✱ **b** Lis et écoute l'interview d'Aboussa. Après chaque aspect sur ta liste, écris **B** si Aboussa a de **bonnes** habitudes, ou **M** si elles sont **mauvaises**. A ton avis, est-ce qu'il a un bon style de vie pour être en forme?

> ## A l'aide!
>
> S'il y a des mots que tu ne comprends pas, cherche-les dans un dictionnaire.

c Laquelle des deux expressions soulignées veut dire: **je ne mange pas** et **je fais un effort pour manger**?

✱ **d** Maintenant écoute les autres interviews. Ecris **B** ou **M** pour les autres personnes. A ton avis, qui a le meilleur style de vie pour être en forme: Florence, Alain ou Gabrielle?

– Aboussa, qu'est-ce que tu fais pour être en forme?

– **Pour être en forme je vais à la piscine trois fois par semaine. La natation, c'est très bon pour le corps. Après une heure à la piscine, je me sens en pleine forme!**

– Est-ce que tu suis un régime?

– **Non, je ne suis pas de régime spécial, mais je fais attention à ce que je mange. En général, j'essaie de manger équilibré, et j'évite de manger trop gras. J'évite aussi le chocolat – le sucre est très mauvais pour les dents et pour la santé. Je me brosse les dents après chaque repas. Je fais très attention aussi à mes heures de sommeil: j'essaie de me coucher de bonne heure, pas trop tard.**

– Est-ce que tu fumes?

– **Non, je ne fume pas, et je ne bois d'ailleurs non plus d'alcool.**

2 ▶ Je répète

Ecoute d'autres jeunes parler de leur style de vie.

a Répète après les jeunes qui ont les mêmes habitudes que toi, bonnes ou mauvaises!

b Réécoute la cassette. Cette fois-ci, répète seulement les bonnes habitudes à avoir pour être en pleine forme!

3 ▶ J'invente

A toi d'examiner ton style de vie! Répond franchement à ces questions et explique tes réponses.

Qu'est-ce que tu fais pour être en forme?

● Est-ce que tu fais de l'exercice? Tu t'entraînes tous les jours?

● Est-ce que tu fumes?

● Est-ce que tu suis un régime? Qu'est-ce que tu manges, d'habitude?

● Est-ce que tu bois de l'alcool?

● Tu fais autre chose pour être en forme?

● Tu essaies de faire attention à tes heures de sommeil?

A l'aide!

Il y a des choses que tu ne sais pas dire?

★ Demande à ton professeur de t'aider.

★ Cherche-les dans un dictionnaire.

Exemple

Pour être en forme, je fais du sport. Je m'entraîne tous les jours. J'essaie de suivre un régime équilibré.

4

Interviewe ton/ta partenaire. Qui a le meilleur style de vie pour être en forme, toi ou lui/elle?
Pour t'aider, regarde les réponses d'Aboussa.

Faut-il changer ton style de vie?

1 ►Je comprends

Nous avons interviewé un couple sur leur style de vie.
Ecoute la cassette.

✳ **a** Qui est le plus honnête, Monsieur ou Madame Brigas?

✳ **b** Comment prennent-ils soin de leur santé et de leur apparence physique?

2 ►J'invente

Et toi? Sois honnête! Est-ce que tu prends soin de ta santé et de ton
apparence physique? Ou est-ce que tu devrais changer certaines de tes
habitudes? Tu vas noter quelques détails et examiner ton style de vie!

Etape 1
Choisis une journée à l'école et une journée du week-end. Pour chaque
journée, décris ta routine et ce que tu fais pour prendre soin de toi:
sommeil; repas; hygiène; exercice; vêtements, etc.

Etape 2
Maintenant, décris plus spécialement ce que tu as fait la semaine dernière.

Jour: Mardi

D'habitude

D'habitude, le mardi, je me lève à sept heures. Je me lave et je m'habille. Pour le petit déjeuner, je mange des biscuits. Je me brosse les dents.

Je vais au collège en autobus. Pendant la récréation du matin, je mange un biscuit au chocolat.

La semaine dernière

Mardi dernier, je me suis levée à sept heures et demie. Je me suis lavée et habillée, mais je n'ai pas pris de petit déjeuner. Je ne me suis pas brossé les dents.

Pendant la récréation, j'ai mangé un biscuit et des bonbons.

Etape 3
Lis ces conseils, pense à tes habitudes et décide si tu dois changer.

● Qu'est-ce que tu fais déjà parmi ce qu'on te conseille ici?

● Qu'est-ce qu'il faudra changer?

Je ne suis pas un régime équilibré. Pour le petit déjeuner, je vais prendre des céréales et du jus de fruit. Je vais faire du sport une fois par semaine et je vais aller au collège à vélo.

Nos conseils

Pour être en bonne santé:

★ Il faut suivre un régime équilibré.

★ Il est important de faire de l'exercice tous les jours.

★ Il faut avoir assez d'heures de sommeil: il ne faut pas se coucher trop tard.

Pour prendre bien soin de ton apparence physique:

★ Il faut se laver matin et soir.

★ Il est essentiel de se brosser les dents au moins deux fois par jour.

★ Il est important de se laver régulièrement les cheveux.

C'est la forme!

Les trucs de la semaine

La musique: Avant de vous coucher, écoutez de la musique calme pour vous relaxer. Vous dormirez bien! Puis, quand vous vous réveillez, écoutez une émission de musique à la radio avant de vous lever!

Le maquillage: Si vous vous maquillez, lavez-vous le visage avant de vous coucher. Ou utilisez une lotion démaquillante.

Etape 4

Explique à ton/ta partenaire ce que tu vas changer dans ton style de vie.

Etape 5

Refais cette activité après deux ou trois semaines. Décris ta routine pour une journée à l'école et une journée du week-end.
Est-ce que tu as vraiment changé tes habitudes?

★ Si oui: Bravo! Tu seras bientôt en pleine forme!

★ Sinon: Tu veux peut-être trop changer trop vite. Essaie de changer une chose à la fois.

A moi, les examens!

1

Tu arrives chez ton correspondant français. Il te montre ta chambre et il te parle de la routine chez lui.

Note l'heure des activités suivantes. L'heure du déjeuner (**C**) est déjà notée.

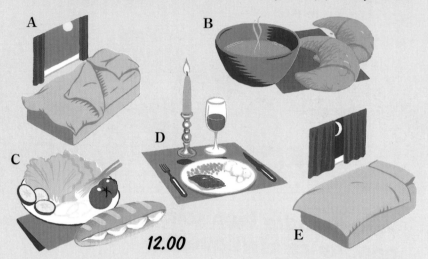

Conseil de l'examinateur

- Avant d'écouter, pense aux mots que tu vas probablement entendre. Par exemple, pour les repas: **mange**, **prend**, **déjeune**. Ça sera plus facile ensuite pour comprendre.

  2

Elsa cherche une fille avec qui partager son appartement. Ecoute les quatre messages sur son répondeur.

✱ **a** Qui Elsa va-t-elle choisir: Katia, Maryse, Delphine ou Agathe?

✱ **b** Pourquoi?

Conseils de l'examinateur

- Avant d'écouter les messages, lis la petite annonce et la description que donne Elsa d'elle-même. Note les détails importants:
  - ★ l'âge de la fille qu'elle recherche. . .
  - ★ sa routine. . .
  - ★ son opinion sur les cigarettes. . .
  - ★ ses centres d'intérêt. . .
- Pour chaque fille, coche les détails qui correspondent ou fais une croix.
- Décide qui convient le mieux à Elsa et pourquoi.

Cherche fille (18 à 25 ans) pour partager appartement. Centre-ville. Téléphoner Elsa: 45.52.37.38 (répondeur automatique).

Je travaille dans un café, donc je me couche très tard. Je ne me lève pas avant dix heures du matin. Je ne fume pas: je déteste ça! Je m'intéresse à la musique et au cinéma. Je cherche une fille qui a un style de vie et des centres d'intérêt similaires.

A moi, les examens!

a Prépare-toi à parler de toi-même, de ce que tu fais pour prendre soin de ta santé et de ton apparence physique.

Utilise ce tableau pour t'aider:

Questions	Conseils	Exemples
C'est important pour toi, la santé?	Ne dis pas tout simplement 'oui' ou 'non'. Donne ton opinion.	Oui, je pense qu'il est très important d'être en pleine forme.
Qu'est-ce que tu fais pour être en bonne santé?	Prépare des exemples détaillés pour plusieurs aspects, comme: – sommeil – régime – exercice.	Je me couche de bonne heure pendant la semaine. J'essaie de manger équilibré. Par exemple, j'évite de manger trop de. . .
	Fais une bonne impression sur l'examinateur: parle du passé et de l'avenir, pas seulement du présent.	Je fais beaucoup de sport. La semaine dernière, par exemple, je suis allé(e) deux fois à la piscine, et j'ai joué au badminton. Ce week-end, s'il fait beau, je vais faire du vélo.
Tu fais attention à ton apparence physique?	Si tu réponds 'oui', donne des exemples. Si tu réponds 'non', dis pourquoi.	Oui, je me lave régulièrement les cheveux. Non, ça ne m'intéresse pas et je n'ai pas le temps.

b Maintenant, pose les questions à ton/ta partenaire. Puis changez de rôle.

c Après, discute de tes réponses avec ton/ta partenaire. Etaient-elles intéressantes et détaillées? Non? Alors essaie de préparer des réponses plus intéressantes.

Idée!

★ Enregistre la conversation, puis écoute ton accent.

Est-ce que tu peux parler avec un meilleur accent? Demande à ton professeur de t'aider.

A moi, les examens!

a   Lis ces conseils, tirés d'un magazine français sur comment se préparer aux examens.

b   Maintenant, lis la routine de Francis, un élève français. Est-elle bonne?

✳ c   Recopie la routine de Francis, et adapte-la pour en faire une routine idéale. Utilise les conseils du magazine.

Préparez-vous physiquement pour vos examens

Tout comme les révisions, votre forme physique joue un grand rôle dans votre réussite aux examens.

■ Dormez plus longtemps et surtout couchez-vous avant minuit. De quatorze à vingt ans, on a besoin d'environ huit heures de sommeil. Pendant le sommeil, la mémoire travaille. Elle se met à stocker les informations reçues pendant la journée.

■ Evitez les excitants comme le café et le thé avant de vous coucher. Pour vous relaxer, prenez un bain.

■ Faites de l'exercice pour être fatigué physiquement. Vous pouvez faire du sport ou, tout simplement, de grandes promenades.

■ Commencez bien la journée. Ecoutez de la musique quand vous vous réveillez, puis, quand vous vous levez, lavez-vous le visage à l'eau froide.

■ Faites attention à votre alimentation. Vous êtes stressé, donc ce n'est pas le moment de changer radicalement votre régime! Mais essayez quand même de manger équilibré: yaourts, laitages, fruits, poisson. Evitez les plats gras. Evitez aussi de manger du chocolat et des biscuits pendant vos révisions!

Conseils de l'examinateur

● Pour connaître le thème de l'article, lis le titre et l'introduction.

● La structure de l'article peut t'aider à le comprendre: chaque section porte sur un conseil différent.

● Lis l'article et la routine de Francis.

● Pour répondre à la question, lis d'abord la première partie de la routine de Francis. Ensuite regarde les conseils. Est-ce qu'il faut changer quelque chose dans sa routine? Continue jusqu'à la fin de sa routine.

Francis Gravillon: ma routine pendant les révisions

7h30	je me lève et je me douche
7h45	je prends mon petit déjeuner
8h30 à 12h	je révise (3 tasses de café)
12h	déjeuner: pizza, frites, coca
12h30 à 18h	je révise (pendant l'après-midi chocolat, biscuits au chocolat, 4 tasses de café)
18h à 19h30	je regarde la télé
19h30 à 20h30	dîner: viande/poisson, légumes
20h30 à 21h00	je révise (1 tasse de café)
21h00 à 00h15	je regarde un film (1 tasse de café)

A moi, les examens!

Tu vas bientôt passer quelques jours chez ton correspondant en France. Il t'écrit cette lettre. Ecris une lettre et réponds à toutes ses questions.

> *Toulouse, le 5 juin*
>
> Salut!
>
> Dans quelques jours, tu seras chez nous. J'attends ta visite avec impatience.
>
> Nous espérons que tu passeras un bon séjour avec nous et que tu feras comme chez toi! Ma mère m'a demandé de te poser quelques questions. Est-ce qu'il y a quelque chose que tu n'aimes pas manger? A quelle heure est-ce que tu te lèves et te couches, d'habitude?
>
> Peux-tu me dire à quelle heure tu arriveras? On viendra te chercher à la gare.
>
> J'ai eu de l'argent pour mon anniversaire, et je vais acheter des vêtements. J'aime être à la mode. Est-ce que tu t'intéresses à la mode, toi aussi? Quels sont tes vêtements préférés?
>
> A bientôt,
>
> Michel.

Conseils de l'examinateur

● Pour t'entraîner, écris ta lettre au brouillon. Discute avec ton/ta partenaire et avec ton professeur.

 ★ Peux-tu améliorer ta lettre? Par exemple, peux-tu ajouter d'autres informations? Est-ce qu'il y a des fautes d'orthographe?

 ★ Quand tu seras prêt(e), prépare la version finale de ta lettre.

● Il y a plusieurs façons de commencer et de terminer une lettre pour un(e) ami(e). En voici quelques-unes.

 ★ **Pour commencer**
 Salut!
 Cher Christophe (si tu écris à un garçon)
 Chère Anne (si tu écris à une fille)
 Chers Christophe et Anne (si tu écris à deux personnes, ou plus)

 ★ **Pour terminer**
 Bon, je te laisse
 Ecris-moi vite
 Réponds-moi vite   PLUS   A bientôt
 Dis bonjour à (tes parents) pour moi.   Amitiés
                                                      Je t'embrasse
                                                      Amicalement

Tu comprends maintenant?

Est-ce que tu sais maintenant parler de tes habitudes, et de comment être en forme? Pour le savoir, fais ces activités. Si tu veux, fais d'abord des révisions.

★ **Vous allez travailler en groupes pour préparer des informations sur la santé.**

Activité 1

Décidez comment vous allez présenter vos informations. Allez-vous préparer une vidéo, une cassette, une brochure. . . ou toutes les trois?
Il faut prendre en considération:

- votre public (c'est pour votre classe/une autre classe/tout le monde à l'école?)
- vos ressources (pouvez-vous emprunter une caméra, par exemple?)
- le temps que vous avez pour la préparation
- votre message (quelle est la meilleure façon de présenter votre message?)

Activité 2

Décidez de quoi vous allez parler en particulier. Du sommeil? Du régime? Ou allez-vous parler de plusieurs aspects?

 ### Activité 3

Ecoute cet extrait d'une émission de radio. Elle peut te donner des idées. C'est une interview avec un acteur qui explique ce qu'il fait pour être en forme.

Activité 4

Ecrivez votre texte au brouillon et vérifiez qu'il n'y a pas d'erreurs.
Il faut distribuer les rôles dans le groupe. Qui va préparer les documents visuels s'il y en a? Si vous faites une vidéo, qui va être le présentateur/la présentatrice?

Activité 5

Quand vous serez prêt(e)s, faites la version finale de votre vidéo, cassette ou brochure.

Tu te rappelles?

■ Je sais parler de mes habitudes

Ma sœur se réveille avant moi.

Je me lève à sept heures, puis je me lave et je m'habille.

Je me douche avant de me coucher.

Tu te brosses les dents après chaque repas?

Je prends soin de mes dents. J'évite le sucre.

Vous vous couchez à quelle heure?

J'ai besoin de huit heures de sommeil, donc je me couche de bonne heure.

Mes frères ne se couchent pas avant minuit.

My sister wakes up before I do.

I get up at seven o'clock, then I get washed and dressed.

I have a shower before going to bed.

Do you brush your teeth after every meal?

I take care of my teeth. I avoid sugar.

What time do you go to bed?

I need eight hours' sleep, so I go to bed early.

My brothers don't go to bed before midnight.

■ Je sais dire ce que je fais pour être en forme

Qu'est-ce que tu fais pour rester en bonne santé?

Pour être en pleine forme, je fais de l'exercice.

Nous faisons du sport: nous nous entraînons trois fois par semaine.

Je fais attention à ce que je mange. Je suis un régime équilibré.

J'essaie de manger beaucoup de fruits et j'évite de manger trop gras.

Je ne fume pas. C'est mauvais pour la santé.

What do you do to keep healthy?

To be on top form, I take exercise.

We play sport: we train three times a week.

I watch what I eat. I follow a balanced diet.

I try to eat a lot of fruit and I try to avoid eating too much fat.

I don't smoke. It's bad for the health.

■ Je sais parler de mon apparence physique

Je me lave régulièrement les cheveux.

Je ne me maquille pas beaucoup.

I wash my hair regularly.

I don't wear much make-up.

Je révise

Utilise ce tableau pour réviser les phrases-clés de cette étape. Voici une activité:

★ Peux-tu décrire la routine de cette personne? Trouve des expressions dans le tableau.

6ème Etape
En voiture

Mes objectifs

Beaucoup de gens partent en vacances à l'étranger en voiture.
Dans cette étape, tu vas apprendre:

- quoi dire dans une station-service
- à demander des renseignements
- à comprendre des panneaux.

Tu pourras:

- aider tes parents si vous allez en France en voiture;
- te préparer pour aller en France plus tard.

1 ▶ Je comprends

Dans une <u>station-service</u>, on peut acheter plusieurs sortes d'<u>essence</u>:

A <u>du super</u>　　**B** <u>du sans-plomb</u>　　**C** <u>du gazole</u>

Il est important de <u>vérifier</u> régulièrement:

D <u>l'huile</u>　　**E** <u>l'eau</u>　　**F** <u>les pneus</u>

Tu comprends tous les mots soulignés? Sinon, cherche-les à la page 80.

✳ 📼 2

Ecoute ces dialogues et écris la lettre de la photo qui correspond à chacun.

A

B

C

D

E

3 ▶ Je comprends et je répète

Recopie la phrase qui correspond à chaque photo. Vérifie le sens des mots soulignés.

> – Trente litres de super, s'il vous plaît.
>
> – *Voulez-vous vérifier l'huile et l'eau, s'il vous plaît?*
>
> – Donnez-moi pour 150F de sans-plomb, s'il vous plaît.
>
> – **Pouvez-vous vérifier la <u>pression</u> des pneus, s'il vous plaît?**
>
> – *Faites le <u>plein</u> de gazole, s'il vous plaît.*

4 ▶ Je répète

Pour être sûr d'être bien servi, il faut être poli!

a Ecoute ces clients dans une station-service et répète seulement ce que disent les clients polis.

b Réécoute la cassette, et répète ce que disent les clients impolis – mais dis-le d'une façon polie! Si nécessaire, ajoute les mots indispensables: 's'il vous plaît'!

5 ▶

Entraîne-toi! Ecoute ce dialogue, puis lis-le avec un(e) partenaire. Ensuite, changez de rôle:

Cliente: **Bonjour, monsieur. Faites le plein de super, s'il vous plaît.**
Pompiste: Oui, madame. Vos clés, s'il vous plaît?
Cliente: **Les voilà.**
Pompiste (décroche le pistolet et fait le plein): Voilà, madame. Ça vous fera 220F.
Cliente: **Merci. Pouvez-vous vérifier la pression des pneus, s'il vous plaît?**
Pompiste: Oui. . . Vous avez besoin d'un peu d'air. Je vous en mets?
Cliente: **Oui, s'il vous plaît.**

6 ▶ J'invente

Inventez d'autres dialogues:

a 100 francs

b 25 litres

c

d à vous de choisir!

Point info

Très souvent, il n'y a pas de pompiste. Beaucoup de stations-service fonctionnent en self-service. Ça s'appelle aussi le 'libre-service'.

A la boutique

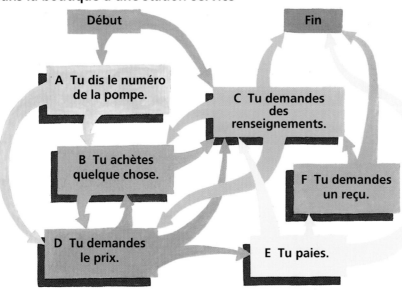

1 ► *Je comprends et je répète*

Voici un diagramme pour t'aider dans la boutique d'une station-service. Ce n'est pas difficile. Tu connais déjà la majorité des phrases.

✱ **a** Trouve et recopie les phrases du client pour chaque étape, de **A** à **F**. Attention! Quelquefois, il y a plus d'une phrase par étape.

✱ **b** Ecoute les dialogues. Pour chaque dialogue, suis le diagramme et écris l'ordre des lettres.

Les phrases du client

– Y a-t-il un téléphone ici?
– C'est la pompe numéro trois.
– Voilà, monsieur/madame.
– Vous acceptez les cartes de crédit?
– Je peux avoir un reçu, s'il vous plaît?
– Avez-vous des cartes routières?
– Ça fait combien?
– Vous vendez des boissons?
– Est-ce qu'il y a des toilettes ici?
– C'est la deux.

Dans la boutique d'une station-service

2 ► *J'invente*

Réécoute le dernier dialogue. Lis-le avec un(e) partenaire. Combien d'autres dialogues pouvez-vous inventer? Utilisez le diagramme pour vous aider.

– Bonjour. C'est quel numéro?
– *C'est la quatre. Est-ce que vous vendez des sandwiches et des boissons?*
– Oui, c'est là, à côté des journaux. Vous les voyez?
– *Ah, oui. Merci. Ça fait combien?*
– Ça vous fait 191F, s'il vous plaît.
– *Vous acceptez les cartes de crédit?*
– Oui, madame. . . Voulez-vous signer ici, s'il vous plaît?
– *Voilà. Je peux avoir un reçu, s'il vous plaît?*
– Bien sûr. Le voilà, et voilà votre carte.
– *Est-ce qu'il y a des toilettes ici, s'il vous plaît?*
– Oui, elles sont derrière la boutique. Vous les trouverez à gauche.

Je peux stationner ici?

1 ▶ *Je comprends*

Imagine! Tu arrives en voiture dans une ville française. Tu veux visiter la ville
à pied, donc tu cherches un parking. Mais est-ce que tu comprends les
réglementations? Voici quelques mots et expressions-clés pour t'aider. Vérifie
le sens des mots soulignés.

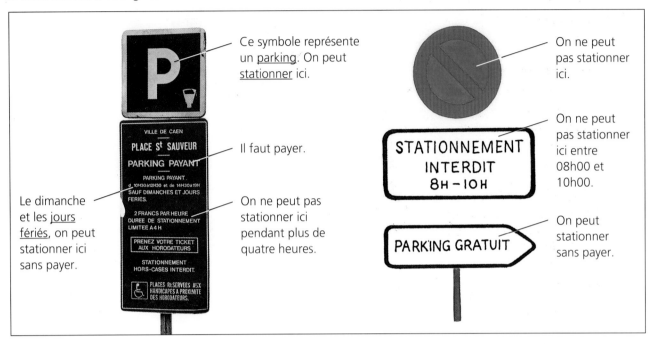

Ce symbole représente un parking. On peut stationner ici.

Il faut payer.

Le dimanche et les jours fériés, on peut stationner ici sans payer.

On ne peut pas stationner ici pendant plus de quatre heures.

On ne peut pas stationner ici.

On ne peut pas stationner ici entre 08h00 et 10h00.

On peut stationner sans payer.

2 ▶

Ecoute les conversations. Pour chaque conversation trouve le bon panneau
sur la Fiche 6.2.

3 ▶ *Je répète*

Explique aux parents de ton correspondant quand on peut stationner ici:

Ça roule!

Point info

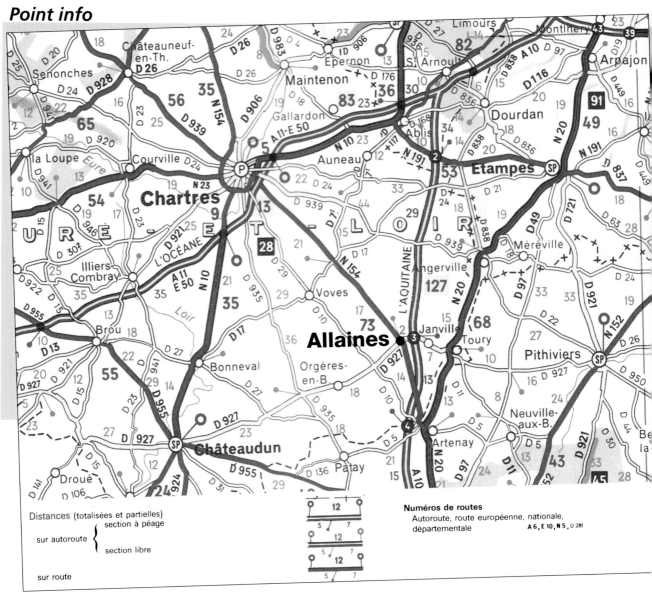

 1 ►**Je comprends**

Dans une station-service, tu entends d'autres clients qui demandent des renseignements.

a Ecoute la cassette. Qui donne les renseignements les plus clairs, la femme ou l'homme?

– Quelle est la
meilleure route
pour Chartres, s'il
vous plaît?
– Alors, vous
prenez la D27
jusqu'à Bonneval,
puis la N10.
– C'est loin?
– C'est assez loin.
C'est à 40 km, à
peu près.

– Pour l'autoroute,
s'il vous plaît,
c'est par où?
– Vous prenez la
première à
gauche, puis vous
continuez tout
droit. Ce n'est pas
loin. C'est à cinq
minutes.

– C'est bien la
route pour
Châteaudun,
monsieur?
– Oui, madame. Ce
n'est pas très loin.
C'est à 20 km.

b Tu comprends les questions soulignées? Cherche-les dans le tableau à la page 80 pour vérifier.

Comme partout dans le monde, il y a différentes sortes de routes en France:

Les autoroutes:

A11

Les autoroutes sont rapides et directes. Elles sont à quatre ou six voies. Elles passent en dehors des villes, et évitent les centre-villes. La plupart des autoroutes françaises sont à péage.

Les routes nationales:

N154

Ce sont les routes principales. Elles sont à deux ou quatre voies, et ont souvent deux chaussées séparées. Elles relient les villes principales d'une région. Elles sont moins directes que les autoroutes et elles passent par les centre-villes.

Les routes départementales:

D17

Ce sont les routes secondaires. Elles sont à deux voies. Elles passent par les petites villes et les villages. Elles ne sont pas rapides, mais elles sont souvent beaucoup plus intéressantes et plus pittoresques que les autoroutes.
Les distances entre les villes et les villages sont souvent indiquées sur les cartes. Sur cette carte, par exemple, on voit qu'Allaines est à deux kilomètres de Janville.

✳ **2 ▶ Je répète**

Imagine! Tu es à Allaines. Recopie les questions et trouve les bonnes réponses. Regarde la carte pour t'aider.

Questions	Réponses
– Quelle est la meilleure route pour Etampes, s'il vous plaît?	– C'est assez loin: c'est à 35 km, à peu près.
– Pour aller à Pithiviers, c'est loin?	– Oui, monsieur.
– Pour aller à Artenay, c'est par où, s'il vous plaît?	– Vous prenez la D927 jusqu'à Toury, puis la N20. C'est à 45 km, à peu près.
– C'est bien la route pour Chartres?	– Non, c'est à cinq minutes.
– Est-ce que l'autoroute est loin d'ici?	– Vous prenez la N154. Ce n'est pas loin.

3 ▶ J'invente

Travaille avec un(e) partenaire. Vous êtes à Toury, à 9 km d'Allaines. Partenaire **A** choisit une ville ou un village à visiter et pose des questions sur la meilleure route à partenaire **B**. Puis changez de rôle.
Qui donne les renseignements les plus clairs?

4 ▶

Tu connais ta région? Imagine! Tu es dans ta ville, ou dans une ville près de chez toi. Ton/Ta partenaire joue le rôle d'un(e) touriste:

● Il/Elle parle seulement français;
● Il/Elle veut visiter une autre ville de la région;
● Il/Elle veut connaître la meilleure route, et si c'est loin.

Peux-tu l'aider?
Changez de rôle. Qui connaît le mieux la région?

Les principaux panneaux

Si on conduit en France, il faut connaître le code de la route pour éviter les accidents. Il faut comprendre la signification des panneaux suivants et ne pas oublier qu'en France, on roule à droite!

1 ▶ Je comprends

a Regarde ces panneaux. Peux-tu deviner la signification de chaque panneau?

b Regarde les panneaux et les situations illustrées ici. Ecoute les explications sur les panneaux sur la cassette. As-tu bien deviné?

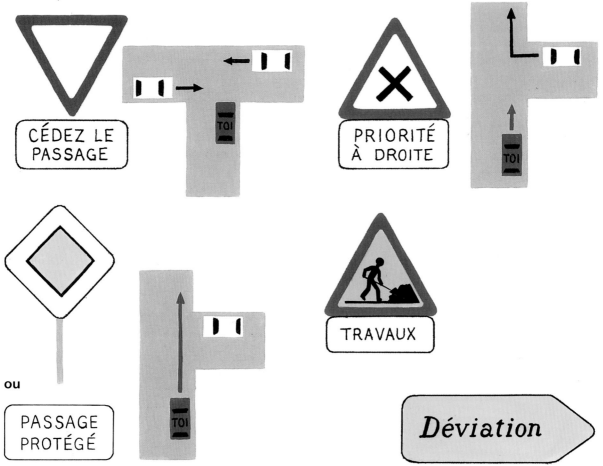

2 ▶ Je répète

Copie les panneaux et les explications qui correspondent:

- Vous n'avez pas la priorité. Un véhicule qui vient de votre droite a la priorité.
- On travaille sur la route.
- Vous avez la priorité. Un véhicule qui vient de votre droite doit s'arrêter.
- Il y a un problème. Vous devez prendre une autre route.
- Vous n'avez pas la priorité. Vous devez vous arrêter.

A moi, les examens!

Tu visites une ville avec la famille de ton correspondant. Vous êtes en voiture. Vous voulez visiter le musée. Vous demandez à l'office du tourisme des renseignements sur les parkings.

a Recopie et complète la grille. Ecoute la cassette. Pour chaque parking, donne *une raison* pour le choisir et *une raison* contre.

	Pour	Contre
Parking 1		
Parking 2		
Parking 3		

b Quel parking est-ce que la famille choisit: **1, 2** ou **3**?

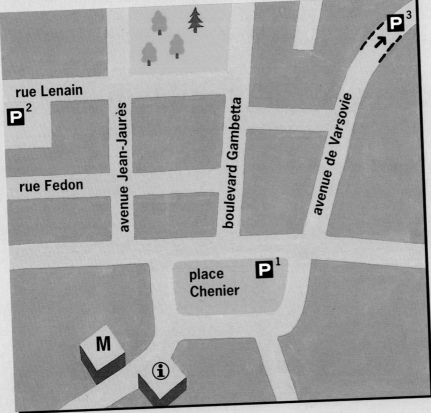

Conseils de l'examinateur

- Lis attentivement les questions pour être sûr(e) de les comprendre.
- Prépare-toi à comprendre la discussion. Comment vas-tu savoir de quel parking on parle? Pour t'aider, regarde le nom des rues où se trouvent les parkings. Pense à l'avance comment prononcer le nom de chaque rue.
- A la première écoute, essaie de noter tes réponses. Puis, à la deuxième, complète tes notes et vérifie tes réponses.

A moi, les examens!

Fais ce jeu de rôles avec un(e) partenaire, puis changez de rôle.

A: Client(e)

Tu es en vacances en France.

Tu demandes deux services au pompiste:

a:

b:

Dans la boutique, tu veux acheter trois choses:

c: Il est midi, et tu as faim et soif.

d: Tu vas à Auxerre, mais tu ne connais pas la route.

e: Tu paies.

Conseils de l'examinateur

● Prépare-toi! Si tu ne trouves pas tout ce que tu veux acheter, qu'est-ce que tu vas faire? Par exemple, vas-tu acheter autre chose, ou vas-tu demander s'il y a un supermarché ou un café près de la station-service?

● Tu ne connais pas la route pour Auxerre. Qu'est-ce que tu vas faire? Demander la route?

B: Pompiste et employé(e)

Pompiste:

a et b: Tu sers le/la client(e).

Employé(e):

c: Tu n'as pas de sandwiches mais tu vends des biscuits. Tu veux vendre tes biscuits au client/à la cliente, mais s'il/si elle te le demande, il y a un café à 100m.

d: Tu n'as pas de cartes routières. Si le client/la cliente te le demande: pour aller à Auxerre: D60 ← A6 ← N6.

e: Si le client/la cliente te le demande: tu acceptes les cartes de crédit.

Comprends-tu les principaux panneaux?

Explique la signification de ces panneaux:

CÉDEZ LE PASSAGE

PASSAGE PROTÉGÉ

P GRATUIT

A moi, les examens!

Ta tante va en France en voiture. Elle voudrait des renseignements, mais elle ne comprend pas très bien le français.

✳ Dans ces extraits trouve les réponses aux questions de ta tante. Réponds-lui en anglais.

- What is the speed limit on the motorway and in towns?
- How much do you have to pay to use the motorway?
- What facilities do they have on the motorway and how frequently do they occur?

En France, comme dans la plupart des pays européens, on roule à droite. Les limites de vitesse varient selon la catégorie de la route:

Vitesses maximales

Autoroutes:	130 km/h
Routes à 2 x 2 voies:	110 km/h
Autres routes:	90 km/h
En ville:	60 km/h

Sur l'autoroute:

Péage:

Il faut payer pour rouler sur la plupart des autoroutes en France. Quand vous entrez sur l'autoroute, vous prenez un ticket au distributeur automatique. Vous conservez le ticket: il servira à calculer la somme à payer. Plus loin, vous verrez un panneau marqué 'Péage'. Un employé vous demandera votre ticket. La somme à payer dépend de la distance voyagée.

Les autoroutes

En cas de trajet de longue durée sur l'autoroute, vous trouverez:

- à intervalles d'une dizaine de kilomètres des aires de stationnement avec eau potable, WC, tables pique-nique;
- tous les 30 à 40 km des stations-service pour l'essence et des lieux de restauration (grill-bars, restaurants self-service);
- tous les 100 km ou plus des Motels (mais pour une nuit, il est préférable de trouver un hôtel en dehors de l'autoroute, c'est moins cher!).

Attention: l'essence est plus chère sur les autoroutes que dans les stations-service du réseau routier normal.

Conseils de l'examinateur

- Lis attentivement les questions.
- Pour trouver les renseignements, cherche des mots-clés, par exemple, **autoroute**, **ville**, **payer**.
- Utilise ton bon sens. Par exemple, tu sais que **km** est une abréviation de **kilomètre(s)**. Il n'est pas difficile de deviner que **130 km/h** signifie **130 kilomètres à l'heure**.
- Fais attention aux petits détails. Par exemple, n'oublie pas que l'expression **une dizaine** veut dire *environ* **dix** (*pas* exactement dix).

A moi, les examens!

Ton correspondant belge va bientôt venir en vacances dans ton pays, avec sa sœur. Ils viendront en voiture. Il t'a écrit pour te demander des renseignements.

a Réponds à toutes les questions de Jean-Philippe.

b Traduis en français pour lui deux autres panneaux, par exemple: 'Give way'; 'No parking'; 'Diversion'.

Conseil de l'examinateur

● Quand tu réponds à une lettre, il y a souvent dans la lettre des mots et des expressions qui peuvent t'aider. Par exemple:
  ★ Tu peux adapter la question, 'Est-ce que vous roulez à droite, comme en Belgique?': 'Oui, nous roulons à droite. . .' ou 'Non, nous roulons à gauche.'
  Si tu as oublié le mot 'gauche' trouve une autre façon de dire la même chose: 'Non, nous ne roulons pas à droite. . . .
  ★ Pour expliquer un panneau anglais comme 'Diversion', tu peux utiliser une autre expression de la lettre: 'Par exemple, avez-vous un panneau avec "P", qui signifie "parking"?'. 'Le panneau "Diversion" signifie en français. . .'

Bruxelles, le 14 juin

Salut!

Je te remercie beaucoup pour ta lettre. Dans quelques semaines, nous serons en vacances. Je les attends avec impatience!

Ce sera la première fois que ma sœur visitera ton pays, et elle a un peu peur de conduire. J'ai quelques questions à te poser.

Est-ce que vous roulez à droite, comme en Belgique?

Est-ce qu'il y a un pompiste dans toutes les stations-service chez vous? Ma sœur met de l'essence sans-plomb dans sa voiture. Est-il facile de trouver des stations-service qui en vendent?

Peux-tu aussi nous aider à comprendre quelques panneaux? Par exemple, avez-vous un panneau avec 'P', qui signifie 'parking'?

Merci beaucoup pour ton invitation à passer quelques jours chez toi. Nous arriverons donc vendredi soir. Où est-ce que nous pourrons stationner?

Bon, je te laisse. Écris-moi vite!

Amicalement,

Jean-Philippe.

Tu comprends maintenant?

Je vérifie

Est-ce que tu saurais maintenant rouler en France avec confiance? Si oui, fais les activités suivantes. Sinon, fais d'abord des révisions.

★ **Tu passes deux semaines avec ta famille dans le nord-ouest de la France. Le dernier week-end, tu vas chez ta correspondante, qui habite à la Flèche. Son oncle, Monsieur Frémy, va te conduire jusqu'à Saint-Malo, où ta famille t'attend, mais il ne connaît pas bien la route.**

Activité 1

Pendant que Monsieur Frémy vérifie les pneus, ta correspondante t'explique la meilleure route pour Saint-Malo. Prends des notes, par exemple le numéro des routes et le nom des villes principales à traverser.

Activité 2

Tu regardes Télétel pour vérifier qu'il n'y a pas de problèmes sur les routes. Regarde aussi la carte pour t'aider.
Est-ce qu'il faut changer votre route? Si oui, prends des notes.

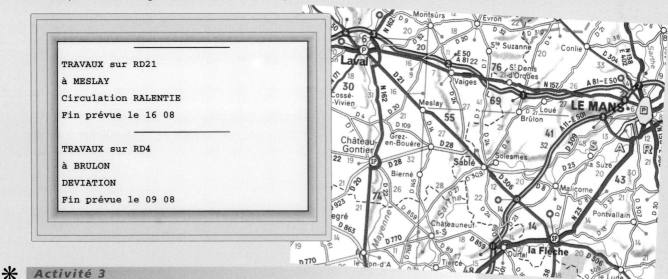

```
TRAVAUX sur RD21
à MESLAY
Circulation RALENTIE
Fin prévue le 16 08

TRAVAUX sur RD4
à BRULON
DEVIATION
Fin prévue le 09 08
```

Activité 3

Maintenant, écris les instructions pour Monsieur Frémy. Elles doivent être correctes et faciles à suivre.

Activité 4

En route, vous avez besoin d'essence. Avec un(e) partenaire, imaginez la conversation à la station-service:

Monsieur Frémy

L'employé(e)
Il est neuf heures du soir, et tu vas fermer. Des clients arrivent et donc tu n'es pas très content(e)!

Tu te rappelles?

■ Je sais quoi dire dans une station-service

Trente litres de super, s'il vous plaît. Voilà les clés.	Thirty litres of four-star, please. Here are the keys.
Faites le plein de sans-plomb, s'il vous plaît.	Fill it up with unleaded, please.
Donnez-moi pour 200F de super, s'il vous plaît.	Give me 200 francs of four-star, please.
Faites le plein de gazole, s'il vous plaît.	Fill it up with diesel, please.
Pour l'essence, c'est libre-service?	Is it self-service for the petrol?
Pouvez-vous vérifier la pression des pneus (l'huile, l'eau), s'il vous plaît?	Could you check the tyre pressure (oil, water), please?
C'est la pompe numéro trois.	It's pump number three.
Ça fait combien?	How much is that?
Vous vendez des boissons (des cartes routières)?	Do you sell drinks (road maps)?
Vous acceptez les cartes de crédit?	Do you accept credit cards?
Je peux avoir un reçu, s'il vous plaît?	Can I have a receipt, please?
Y a-t-il un téléphone (des toilettes) ici?	Is there a telephone (toilets) here?

■ Je sais demander des renseignements

Quelle est la meilleure route pour Chartres, s'il vous plaît?	Which is the best route for Chartres, please?
Vous prenez la D27 jusqu'à Bonneval, puis la N10.	You take the D27 to Bonneval, then the N10.
C'est loin?	Is it far?
C'est à 40 km, à peu près.	It's about 40 km.
Pour l'autoroute, s'il vous plaît, c'est par où?	Which way is it for the motorway, please?
Ce n'est pas loin. C'est à cinq minutes.	It's not far. It's five minutes away.
C'est bien la route pour Châteaudun?	It this the right road for Châteaudun?
Est-ce que je peux stationner ici?	Can I park here?

■ Je comprends les panneaux

Parking gratuit (payant)	Free (paying) car park
Stationnement interdit tous les jours sauf dimanche	No parking every day except Sunday
Cédez le passage	Give way
Priorité à droite	Vehicles joining the road from the right have priority
Passage protégé	Traffic on this road has priority.
Travaux	Roadworks
Déviation	Diversion

■ Je sais louer une voiture

Je voudrais louer une voiture pour sept jours.	I'd like to hire a car for seven days.
Voilà mon permis de conduire.	Here is my driving licence.

Je révise

Utilise ce tableau pour réviser les phrases-clés de cette étape. Voici une activité:

★ Trouve dans le tableau les mots ou les phrases qui correspondent à ces illustrations:

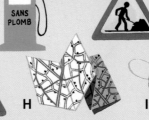

7ème *Etape*
Changer de l'argent

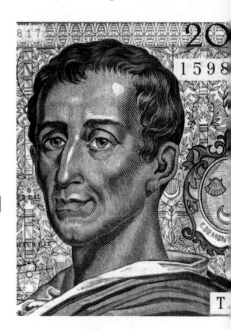

Mes objectifs

Si tu voyages dans un pays où l'on parle français, il faut savoir changer de l'argent!

■ Dans cette étape, nous allons parler d'argent et nous allons apprendre comment changer de l'argent.

Tu aimerais visiter la France?
Si un jour tu vas en France, tu devras emporter de l'argent. Tu pourrais partir avec des livres sterling, mais moi, à ta place, je prendrais des chèques de voyage. Si tu partais avec des livres sterling, tu pourrais les perdre. Tu sais, avec les chèques de voyage tu aurais moins de problèmes. C'est plus sûr.

Avant de partir, tu devrais aussi apprendre à changer de l'argent . . .

dans une banque . . .

ou dans un bureau de change.

Je voudrais changer de l'argent

1 ► Je comprends

a Lis et écoute ces dialogues dans une banque.

1

Je voudrais changer de l'argent. C'est à quel guichet?

3

Je voudrais changer des chèques de voyage.

Vous avez une pièce d'identité?

J'ai un passeport.

Pouvez-vous les signer?

Est-ce que je pourrais avoir un reçu?

2

Je voudrais changer quarante livres sterling.

Je pourrais avoir des billets de cent francs?

b Ces illustrations correspondent à quels dialogues?

A

B

C

c Ecoute la cassette. Pour chaque dialogue, réponds oui ou non à ces trois questions.

★ Est-ce que l'employé(e) est poli(e)?

★ Est-ce que le/la client(e) est poli(e)?

★ Est-ce que le/la client(e) est bien organisé(e)?

2 ► Je répète

Ecoute la cassette.

a La première fois, répète après les gens qui veulent changer des chèques de voyage.

b La deuxième fois, répète après les gens qui veulent changer de l'argent de ton pays.

3 ► Je répète et j'invente

Travaille avec un(e) partenaire.

a Réécoutez la cassette (voir **1** ►). Regardez les illustrations et réécrivez les trois dialogues.

b Inventez un dialogue. Imaginez que c'est une publicité pour une banque. N'oubliez pas d'être poli(e)s!

Et s'il y a un problème?

1 ► *Je comprends*

Voici quatre situations possibles:

A Il y a une erreur.

B La banque ferme.

C La banque n'a pas de bureau de change.

D La banque prend une commission.

Ecoute la cassette. Ce touriste a des problèmes! Note les lettres des problèmes dans le bon ordre.

2 ► *Je répète*

Réécoute la cassette et lis les dialogues. Recopie les phrases-clés.

 ► *J'invente*

Travaille avec un(e) partenaire. Réécoutez la cassette et inventez deux dialogues. Jouez les dialogues, puis changez de rôle.

a Le/La client(e) est fatigué(e).

b Le/La client(e) n'est pas très gentil(le).

4

Inventez ensemble un sketch amusant: un(e) touriste voudrait changer de l'argent, mais il/elle a beaucoup de problèmes.

Avez-vous de la monnaie?

Quelquefois, il faut de la monnaie, par exemple pour le téléphone ou pour acheter une boisson.

1 ▶ Je comprends

Lis ces dialogues. Cherche les trois expressions utilisées pour demander de la monnaie.

– Pourriez-vous me donner de la monnaie pour acheter des timbres, s'il vous plaît?

– Qu'est-ce qu'il te faut?

– Vous avez des pièces de deux francs?

– Oui.

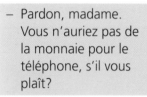

– Pardon, madame. Vous n'auriez pas de la monnaie pour le téléphone, s'il vous plaît?

– Il vous faut combien?

– Cinq pièces d'un franc.

– Tu as de la monnaie pour le distributeur de boissons, s'il te plaît?

– J'ai une pièce de cinq francs.

2

Ecoute la cassette. Qu'est-ce que tu dis pour demander de la monnaie à: ton/ta correspondant(e); sa mère; un(e) vendeur/euse?

3 ▶ Je répète

Ecoute la cassette.

a La première fois, répète après les jeunes qui demandent de la monnaie à un jeune.

b La deuxième fois, répète après les jeunes qui demandent de la monnaie à un adulte.

4 ▶ J'invente

Tu as besoin de monnaie pour le téléphone. Comment vas-tu en demander à ces gens? Avec un(e) partenaire, invente deux dialogues.

A moi, les examens!

 Ecoute la cassette. Note l'illustration qui correspond à chaque dialogue.

Conseils de l'examinateur

● Prépare-toi! Regarde les illustrations **avant** d'écouter. Comment pourrais-tu décrire chaque illustration en français?

● Ecoute **tous** les détails qui pourraient t'aider à identifier l'illustration correcte. Par exemple, si le/la client(e) doit signer son nom et donner une pièce d'identité, c'est un chèque de voyage qu'il/elle change.

A

B

C

D

E

F

A moi, les examens!

Fais ces jeux de rôles avec un(e) partenaire.

Conseil de l'examinateur

● Prépare-toi! Essaie de poser toutes les questions et de donner tous les détails.

Conseils de l'examinateur

● Explique ce que tu voudrais faire.

● Il y a un problème: quelles sont les stratégies possibles?

Exemples

★ La banque ouvre à quelle heure l'après-midi?

★ Il y a une autre banque ou un autre bureau de change?

★ Où peux-tu changer de l'argent?

Client(e) 1A

Tu es en vacances en France. Il est midi. Tu vas prendre un train à 14h30, mais tu n'as pas de francs français pour acheter ton billet. Tu vas dans une banque. . . Commence la conversation.

Employé(e) 1B

Un(e) client(e) arrive à la banque où tu travailles. Il est midi, et vous fermez.

Si le/la client(e) te pose des questions, tu peux donner ces informations:

★ Vous ouvrez à 14h45 cet après-midi.

★ Il y a un bureau de change qui ne ferme pas à midi à la gare.

Conseils de l'examinateur

● Explique ce que tu voudrais faire.

● Il y a un problème: qu'est-ce que tu vas dire? N'oublie pas que: 'Je pense/crois qu'il y a une erreur' est plus poli que: 'Il y a une erreur'.

● Si tu oublies un mot, par exemple, 'erreur', donne un équivalent: 'Je pense qu'il y a un problème' ou 'Je pense qu'il manque de l'argent'.

Client(e) 2A

★ Tu es dans une banque. Explique ce que tu voudrais faire:

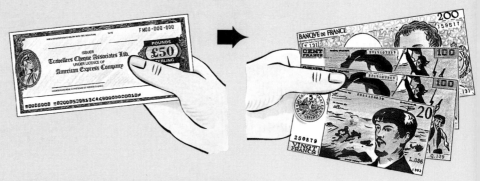

★ Réponds aux questions de l'employé(e).

★ Tu penses que l'employé(e) ne te donne pas la somme d'argent correcte.

★ Commence la conversation.

Employé(e) 2B

Un(e) client(e) change un chèque de voyage.

★ Demande au/à la client(e) de signer le chèque.

★ Demande une pièce d'identité.

★ Le/La client(e) pense que tu as fait une erreur. Il/Elle a raison. Il manque 15F. Dis-lui que tu es désolé(e).

A moi, les examens!

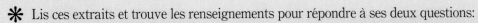

Une amie de tes parents va passer deux semaines en France. Elle a deux livres français avec des renseignements pour les visiteurs en France, mais elle ne parle pas français.

✳ Lis ces extraits et trouve les renseignements pour répondre à ses deux questions:

★ When are banks normally open?

★ What are the options if I want to change money outside normal banking hours?

Les Banques

Banques ouvertes plus tard que la normale (le samedi et jusqu'à 16h30):

– *C.C.F.* Crédit Commercial de France, Agence Élysées, 103, Champs-Élysées, 8ᵉ, Ⓜ George-V ☎ 47.20.92.00: ouverte tous les jours de 8h30 à 20h sauf dimanche.

– *Crédit Lyonnais,* Agence Élysées, 55, Champs-Élysées, Ⓜ F.D.-Roosevelt, ☎ 42.76.51.81: ouverte le samedi de 9h à 11h30.

Beaucoup de banques disposent de distributeurs automatiques de billets.

Voir aussi les Bureaux de change de la Gare de l'Est ☎ 42.06.51.97, de la Gare Saint-Lazare ☎ 43.87.72.51 et de la Gare du Nord ☎ 42.80.11.50, ouverts de 7h à 21h30.

Conseils de l'examinateur

● Lis les deux extraits en entier. Dans quelles sections vas-tu trouver les renseignements que tu cherches?

● Lis ces sections plus attentivement.

● Il y a beaucoup de renseignements dans les deux extraits. Essaie de les classer en catégories.
  Exemples
  ★ les banques qui sont ouvertes plus tard que la normale
  ★ les bureaux de change
  ★ les changeurs automatiques.

● Trouve les renseignements principaux pour chaque catégorie, par exemple: nom; situation; heures d'ouverture.

En règle générale, les banques sont ouvertes du lundi au vendredi à Paris et du mardi au samedi en banlieue et en province, en principe de 9h à 17h. Certaines agences font toutefois des nocturnes jusqu'à 19h ou 20h. Attention: les veilles de fêtes, les banques ferment généralement beaucoup plus tôt, et lorsqu'une fête tombe un jeudi, à Paris, elles font souvent le 'pont'.

LE SERVICE DE CHANGE

Il est normalement assuré dans toutes les agences bancaires, ainsi que dans les 'bureaux de change' situés à l'intérieur ou à proximité des aéroports et des gares (ces derniers sont les seuls à offrir des horaires plus souples: 7h à 22h ou plus). Vous obtiendrez des francs français au guichet signalé par l'écriteau 'change', en échange de vos Travellers, de vos Eurochèques ou de vos billets nationaux.

Une banque réputée pour son esprit d'innovation, la BRED, a cherché à améliorer ce service en installant sur les Champs-Elysées à Paris, le premier changeur automatique de devises. Cette billeterie d'un genre un peu particulier avale 2 types de coupures pour chacune des quatre devises traitées (dollar, livre, lire et deutsche mark) et rend la monnaie en francs, à dix centimes près. Le montant de l'opération n'est pas limité et la commission est du même ordre que celle perçue sur une opération de change au guichet. Le même service existe actuellement à l'aéroport de Roissy (Aérogare n°1 – niveau arrivée – porte 16 près du CCF).

A moi, les examens!

Tu vois cette publicité pour un concours dans un magazine. Tu voudrais gagner le prix. Ecris un article pour ce concours.

Concours!

Imagine: si tu avais 1 000 000 francs . . .

Ecris un article de cent mots pour décrire ta situation si tu devenais riche.

★ Comment est-ce que ta vie changerait?

Par exemple:

– Où habiterais-tu?

– Qu'est-ce que tu achèterais?

– Qu'est-ce que tu ferais?

★ A ton avis, serais-tu plus ou moins heureux (-euse) que maintenant?

Conseils de l'examinateur

● Réfléchis: un million de francs, c'est combien d'argent dans ton pays?

● Note tes idées.

● Invente un titre pour ton article. Exemple: 'Si j'étais riche' ou 'Etre millionnaire'.

● Ecris une courte introduction. Exemple:
  'Si j'étais riche, ma vie changerait beaucoup.'

● Ecris ton article en paragraphes: un paragraphe pour chaque sujet. Exemple: où tu habiterais; les choses que tu achèterais, etc. Comme ça, l'article sera plus facile à lire.

● N'oublie pas de répondre à toutes les questions.

● Utilise ton imagination. Exemple:
  Quelle est la description la plus intéressante, **A** ou **B**?

  A J'achèterais une grande maison.

  B J'achèterais une vieille maison immense à la campagne. Elle aurait un joli jardin plein de fleurs, et une piscine. . .

Tu comprends maintenant? BANQVE DE FRANCE

Est-ce que tu serais capable de changer de l'argent en France? Fais ce test! Si tu veux, tu peux d'abord réviser un peu.

★ **Vous allez travailler en groupes et préparer un guide pour expliquer comment changer de l'argent ou des chèques de voyage en France.**

Activité 1

Décidez de la présentation de votre guide. Discutez de ces questions:

● C'est pour qui? C'est pour votre classe ou pour une autre classe?
● Quelle est la meilleure façon de présenter vos renseignements?

A mon avis, une vidéo serait plus utile. Ça montre les choses plus clairement.

Je ne suis pas d'accord: une brochure serait plus pratique. On pourrait l'emporter en France.

On pourrait faire une cassette, pour montrer comment prononcer les mots.

Activité 2

Faites une liste des expressions et des renseignements que vous allez donner.

Activité 3

Pour vous aider à préparer votre liste, écoutez ces dialogues. Faites un résumé de chaque dialogue.
Est-ce que ces dialogues vous aident à préparer votre liste pour l'Activité 2?
Il y a des expressions que vous voulez ajouter?

✳ Activité 4

Donnez d'autres renseignements utiles.
Lisez, par exemple, ces renseignements sur une autre façon d'avoir de l'argent en France.

● Qu'est-ce qu'il faut présenter pour avoir ce service?
● Où et quand peut-on avoir ce service?
● Est-ce qu'il faut payer?

LES RETRAITS DE BILLETS

Si vous possédez une carte **Visa** ou **Mastercard/Eurocard**, vous pourrez sur simple présentation de la carte et d'une pièce d'identité, retirer jusqu'à 3 000F par semaine:
– soit **aux guichets des banques affiliées** à ces deux réseaux internationaux, aux heures d'ouverture de ces derniers, et sur présentation de votre carte d'identité ou de votre passeport
– soit dans un **distributeur automatique de billets** où figure l'affiche de la carte que vous possédez. Principal avantage de ces billeteries: elles sont accessibles 24h/24, à condition d'être approvisionnées, ce qui n'est pas toujours le cas le week-end! Dans les deux cas, on vous prélèvera à chaque retrait une commission de 15F.

Activité 5

a Ecrivez votre texte au brouillon, discutez-en et vérifiez-le. Puis, corrigez les erreurs et faites des changements pour l'améliorer.

b Préparez la version finale.

Tu te rappelles?

159817 DEUX CENTS FRANCS 1993

■ Je sais changer de l'argent

Il y a une banque ou un bureau de change près d'ici?	Is there a bank or a foreign exchange bureau near here?
C'est quel guichet pour changer de l'argent?	Which counter is it to change some money?
Je voudrais changer quarante livres sterling (des chèques de voyage, des dollars).	I'd like to change £40 (some travellers' cheques, some dollars).
Est-ce que vous prenez une commission?	Do you take a commission?
Pouvez-vous signer vos chèques, s'il vous plaît?	Could you sign your cheques, please?
Quelle est la date aujourd'hui?	What is the date today?
Avez-vous une pièce d'identité?	Do you have some identification?
Voilà mon passeport.	Here's my passport.
Je pourrais avoir des billets de cent francs, s'il vous plaît?	Could I have some one hundred franc notes, please?
Excusez-moi, mais je crois qu'il y a une erreur. Il manque dix francs.	Excuse me, but I think there's a mistake. It's ten francs short.
Pourriez-vous vérifier?	Could you check?

■ Je sais demander de la monnaie

Marc, as-tu de la monnaie, s'il te plaît?	Marc, do you have any change, please?
Pourriez-vous me donner de la monnaie, s'il vous plaît?	Could you give me some change, please?
Pardon, madame, vous n'auriez pas de la monnaie pour le téléphone?	Excuse me. You wouldn't happen to have some change for the telephone?
Il vous faut combien?	How much do you need?
Une pièce de cinq francs.	A five franc piece.

Je révise

Utilise ce tableau pour réviser les phrases-clés de cette étape. Voici une activité:

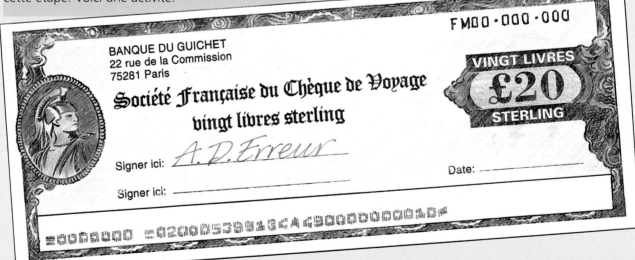

★ Trouve dans ce 'chèque de voyage' des mots-clés du tableau. Peux-tu les trouver plus vite que ton/ta partenaire?

★ Recopie la phrase du tableau qui correspond à chaque mot.

★ Avec ton/ta partenaire, invente un dialogue avec les phrases.

8ème Etape
Projets de vacances

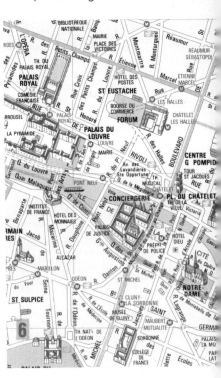

Mes objectifs

**Imagine! Tu voudrais passer tes vacances en France, mais tu n'as pas décidé quelle ville ou quelle région tu voudrais visiter. Pour t'aider à décider, tu pourrais demander des renseignements à l'office du tourisme, ou à quelqu'un qui connaît la région.
Dans cette étape, tu vas apprendre:**

■ **à parler de villes et de régions en France**

■ **à parler de ta région et de ta ville ou de ton village.**

Quand on décrit une ville ou une région, on parle souvent des endroits suivants:

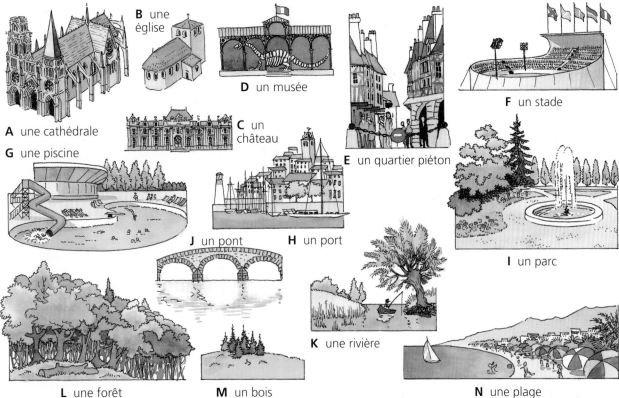

A une cathédrale
B une église
C un château
D un musée
E un quartier piéton
F un stade
G une piscine
H un port
I un parc
J un pont
K une rivière
L une forêt
M un bois
N une plage

1 ▶ **Je comprends**

Ecoute la cassette. Des gens parlent de leur ville. Pour chaque personne, écris la lettre correspondant aux endroits mentionnés.

2 ▶ **Je répète**

a Quels endroits aimes-tu visiter pendant tes vacances? Fais trois listes avec les noms des endroits de l'activité **1** ▶ :

● endroits très importants
● assez importants
● pas importants.

b Peux-tu deviner ce qu'il y a dans les trois listes de ton/ta partenaire?

Un peu de géographie

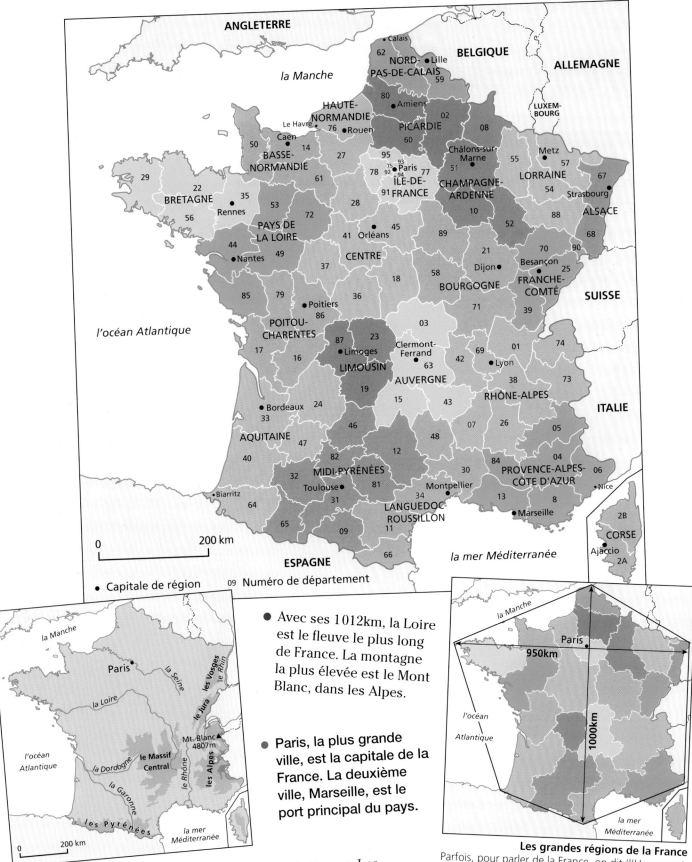

Capitale de région   09 **Numéro de département**

Les grandes régions de la Etape
Parfois, pour parler de la France, on dit 'l'Hexagone'.
Peux-tu dire pourquoi?

● Avec ses 1012km, la Loire est le fleuve le plus long de France. La montagne la plus élevée est le Mont Blanc, dans les Alpes.

● Paris, la plus grande ville, est la capitale de la France. La deuxième ville, Marseille, est le port principal du pays.

● Le tourisme est une industrie importante pour la France. Les vacances d'été à la mer sont les plus populaires, mais en hiver, c'est le tourisme de montagne qui attire le plus grand nombre de Français et d'étrangers. L'agriculture, la construction automobile et l'aérospatiale sont d'autres industries importantes.

● Deux Français, Jean Monnet et Robert Schuman, ont été à l'origine de l'Union Européenne en 1957. Aujourd'hui, le Parlement Européen siège à Strasbourg.

Cette carte explique le climat de la France. Il y a quatre types principaux de climats en France:

- le climat océanique, à l'ouest;
- le climat continental, à l'est;
- le climat de montagne, au-dessus de 1500m;
- le climat méditerranéen, au sud.

1 ▶ Je comprends

a Tu comprends tous les mots et expressions soulignés? Sinon, cherche-les dans le dictionnaire.

b Et toi? Quel climat est-ce que tu préfères? Est-ce que ton/ta partenaire préfère le même climat que toi?

La France a un climat varié, mais tempéré avec des températures modérées, et quatre saisons.

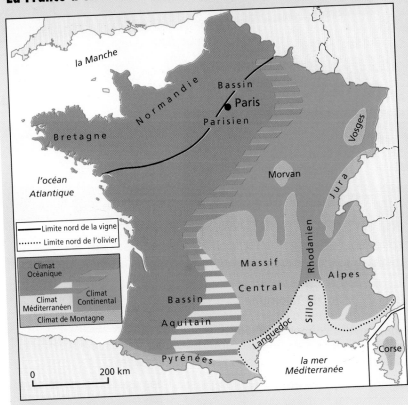

Le climat océanique

Dans les régions océaniques, les saisons sont peu marquées. En hiver, il ne fait pas trop froid et il gèle rarement, mais les étés sont frais. Il pleut souvent pendant l'année, et le ciel est souvent couvert. En automne, il y a souvent du brouillard.

Le climat continental

Ici, les hivers sont, en général, secs et froids, avec du vent et de la neige. Les étés sont chauds et lourds. Quand il fait très chaud, il y a souvent des orages.

Le climat de montagne

A la montagne, les hivers sont longs et durs. Il fait très froid et il neige beaucoup. Les étés, par contre, sont courts et pluvieux.

Le climat méditerranéen

Les hivers sont doux et courts et il gèle rarement. Les étés sont longs. Il y a du soleil, et il fait souvent très chaud. Un vent froid, sec et fort, qui s'appelle le Mistral, arrive dans le sud par la vallée du Rhône, et chasse les nuages. En été, il pleut rarement, mais en automne, il y a souvent des averses.

2 ▶ Je répète

Tout le monde est différent. Certains adorent le climat méditerranéen. Pour d'autres, ce climat est beaucoup trop chaud.
Fais deux listes avec les expressions qui décrivent le climat de la France:

- le temps que tu aimes
- le temps que tu n'aimes pas.

3 ▶ J'invente

Décris le climat de ton pays en hiver et en été. Peux-tu décrire aussi le temps au printemps et en automne?

4

Invente un climat qui serait idéal pour toi. Décris ce climat à ton/ta partenaire. Est-ce que son climat idéal est similaire ou complètement différent?

Connais-tu Paris?

Située sur la Seine, Paris est la capitale de la France, et la plus grande ville du pays. Visitée chaque année par des millions de touristes, c'est une des villes les plus belles et les plus célèbres du monde.

La Joconde, peut-être la peinture la plus célèbre du monde.

Le Louvre

Ancien palais royal, le Louvre est aujourd'hui un des musées les plus riches du monde. Il abrite une immense collection de peintures, de sculptures et d'objets d'art. Devant le Louvre se trouve le Jardin des Tuileries.

La Tour Eiffel

Construite par l'ingénieur Gustave Eiffel pour l'Exposition Universelle de 1889, la Tour Eiffel est devenue le symbole de Paris. Haut de 307 mètres, ce bâtiment (le plus haut de Paris) est maintenant l'émetteur de télévision de la région parisienne. Du troisième étage, on a la meilleure vue sur la capitale.

L'Arc de Triomphe

Edifié en 1836 à la gloire de l'armée de Napoléon 1er, ce monument célèbre est haut de 50 mètres. Il abrite la tombe du Soldat Inconnu.

L'avenue des Champs-Elysées

Cette avenue est la plus célèbre de Paris. Elle relie la place de la Concorde à la place de l'Etoile, où se trouve l'Arc de Triomphe. En descendant l'avenue des Champs Elysées, on passe devant des magasins chics et des cafés chers. Plus loin, il y a de beaux jardins et des maisons élégantes.

La Défense: Arche de la Fraternité

Cette arche colossale, dédiée à la fraternité, se trouve dans un quartier moderne, le quartier de la Défense.

La basilique du Sacré-Cœur

L'imposante basilique du Sacré-Cœur se trouve à Montmartre, quartier touristique dans le nord de Paris. Située sur une colline, la basilique offre un panorama exceptionnel sur la capitale.

La cathédrale Notre-Dame

Un des plus beaux exemples de l'architecture gothique, Notre-Dame est située au cœur de Paris. Les distances routières de France sont calculées à partir du point '0 km' devant la cathédrale.

La Villette

Dans la Cité des Sciences et de l'Industrie, il y a une grande exposition sur la technologie d'aujourd'hui.

Le plus vieux pont sur la Seine s'appelle le Pont Neuf!

Le Centre National d'Art et de Culture Georges Pompidou

Exemple controversé de l'architecture contemporaine, le Centre Pompidou est un musée d'art moderne. La place devant le centre est animée par des artistes et des musiciens.

Le Musée d'Orsay

 musée très populaire a été créé à l'intérieur d'une ancienne re de chemin de fer. Des milliers de touristes visitent sa lection d'œuvres de peintres impressionnistes.

La place de la Concorde

Cette grande place spacieuse a deux belles fontaines. Entre ces fontaines, on voit le plus vieux monument de Paris. . . qui vient d'Egypte! C'est un obélisque couvert de hiéroglyphes, qui date du treizième siècle avant Jésus-Christ.

Quelques destinations possibles

Si tu veux passer tes vacances en France, tu peux trouver des renseignements dans des brochures touristiques. Tu peux aussi demander à des Français. Tu trouveras des messages reçus par courrier électronique sur la Fiche 8.2.

1 ▶ *Je comprends et je répète*

a Lis les messages (Fiche 8.2) et ces extraits de brochures touristiques pour faire tes recherches.

Bretagne: Perros-Guirec

Au cœur de la Côte de Granit Rose ouverte sur l'une des principales réserves d'oiseaux de France, Perros-Guirec jouit d'une vue exceptionnelle sur la baie de Trestraou et l'Archipel des Sept-Iles. Perros-Guirec, c'est aussi trois grandes plages de sable fin, une activité économique, commerciale et de loisirs toute l'année.

Equipements

Port de plaisance aménagé de pontons et corps morts (600 places) – Port naturel ouvert toute l'année à Ploumanac'h (300 places) – Centre nautique – Casino avec machines à sous – Palais des congrès – Centre culturel polyvalent – Centre de thalassothérapie – Complexe sportif – Golf 18 trous (5 km) – Salles de cinéma – De nombreux espaces verts et jardins publics.

Chambéry, dans le sud-est de la France

Capitale de la Savoie, Chambéry fut pendant plusieurs siècles le siège d'un Etat souverain. Ville active et dynamique, Chambéry est d'un accès facile et dispose d'une hôtellerie confortable et d'une restauration de qualité. Visites guidées de la ville, riche programme culturel, musées, maison de Jean-Jacques Rousseau aux Charmettes, séduisent les amateurs.

Chambéry offre une large gamme de sports et loisirs en toutes saisons: natation, tennis, équitation, vol à voile, parachutisme, deltaplane, parapente, randonnées pédestres. En hiver: patin à glace, ski alpin et ski de fond, dans les stades de neige des massifs des Bauges (La Féclaz et le Grand Plateau Nordique) et de la Chartreuse (vallée des Entremonts). En été, à 15 minutes, tous les plaisirs de l'eau et de la plage, sur les bords du lac du Bourget et d'Aiguebelette.

Annonay

Sites et monuments: Patrie des Frères Montgolfier et de Marc Seguin (Statues) – Ville d'adoption de Boissy d'Anglas – Vieux quartiers: maisons médiévales et Louis XIV; porte du Château (1574); Pont Valgelas (XIIIe siècle); Tour des Martyrs (restes de fortifications XIe siècle); Chapelle Ste-Marie; Chapelle de Trachin et son clocher hexagonal (XIVe siècle) – Musée César Filhol – Musée Canson et Montgolfier (musée de la papeterie) – Roche Péréandre – Barrage du Ternay – Château de Gourdan (visite extérieure.).

Loisirs: Golf de Gourdan (18 trous) – Piscine couverte (animations – bassins d'été) – Tennis privés et municipaux – Sentier botanique – Sentiers de petites randonnées – Locations vélos et V.T.T. – Pêche – Boulodrome – Parc d'agrément et de détente – Equitation – Complexe sportif – Moto Club – Aéro Club et Aéro Rétro – Clubs de montgolfières (vols captifs et en découverte) – Deltaplane – Discothèques – Cinémas – Bibliothèque – Théâtre.

b Tu vas prendre des notes pour chacun des points suivants:

> 1 Situation, caractère
> 2 A faire / à voir dans la ville
> 3 A faire / à voir dans la région
> 4 Climat
> 5 Opinion

✳ c Ecoute ce jeune Belge qui prend des notes. Peux-tu identifier la ville?

d A toi de prendre des notes.

 2

Ecoute ces deux jeunes, Véronique et Hugo, qui jouent au 'dix questions'.
Véronique peut poser dix questions pour identifier la ville. Hugo doit répondre
'oui' ou 'non'.

a Peux-tu identifier la ville avant Véronique?

b Maintenant, Hugo pose les questions. Peux-tu identifier la ville?

c Joue au 'dix questions' avec ton/ta partenaire. Il te faut combien de
questions pour identifier la ville?

3 ▶ *J'invente*

Prends des notes.

a Quelle ville aimerais-tu le plus visiter, et pourquoi? Qu'est-ce que tu
y ferais pendant tes vacances?

b Quelle ville t'intéresse le moins? Pourquoi?

4

Discutez des destinations possibles en groupes.
Quelles sont les destinations les plus et les moins populaires, et pourquoi?

5

Tu peux préparer des renseignements pour aider tes amis français!
Travaille avec un(e) partenaire. Faites une description par écrit de votre région
et de votre ville (ou d'une ville voisine) pour envoyer par lettre ou par courrier
électronique.

A l'aide!

★ Pour commencer, écrivez votre description au brouillon.
★ Discutez de votre description avec des amis. Est-elle intéressante? Les
détails sont-ils corrects?
★ Vérifie qu'il n'y a pas de fautes de grammaire et d'orthographe.
★ Ecrivez votre description au propre.

 6

Les villes touristiques ne sont pas toujours idéales pour les gens qui y habitent!
Ecoute ces jeunes qui parlent de leur ville. Est-ce qu'ils aiment habiter dans
cette ville? Pourquoi ou pourquoi pas?

7

Et toi, est-ce que tu aimes la ville ou le village où tu habites? Qu'est-ce que
tu y aimes et qu'est-ce que tu n'y aimes pas?

a Discutez en groupes, puis comparez vos opinions et vos raisons avec celles
des autres groupes.

b Avec un(e) partenaire, prépare une cassette pour envoyer à ta classe-
partenaire en France. Donnez votre opinion sur votre ville du point de vue
des touristes et des habitants.

Demander des renseignements

Tu peux demander des renseignements à l'office du tourisme sur place, ou
par lettre avant de partir.
Attention! Souvent, on appelle l'office du tourisme 'le syndicat d'initiative' (S.I.).

1 ► Je comprends et je répète

Voici quelques renseignements que tu pourrais demander.

a Cherche dans le dictionnaire les mots que tu ne comprends pas.

b Quels renseignements est-ce que tu préférerais avoir avant de partir?

une liste des campings

les programmes de cinéma

une brochure sur la ville

un plan de la ville

une liste des hôtels

une brochure sur la région et une carte de la région

des dépliants sur les distractions principales et sur les excursions possibles

une liste des restaurants

2 ► Je répète et j'invente

Ecoute et lis cette conversation dans un syndicat d'initiative.

a Avec un(e) partenaire, lis la conversation. Puis, changez les
expressions soulignées pour demander les choses illustrées.

– Bonjour, monsieur. Auriez-vous <u>une brochure sur la ville</u>, s'il vous plaît?
– Oui, madame. Prenez <u>cette brochure-ci</u>.
– Et est-ce que vous auriez <u>des renseignements sur la région</u>?
– Oui, voilà <u>quelques dépliants</u>.
– Merci beaucoup.
– Au revoir, madame, et bon séjour.

b Si tu voulais avoir des renseignements à l'avance, tu pourrais écrire
au syndicat d'initiative.
Imagine! Tu veux passer tes vacances en Bretagne cet été.
Tu voudrais avoir des renseignements sur la région, les hôtels
et la ville de Rennes, et tu as besoin d'une carte de la région.
Recopie et adapte cette lettre:

Leicester, le 6 avril
Monsieur/Madame,
J'ai l'intention de passer trois
semaines à Bordeaux cet été.
Pourriez-vous m'envoyer <u>quelques
renseignements sur la ville</u> et
<u>une liste des campings</u>.
J'aimerais aussi avoir <u>des
dépliants sur les châteaux dans
la région</u>.
Vous trouverez ci-joint un
coupon de réponse.
En vous remerciant d'avance, je
vous prie de croire,
Monsieur/Madame, à l'expression
de mes meilleurs sentiments.
Grace Howie

A moi, les examens!

Alexis veut partir en vacances au mois d'août, mais il n'a pas décidé où aller. Voici ce qu'il aime faire.

> J'aime passer mes vacances dans une jolie ville, calme, et pas trop grande. Je m'intéresse à l'histoire. Je n'aime pas beaucoup le sport. Pour moi, le climat idéal n'est pas trop chaud, et je n'aime pas la pluie!

Sur la cassette, trois jeunes, Elisabeth, Mehdi et Suzanne parlent de leur ville.

 a Ecoute les interviews. Est-ce que tu recommanderais à Alexis de visiter:

- la ville d'Elisabeth
- la ville de Mehdi
- ou la ville de Suzanne?

✳ **b** Explique pourquoi tu as choisi cette ville, et pas les autres. (Donne quatre raisons.)

Conseils de l'examinateur

- Qu'est-ce qu'il faut faire? Pour commencer, lis la question attentivement. Attention! Il y a deux parties: il faut choisir la meilleure ville pour les vacances d'Alexis, et il faut aussi dire pourquoi. Il faut donc savoir pourquoi une des villes est idéale, et pourquoi elle est mieux que les autres.

- Prépare-toi à écouter. Prends des notes sur les préférences d'Alexis. Comme ça, quand tu écouteras la cassette, tu sauras ce que tu recherches.

- Pense tout le temps aux préférences d'Alexis et, pour chaque ville, note les points positifs et les points négatifs. N'oublie pas de dire pourquoi tu as choisi une ville, et pourquoi tu n'as pas choisi une autre ville.

- Ecoute attentivement. Si tu entends le mot 'château', ca ne veut pas dire qu'il y a un château. Par exemple, la phrase, c'est peut-être: 'Dans notre ville, il n'y a pas de château.' Alors fais bien attention!

A moi, les examens!

Un exposé

a Tu dois parler pendant deux ou trois minutes sur ce thème: **une ville que tu as visitée, et que tu as aimée.** Tu dois faire ton exposé sans notes, mais tu peux le préparer à l'avance.

C'est une ville touristique dans le sud. . .

b Quand tu es prêt(e), présente ton exposé à ta classe ou à ton groupe. Après, invite les autres à te poser des questions.

Conseils de l'examinateur

- Prépare-toi bien! Tout d'abord, choisis la ville. Attention! Est-ce que tu as beaucoup de choses à dire sur cette ville?
- Ton exposé sera plus intéressant et plus facile à comprendre s'il est bien organisé et structuré. Prépare des notes sur différents aspects, par exemple:
  - ★ où se trouve la ville (dans l'est de l'Espagne? dans le nord de l'Angleterre?)
  - ★ son caractère (historique? pittoresque?)
  - ★ son climat
  - ★ ses distractions
  - ★ ce que tu y as vu et ce que tu y as fait
  - ★ ce que tu en as pensé.
- N'oublie pas de dire pourquoi tu as aimé cette ville.
- Apprends ce que tu vas dire.
- Si tu veux, apporte des photos, des brochures ou d'autres souvenirs pour illustrer ton exposé.
- Parle avec assurance! Ce n'est pas facile d'être à l'aise quand on fait un exposé.
  - ★ Calme-toi et souris.
  - ★ Essaie de ne pas parler trop vite. Parle assez fort et d'une voix calme et claire.

  Tout le monde pensera que tu es très à l'aise!
- Essaie d'impressionner l'examinateur! Utilise des mots sophistiqués et des structures complexes.

  Par exemple, ne dis pas: 'J'aime Blackpool. C'est une ville touristique. Elle se trouve dans le nord-ouest de l'Angleterre.'

  Une phrase complexe est plus impressionnante: 'L'année dernière, j'ai visité Blackpool, une ville touristique, qui se trouve dans le nord-ouest de l'Angleterre.'

A moi, les examens!

✳ Tu es en vacances avec ta mère et ton petit frère de neuf ans. C'est dimanche soir.

Qu'est-ce que vous pouvez faire demain?

a Vous avez combien d'options pour demain?

b Explique les options en anglais à ta mère.

c Pour chaque option, est-ce qu'il y a une réduction pour ton frère?

Visite de la vieille ville en mini-train

La compagnie CMT vous propose une visite commentée de la vieille ville, en petit train touristique. Possibilité de commentaires en anglais, allemand et italien.

Départ: hôtel de ville.
Tous les jours de 10h à 17h sauf lundi. Un départ toutes les demi-heures. 31F, tarif réduit enfants – 15F.

PARC ZOOLOGIQUE

Promenez-vous dans un parc de 10 hectares et découvrez la vie secrète de douzaines d'animaux exotiques. Visitez la petite ferme où vous pourrez aider à donner à manger aux animaux.

Fermé le mardi. Entrée 42F; Tarif réduit (moins de 12 ans) 22F.

Samedi et dimanche, 15h: spectacle singes – 12F.

Visitez la ville en bateau!

Passez un après-midi sur la rivière, et visitez la ville en même temps.

Tous les jours. Toutes les demi-heures de 9h à 17h et de 18h à 22h. Tarifs: 38,00F (jour) – 19,00F (soir)
Tarifs groupes: nous consulter. Les chiens ne sont pas admis.

Conseils de l'examinateur

● Pour savoir ce que vous pouvez faire demain, il faut réfléchir: c'est dimanche aujourd'hui, donc demain, c'est quel jour?

● Quand tu expliques les options à ta mère, donne tous les détails, pour l'aider à décider.

● Pour t'aider à trouver les prix, cherche un nombre, suivi par 'F' ou 'francs'. Attention! Tu as trouvé le prix que tu cherches? Vérifie les mots-clés, par exemple, cherche le mot 'tarif'.

A moi, les examens!

Ton correspondant français t'a écrit cette lettre.

Ecris une réponse à ton correspondant.

a Décris ta ville ou ton village.

b Décris ta région.

c Réponds aux questions de ton correspondant.

Ecris approximativement 100 mots.

> Strasbourg, le 9 février
>
> Salut!
>
> Merci beaucoup pour ta dernière lettre.
> J'espère que ta mère va mieux maintenant.
> Comme tu me l'as demandé, je t'envoie des
> brochures et des photos de ma ville. Est-ce
> que tu pourrais me décrire ta ville et ta
> région? Qu'est-ce qu'il y a pour les jeunes?
> Est-ce que tu aimes y habiter? Qu'est-ce
> que tu y aimes? Et qu'est-ce que tu n'y
> aimes pas?
> Je t'écrirai bientôt pour te parler de mes
> vacances. Je vais passer une semaine
> chez ma tante.
> Toutes mes amitiés,
>   Jean-Michel

Conseils de l'examinateur

- Note les instructions. Tu dois décrire ta ville (ton village) et ta région, et tu dois répondre aux questions de Jean-Michel. Lis la lettre et fais une liste de ces questions.

- Réponds à chaque question, même si tu n'as pas beaucoup à dire pour chacune.

- Après, lis ta lettre. Est-elle intéressante? Peux-tu ajouter des détails? Y a-t-il des fautes de grammaire et d'orthographe? Peux-tu utiliser des mots et des expressions plus variés et plus sophistiqués?

Tu comprends maintenant?

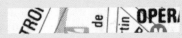

Je vérifie

Est-ce que tu es prêt(e) à décrire ta ville et ta région en français? Fais ce test! Si tu veux, tu peux d'abord faire un peu de révision.

★ Tu vas préparer des renseignements en français pour des touristes qui visitent ta ville et ta région. Travaille avec un(e) partenaire ou en groupe.

Activité 1

Quels renseignements allez-vous donner?

✱ a Ecoutez ces interviews avec quelques touristes. Notez les renseignements qu'ils voudraient avoir.

✱ b Lisez cet extrait d'une brochure sur la ville de Caen. Notez le genre de renseignements donnés.

Duc de Normandie et roi d'Angleterre, Guillaume Le Conquérant (1027-1087) fut le fondateur de Caen.
Situé au cœur de la ville, le château a été commencé sous son règne. Il loge dans son enceinte les musées de Normandie et des Beaux-Arts.
L'Abbaye aux Hommes et l'Abbaye aux Dames, épargnées dans la bataille de juin 1944 sont aujourd'hui visitées comme des témoins de ce glorieux passé.
C'est également le cas de vieux et pittoresques quartiers: le Vaugueux, la rue Froide, la place Saint-Sauveur et de splendides hôtels particuliers comme ceux de Than et d'Escoville (XVIe siècle).

Colombages-Quartier Vaugueux

Festival de la Paix

Ville jeune et active, Caen propose aux noctambules ses nombreux cinémas, son théâtre, ses bars et restaurants.
C'est un centre de vie culturelle animé avec le Conservatoire Régional de Musique, la Compagnie de Danse Contemporaine, les Centres d'Art Dramatique, l'Ecole des Beaux Arts et bien sûr ses structures de formation dont l'Université fondée en 1432 qui enregistre plus de 20 000 étudiants.
Port de plaisance, patinoire, piscine, golf, équitation sont des exemples d'une ville de sports et de loisirs qui offrent à chacun la possibilité de pratiquer ses activités favorites.

c Regardez vos listes. Pouvez-vous ajouter d'autres renseignements?

Activité 2

Comment allez-vous présenter vos renseignements?
Par exemple, vous pourriez faire une brochure ou des dépliants avec des photos ou des illustrations, vous pourriez faire une cassette pour les accompagner, ou vous pourriez faire une vidéo.
Pour vous aider à décider, pensez aux avantages et aux inconvénients de chaque moyen de présentation.

Activité 3

Préparez les renseignements.

a Ecrivez le texte au brouillon. Discutez-en! Est-il facile à comprendre? Y a-t-il assez de renseignements? Sont-ils corrects? Pourriez-vous améliorer le français?

b Préparez la version finale.

Tu te rappelles?

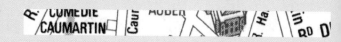

■ Je sais parler d'une ville ou d'une région

La ville se trouve dans le nord (le sud, l'est, l'ouest) de la Grande-Bretagne.	The town is situated in the north (the south, the east, the west) of Great Britain.
C'est une ville assez grande et industrielle (historique, touristique).	It's quite a big and industrial (historical, tourist) town.
Le quartier piéton est calme et pittoresque.	The pedestrian quarter is quiet and picturesque.
Il y a une rivière et le plus joli pont de la région.	There's a river and the prettiest bridge in the region.
Il y a beaucoup de distractions.	There are a lot of things to do.
Il y a des monuments historiques (un château, une cathédrale, une église, un port).	There are historical monuments (a castle, a cathedral, a church, a port).
On peut faire des randonnées dans les bois et les forêts.	You can go on hikes in the woods and forests.
Il n'y a pas grand-chose pour les jeunes. On s'ennuie.	There's not much for young people. It's boring.

■ Je sais parler du climat

Les étés sont frais (pluvieux, lourds). Le ciel est souvent couvert.	The summers are cool (rainy, heavy). The sky is often clouded over.
On a le meilleur climat ici: les hivers sont doux (courts, secs). Il gèle rarement.	We have the best climate here: the winters are mild (short, dry). It rarely freezes.
En automne, il y a souvent des averses (orages).	In autumn, there are often showers (storms).

■ Je sais demander des renseignements

Avez-vous un plan de la ville (le programme du cinéma, une brochure sur la ville, une liste des hôtels et des restaurants, des dépliants sur les distractions principales)?	Do you have a map of the town (a cinema programme, a brochure about the town, a list of the hotels and restaurants, any leaflets on the main things to do)?
Quand est-ce que c'est fermé?	When is it closed?
Le musée est ouvert tous les jours, sauf le mardi.	The museum is open every day, except Tuesdays.
C'est combien, l'entrée? (Ça coûte combien?)	How much is it to get in? (How much is it?)
Il y a des réductions?	Are there any reductions?
Ça se trouve où? (On part d'où?)	Where is it? (Where do you leave from?)
Ça commence à quelle heure? (On part à quelle heure?)	What time does it start? (What time do you set off?)
Ça dure combien de temps?	How long does it last?

Je révise

Utilise ce tableau pour réviser les phrases-clés de cette étape. Voici une activité:

★ Partenaire **A** fait un dessin. Partenaire **B** essaie d'identifier la phrase qui correspond.

On peut visiter le port.

9ème Etape
En vacances

Mes objectifs

Pour beaucoup de gens, les vacances sont très importantes. Et toi, est-ce que tu aimes partir en vacances?
Dans cette étape, tu vas parler des vacances:

■ de tes habitudes et de tes préférences

■ des vacances que tu as déjà passées.

 Trois personnes parlent de leur vacances. Tu préfères les vacances de quelle personne?

En général, je passe mes vacances au bord de la mer. L'année dernière, j'ai fait du camping. Il a fait très chaud, mais je m'ennuyais un peu.

Je pars en famille. Normalement, nous allons à l'étranger. L'année dernière, nous avons passé quinze jours en Espagne. Je me suis très bien amusée.

J'aime faire du tourisme, mais je n'aime pas les voyages organisés. Je préfère être plus indépendante. L'année dernière, je suis allée en Italie. J'ai visité des monuments historiques tous les jours.

Où vas-tu en vacances?

1 ▶ Je comprends

Un élève britannique a demandé à des élèves français de lui parler de ce qu'ils font habituellement pendant leurs vacances. Lis la lettre sur cette page, et les messages qu'ils ont envoyés par courrier électronique sur la Fiche 9.1.

a Pour t'aider à comprendre la réponse de chaque personne, identifie et note les mots et les expressions-clés pour répondre aux questions suivantes:

- Où va-t-il/elle, en général?
- Il/Elle part pour combien de temps?
- Il/Elle passe ses vacances avec qui?

b Il y a quelqu'un qui a les mêmes habitudes que toi?

> Limoges, le 3 avril
>
> Salut!
>
> Tu m'as demandé de parler de mes vacances. En général, je passe mes vacances avec mes parents. On va toujours au même endroit. Chaque été, on loue un gîte au bord de la mer, et on va à la plage tous les jours. Je t'en envoie une photo.
> Et puis, chaque Noël, je passe une semaine chez mes grands-parents à la campagne. C'est génial.
> Et toi, qu'est-ce que tu fais?
> Ecris-moi bientôt.
>
> Claude

2 ▶ Je répète

a Lis chaque message et mémorise le nom de la personne qui l'a écrit. Joue avec un(e) partenaire. Le partenaire **A** ne regarde pas les messages. Partenaire **B** lit un des messages à voix haute, et partenaire **A** dit le nom de la personne qui a écrit le message. Puis, vous changez de rôle.

b Fais la même chose, mais cette fois, partenaire **B** change un mot du message, par exemple la destination ou la durée des vacances. Partenaire **A** essaie d'identifier ce qui a changé.

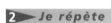

3 ▶ J'invente

Ecris un message aux élèves français pour répondre aux questions suivantes. Réponds la vérité, ou invente des réponses si tu veux.

- Où vas-tu en vacances, en général?
- Tu pars avec qui?
- Tu pars pour combien de temps?

Pour t'aider, utilise les mots et les expressions-clés des messages des jeunes Français.

Qu'est-ce que tu fais en vacances?

Pour comparer deux lieux de vacances très différents, *En vacances!*, une émission de radio, a interviewé des vacanciers.
Voici un extrait de la brochure sur chaque lieu de vacances:

CARIGNAN DE BORDEAUX

MAIRIE: RUE DE VERDUN - 56 21 21 62
Habitants: 2 940

Infrastructures sportives:
1 salle de sport
4 courts de tennis
1 centre équestre
1 stade
Chemins pédestres

*Son **église romane du XIIᵉ siècle**, ses châteaux – le **château de Carignan**, qui conserve des parties construites au XVᵉ siècle et le **château de Canteloup**, qui domine la vallée de la Pimpine – son vignoble de réputation internationale, ses bois, ses chemins pédestres, ses points de vue sur la vallée de la Garonne font de Carignan une halte agréable.*

Villers-sur-mer

LA STATION: Station balnéaire et climatique, **Villers-sur-mer** est de plus en plus animée pendant toute l'année. La vaste plage de sable fin, bordée de digues-promenade, est le centre de loisirs de la station.

ACTIVITÉS, LOISIRS: Tennis et club house, équitation, cercle nautique, école de voile, planche à voile, volley-ball, ensemble sportif avec salle omnisports, piscine. 'Complexe attractif' avec bar, restaurant, night-club, cinémas, golf miniature, bibliothèque. Saison musicale, conférences, expositions, concerts, manifestations folkloriques.

1 ▶ Je comprends

a Lis ces extraits des interviews et vérifie le sens de toutes les activités mentionnées.

– Je passe <u>toujours</u> mes vacances au bord de la mer. Je bronze sur la plage <u>tous les jours</u>. Je me baigne dans la mer. Je fais les magasins <u>de temps en temps</u>.

– <u>D'habitude</u>, en vacances, je fais du tourisme. Ici, je visite <u>souvent</u> des monuments historiques. J'aime visiter les châteaux.

– Moi, je fais du sport. <u>Normalement</u>, je vais à la plage, et je fais de la voile et de la planche à voile.

– <u>En général</u>, je me repose. Je lis un livre ou le journal. J'adore danser, et je vais en boîte de nuit <u>tous les soirs</u>.

– <u>Chaque année</u>, je passe mes vacances à la campagne. Je fais des randonnées et, <u>quelquefois</u>, je fais de l'équitation. <u>De temps en temps</u>, je loue un vélo tout terrain et je fais du VTT.

✳ b Ecoute les cinq interviews sur la cassette. Peux-tu identifier l'endroit où chaque vacancier passe ses vacances?

2 ▶ Je répète

Les mots et les expressions soulignés représentent la fréquence de certaines activités. Vérifie le sens de ces mots utiles. Pour t'aider à les mémoriser, recopie-les dans l'ordre de fréquence.

3 ▶ J'invente

Que fais-tu en vacances?
Discute avec ton/ta partenaire. Est-ce que vous aimez faire les mêmes choses?
N'oublie pas d'utiliser les expressions de fréquence.

Comment sont tes vacances idéales?

1 ► *Je comprends*

En vacances! a interviewé des gens pour connaître leurs préférences. Voici une liste de genres de vacances. A ton avis, quelles descriptions pourraient correspondre à chacun (pour ou contre)?

Genres de vacances	Descriptions (pour ou contre)
1 faire un voyage organisé	a c'est plus confortable
2 louer une maison/un appartement/un gîte	b c'est moins confortable
	c c'est plus cher
3 faire du camping (tente)	d c'est moins cher
4 faire du camping (caravane)	e c'est plus décontracté
5 dormir à l'hôtel	f c'est moins décontracté
6 dormir à l'auberge de jeunesse	g on est indépendant
7 aller chez des grands-parents, cousins, etc	h on n'est pas indépendant
	i il y a des règlements
	j on est avec sa famille

 2 ►

✱ a Ecoute les interviews. Pour chaque personne, note le(s) genre(s) de vacances qu'elle préfère, ou qu'elle n'aime pas.

✱ b Ecoute une deuxième fois, et note deux raisons pour chaque personne.

c Est-ce que quelqu'un a les mêmes préférences que toi?

3 ► *Je répète*

Recopie les genres de vacances que tu préfères, et ceux que tu n'aimes pas. Donne tes raisons.

4 ► *J'invente*

a Essaie d'ajouter d'autres détails:
  ● d'autres choses que tu aimes ou que tu n'aimes pas
  ● d'autres raisons.

b Pose des questions à ton/ta partenaire pour connaître son opinion.
  Que penses-tu des voyages organisés?   *Tu aimes faire du camping?*

5 ►

Travaille avec un(e) partenaire ou en groupe. Pour chaque genre de vacances, donnez un, deux, trois ou quatre points pour:

● le confort   ● le prix   ● l'indépendance.

Quel genre de vacances recommandez-vous pour chaque catégorie?

Louer une maison, c'est assez cher.

Oui, mais dormir à l'hôtel, c'est encore plus cher. Alors l'hôtel, quatre points?

Bonnes vacances?

On dit 'Bonnes vacances!' à un ami qui part en vacances, mais il n'est pas nécessaire de passer des vacances exotiques pour bien s'amuser. On peut passer de bonnes vacances à la maison!

 1 ► **Je comprends**

Ecoute ces gens qui parlent de leurs vacances l'année dernière. Qui a passé de bonnes vacances?

2 ►

Réécoute les interviews. Est-ce que tout le monde répond bien aux questions? Par exemple, est-ce que quelqu'un ne donne pas assez d'informations, ou au contraire parle trop? Que fait l'interviewer?

 3 ► **Je répète**

Ecoute des gens parler de vacances qu'ils ont passées. Répète après ceux qui, à ton avis, ont fait des choses intéressantes.

4 ► **J'invente**

Cette interview n'est pas très intéressante, parce que la personne interviewée ne dit pas grand-chose.
Avec un(e) partenaire, regarde l'extrait de la brochure et adapte l'interview pour la rendre plus intéressante. Vous pouvez inventer d'autres détails aussi.
Pour vous aider, réécoutez les interviews intéressantes de l'activité **1** ►

– Où as-tu passé tes vacances, l'année dernière?
– *Je suis allé(e) au bord de la Méditerranée, à Beaulieu.*
– Tu es parti(e) avec qui?
– *Avec ma famille.*
– Tu as passé combien de temps à Beaulieu?
– *Une quinzaine de jours.*
– Tu as fait du camping?
– *Non.*
– Tu t'es bien amusé(e)?
– *Oui.*
– Qu'est-ce que tu as fait?
– *Du sport.*

Frantour Victoria ★★

SITUATION
Au cœur du centre-ville à 300 m de la plage et du casino, l'hôtel Victoria bénéficie d'une situation exceptionnelle.

L'HOTEL 2 ETOILES
Cet établissement en pierre de taille s'élève sur 4 étages et a été entièrement rénové en 1990. 2 ascenseurs, bar, salle de billard, salon, jardin arboré

de palmiers, orangers, citronniers, mandariniers et bananiers.
Animation de la station:
Salle de jeux, cinéma, promenades entre Beaulieu et Villefranche, sans oublier le Casino et ses jardins.
Sports: *(A proximité)*
Tennis, yachting, voile, promenades en mer, mini-golf, boules, pétanque.

5

Tu vas décrire à ton groupe ou à ta classe:
● les meilleures vacances de ta vie;
● les pires vacances de ta vie.
Les vacances peuvent être réelles ou, si tu préfères, inventées.

a De quoi vas-tu parler? Fais une liste.

b Ensuite, prépare des notes. N'oublie pas d'ajouter des détails intéressants et, si possible, amusants.

c Peux-tu illustrer ton exposé, avec des photos, des brochures ou des souvenirs?

d N'oublie pas les expressions de fréquence, comme **souvent** et **de temps en temps**.

e Prépare-toi à parler! Rappelle-toi les stratégies que tu connais déjà. Parle lentement et clairement.

destination
logement
durée
gens
activités
temps
opinion

A moi, les examens!

 1

Serge, ton correspondant belge, te parle de ses vacances de l'année dernière.

Regarde ces trois cartes postales.

Quelle carte postale a-t-il acheté en vacances, **A**, **B** ou **C**?

Donne trois raisons pour expliquer ta réponse.

A

B

C

Conseil de l'examinateur

● Avant d'écouter, regarde les trois cartes postales et essaie de penser à ce que Serge pourrait dire. Par exemple, il pourrait parler du temps ou de ce qu'il a fait.

 2

Tu écoutes une émission de radio sur les vacances. Un homme et une femme parlent de leurs habitudes et de leurs préférences.

Pour l'homme et la femme, note:

● le type de vacances qu'il/elle préfère et une raison donnée

● le type de vacances qu'il/elle n'aime pas et une raison donnée.

Conseil de l'examinateur

● Tu vas entendre la conversation deux fois, donc il n'est pas nécessaire de noter tout à la fois.

★ La première fois, note ce que chaque personne aime et n'aime pas. Attention aux expressions négatives (ne... pas; pas du tout; pas beaucoup) et au vocabulaire (aime/adore/préfère; déteste).

★ La deuxième fois, note les raisons données.

A moi, les examens!

1

L'exposé

Tu dois parler pendant deux ou trois minutes sur ce thème: **les vacances que je préfère**. Tu peux te préparer à l'avance.

Conseils de l'examinateur

- Tout d'abord, décide quelles sont les vacances que tu préfères. Ce sont des vacances au bord de la mer? En ville? Des voyages organisés à l'hôtel?

- Prépare-toi à expliquer tes préférences. Tu aimes être indépendant(e)? Tu préfères le confort? Tu as des centres d'intérêt particuliers?

- Pense à ce qui contribue à de bonnes vacances. Par exemple, le temps qu'il fait dans certains pays, les choses qu'on peut y faire ou voir.

- Organise tes idées. Parle d'abord, par exemple, de ta destination préférée, et donne les raisons.

- Essaie d'impressionner l'examinateur! Utilise des mots sophistiqués et des structures complexes.
    - ★ Ne répète pas toujours les mêmes expressions, comme **'j'aime. . .'**. Tu pourrais dire **'je m'intéresse aux monuments historiques'** ou **'je trouve les musées intéressants'**.
    - ★ Si possible, utilise une variété de temps, par exemple: 'Je préfère les voyages organisés. Si **j'avais** de l'argent, **j'irais** en Egypte et **je visiterais** les pyramides. L'année dernière, **je suis allé(e)** en Espagne et **je me suis bien amusé(e).'**

2

La conversation

Ensuite, ton/ta partenaire te posera des questions.

Partenaire A	**Partenaire B**
Pose les questions suivantes à **B**.	Pose les questions suivantes à **A**.
Si tu veux, tu peux ajouter d'autres questions.	Si tu veux, tu peux ajouter d'autres questions.
★ Est-ce que tu es parti(e) en vacances l'année dernière? Qu'est-ce que tu as fait?	★ Est-ce que tu es parti(e) en vacances l'année dernière? Qu'est-ce que tu as fait?
★ Quelles ont été les meilleures vacances de ta vie? Pourquoi?	★ As-tu déjà passé des vacances horribles? Parle-moi de ces vacances.
★ Et l'année prochaine?	

Conseils de l'examinateur

- Quand on te pose des questions qui te surprennent, réfléchis avant de répondre:
- ★ As-tu bien compris la question? Par exemple, pense au verbe: 'Est-ce que tu es parti(e). . .' est le passé composé qui veut dire qu'on parle du passé. L'expression 'l'année dernière' le confirme!
- ★ Quelquefois, il est difficile de penser à une réponse. Pour avoir un peu plus de temps, répète la question:
    - – Les meilleures vacances de ma vie? Mmm, c'est difficile à dire. J'ai passé de très bonnes vacances à l'âge de douze ans. . . .

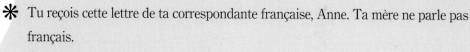

A moi, les examens!

✳ Tu reçois cette lettre de ta correspondante française, Anne. Ta mère ne parle pas français.

Réponds, en anglais, à ses questions:

★ Where did Anne and her family spend their holiday?

★ When did they go there?

★ What activities did Anne do during the holiday?

★ What did she think of the holiday?

Conseils de l'examinateur

● Pour commencer, lis les questions. Elles t'aideront à comprendre la lettre, et tu sauras ce qu'on te demande.

● Puis, lis la lettre en entier. Ne t'inquiète pas s'il y a des mots ou des expressions difficiles. Très souvent, il n'est pas nécessaire de comprendre chaque mot.

● Ensuite, cherche les réponses aux questions, une à la fois. En général, tu trouveras les réponses dans le même ordre que les questions.

● Pour chaque question, donne le plus d'informations possibles.

Salut! Orange, le 10 Janvier

Je viens de recevoir ta lettre et les photos. Merci beaucoup.

Pendant les vacances de Noël, on est allé en famille passer une semaine chez mes grands-parents à la montagne.

Nous avons fait du ski tous les matins ce qui était fatigant, mais génial. De temps en temps, nous avons fait des randonnées dans la neige. Le soir, on s'ennuyait un peu, parce qu'il n'y avait pas grand-chose à faire. On a joué aux cartes presque tous les soirs.

Ecris-moi bientôt. J'aimerais savoir ce que tu as fait pendant tes vacances.

Je t'embrasse,

Anne

A moi, les examens!

Tu as participé à un concours dans un magazine. A ta grande surprise, tu as gagné un week-end pour deux à Paris. Le magazine te demande de décrire ton week-end. Fais la description pour le magazine. Tu dois donner les informations suivantes:

★ Qui est allé à Paris avec toi? Pourquoi as-tu choisi cette personne?

★ Quel temps a-t-il fait?

★ Qu'est-ce que tu as fait samedi?

★ Qu'est-ce que tu as fait dimanche?

★ Que penses-tu du week-end?

Concours! Jouez et gagnez!

★ ★

Gagnez un week-end pour deux à Paris!

Visitez les monuments de la capitale:

la Tour Eiffel

la cathédrale Notre-Dame

le musée du Louvre

la place de la Concorde

l'avenue des Champs-Elysées

Conseils de l'examinateur

- Avant de commencer ta description, prends des notes pour chaque question.

- Il est important de répondre à **toutes** les questions, même si tes réponses sont très courtes.

- Essaie de rendre ta description aussi intéressante que possible. Utilise différents adjectifs. Donne des détails. Ecris plus que le minimum!

- Si tu ne sais pas le bon mot en français, tu peux changer ce que tu écris! Surtout, n'écris pas en anglais!
  Imagine! Tu ne sais pas comment dire en français que tu as fait une promenade en bateau sur la Seine.
  Pas de problème! Tu dis autre chose. Par exemple, tu dis que tu as visité le Louvre.

Tu comprends maintenant?

Je vérifie

**Est-ce que tu sais parler de tes vacances avec assurance? Fais ce test!
Si tu veux, tu peux d'abord faire un peu de révision.**

★ **Travaillez en groupes. Imaginez! Vous voudriez travailler pendant les
vacances d'été pour une agence de voyages en France. Pour trouver
les meilleurs candidats, l'agence vous fait passer un petit test.**

 Agence Passe-partout

Vous allez trouver des vacances idéales à
recommander à trois clients.

Activité 1

 Ecoutez ces trois personnes qui parlent de leurs vacances
habituelles, et de leurs préférences. Prenez des notes pour
vous aider à trouver leurs vacances idéales.

Activité 2

Faites des recherches pour trouver des vacances idéales
pour chaque client(e). Vous trouverez quelques suggestions
sur la fiche (ci-jointe).

Activité 3

Discutez de vos suggestions avec les autres membres du
groupe. Dites ce que vous pensez et essayez de vous mettre
d'accord.
Dans notre travail, il est très important de pouvoir
travailler harmonieusement en équipe.

Activité 4

Chaque personne du groupe doit écrire un rapport pour un(e)
des client(e)s pour lui dire quelles vacances vous lui
recommandez, et pourquoi.
N'oubliez pas: nous vendons des vacances! Vous devez être
enthousiastes et convaincre les clients. Il faut les
persuader que ces vacances sont idéales!
Décrivez les vacances et expliquez pourquoi vous avez
choisi ces vacances pour eux.

Tu te rappelles?

■ Je sais parler de ce que je fais habituellement pendant mes vacances

Je vais à la campagne pendant quinze jours. On fait du camping.

I go to the countryside for a fortnight. We go camping.

Chaque année (été), je passe quelques jours au bord de la mer avec mes amis.

Every year (summer), I spend a few days at the seaside with my friends.

Normalement, je reste chez moi et je sors avec mes copains.

I normally stay at home and go out with my mates.

Je passe un mois chez mon père. Pendant les vacances de Noël, je passe une semaine à la montagne.

I stay with my father for a month. During the Christmas holidays, I spend a week in the mountains.

■ Je sais parler de mes préférences

Je vais à la plage tous les jours. Je bronze et je me baigne dans la mer. De temps en temps, je fais de la voile et de la planche à voile.

I go to the beach every day. I sunbathe and swim in the sea. From time to time, I go sailing and windsurfing.

Je fais des randonnées. Je fais quelquefois du vélo tout terrain.

I go hiking. I sometimes go mountain-biking.

J'aime faire du tourisme. Je visite souvent des monuments historiques.

I like sight-seeing. I often visit places of historical interest.

Pendant les vacances, je lis toujours un bon livre, et je me repose!

During the holidays, I always read a good book and have a rest!

En général, je préfère dormir à l'hôtel. C'est plus confortable.

In general, I prefer to stay in a hotel. It's more comfortable.

Je vais toujours dans une auberge de jeunesse. C'est moins cher, et plus décontracté.

I always go to a youth hostel. It's cheaper and more relaxed.

Je n'aime pas les voyages organisés. Je préfère louer un gîte. On est plus indépendant.

I don't like package tours. I prefer to rent a holiday house. You're more independent.

■ Je sais parler des vacances que j'ai passées

L'année dernière, je suis parti(e) en famille. Nous avons passé une quinzaine de jours à l'étranger. Il a fait très beau.

Last year, I went away with my family. We spent a fortnight abroad. The weather was very good.

Je me suis bien amusé(e). C'était très intéressant. (Je m'ennuyais un peu.)

I enjoyed myself. It was really interesting. (I was a bit bored.)

Pendant mes vacances, j'allais en boîte de nuit avec ma copine tous les soirs. C'était super!

During my holidays, I went to a nightclub with my friend every evening. It was great!

Je révise

Utilise ce tableau pour réviser les phrases-clés de cette étape. Voici une activité:

★ Trouve des phrases pour décrire ce que cette personne fait habituellement pendant ses vacances:

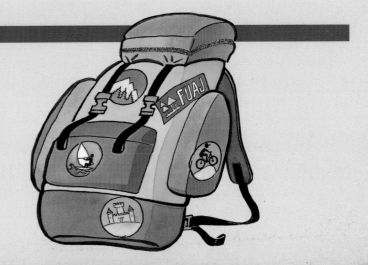

10ème Etape
Les stéréotypes nationaux

Mes objectifs

Beaucoup de gens ont des préjugés sur les habitants de certains pays. Est-ce que ces stéréotypes sont vrais? D'où viennent-ils? Sont-ils dangereux?
Dans cette étape, tu vas:

- examiner les stéréotypes de plusieurs nationalités
- donner ton opinion sur les stéréotypes.

LES FRANÇAIS

ILS SONT ARROGANTS ET IMPOLIS. ILS CONDUISENT COMME DES FOUS, MAIS MIEUX QUE LES ITALIENS! ILS SONT EGOISTES ET TRES FIERS DE LEUR CUISINE. EN FRANCE, LES GENS NE MANGENT QUE DES ESCARGOTS ET NE BOIVENT QUE DU VIN.

LES AMERICAINS

LES AMERICAINS SONT GROS ET DESAGREABLES. ILS SONT BEAUCOUP MOINS TIMIDES QUE NOUS. LES GRANDES VILLES AUX ETATS-UNIS SONT DANGEREUSES. LES GENS NE SORTENT JAMAIS SANS LEUR REVOLVER!

LES BRITANNIQUES

LES ANGLAIS SONT TRES CONSCIENTS DES CLASSES SOCIALES. ILS SONT TRES POLIS, MAIS ARROGANTS. ILS NE PARLENT QUE DE LA FAMILLE ROYALE ET DU TEMPS. L'HUMOUR ANGLAIS EST ASSEZ DROLE. IL NE FAIT JAMAIS BEAU EN ANGLETERRE. LES GALLOIS ADORENT CHANTER. ILS SONT TRES FIERS DE LEUR LANGUE. LES ECOSSAIS SONT TRES FIERS DE LEUR CULTURE ET DE LEURS TRADITIONS. ILS HABITENT DANS DES CHATEAUX HANTES! EN ECOSSE, LE TEMPS EST PIRE QU'EN ANGLETERRE.

Des élèves de plusieurs pays nous ont envoyé des messages par courrier électronique. En voici quelques-uns. Il y en a d'autres sur la Fiche 9.1.

1 ▶ *Je comprends*

a N'oublie pas les stratégies pour mieux comprendre:
- essaie de deviner le sens de certains mots et cherche les autres dans le dictionnaire
- vérifie que le sens correspond bien au contexte.

b Trouve dans les messages des expressions qui veulent dire:
- les gens mangent **seulement** des escargots
- les gens sortent **toujours** avec leur revolver
- le contraire de l'expression: ils font beaucoup de choses.

Travail de détective

Tu comprends l'expression **aussi. . . que. . .**? Pense au contexte pour t'aider.

Les Américains sont **plus** gros **que** les Français.

Les Irlandais sont **moins** sérieux **que** les Allemands.

Les Australiens sont **aussi** paresseux **que** les Espagnols.

---

c Est-ce que tu reconnais certains des stéréotypes dans les messages? Lesquels?

2 ▶ *Je répète et j'invente*

a Est-ce que tu as des préjugés? Lesquels? Cherche dans tous les messages des caractéristiques et des expressions pour décrire tes préjugés sur chaque pays/nationalité dans la boîte.

b Est-ce que tu as les mêmes préjugés que ton/ta partenaire?

la Grande-Bretagne/les Britanniques

la France/les Français

la Belgique/les Belges

l'Espagne/les Espagnols

l'Allemagne/les Allemands

le Danemark/les Danois

les Pays-Bas/les Hollandais

le Portugal/les Portugais

la Grèce/les Grecs   l'Italie/les Italiens

l'Australie/les Australiens   les Etats-Unis/les Américains

3 ▶ *J'invente*

En groupes, écrivez **votre** description de trois pays et de leurs habitants.
C'est facile? Etes-vous tous d'accord?

Ces images sont vraies?

1 ► *Je comprends et je répète*

a Ton correspondant français et ses amis discutent des stéréotypes. Ecoute la conversation. Deux jeunes ne sont pas d'accord avec les stéréotypes. Pourquoi?

b Entraîne-toi à participer à une conversation similaire! Note les expressions-clés dans ce dialogue:

– <u>On dit que</u> les Français sont impolis. <u>Qu'en penses-tu</u>? <u>Tu crois que c'est vrai</u>?

– <u>Je ne suis pas d'accord</u>. <u>A mon avis</u>, <u>c'est tout à fait faux</u>. Moi, j'ai visité la France. <u>Je crois que</u> les Français sont aussi polis que nous. <u>J'ai trouvé</u> les parents de mon correspondant charmants. <u>On ne peut pas généraliser</u>.

– <u>C'est vrai qu'</u>ils ne mangent que des escargots?

– <u>Pas du tout</u>! <u>Ça, c'est une exagération</u>! Ils mangent des escargots de temps en temps. Pendant que j'étais là, nous n'en avons pas mangé.

2 ► *J'invente*

a Avec un(e) partenaire, adapte le dialogue pour discuter des Espagnols.

Ils ne mangent que de la paëlla.

Ils sont paresseux.

Les magasins sont fermés entre 2h et 5h.

Point-info

En Espagne, il fait très chaud l'après-midi, et les Espagnols font la sieste. Beaucoup de magasins ferment l'après-midi, mais ils sont ouverts de 8h du matin jusqu'à 2h, et de 5h jusqu'à 8h30 le soir.

b Avec un(e) partenaire, décris les stéréotypes sur ton pays.

c En groupes, comparez et discutez de vos descriptions.

Tout comprendre, c'est tout pardonner (proverbe français)

Les Néo-Zélandais sont très impolis. Ils ne vous serrent pas la main!

Que penses-tu des stéréotypes?

 1 ▶ *Je comprends*

Ces jeunes Français discutent des stéréotypes.

a   Vérifie les mots que tu ne comprends pas.

b   Ecoute la cassette et identifie chaque personne qui parle. Tu es d'accord
avec qui?

Les blagues sont amusantes, et elles ne font pas de mal.

Les stéréotypes sont faux.

Les stéréotypes sont dangereux. Ils sont souvent racistes.

Les stéréotypes sont des exagérations, c'est tout.

On ne peut pas généraliser. Tout le monde est différent.

Il faut accepter les différences et essayer de comprendre les autres cultures. Il faut avoir l'esprit ouvert.

2 ▶ *Je répète et j'invente*

a   Recopie les opinions ci-dessus. Fais deux listes:

> *1 Je suis d'accord   2 Je ne suis pas d'accord*

b   Peux-tu ajouter d'autres opinions sur les stéréotypes?

3 ▶

Travaillez en groupes. Discutez: que pensez-vous des stéréotypes?

4 ▶

Comment peut-on mieux comprendre les gens d'un autre pays?
Voici quelques suggestions.
Peux-tu en ajouter d'autres?

> ● *Passer des vacances dans le pays.*
> ● *Trouver un(e) correspondant(e).*

5 ▶

Pendant la deuxième guerre mondiale,
des millions de gens ont été tués par les
Nazis, dans des camps de concentration,
à cause de leur nationalité, de leur
mode de vie, ou de leurs opinions.
Martin Niemoller, un pasteur
allemand, a écrit ce poème dans le
camp de Dachau, juste avant sa mort: ▶

> Quand ils sont venus
> chercher les communistes,
> Je n'ai rien dit,
> Je n'étais pas communiste.
>
> Quand ils sont venus
> chercher les syndicalistes,
> Je n'ai rien dit,
> Je n'étais pas syndicaliste.
>
> Quand ils sont venus
> chercher les juifs,
> Je n'ai rien dit,
> Je n'étais pas juif.
>
> Quand ils sont venus
> chercher les catholiques,
> Je n'ai rien dit,
> Je n'étais pas catholique.
>
> Puis ils sont venus
> me chercher
> Et il ne restait personne
> pour dire quelque chose.

A moi, les examens!

 1

En France, tu entends une femme et un homme qui parlent de vacances à l'étranger. Ils n'ont pas la même opinion.

a Est-ce que la femme aime voyager à l'étranger?

Et l'homme, est-ce qu'il aime voyager à l'étranger?

Pour quelle raison majeure pensent-ils ainsi?

b Donne des raisons plus précises:

★ pour expliquer l'opinion de la femme (deux raisons)

★ pour expliquer l'opinion de l'homme (deux raisons).

Conseils de l'examinateur

- Pour la section **a**, ta réponse devrait être courte. Ecoute les raisons données par chaque personne. Essaie de les résumer en un ou deux mots.

- Pour la section **b**, il faut écouter attentivement les détails. Note les deux raisons que tu comprends le mieux. Ne donne pas plus de deux raisons parce que l'examinateur lira seulement les deux premières.

 2

Deux jeunes Français, Elodie et Marc, discutent de l'Irlande. Elodie va y passer ses vacances l'année prochaine.

a Est-ce qu'Elodie a une image stéréotypée de l'Irlande?

b Explique ta réponse.

c Est-ce que Marc a une image stéréotypée de l'Irlande?

d Explique ta réponse.

Conseils de l'examinateur

- Pour identifier un stéréotype, trouve **les exagérations** et **les généralisations**, par exemple:

★ ils **ne** mangent **que**. . .

★ **tous** les Irlandais sont. . .

★ ils ne font **jamais**. . .

- Beaucoup de gens ont des préjugés sur une nationalité parce qu'ils la connaissent mal. Par exemple, ils n'ont jamais visité le pays, ni rencontré d'habitants de ce pays.

A moi, les examens!

Ta correspondante française t'a envoyé cette blague:

A l'aide!

L'enfer, c'est le contraire du paradis.

Lis la blague, et prépare-toi à répondre aux questions suivantes:

a Est-ce que tu trouves la blague amusante?

b Peux-tu expliquer les stéréotypes contenus dans cette blague?

c Que penses-tu de ce genre de blagues en général?

d Que penses-tu des stéréotypes?

Conseils de l'examinateur

● Si l'examinateur te demande de donner ton opinion, n'oublie pas d'utiliser des phrases comme:

★ A mon avis. . .

★ Je trouve que. . .

★ Moi, je pense que. . .

★ Il est vrai que. . .

★ Je crois que. . .

★ Je (ne) suis (pas) d'accord.

● Entraîne-toi régulièrement pour l'examen! Par exemple, prépare des notes pour répondre à ces questions, puis enregistre-toi sur cassette. Ecoute l'enregistrement. Peux-tu l'améliorer? Demande à ton professeur de t'aider.

A moi, les examens!

✳ Tu lis cette lettre dans *Okapi*, un magazine français pour les jeunes. Ta sœur, qui ne lit pas très bien le français, voudrait savoir pourquoi Marie a écrit la lettre. Explique en anglais, à ta sœur, l'opinion de Marie:

★ sur les médias (la télévision et les journaux)

★ sur les citadins (les gens qui habitent dans les grandes villes):
  – comment ils sont;
  – comment ils devraient être.

«SOYEZ TOLÉRANTS»

«Cher Okapi. Je m'appelle Marie, j'ai 14 ans et j'habite à Megève. Il y a quelque chose que je ne comprends pas et qui m'énerve. Lorsque je regarde la télévision ou que je lis n'importe quel journal, j'ai l'impression que la France entière habite en ville et tout particulièrement à Paris.

J'ai l'impression que les médias pensent que ceux qui habitent en montagne, comme moi, ou à la campagne, comme les paysans, ne sont pas cultivés. . . Je ne sais pas si c'est le cas, mais c'est mon impression. Lorsque je vais en cours, l'hiver, et que les Parisiens sont en vacances à Megève, j'ai l'impression d'être 'sous-développée'.

Mais je pourrais aussi me moquer des citadins lorsqu'ils font du ski ou du surf, parce que j'en fais mieux qu'eux, ou quand ils se baladent avec leurs après-skis, sur une route sèche. Mais je ne le fais pas, par respect, et on dirait que, malgré leur grande culture, ils sont intolérants par rapport à nous.

Alors que, soi-disant, **lorsque quelqu'un est cultivé, il doit avoir l'esprit ouvert. · ·** J'espère que vous comprendrez ce que je veux dire. En tout cas, merci et bravo pour Okapi que j'attends toujours avec impatience.»

Marie, 14 ans
Megève (74)

Point-info

Megève est une ville dans les Alpes, dans l'est de la France.

Conseils de l'examinateur

● Prépare-toi! Lis le titre de la lettre, et les questions, pour avoir une idée du sujet de la lettre.

● D'autres aspects peuvent aussi t'aider à comprendre. Par exemple, dans un magazine, les sections **en caractères gras** contiennent souvent les idées les plus importantes.

● Lis la lettre en entier assez vite, pour la comprendre d'une façon générale.

● Maintenant, lis la lettre en détail, pour répondre aux questions.

A moi, les examens!

Tu reçois cette lettre d'Yves, ton correspondant français.

Réponds à sa lettre, et décris les préjugés sur les jeunes qui existent dans ton pays.

Lyon, le 15 avril.

Salut!

Merci pour ta dernière lettre; j'ai trouvé les blagues très amusantes!

Je voudrais te demander si les adultes dans ton pays ont des préjugés sur les jeunes? Chez nous, il y en a beaucoup. Je t'envoie des illustrations pour t'en donner quelques exemples.

S'il te plaît, dans ta prochaine lettre, parle-moi des préjugés sur les jeunes qui existent dans ton pays.

J'espère que tu vas bien.

Ecris-moi bientôt,

Yves.

Les jeunes d'aujourd'hui?

Conseils de l'examinateur

- Lis attentivement la lettre. Souvent, tu y trouveras des mots, des expressions ou des idées utiles. Quelques exemples sont soulignés dans la lettre d'Yves.
- Les illustrations t'aideront à penser à des stéréotypes.

Tu comprends maintenant?

Sais-tu maintenant parler des stéréotypes? Si tu es prêt(e), fais ces activités. Sinon, révise d'abord un peu.

★ **Tu reçois une cassette de tes amis français, Sandrine et Michel. Ecoute-la attentivement. Ils te posent des questions. Pour t'aider à comprendre et à écrire, tu peux utiliser un dictionnaire.**

 ★ Qu'est-ce qu'ils te demandent de faire? Prends des notes pour ne pas oublier.

★ Voici la blague qu'ils t'ont envoyée.

Un bateau prend feu, avec à son bord des passagers de nombreuses nationalités. Le capitaine demande à son second d'aller demander à tous les passagers de se jeter à l'eau. Dix minutes plus tard, le second revient. Tous ont refusé. « Je m'en charge », dit le capitaine. Cinq minutes plus tard, le capitaine revient. Tous les passagers ont sauté.

« Comment avez-vous fait? », demande le second, admiratif.

« C'est simple, dit le capitaine. J'ai dit aux Anglais que se jeter à l'eau était traditionnel; aux Français que c'était chic; aux Américains qu'ils étaient assurés; aux Allemands que c'était un ordre; et aux Italiens que c'était défendu! »

★ N'oublie pas de discuter avec tes amis, pour connaître leurs opinions.

Tu te rappelles?

■ **Je sais parler des stéréotypes nationaux**

C'est vrai que les Espagnols sont paresseux?	Is it true that the Spanish are lazy?
C'est tout à fait faux. En Espagne, les gens sont aussi travailleurs que chez nous!	It's completely false. In Spain, the people are as hard-working as people here.
On dit que les Allemands sont sérieux et arrogants.	They say that the Germans are serious and arrogant.
Je ne suis pas d'accord. J'ai visité l'Allemagne, et j'ai trouvé les gens très aimables. Je ne pense plus qu'ils sont arrogants.	I don't agree. I've visited Germany and I found the people very nice. I no longer think that they're arrogant.
Est-ce que les Grecs sont gentils?	Are the Greeks nice?
Je ne suis jamais allé(e) en Grèce. Je ne connais personne là-bas.	I've never been to Greece. I don't know anyone there.
On dit que les Italiens sont très actifs. Tu crois que c'est vrai?	They say that Italians are very active. Do you think it's true?
A mon avis, on ne peut pas généraliser.	In my opinion, you can't generalise.
C'est vrai que les Anglais ne font rien comme tout le monde?	Is it true that the British do nothing like anyone else?
Ça, c'est une exagération!	That's an exaggeration!
On dit que les Danois et les Hollandais sont très fiers de leur culture.	They say that the Danish and the Dutch are very proud of their culture.
Je n'ai visité ni le Danemark, ni les Pays-Bas.	I've visited neither Denmark nor Holland.
Tu penses qu'on ne mange que des spaghettis en Italie?	Do you think they eat nothing but spaghetti in Italy?
Pas du tout! Ça, c'est exagéré!	Not at all! That's exaggerated!
Tu penses que les Portugais sont désagréables?	Do you think the Portugese are unpleasant?
J'ai un correspondant au Portugal qui est très agréable.	I've got a penfriend in Portugal who is very pleasant.
Je crois que les stéréotypes sont dangereux. Tout le monde est différent. Il faut avoir l'esprit ouvert.	I think that stereotypes are dangerous. Everyone is different. You should have an open mind.

Je révise

Utilise ce tableau pour réviser les phrases-clés de cette étape. Voici une activité:

★ Travaille avec un(e) partenaire. Reconnaissez-vous ces stéréotypes? Etes-vous d'accord avec ces stéréotypes?

11ème Etape
Sondages sur la famille

Mes objectifs

L'adolescence, c'est souvent une période de conflits entre parents et jeunes.

Dans cette étape, tu vas parler:

■ de la personnalité des gens de ta famille

■ des rapports entre les jeunes et leurs parents.

---

1 ▶ **Je comprends**

Lis les descriptions des différents signes du zodiaque.

a Tous les adjectifs sont soulignés. Tu en connais déjà la majorité. Vérifie le sens de ceux que tu ne connais pas.

b Est-ce que la description de ton signe te correspond bien?

c Peux-tu deviner de quels signes sont les gens de ta classe?

 ## Bélier
21 mars – 20 avril

Vous êtes <u>optimiste</u> et <u>actif/active</u>, mais quelquefois <u>impoli(e)</u>, et même un peu <u>agressif/agressive</u>. Vous aimez faire des projets!

 ## Cancer
22 juin – 22 juillet

Vous êtes <u>sympathique</u>, et assez <u>sérieux/sérieuse</u>. Vous avez beaucoup d'imagination. Vous aimez rester chez vous.

 ## Taureau
21 avril – 21 mai

En général, vous êtes <u>aimable</u> et <u>calme</u>, mais si vous vous mettez en colère… attention! Vous aimez le confort et l'argent.

 ## Lion
23 juillet – 22 août

Vous êtes <u>amusant(e)</u> et <u>généreux/généreuse</u>, mais vous êtes <u>strict(e)</u> avec les enfants. Vous voudriez être <u>célèbre</u>.

 ## Gémeaux
22 mai – 21 juin

Vous êtes <u>optimiste</u> et <u>charmant(e)</u>, mais vous êtes souvent <u>nerveux/nerveuse</u>. Vous aimez discuter.

 ## Vierge
23 août – 22 septembre

Vous êtes <u>gentil(le)</u>, <u>poli(e)</u> et <u>honnête</u>. Vous aimez aider les autres. Vous n'aimez pas être en retard.

2 ▶ Je répète

Recopie les adjectifs en deux catégories: les caractéristiques positives et les caractéristiques négatives. Puis, compare tes listes avec celles de cinq autres personnes. Avez-vous tous la même opinion?

3 ▶ Je comprends et je répète

Ecoute ces jeunes qui parlent de membres de leur famille. Ils s'entendent bien, assez bien, ou mal avec eux? Pourquoi?

Ma sœur est calme et gentille, en général. Elle n'est pas toujours très raisonnable, mais je m'entends assez bien avec elle.

4 ▶ J'invente

a Ecris une description de la personnalité de chaque membre de ta famille. A ton avis, est-ce que la description de leur signe du zodiaque correspond à leur personnalité?

b Parle avec ton/ta partenaire de quelqu'un de ta famille:
  ● Il/Elle a quel caractère?
  ● Tu t'entends bien avec lui/elle?
  Si tu veux, tu peux parler de tous les membres de ta famille!

 ## Balance
23 septembre – 22 octobre

Vous êtes <u>charmant(e)</u> et <u>intelligent(e)</u>, mais vous n'aimez pas prendre de décisions!

 ## Scorpion
23 octobre – 21 novembre

Vous êtes <u>charmant(e)</u>, mais vous pouvez être <u>égoïste</u> et quelquefois <u>méchant(e)</u>! Vous adorez les mystères.

 ## Sagittaire
22 novembre – 20 décembre

En général, vous êtes <u>heureux/heureuse</u> et <u>optimiste</u>, mais, de temps en temps, vous parlez sans réfléchir! Vous aimez les voyages.

 ## Capricorne
21 décembre – 19 janvier

Vous êtes <u>honnête</u> et <u>travailleur/ travailleuse</u>, mais quelquefois <u>pessimiste</u>. Vous aimez le succès.

 ## Verseau
20 janvier – 19 février

Vous êtes <u>intelligent(e)</u> et <u>raisonnable</u>, mais un peu <u>bizarre</u>. Vous détestez l'injustice.

 ## Poissons
20 février – 20 mars

Vous êtes <u>agréable</u>, <u>calme</u>, et un peu <u>timide</u>. Vous avez beaucoup d'imagination. Vous aimez les films.

Un conflit de générations?

Nous avons fait un sondage auprès de jeunes Français sur leurs relations avec leurs parents. Voici quelques résultats:

Question 1: En général, quelles sont tes relations avec tes parents?

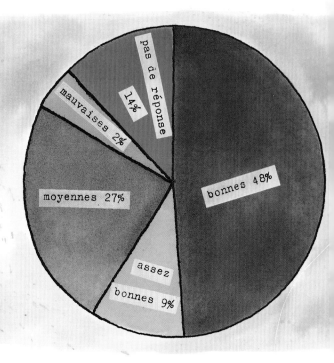

pas de réponse 14%

mauvaises 2%

bonnes 48%

moyennes 27%

assez bonnes 9%

 1 ► *Je comprends et je répète*

a Choisis les réponses que toi, tu donnerais à ces questions.

b Essaie de deviner les réponses à la question 2. A ton avis, quelles sont les raisons les plus fréquentes et les moins fréquentes? Recopie-les dans l'ordre.

✳ **c** Maintenant, écoute deux jeunes qui discutent des résultats. Note les pourcentages que tu entends sur ta liste. Est-ce que tu as deviné le bon ordre pour les réponses à la question 2? Est-ce que tu es surpris(e)?

 2

Quels sont les principaux problèmes entre les générations? Nous avons posé cette question à des jeunes. Voici quelques-unes de leurs réponses:

A Les parents sont trop stricts.	**E** Ils n'aiment pas les amis de leurs enfants.
B Ils oublient qu'ils ont été jeunes, eux aussi.	**F** Ils n'aiment pas les vêtements de leurs enfants.
C Ils ne comprennent pas les adolescents.	**G** Ils ne sont pas raisonnables.
D Ils n'écoutent pas leurs enfants.	

a Est-ce que ces problèmes sont fréquents?
Lis les messages sur la Fiche 11.1, et écoute les jeunes interviewés sur la cassette. Note les problèmes qui sont mentionnés.
Quels problèmes sont les plus fréquents?

b Discute de chaque problème avec un(e) partenaire: pensez-vous que c'est vraiment un problème sérieux?

3 ► *J'invente*

Travaillez en groupes. A votre avis, quels sont les cinq problèmes les plus sérieux entre les jeunes et leurs parents? Faites une liste. Puis comparez votre liste avec celles des autres groupes.

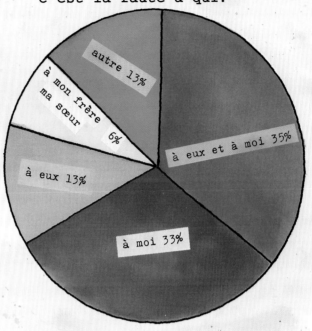

Question 2: D'habitude,
pour quelles raisons te
disputes-tu avec tes parents?

Question 3: Normalement,
c'est la faute à qui?

les vêtements
les opinions différentes
les notes scolaires
l'argent de poche
un frère/une sœur
l'heure de retour le soir
la télévision
la discipline
un objet
les sorties
autres
les travaux ménagers

Pie chart labels:
autre 13%
à mon frère / ma sœur 6%
à eux et à moi 35%
à eux 13%
à moi 33%

4

Les valeurs, les choses qu'on considère comme très importantes, c'est une autre source de conflits entre les générations. Voici un sondage tiré de la revue, *Phosphore*.
Est-ce qu'il y a plus de similarités ou de différences entre les générations?

Quelles sont les valeurs qui comptent le plus pour vous, qui vous paraissent les plus fondamentales?

les 15-20 ans répondent	%
La tolérance, le respect des autres	46%
L'honnêteté	44%
La politesse, les bonnes manières	39%
Le respect de l'environnement, de la nature	32%
L'obéissance	26%
La générosité	25%
Le goût de l'effort, du travail	21%
La solidarité avec les gens, avec les peuples	19%
Le sens de la famille	17%
La réussite sociale, l'esprit de compétition	16%
Le courage	15%
La patience, la persévérance	13%
La fidélité, la loyauté	13%
Le sens de la justice	10%

Quelles sont les valeurs qui comptent le plus pour vous, qui vous paraissent les plus fondamentales?

les 21-49 ans répondent	%	les 50 ans et plus répondent	%
La tolérance, le respect des autres	45%	Le goût de l'effort, du travail	47%
L'honnêteté	41%	L'honnêteté	47%
La politesse, les bonnes manières	39%	La politesse, les bonnes manières	37%
Le goût de l'effort, du travail	34%	La tolérance, le respect des autres	33%
Le sens de la famille	30%	Le sens de la famille	29%
Le respect de l'environnement, de la nature	28%	Le courage	21%

Ça existe, les parents idéaux?

 1 ► Je comprends et je répète

Travaille avec un(e) partenaire.
Ces jeunes Français discutent des
parents idéaux.
Etes-vous d'accord avec eux?

2 ► J'invente

Avez-vous d'autres idées?
A votre avis, quelles sont les cinq
qualités les plus importantes chez
les parents?

> *Pour moi, les parents idéaux feraient confiance à leurs enfant. Ils leur permettraient de rentrer tard.*

> *Je pense que les parents devraient essayer de comprendre les jeunes. Ils devraient être assez stricts, mais pas trop.*

> *Les parents idéaux seraient calmes et raisonnables. Ils écouteraient leurs enfants. Ils les aideraient à résoudre leurs problèmes.*

3 ► Je comprends

Une mère a écrit cette lettre au magazine *Okapi*. Elle donne un autre point
de vue.

a A son avis, est-ce que les parents idéaux existent?

b Es-tu d'accord avec elle?

UNE MERE PARLE: ETRE PARENTS, CE N'EST PAS UN METIER

«J'ai pu constater que je n'étais pas la seule maman à lire *Okapi*. Est-ce parce que nous trouvons ce journal intéressant ou parce que nous voulons mieux comprendre nos enfants?

Je voudrais réagir au débat sur «Vos parents vous comprennent-ils?». C'est vrai que les parents ne sont pas toujours très patients et disponibles, car ils ont leurs propres soucis et voudraient aussi parfois avoir un petit moment à eux. Etre parents, ce n'est pas un métier, ni quelque chose qu'on apprend à l'école; notre rôle, on l'apprend «sur le tas». Alors parfois, on tâtonne, on fait des erreurs. Les parents parfaits, je crois que ça n'existe pas, car nous aussi nous avons notre histoire.

J'ai 40 ans, et je n'ai pas eu la vie trop dure, mais j'ai quand même été beaucoup moins gâtée que mes filles. J'ai aussi beaucoup voyagé, j'ai vu la misère de certains enfants. Aussi, quand les nôtres refusent un plat ou un repas pour plonger dans le frigidaire, réclament toujours plus d'argent de poche, exigent des vêtements et des chaussures de marque à des prix exorbitants (au fait, à quand un dossier sur la consommation et la publicité?), veulent tout et tout de suite, sans faire aucun effort (est-ce notre exemple?), cela me révolte. Moi, je voudrais que mes enfants soient le plus heureux possible, et pas seulement les miens, mais tous les enfants du monde. Je voudrais qu'ils fassent un métier qui soit pour eux une passion, qu'ils n'aient pas envie de se recoucher le matin en se réveillant, qu'ils créent un monde meilleur. . .

Merci de m'avoir lue jusqu'au bout.»

*Une mère, Aberdeen
(Royaume-Uni)*

4 ► J'invente

Comment seraient les enfants idéaux? Par exemple, devraient-ils être moins
égoïstes, plus honnêtes avec leurs parents?
Discute de cette question avec un(e) partenaire.

 5 ►

Travaillez en groupes. Inventez une liste de suggestions pour des relations
idéales entre parents et adolescents.

Les frères et sœurs, sont-ils amis?

Est-ce que les jeunes Français s'entendent bien avec leurs frères et leurs sœurs? Ton ami français t'a écrit cette lettre, et il t'a envoyé une cassette avec cinq interviews qu'il a faites.

1 ► Je comprends

a Lis la lettre et écoute la cassette plusieurs fois.

✳ **b** Est-ce que les jeunes s'entendent bien avec leurs frères et sœurs?
Pourquoi ou pourquoi pas?
Qui te ressemble le plus?

c A leur avis, comment sont les frères et sœurs idéaux? Es-tu d'accord?

Rouen, le 3 mai

Salut!

Tu m'as demandé de te parler de ma famille. J'ai deux sœurs qui sont plus âgées que moi. On s'entend assez bien.

Par contre, je ne m'entends pas bien avec mon frère jumeau. Il est égoïste et paresseux. Nous, on se dispute souvent, parce qu'il veut toujours écouter mes CD, ou jouer avec mes jeux vidéo, ou emprunter mes vêtements. Je partage ma chambre avec lui, et il m'énerve. Quelquefois, je me dispute avec lui pour des raisons bêtes.

Pour moi, un frère idéal serait sympathique et amusant. On pourrait sortir et s'amuser ensemble. Et il ne m'emprunterait pas toujours mes affaires!

Et toi, as-tu des frères ou des sœurs? Comment sont-ils? Est-ce que tu t'entends bien avec eux, ou est-ce qu'ils t'énervent? Pourquoi? Comment serait ton frère idéal ou ta sœur idéale?

Ecris-moi vite.

Amitiés,

Jean-François

2 ► J'invente

Prépare une lettre ou une cassette pour Jean-François.

a Fais-lui la description de ton frère idéal ou de ta sœur idéale.

b Parle-lui de tes frères et de tes sœurs. Réponds à ses questions. Si tu es enfant unique, parle-lui de ton/ta meilleur(e) ami(e).

A moi, les examens!

 Ecoute six jeunes qui parlent de leurs relations avec des membres de leur famille.

Note le numéro de chaque personne:

a qui parle de quelqu'un avec qui il/elle s'entend toujours très bien

b qui parle de quelqu'un avec qui il/elle s'entend assez bien, en général

c qui parle de quelqu'un avec qui il/elle s'entend vraiment mal.

Conseils de l'examinateur

● Si les gens ne disent pas tout simplement, 'Je m'entends très bien avec. . .', comment vas-tu connaître leur attitude ou leur opinion? Il faudra 'lire entre les lignes':

● Ecoute attentivement ce qu'ils disent et essaie d'en tirer des conclusions. Par exemple, si quelqu'un dit, 'Je ne parle jamais à mon frère', il est évident qu'il s'entend très mal avec son frère!

● Des descriptions peuvent t'aider. Si quelqu'un dit que sa mère est 'vraiment gentille', il/elle a une attitude plutôt positive envers sa mère.

● Fais aussi attention aux détails! Quels mots utilisent-ils?

★ Par exemple, s'ils ont une attitude plutôt extrême (s'ils s'entendent **très bien** ou **très mal** avec quelqu'un), ils utiliseront des mots comme: **toujours**, **jamais**, **tout le temps**, **pas du tout**, **très**.

★ S'ils ont une attitude plutôt modérée (s'ils s'entendent **assez bien** avec quelqu'un), ils utiliseront des mots plus modérés, comme:
en général, **quelquefois**, **souvent**, **mais**, **d'un côté/de l'autre**.
(Si tu ne comprends pas tous les mots **en gras**, cherche-les dans un dictionnaire.)

● Fais attention à la voix de chaque personne. Elle peut t'aider à confirmer tes idées.

● Fais bien attention aux négatifs. Ils changent tout! Par exemple, 'Je **ne** m'entends **pas** bien avec elle' est le contraire de 'Je m'entends bien avec elle'!

A moi, les examens!

Prépare-toi pour une conversation sur:

a ta famille, et ta famille idéale

ou

b ton/ta meilleur(e) ami(e), et ton ami(e) idéal(e).

A toi de choisir!

Entraîne-toi avec un(e) partenaire. Jouez les rôles de l'examinateur et du candidat, puis changez de rôle.

'L'examinateur' ne doit pas oublier d'avoir des réactions normales, et de dire par exemple: 'Ah bon?', 'Oui. . .', 'C'est intéressant', 'Pourquoi?'.

Conseils de l'examinateur

- Pendant l'examen, écoute attentivement pour bien comprendre les questions. Tu devrais reconnaître des mots-clés, par exemple:
  - ★ Tu as **combien** de frères et sœurs? (how many?)
    Tu vis avec **qui**? (who?)
  - ★ Elle est **comment**, ta sœur? (what is she like?)
  - ★ Vous vous disputez pour **quelles** raisons? (what reasons?)
  - ★ **Qu'est-ce que** vous faites ensemble? (what?)
  - ★ **Décris-moi** ton ami(e) idéal(e). (describe to me)
  - ★ **Parle-moi** de ton père. (tell me about)

  Peux-tu trouver d'autres mots importants?

- Pour répondre aux questions, essaie de dire plus que le minimum. La conversation sera plus intéressante, et tu impressionneras l'examinateur!

- Si tu fais une erreur, ne t'inquiète pas. Corrige-la, puis continue.

- Essaie de trouver des moyens de dire ce que tu **veux** dire et ce que tu **sais** dire. Utilise, par exemple, la technique 'Oui. . ., et. . .' ou 'Non. . ., mais. . .', par exemple:

  'Je vis avec mes parents et ma sœur, et nous avons aussi un gros chien. . .'.
  'Je n'ai pas de frère ni de sœur, mais j'ai beaucoup de bons amis. On sort tout le temps ensemble. . .';

- Essaie de penser à l'avance aux questions que l'on pourrait te poser, et prépare tes réponses.

- Demande à ton professeur de corriger tes réponses, puis enregistre les questions et les réponses sur cassette. Tu pourras écouter la cassette quand tu feras ta révision.

Je vis avec mes parents, mon frère et ma grand-mère. En général, je m'entends bien avec eux. . .

A moi, les examens!

✳ Tu trouves cette lettre dans le magazine *Phosphore*. Ta sœur ne comprend pas le français. Explique-lui, en anglais, les quatre points principaux de la lettre.

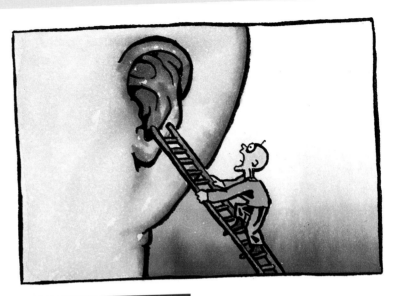

COURRIER

LES ADULTES NE NOUS ÉCOUTENT PAS

Je voudrais répondre à Marie (*Phosphore*, n° 109-février) qui se sent méprisée.

Ta lettre Marie, m'a beaucoup intéressée car je ressens souvent la même chose que toi. . . Tu dis que ton problème n'en est pas un, mais moi je pense le contraire. . . Il est très important car je crois qu'il concerne tous les jeunes d'aujourd'hui. Toi, tu es une personne à part entière qui a le droit de s'exprimer comme tout le monde. Les adultes ont tendance à penser que nous les jeunes, nous ne savons pas de quoi nous parlons et que nous sommes incapables d'avoir des idées précises, il nous sous-estiment! Alors ils nous laissent de côté en nous répétant de nous taire car nous n'y connaissons rien. . . Eh bien moi je dis non! Je crois que la société doit nous écouter, car nous avons des choses à dire! Je ne dis pas que toutes nos idées sont justes, mais que c'est par la confrontation avec les adultes que nos pensées pourront évoluer et s'épanouir. Il y a des adultes qui «se la jouent» un peu trop et qui feraient mieux d'écouter ce que pensent les jeunes. . . Je suis sûre qu'ils pourraient apprendre beaucoup. Car nous voyons les choses d'une autre manière et cela peut toujours apporter des éléments de réponse à certains problèmes.

Cécile, 1ʳᵉ S.

Conseils de l'examinateur

- Avant de lire la lettre, lis le titre. Il te donnera une idée du thème de la lettre.

- Lis la lettre en entier d'abord, puis relis-la et essaie d'identifier les points principaux.

- Dans cette lettre, il n'y a pas de paragraphes pour t'aider. Alors, examine chaque phrase attentivement. Quand tu trouves une idée, vérifie si la phrase suivante ne contient pas le développement de la même idée.

- Il est dangereux de baser ta réponse sur une illustration, mais elle peut t'aider à la confirmer. Au moins, l'illustration ne devrait pas contredire ta réponse.

A moi, les examens!

Tu vois cette lettre dans une revue française. Tu décides d'y répondre.

Ecris ta lettre et réponds aux trois questions de Frédéric.

Le conflit des générations

J'ai seize ans et j'ai un frère de dix-sept ans. Je m'entends bien avec mon frère, mais j'ai de très mauvaises relations avec mes parents. Ils ne me comprennent pas, et nous nous disputons tout le temps.

Je voudrais savoir ce que d'autres jeunes pensent du conflit des générations. A votre avis, quels sont les principaux problèmes entre les deux générations? Pour trouver une solution à ces problèmes, qui devrait changer, à votre avis: les parents, les enfants, ou les deux? Et comment devraient-ils changer?

Frédéric (Boulogne)

Conseils de l'examinateur

- Lis attentivement la lettre. Tu dois répondre à trois questions. Note-les.

- Dans un examen, tu trouveras souvent des mots et des expressions utiles dans la lettre ou l'article. Mais il faudra quelquefois les changer. N'oublie pas les principes de la grammaire!

  Par exemple, ici, tu peux utiliser ou adapter les expressions suivantes:

  ★ **Je m'entends bien avec**
  (**s'entendre**: Beaucoup de jeunes s'entendent mal avec leurs parents.)

  ★ **Ils ne me comprennent pas**
  (**comprendre**: Souvent, les jeunes ne comprennent pas leurs parents. Ils devraient essayer de les comprendre.)

  Peux-tu trouver d'autres expressions utiles dans cet article?

Tu comprends maintenant?

Je vérifie

Est-ce que tu sais maintenant parler de la famille? Vérifie avec ces activités. Si tu préfères, révise un peu d'abord.

★ **Votre classe-partenaire voudrait savoir si, dans ton pays, vous avez les mêmes problèmes de générations qu'en France.**

Activité 1

Quels sont les problèmes en France? Ecoute la cassette, lis la lettre et prends des notes.

> Calais, le 30 avril
>
> Chers amis,
>
> Nous avons promis de vous envoyer les interviews que nous avons faites sur les problèmes de générations. Voici la cassette.
>
> Moi, personnellement, je pense que s'il y a des problèmes, c'est de la faute de tout le monde. Je crois que les parents n'aiment pas l'idée de nous voir grandir et changer. Ils trouvent étrange quand on ne leur raconte plus tous nos problèmes. Ils ont peut-être oublié qu'eux aussi, ils sont passés par là – En même temps, il me semble qu'ils ont besoin d'être compris, à leur tour.
>
> Avez-vous les mêmes problèmes chez vous?
> Nous attendons votre réponse avec impatience.
>
> A bientôt,
>
> Vanessa

Activité 2

Discute avec deux ou trois amis de ce que pensent les élèves français. Pensez-vous qu'il y a les mêmes problèmes dans votre pays? Est-ce qu'il y en a d'autres?

Activité 3

Préparez ensemble un rapport à envoyer à votre classe-partenaire française.

a Préparez des notes sur:
   - les problèmes en France
   - les problèmes dans votre pays
   - vos conclusions: avez-vous les mêmes problèmes?

b Faites un brouillon, puis vérifiez-le. Pouvez-vous l'améliorer?

c Ecrivez votre rapport.

Tu te rappelles?

■ Je sais parler de ma famille

Je me dispute beaucoup avec mon frère. Il est agressif et quelquefois assez méchant.	I argue a lot with my brother. He's aggressive and sometimes quite nasty.
Et vous, vous vous entendez bien dans ta famille?	What about you, do you get on well in your family?
Oui. Nous, on s'entend très bien.	Yes, we get on very well.
Et toi? Tu as de bons rapports avec tes sœurs?	What about you? Do you have a good relationship with your sisters?
Oui, je me confie à elles, si j'ai un problème.	Yes, I confide in them, if I have a problem.
Mes parents sont séparés et je vis avec mon père. Je m'entends très bien avec lui. Il est sympathique et amusant. On se dispute rarement.	My parents are separated and I live with my father. I get on very well with him. He's nice, and funny. We rarely argue.
Ma mère est calme et charmante. Mon père est plus nerveux qu'elle.	My mother is calm and charming. My father is more touchy than she is.
Je partage une chambre avec ma petite sœur. Elle m'énerve! On se dispute pour des raisons bêtes, par exemple quand elle veut emprunter mes affaires.	I share a room with my little sister. She gets on my nerves! We argue for stupid reasons, for example when she wants to borrow my things.

■ Je sais parler des relations entre les générations

Je crois que les parents oublient qu'ils ont été jeunes, eux aussi.	I think that parents forget that they too were young.
Ils ne comprennent pas les problèmes des adolescents.	They don't understand teenagers' problems.
Je ne suis pas d'accord. Moi, mes parents m'écoutent et m'aident à résoudre mes problèmes.	I don't agree. My parents listen to me and help me with my problems.
Les parents idéaux seraient stricts, mais raisonnables.	The ideal parents would be strict but reasonable.
Les enfants devraient, eux aussi, essayer de comprendre leurs parents.	Children should try to understand their parents, too.
Ils devraient être plus honnêtes avec eux.	They should be more honest with them.

Je révise

Utilise ce tableau pour réviser les phrases-clés de cette étape. Voici une activité:

★ Trouve dans le tableau des phrases qui correspondent aux illustrations **A** et **B**.

A   B

12ème Etape

Dans une famille

Mes objectifs

Si tu as la possibilité de passer quelques jours dans une famille, tu as de la chance! Tu feras sûrement de grands progrès en français, et tu verras comment vit une famille française!

Mais, certains jeunes hésitent à faire un échange. Ils pensent qu'ils ne sauront pas quoi faire ni quoi dire.

Pas de problème! Dans cette étape, tu vas apprendre les mots et les expressions qui t'aideront à être un(e) invité(e) idéal(e) dans une famille. Ainsi, tu pourras sans problème:

- arriver dans la famille
- demander où se trouve quelque chose
- emprunter quelque chose
- demander la permission de faire quelque chose
- prendre des repas en famille
- aider à la maison
- offrir un cadeau
- partir et remercier la famille.

B

Je comprends

Il n'est pas difficile d'être un(e) invité(e) idéal(e)! Regarde les photos et écoute Ahmed, un élève français, qui a passé une semaine chez les Jaubert, en Belgique.

Attention! Les conversations ne sont pas dans le bon ordre. Peux-tu identifier la photo qui correspond à chaque conversation?

A

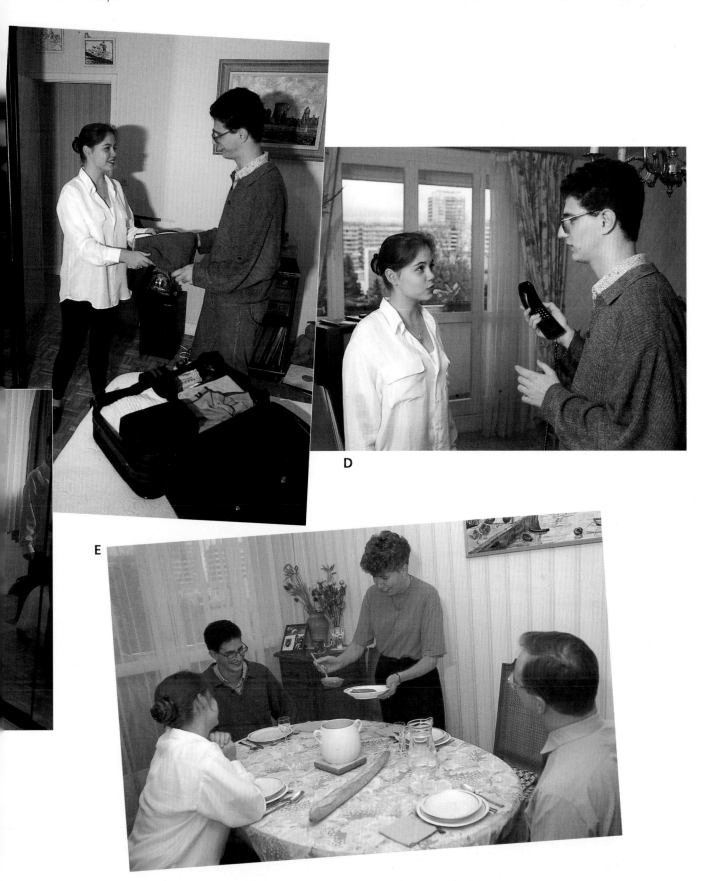

D

E

A ton avis, pourrais-tu parler avec assurance dans toutes ces situations? Si oui, bravo! Sinon, tu trouveras des exercices pour t'aider dans le Livre de révision (A table!, page 23 et A la maison, page 33).

Dans cette étape, tu vas apprendre des mots et expressions utiles dans trois autres situations:

■ **aider à la maison**
■ **offrir un cadeau**
■ **partir et remercier la famille.**

Tu apprendras aussi comment dire ce que tu fais pour aider à la maison.

Je peux vous aider?

1 ► *Je comprends et je répète*

Pour être un(e) invité(e) idéal(e) dans une famille, tu peux aider à la maison.
Voici ce que tu pourrais faire pour aider:

A faire le ménage

B faire la vaisselle

C essuyer la vaisselle

D faire la cuisine

E mettre la table

F débarrasser la table

G faire la lessive

H repasser le linge

I passer l'aspirateur

J ranger le salon

K faire les courses

L promener le chien

M laver la voiture

a Ecoute la cassette. Ces invités proposent de faire quelles tâches? Pour chaque personne, écris la lettre de l'illustration qui correspond.

b Réécoute la cassette.
- La première fois, répète ce que disent les gens qui proposent de faire les tâches que tu voudrais faire.
- La deuxième fois, répète ce que disent les gens qui proposent de faire les tâches que tu ne voudrais pas faire.

A l'aide!

une tâche ménagère: un travail domestique

2 ► *Je comprends et je répète*

Tu vois! Proposer d'aider quelqu'un est très simple. Tu peux tout simplement demander: 'Je peux. . . ?'. Mais tu peux utiliser d'autres expressions si tu veux.

a Ecoute et lis les conversations suivantes et trouve trois autres moyens de proposer ton aide:

> – Je peux vous aider?
> – Ah oui, c'est très gentil. Tu peux essuyer la vaisselle si tu veux.

> – Je peux vous aider à mettre la table?
> – Merci, mais c'est déjà fait.

> – Je peux vous donner un coup de main pour faire le ménage?
> – Merci, c'est gentil. Veux-tu passer l'aspirateur dans le salon?

A l'aide!

Tu connais déjà le mot 'main'. Peux-tu deviner le sens de 'donner un coup de main'? Pour vérifier, regarde dans le dictionnaire.

b Lis les conversations avec un(e) partenaire.

3

Pour être poli, on propose souvent de faire des choses qu'on ne veut pas faire! Il faut quand même parler avec enthousiasme!
Ecoute ces invités. Répète ce que disent ceux qui sont les plus polis et qui proposent d'aider avec enthousiasme.

4 ►

Jeu

Travaille avec un(e) partenaire.
Partenaire **A** (l'hôte(sse)) fait une liste de sept tâches à faire à la maison.
Partenaire **B** (l'invité(e)) fait une liste de sept tâches qu'il/elle veut faire pour aider à la maison.
B propose à **A** de faire ces sept tâches. Pour chaque tâche qui est sur sa liste, **A** répond: 'Merci, c'est gentil!' et **B** gagne un point. Pour les tâches qui ne sont pas sur sa liste, **A** répond: 'Merci, mais c'est déjà fait!', et **A** gagne le point.

A l'aide!

Les phrases-clés:

Je peux vous aider?
Je peux vous donner un coup de main?
Je peux vous aider à faire le ménage?
Je peux mettre la table?

Exemple

> Je peux vous donner un coup de main? Je peux faire la vaisselle?

> Merci, mais c'est déjà fait!

5 ► *J'invente*

Travaillez en groupes de trois ou quatre.
Regardez les images sur la Fiche 12.1B et faites une liste des tâches qu'il faut faire.
Puis décidez qui va faire chaque tâche.

Exemple

– Jon, tu veux passer l'aspirateur?

– Ah, non! Je déteste passer l'aspirateur! Est-ce que je peux débarrasser la table?

– Moi, j'aime bien passer l'aspirateur. Je le ferai.

– D'accord.

Que fais-tu pour aider à la maison?

1 ► *Je comprends*

Travaille sur la Fiche 12.3. Quelques jeunes expliquent ce qu'ils font pour aider à la maison.

2 ► *J'invente*

Et toi? Quelles tâches fais-tu pour aider à la maison? Quand est-ce que tu les fais? Tous les jours, souvent, une ou deux fois par semaine, quelquefois ou rarement?
Fais une liste de toutes les tâches et dis quand tu les fais. Commence par les tâches que tu fais le plus souvent, et finis par les tâches que tu ne fais jamais.

> Je fais mon lit et je promène le chien tous les jours.
> Je mets et je débarrasse la table quatre à cinq fois par semaine.
> Je range et souvent je fais le ménage dans ma chambre.
> Je passe rarement l'aspirateur.
> Je ne repasse jamais le linge.
> Je ne lave jamais la voiture. ...

3 ►

Qui travaille le plus à la maison: les femmes/les filles ou les hommes/les garçons?

a Invente un questionnaire pour faire un sondage dans ta classe. Essaie de deviner les résultats!
C'est à toi de décider de la forme du questionnaire.
Voici deux exemples:

A

Nom: _____

Qui fait les tâches suivantes chez toi? Coche la réponse correcte.
Tu peux cocher plus d'une personne pour chaque tâche.

	moi	ma mère/ ma belle-mère	mon père/ mon beau-père	mon frère	ma sœur	autre
Qui fait la cuisine?						
Qui fait la vaisselle?						

B

Nom: _____

Qui fait le ménage chez toi? Réponds aux questions suivantes:
En général:

Qui met la table? _____

Qui débarrasse la table? _____

b Distribue les questionnaires.

c Analyse les résultats. Fais le total des tâches ménagères faites par les femmes/les filles et les hommes/les garçons. Qui travaille le plus à la maison? Quelles tâches sont faites le plus souvent par les femmes/les filles et par les hommes/les garçons? Tu as deviné juste?

A l'aide!

N'oublie pas les différentes formes des verbes, par exemple:

Je **fais** la vaisselle et mon frère **fait** les courses.

Je **mets** souvent la table, mais ma sœur ne **met** jamais la table.

Mes deux frères **débarrassent** la table.

4 ►

Réponds à la lettre de Martin sur la Fiche 12.3. Réponds à toutes ses questions.

Voici un cadeau pour vous

 1 ▸ *Je comprends*

Un(e) invité(e) poli(e) dit toujours merci! C'est aussi une bonne idée d'offrir
un cadeau à ses hôtes. On peut l'offrir quand on arrive ou quand on part.

a Lis et écoute ces deux conversations. Dans chaque conversation, est-ce
que l'invitée vient d'arriver ou est-elle en train de partir?

A		**B**	
Mère:	Eh bien. . . bon retour, Sandra.	*Correspondante:*	Maman, je te présente Sandra.
Invitée:	Merci. . . et merci beaucoup pour votre hospitalité. J'ai passé un très bon séjour avec vous.	*Mère:*	Bienvenue, Sandra. Tu as fait bon voyage?
Mère:	Ça nous a fait plaisir!	*Invitée:*	Oui, merci. Je vous ai apporté un cadeau.
Invitée:	Voici un petit cadeau pour vous.	*Mère:*	Oh, c'est très gentil! Merci!
Mère:	Oh, merci beaucoup!	*Invitée:*	Et voici un cadeau pour toi, Nadège.
		Correspondante:	Merci beaucoup, Sandra!

b Trouve dans les conversations des expressions utiles pour:
- remercier l'hôte(sse) avant de partir
- offrir un cadeau à quelqu'un.

c Tu comprends tous les mots? Par exemple, peux-tu deviner le sens des
mots **séjour** et **apporté**? Pour vérifier, cherche-les dans un dictionnaire.

2 ▸ *Je répète*

Voici quatre expressions utiles pour offrir un cadeau. Quelles
expressions pourrais-tu utiliser pour parler à ton/ta correspondant(e)?
Et à ses parents? Pourquoi?

> Je vous ai apporté un petit cadeau.
>
> Voici un petit cadeau pour toi.
>
> Je t'ai apporté un petit cadeau.
>
> Voici un petit cadeau pour vous.

  3

As-tu beaucoup d'assurance ou es-tu un peu timide? Ça n'a pas d'importance!
L'important, c'est d'être sincère!
Ecoute la cassette. La première fois, répète ce que disent les invités qui ont
beaucoup d'assurance.
La deuxième fois, répète ce que disent les invités qui sont un peu timides.
Mais ne répète pas ce que disent ceux qui n'ont pas l'air sincère!

4 ▸ *J'invente*

Travaille avec un(e) partenaire. Inventez des conversations pour les situations
suivantes:
Rôle A: l'invité(e)
Rôle B: le/la correspondant(e) français(e)
Rôle C: le père/la mère.

a **A** arrive dans la famille française. Il/Elle a apporté un cadeau pour **C**.
b **B** va chercher **A** à la gare. **A** a apporté un cadeau pour **B**.
c C'est la fin du séjour. **A** offre un cadeau aux parents de **B**, et les remercie.

Apprenez vos conversations et jouez-les devant vos amis, sans regarder vos notes!

A moi, les examens!

 1

Tu es en France avec ton frère. Tu écoutes la radio: c'est une interview avec une femme. Ton frère ne comprend pas bien le français. Réponds à ses questions:

a What is the woman talking about?

b What is her attitude towards her family?

c Why does she have this attitude? (Explain in detail.)

Conseils de l'examinateur

- Avant d'écouter, lis les questions attentivement, pour savoir ce qu'on te demande.

- La première fois que tu écoutes la cassette, note le sujet de l'interview, pour la question **a**.

- Ecoute ce que dit la femme. A ton avis, quelle est son attitude (question **b**)? Pour connaître l'attitude de quelqu'un, il faut souvent 'lire entre les lignes'. Par exemple:
  - ★ Il/Elle pourrait faire des commentaires, comme: 'Ça m'énerve! J'en ai vraiment marre!', ou 'C'est génial!'.
  - ★ Il/Elle pourrait aussi décrire la situation: à toi de tirer tes conclusions! Exemples:
    'Ils ne disent jamais merci.'
    'Elle fait les courses pour moi tous les jours.'
  - ★ Fais attention à la voix de la personne. Est-ce qu'il/elle parle d'un ton fâché, content, triste, etc?

- La deuxième fois que tu écoutes la cassette, note les raisons de l'attitude de la femme avec sa famille.

 2

Ecoute ces cinq jeunes. Pour chaque personne, note la lettre de la meilleure description:

A poli(e)

B timide

C impoli(e)

D peu enthousiaste

E fâché(e)

F fatigué(e)

G enthousiaste

Conseils de l'examinateur

- Avant d'écouter, prépare-toi. Lis les sept descriptions. Qu'est-ce que ces mots veulent dire en anglais?

- Attention! As-tu remarqué? Il y a cinq personnes, mais sept descriptions.

A moi, les examens!

1 ►

Jeux de rôles

Travaille avec un(e) partenaire.

Partenaire **A** a passé une semaine chez sa correspondante belge. C'est la fin du séjour, et partenaire **B**, la mère/le père de la correspondante, dit au revoir à **A**.

a Lis ton scénario, mais ne lis pas le scénario de ton/ta partenaire!

Scénario A: l'invité(e)

Tu remercies **B** avant de partir. Tu as passé un très bon séjour avec la famille. Tu veux être très poli(e). Mais, l'autobus pour la gare devrait arriver dans dix minutes et l'arrêt d'autobus est à cinq minutes de la maison. . .

Conseil de l'examinateur

● Avant de jouer, prépare quelques expressions que tu peux utiliser.
Comment vas-tu remercier **B** d'une façon polie et sincère? Qu'est-ce que tu peux faire pour ne pas être en retard pour ton bus, sans être impoli(e)? Exemple: 'Je suis désolé(e), mais je dois vraiment partir.'

Scénario B: l'hôte(sse)

A est prêt(e) à partir. Ta fille lui a acheté un cadeau, mais elle ne le trouve pas. Essaie de parler à **A** pendant que ta fille cherche le cadeau.

Conseil de l'examinateur

● Avant de jouer, prépare quelques expressions que tu peux utiliser.
Qu'est-ce que tu peux faire pour empêcher **A** de partir? Tu pourrais, par exemple, lui demander s'il/ si elle n'a rien oublié, ou s'il/si elle voudrait des sandwiches pour le train. . .

b Ensuite, discutez de vos stratégies. Comment pourriez-vous les changer pour les améliorer? Puis, changez de rôle. Vous avez fait des progrès?

2 ►

Conversation

a Prépare-toi pour une conversation au sujet des tâches ménagères.

Conseils de l'examinateur

● Prépare des réponses aux questions qu'on pourrait te poser, par exemple:
  ★ Qu'est-ce que tu fais pour aider à la maison?
  ★ Que font les autres membres de ta famille?
  ★ A ton avis, est-ce que les femmes devraient faire plus de tâches ménagères que les hommes? Pourquoi ou pourquoi pas?

● N'oublie pas de donner des réponses intéressantes, avec des informations supplémentaires. Par exemple:
  'Je fais mon lit tous les jours, et je range ma chambre une fois par semaine. Je n'aime pas passer l'aspirateur, mais je le fais de temps en temps. . .'
  est plus intéressante que la réponse:
  'Je fais mon lit, je range ma chambre et je passe l'aspirateur'.

● N'oublie pas que dans une vraie conversation, on pose des questions aussi. Prépare des questions à poser.

b Discute des tâches ménagères avec ton/ta partenaire. Est-ce qu'il/elle fait les mêmes choses que toi? Est-ce qu'il/elle en fait plus ou moins que toi à la maison? Qu'est-ce qu'il/elle aime et n'aime pas faire?

A moi, les examens!

✱ Pendant un cours au collège, vous discutez des tâches ménagères. Tu as trouvé cet article dans un magazine français. Prends des notes en anglais pour résumer à ta classe les opinions des jeunes Français.

Qui devrait faire les tâches ménagères?
Des jeunes donnent leurs points de vue...

'Moi, je pense que c'est à la femme de faire les tâches ménagères parce que c'est le rôle d'une femme de s'occuper de la maison. Si elle veut travailler aussi, c'est son choix.

De toute façon, il n'y a pas beaucoup de travail à faire à la maison – ce n'est pas difficile, quand même!

Quant aux enfants, à mon avis, ils ne devraient pas aider à la maison. Ils ont beaucoup de devoirs à faire et le travail scolaire, c'est très important pour eux.

En plus, quand on est jeune, on devrait s'amuser, jouer, et lire. On aura assez de travail plus tard!'

Nathalie Catélan

'A mon avis, si on vit en famille, on doit tout faire pour en assurer l'harmonie.

En ce qui concerne les tâches ménagères, je pense que tout le monde devrait participer. Sinon, il y a toujours une personne qui en fait beaucoup plus que les autres, et ça, ce n'est pas juste, surtout dans une famille où tous les adultes travaillent.

Selon moi, les enfants devraient aider. Ils devraient apprendre qu'ils ont des responsabilités envers la famille, eux aussi.

Si tout le monde participe, les tâches sont faites plus rapidement, et tout le monde peut s'amuser.'

Patrick Dulle

Conseils de l'examinateur

● Tu dois résumer les opinions, donc il n'est pas nécessaire de traduire tout l'article. Essaie d'identifier et de noter les idées principales.

● N'oublie pas que la structure d'un article peut t'aider à le comprendre et à identifier les idées principales. Tu trouveras souvent que chaque paragraphe contient une idée.

A moi, les examens!

Tu viens de passer une semaine géniale chez Franck, ton correspondant français.

Il t'a envoyé cette lettre.

a Ecris une lettre à toute sa famille pour les remercier.

b Donne ta réaction aux photos que Franck t'a envoyées.

c Réponds aussi à toutes les questions de Franck.

Paris, le 4 septembre

Salut, Chris!

Je t'écris pour t'envoyer les photos que j'ai prises pendant ton séjour ici. Je trouve qu'elles sont super.

J'ai passé une très bonne semaine avec toi. On s'est bien amusé, non? Qu'est-ce que tu as aimé le plus?

Est-ce que ton voyage s'est bien passé? Tes parents sont venus te chercher à la gare?

Je te remercie beaucoup de m'avoir invité chez toi à Pâques. Je n'ai jamais visité ton pays. Peux-tu me décrire un peu ta ville?

Ecris-moi vite,

Amitiés,

Franck

Conseils de l'examinateur

● Lis attentivement les instructions. Tu dois:
   ★ écrire à toute la famille pour les remercier
   ★ donner ta réaction aux photos
   ★ répondre à toutes les questions de Franck (cherche-les!).
   Il faut faire tout ce qu'on te demande. Sinon, tu perdras des points.

● Si tu trouves que c'est difficile de répondre à une des questions, écris quand-même quelques mots.

● Quand tu auras fini, lis et vérifie ta lettre. Tu as bien répondu à tout ce qu'on te demande? Tu n'as pas fait d'erreurs?

Tu comprends maintenant?

Je vérifie

As-tu maintenant plus confiance en toi pour être l'invité(e) idéal(e) dans une famille? Fais ce petit test pour le savoir. En même temps, tu aideras d'autres élèves à avoir plus confiance en eux. . .

★ **Tu vas donner des conseils à une Française et à des élèves de ton pays qui vont faire un échange.**

Activité 1

Une amie française vous envoie ce message par courrier électronique. Discutez en groupes de son problème, puis écrivez une réponse, avec des conseils.

```
SALUT!
DANS QUELQUES SEMAINES, JE FAIS UN ECHANGE AVEC
MON PARTENAIRE DANS VOTRE REGION. JE M'INQUIETE UN
PEU, PARCE QUE JE NE SAIS PAS CE QUE JE DEVRAIS
FAIRE ET DIRE POUR ETRE VRAIMENT POLIE.
EST-CE QUE JE DEVRAIS APPORTER UN CADEAU, PAR
EXEMPLE? LA FAMILLE DE MON PARTENAIRE PARLE
FRANCAIS. EST-CE QUE JE DEVRAIS PARLER EN ANGLAIS
OU EN FRANCAIS AVEC EUX?
POUVEZ-VOUS ME DONNER DES CONSEILS POUR ETRE UNE
INVITEE PARFAITE (ET QUELQUES EXPRESSIONS ANGLAISES
POUR M'AIDER!)?
MERCI D'AVANCE.
AMITIES,
AXIANE
```

Activité 2

Maintenant, faites une liste de conseils pour des élèves de votre pays qui vont participer à un échange en France.

a Préparez vos idées.

Discutez des conseils les plus importants, et faites-en une liste.

b Ecrivez des conseils.

Vous pourriez faire une liste ou inventer des dialogues qui pourront vous servir d'exemples.

Exemples

Pour être un(e) invité(e) idéal(e):
- Offre un cadeau à tes hôtes.
- Fais ton lit.
- Propose d'aider à

Pour être un(e) invité(e) idéal(e), tu peux offrir un cadeau à tes hôtes:
- Voici un cadeau pour vous.
- C'est gentil! Merci!

c Inventez des sketchs.

Inventez une série de sketchs, avec des expressions-clés, où l'invité(e) est très poli(e).

Apprenez vos rôles et répétez vos sketchs. Si possible, jouez vos sketchs devant des élèves plus jeunes que vous, pour leur montrer que ce n'est pas difficile d'être un(e) invité(e) parfait(e)!

Tu te rappelles?

Je sais être un(e) invité(e) idéal(e)!

■ Je sais parler des tâches ménagères

Pour aider mes parents, je passe l'aspirateur et je promène le chien.	To help my parents, I vacuum and I walk the dog.
Quelquefois, je lave la voiture.	I sometimes wash the car.
Je range et je fais le ménage dans ma chambre, et je fais mon lit tous les jours.	I clean and tidy my room and I make my bed every day.
Je ne fais jamais la lessive (les courses).	I never do the washing (the shopping).
Mon frère repasse le linge et mon père fait la cuisine.	My brother does the ironing and my father does the cooking.
Je déteste faire le ménage (et essuyer la vaisselle)!	I hate doing housework (and drying the dishes)!

■ Je sais proposer mon aide à la maison

Je peux vous donner un coup de main?	Can I give you a hand?
Je peux vous aider?	Can I help you?
Je peux débarrasser la table?	Can I clear the table?
Est-ce que je peux vous aider à faire la vaisselle (à mettre la table)?	Can I help you do the dishes (set the table)?

■ Je sais offrir un cadeau

Je vous ai apporté un cadeau.	I've brought you a present.
Madame Jouan, voici un petit cadeau pour vous.	Madame Jouan, here's a small present for you.
Claude, je t'ai apporté un cadeau.	Claude, I've brought you a present.
Voici un cadeau pour toi.	Here's a present for you.

■ Je sais remercier mes hôtes

Merci beaucoup pour votre hospitalité.	Thank you very much for your hospitality.
J'ai passé un très bon séjour ici.	I've really enjoyed my stay here.

Je révise

Tu peux utiliser ce tableau pour réviser les phrases-clés de cette étape. Voici quelques activités:

● Combien de choses y a-t-il dans l'illustration? Trouve dans le tableau une phrase pour chaque objet.

● Travaille avec un(e) partenaire. Mime une tâche ménagère. Ton/Ta partenaire devine quelle tâche tu fais et propose de t'aider.

Pages jaunes: grammaire

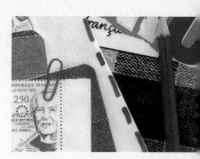

1ère Etape
the future tense (1)

On parle souvent de l'avenir. Par exemple, on lit son horoscope et on écoute la météo pour savoir quel temps il fera.

En anglais et en français, on emploie souvent **le futur**. C'est très utile. Par exemple, on peut l'employer:

★ pour parler de l'**avenir** (predictions)
★ pour faire des **projets** (plans)
★ pour prendre des **résolutions** (resolutions).

Peux-tu identifier les prédictions, les projets et les résolutions?

A *Je passerai chez toi à 9h, d'accord?*

B *Lis ton horoscope. Tu partiras en vacances avec l'homme de ta vie!*

C *Je ne sortirai pas avec mes parents ce soir, je déteste l'opéra!*

D *Pour être en bonne santé, je mangerai plus de fruits et de légumes. Je ne mangerai pas de frites.*

E *Tu n'aimeras pas ce film. Je l'ai vu, il est ennuyeux.*

F *J'apprendrai à parler italien cette année.*

Le principe

● It is very easy to form the future tense! Look at examples **A** to **F** above. Can you identify the endings (the last two letters) which go with **je** and **tu**?

Answer

★ **je** takes **-ai**; **tu** takes **-as**.

● But what do you add the endings to? Look carefully at the examples above.

Answer

● Take the infinitive form of the verb.
● For verbs ending in **-er** or **-ir**, simply add the appropriate ending:
  ★ passer → je passer**ai**
  ★ partir → tu partir**as**
● For verbs ending in **-re**, remove the final 'e' before adding the ending:
  ★ apprendre → j'apprendr**ai**

✳ 2

a Tu fais des projets pour le week-end prochain. Voici quelques idées d'activités que tu pourras faire si tu as du temps libre.
Choisis-en cinq, et note-les.

Exemple

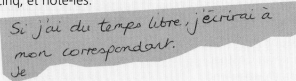

Ce week-end, je peux:
– écrire à mon correspondant
– laver la voiture
– regarder la télé
– jouer avec mon ordinateur
– écouter de la musique
– sortir avec mes amis
– visiter un musée
– lire un bon livre
– jouer au ping-pong.

the future tense (2)

Le principe

- How do you say what you **will not** do? Look back at the examples in activity **1** ► to find out.

- It is simple. Just put **ne** or **n'** and **pas** around the verb as usual:
  - ★ tu **n'**aimeras **pas** ce film: you won't like this film
  - ★ je **ne** laverai **pas** la voiture: I won't wash the car

b Maintenant, écris les activités que tu ne feras pas.

c Tu as choisi les mêmes activités que ton/ta partenaire? Pose-lui des questions.

Tu regarderas la télé, si tu as du temps libre?

Non, je ne regarderai pas la télé, mais j'écouterai des disques.

Le principe

- You have also been using four verbs which do not follow the regular pattern:
  - ★ faire → je **fer**ai (I will do)
  - ★ être → je **ser**ai (I will be)
  - ★ avoir → j'**aur**ai (I will have)
  - ★ aller → j'**ir**ai (I will go)

- The endings are the same for all verbs in the future tense, but the first part of the verb is sometimes irregular. You need to learn these irregular verbs.

✳ **3**

Entraîne-toi à utiliser ces verbes. Recopie et complète les réponses des questions suivantes.

1 Tu penses que tu seras marié(e) dans dix ans?
    Non, je pense que _____ célibataire.
2 Tu auras des animaux à la maison plus tard?
    Oui, _____ deux chats.
3 Tu as fait tes devoirs?
    Non, _____ mes devoirs ce soir.
4 Tu es allé(e) voir le nouveau film de Kevin Costner?
    Non, mais _____ au cinéma ce week-end.

4

Tu as déjà écrit quelques résolutions pour la nouvelle année scolaire. Tu peux maintenant ajouter d'autres résolutions à ta liste. Recopie et complète ces phrases:

Cette année, je ferai. . .   **J'apprendrai. . .**   **J'irai. . .**

the future tense (3)

Deuxième partie

Tu sais déjà qu'on emploie **le futur**, en français comme en anglais:

★ pour parler de l'avenir   ★ pour faire des projets   ★ et pour prendre des résolutions

On peut aussi l'employer, en français comme en anglais:

★ pour donner des **ordres** (orders)

★ pour faire des **promesses** (promises)

★ pour parler d'**intentions** (intentions)

★ pour donner des **avertissements** (warnings)

> *Vous ferez vos devoirs pour lundi, d'accord?*

> *Oui, madame, nous ferons nos devoirs pour lundi.*

> *Mes parents iront en France pendant les vacances, et ma sœur ira en Irlande.*

> *Si vous ne partez pas maintenant, vous serez en retard!*

Tu sais déjà employer le futur avec **je** et **tu**. Regarde les exemples ci-dessus pour savoir comment le faire avec **il/elle, nous**, **vous** et **ils/elles**. Regarde le résumé pour vérifier.

5

Nos projets dépendent souvent du temps qu'il fera.
Recopie et complète cette conversation:

– Que fais-tu ce week-end?
– Ben. . . s'il fait beau, je
  et ma sœur
  avec ses amis. Et toi?
– S'il fait beau, mon frère et moi, nous
  Mais s'il pleut, nous
– Et dimanche?
– Mes parents aiment sortir. S'il fait beau, ils
  Moi, je n'aime pas ça. S'il y a un bon film, j'

faire une promenade

aller au cinéma

jouer au tennis

aller à la pêche

faire un pique-nique

regarder la télé

Résumé

● To form the future tense, add endings to the infinitive of the verb. For verbs ending in **-re**, first remove the 'e'.

manger	**partir**	**apprendre**
je manger**ai**	je partir**ai**	j'apprendr**ai**
tu manger**as**	tu partir**as**	tu apprendr**as**
il manger**a**	il partir**a**	il apprendr**a**
elle manger**a**	elle partir**a**	elle apprendr**a**
on manger**a**	on partir**a**	on apprendr**a**
nous manger**ons**	nous partir**ons**	nous apprendr**ons**
vous manger**ez**	vous partir**ez**	vous apprendr**ez**
ils manger**ont**	ils partir**ont**	ils apprendr**ont**
elles manger**ont**	elles partir**ont**	elles apprendr**ont**

● *Tip:* a good way of remembering the future tense endings is to think of the endings of the present tense of **avoir**: j'**ai**; tu **as**; il **a**; nous av**ons**; vous av**ez**; ils **ont**.

● For a few verbs, you do not add the endings to the infinitive form, but to a different root. You need to learn these by heart. Here are the most common ones:

être: je **ser**ai   voir: on **verr**a   savoir: elles **saur**ont
avoir: tu **aur**as   pouvoir: nous **pourr**ons   devoir: je **devr**ai
aller: il **ir**a   vouloir: vous **voudr**ez   acheter: tu **achèter**as
faire: elle **fer**a   venir: ils **viendr**ont   il faut: il **faudr**a

1

✱ **a** Regarde ces renseignements sur le camping
Saint-Grégoire et choisis les réponses correctes.

1 Vous avez des machines à laver?
  a Oui, nous en avons cinq.
  b Je suis désolé, nous n'en avons pas.

2 Il y a un bar au camping?
  a Non, mais il y en a un à la plage.
  b Oui, il y en a deux.

3 Vous avez des douches chaudes?
  a Oui, il y en a au bloc sanitaire.
  b Non, il n'y en a pas.

4 Il y a de l'eau chaude?
  a Non, il n'y en a pas.
  b Oui, il y en a, aux douches et aux lavabos.

> **Camping Saint-Grégoire**
> **Installations**
> magasin
> restaurant
> 2 bars
> terrain de jeux
> douches chaudes
> lavabos avec eau chaude
> prises de courant

b Trouve les expressions françaises dans la section **a** qui veulent dire:

★ Il n'y a pas <u>de douches chaudes</u>.
★ Il y a deux <u>bars</u>.
★ Il y a <u>de l'eau chaude</u> aux douches et aux lavabos.
★ Nous avons cinq <u>machines à laver</u>.
★ Il n'y a pas <u>d'eau chaude</u>.
★ Il y a <u>des douches chaudes</u> au bloc sanitaire.
★ Non, mais il y a un <u>bar</u> à la plage.
★ Nous n'avons pas de <u>machines à laver</u>.

Dans chaque phrase, les mots soulignés sont représentés dans la section **a**
par quel mot? Quelle est la position de ce mot dans la phrase?

Le principe

● The word **en** can save you repeating a longer word or a whole phrase.
We do something similar in English, when we say 'some', 'any', 'of it'
and 'of them'.
Find the phrases above which mean:

★ there are some
★ there is one
★ there aren't any (of them)
★ we have five of them

★ there are two of them
★ there is some
★ we don't have any
★ there isn't any (of that)

● Notice that the word **en** goes directly before the verb:

★ je n'en **ai** pas
★ il y en **a** deux
★ nous n'en **avons** pas

★ il n'y en **a** pas
★ nous en **avons** deux
★ j'en **ai** trois

2

Tu peux utiliser le mot **en** pour parler d'autres choses! Par exemple, réponds
à ces questions:

1 As-tu des frères?
2 Avez-vous un chien à la maison?
3 Il y a une piscine dans ta ville?
4 As-tu des sœurs?
5 Il y a une plage près de chez toi?

Exemple
1 As-tu des frères?
Oui, j'en ai deux.
ou Non, je n'en ai pas.

ce/cet/cette/ces (1)

1

a Un campeur est dans un magasin de matériel de camping:

Campeur: Cette lampe de poche coûte combien?

Vendeuse: Elle coûte 80F.

Campeur: Et ces piles?

Vendeuse: Elles sont à 42F le paquet.

Campeur: Ces sacs de couchage à gauche, ils coûtent combien?

Vendeuse: Ils coûtent 160F.

Campeur: Est-ce que je peux voir ce sac de couchage à droite?

Vendeuse: Oui, monsieur. Il est de très bonne qualité.

Campeur: Oui, mais il est assez cher. Je vais devoir aller à la banque. Je reviendrai cet après-midi.

b Peux-tu trouver des mots qui veulent dire 'this/that' et 'these'? Tu comprends le principe?

Le principe

- There are three words for 'this/that':
  - ★ with **masculine** words (un):

    ce   Est-ce que je peux voir **ce** sac de couchage?
  - ★ with **masculine words which begin with a vowel** (a,e,i,o,u) or **h**:

    cet   Je reviendrai **cet** après-midi.

    Où est **cet** hôtel?
  - ★ with **feminine** words (une):

    cette   Elle coûte combien, **cette** lampe de poche?
- There is one word for 'these', whether the following word is masculine or feminine:

    ces   Elles coûtent combien, **ces** piles?

    Je peux voir **ces** sacs de couchage?

2

Prépare-toi à acheter du matériel de camping. N'oublie pas, pour être sûr(e), tu peux:

★ demander de voir l'article que tu veux acheter:
  - Est-ce que je peux voir cette lampe, s'il vous plaît?

★ demander le prix:
  - Ce bol coûte combien?
  - Ces assiettes en plastique coûtent combien?

a Tu voudrais voir ces articles. Que dis-tu?

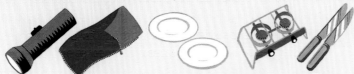

b Tu voudrais savoir le prix de ces articles. Que dis-tu?

ce/cet/cette/ces (2)

COULEURS ET
75 - PARIS
Coucher de Soleil sur la Sei
Serge Le Manouri

Deuxième partie

3

✳ **a** Ce campeur a le choix. Qu'est-ce qu'il achète?

  – Avez-vous des lampes, madame?
  – Oui, monsieur. Il y a **cette** lampe-**ci** qui est assez petite, et **cette** lampe-**là**, qui est plus grande.
  – Je prends **cette** lampe-**ci**: elle est moins chère. Je voudrais aussi des piles pour ma lampe de poche.
  – Nous avons **ces** piles-**ci**, en paquets de deux, et **ces** piles-**là**, en paquets de huit.
  – Je prends **ces** piles-**là**: j'en ai besoin de six.

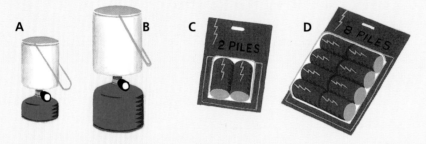

b Peux-tu trouver les mots qui veulent dire 'this one', 'that one', 'these ones', 'those ones'?

4

Tu as besoin de tous ces articles, mais tu as seulement 250F. Qu'est-ce que tu prends? Explique-le à ton/ta partenaire.

Exemple
– Je préfère ce bol-ci, mais ce bol-là est moins cher.

3ème Etape
le/la/les (1)

Première partie

1 ▶

Lis ces dialogues et note les lettres des vêtements qu'on achète:

1
– Vous aimez ces pulls?
– Oui, je les aime bien.
– Ce pull bleu, je peux l'essayer?. . . Bon, ça va, je le prends.

2
– Ces chaussures grises, je peux les essayer?
– Oui, madame.
– Elles sont très confortables, je les prends.

3
– Vous aimez cette cravate rayée?
– Oui, je l'aime beaucoup. Je la prends.

Travail de détective! Comment dit-on en français:

Regarde les exemples ci-dessus. Peux-tu deviner le principe?

I like	**it**
Can I try	
I'll take	**them**

Le principe

● **Singular** (one only) **it**
  ★ Masculine words (e.g. **le** pull)
    je **le** prends   I'll take **it**
  ★ Feminine words (e.g. **la** robe)
    je **la** prends   I'll take **it**
  ★ Masculine and feminine before a word beginning with a vowel
    je **l'**aime   I like it

● **Plural** (more than one) **them**
  ★ Masculine and feminine
    je **les** prends   I'll take **them**
● Have you noticed where the words 'it' and 'them' come? In English they come *after* the verb: I'll take **it**
  In French they come *before* the verb: je **le** prends

2 ▶

Tu vas tout acheter! Comment réponds-tu à la vendeuse?

Exemple
– Vous prenez cette robe?
– Oui, je la prends.

1 Vous prenez cette cravate?
2 Vous prenez ce jean?
3 Vous aimez ces chaussures vertes?
4 Vous aimez cet imperméable?
5 Vous prenez ces bottes?
6 Vous aimez cette ceinture?

3 ▶

Qu'est-ce qu'on dit si on n'aime pas un vêtement? Regarde l'illustration..

Le principe

● You already know that to say what you **do not** like or what you **will not** do, you put **ne** and **pas** around the verb. It is the same here, except you keep the word for 'it' or 'them' next to the verb, in front of it:

  ★ Je **ne** les aime **pas**
  ★ Je **ne** le prends **pas**

4 ▶

Réponds aux questions de la vendeuse (✓ = oui; ✗ = non):

1 Vous prenez cette chemise? ✗
2 Vous prenez ce gilet? ✗
3 Vous aimez ces sandales? ✓
4 Vous prenez ces chaussettes? ✗
5 Vous aimez cet imperméable? ✓
6 Vous aimez cette jupe? ✗

le/la/les (2)

Deuxième partie

5

Parler du passé, c'est facile aussi! Regarde ces exemples et note la position des mots **l'** et **les**.

> Je voudrais me plaindre de ce jean. Je l'ai acheté hier.

> Je voudrais me plaindre de ces chaussures. Je les ai achetées ce matin.

> Tu as vu mes nouveaux tee-shirts ? Je les ai reçus pour mon anniversaire.

> J'aime ta cravate. Merci, je l'ai achetée aux Galeries Goncourt.

Est-ce que tu remarques autre chose? (Regarde le mot **acheté**.)

Le principe

- As you know, the perfect tense is made up of two parts:
  - ★ **avoir** (or **être**) and the main verb, e.g.: j'**ai acheté**.
- In the perfect tense, the word for 'it' or 'them' comes *before* avoir.
- Did you also notice that the main verb has letters added, depending on what 'it' or 'them' stands for?
  - ★ **it: masculine**:
    Tu as vu mon pull? Je **l'**ai acheté hier.
  - ★ **it: feminine**:
    Voilà ma nouvelle jupe. Je **l'**ai acheté**e** ce matin.
  - ★ **them: masculine**:
    Tu aimes ces crayons? Je **les** ai acheté**s** pour ma petite sœur.
  - ★ **them: feminine**:
    Et ces chaussettes, je **les** ai acheté**es** pour mon père.

celui-ci/celui-là. . . (1)

1

Quels vêtements préfèrent-ils?

1
- Qu'est-ce que vous avez comme cravates?
- Nous avons celles-ci en laine, et celles-là en soie.
- Euh. . . je préfère celles-là.

2
- Je cherche une ceinture verte.
- Oui, madame. Nous avons celle-ci, en vert clair, et celle-là, en vert foncé.
- Je préfère celle-ci.

3
- Bonjour, madame. Vous avez des blousons?
- Oui, monsieur. Il y a ceux-ci, en cuir. Ou préférez-vous ceux-là, en laine?
- Je préfère ceux-là.

4
- Je cherche un imperméable. Est-ce que je peux essayer celui-ci?
- Bien sûr, madame. Le voilà. Nous avons aussi celui-là, en gris. Voulez-vous l'essayer?
- Non, je préfère celui-ci.

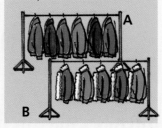

Travail de détective! Comment dit-on en français 'this one', 'that one', 'these ones' et 'those ones'? Peux-tu deviner le principe?

celui-ci/celui-là. . . (2)

Le principe

● It all depends on whether the item(s) you are referring to is (are) masculine or feminine:

	masculine	feminine	
singular	**celui-ci**	**celle-ci**	this one
	celui-là	**celle-là**	that one
plural	**ceux-ci**	**celles-ci**	these ones
	ceux-là	**celles-là**	those ones

2

Avec un(e) partenaire, adapte et joue le dialogue **2** (à la page 158) pour les vêtements suivants:

Le principe

● You can also use these words to say 'the _____ one(s)', e.g.:
  ★ Vous aimez ce pull en laine? (**un** pull)
    Oui, mais je préfère **celui** en coton. (I prefer **the** cotton **one**.)
  ★ Voici une jolie robe rose. (**une** robe)
    Je préfère **celle** en jaune. (I prefer **the** yellow one.)
  ★ Vous voudriez quels mouchoirs? (**un** mouchoir)
    Je voudrais **ceux** en soie. (I'd like **the** silk **ones**.)
  ★ Vous prenez les chaussettes en nylon? (**une** chaussette)
    Non, je prends **celles** en laine. (I'll take **the** woollen **ones**.)

✳ 3

Trouve une phrase pour chaque illustration de l'activité :

1 Je préfère celle en vert foncé.
2 Je prends celui en coton.
3 J'aime mieux celles en coton jaune.
4 Je préfère ceux en vert foncé.
5 Je prends celle en cuir bleu.
6 Je peux essayer celles en rouge et bleu?

the imperfect tense (1)

1

Les inventions ont-elles toujours des effets positifs? Voici deux inventions.
Recopie la phrase qui pour toi définie le mieux l'invention.

la télévision

a Avant la télévision, on s'ennuyait, le soir.

b Avant la télé, les gens jouaient et parlaient ensemble.

l'ordinateur

a Avant, on faisait des calculs longs et difficiles tandis que maintenant, les
maths, c'est plus facile.

b A cause des ordinateurs, nous avons maintenant des machines pour faire
notre travail. Avant, il y avait moins de chômage.

c Avant l'ordinateur, les gens n'avaient pas de jeux vidéo.

Le principe

- When we talk in French about what **used to happen** in the past, we
  use the **imperfect tense**. Find examples in the sentences above of
  verbs indicating the way things **used to be**. Can you work out the
  two endings for **il/elle/on** and **ils/elles**?

- To form the imperfect tense:
  - ★ Take the **nous** form of the verb
    in the present tense, and take off
    the **-ons**, e.g.:
    (nous) **pren**(ons)
    (nous) **av**(ons)
    (nous) **all**(ons)
    (nous) **fais**(ons)
    (nous) **finiss**(ons)

  - ★ Add the following endings:
    (je) - **ais**
    (tu) - **ais**
    (il, elle, on) - **ait**
    (nous) - **ions**
    (vous) - **iez**
    (ils, elles) - **aient**

avoir	j'**avais**
dire	tu **disais**
pouvoir	il **pouvait**
faire	elle **faisait**
être	on **était**
devoir	nous **devions**
savoir	vous **saviez**
finir	ils **finissaient**
jouer	elles **jouaient**
écrire	elles **écrivaient**

- As usual, the verb **être** is an exception: j'**ét**ais; tu **ét**ais; il **ét**ait;
  nous **ét**ions; vous **ét**iez; ils **ét**aient.

2

Ecris une phrase pour décrire la situation avant ces inventions:

Exemple
Avant l'invention du disque, on allait aux concerts pour écouter de la
musique.

Voici quelques expressions pour t'aider:
Grâce à ces inventions, il n'est plus
nécessaire:
- de voyager en bateau
- d'aller aux concerts pour écouter de
  la musique
- de lire les journaux pour les nouvelles
- d'aller partout à pied ou à cheval
- d'aller au cinéma pour voir des films.

the imperfect tense (2)

3

Lis les lettres sur la Fiche 4.2. Qui a le plus changé? Pour t'aider, souligne au crayon les phrases qui décrivent chaque personne **maintenant**; et souligne au stylo les descriptions de chaque personne **il y a cinq ans**.

Le principe

Tu as remarqué?

Infinitif	Présent	Imparfait
★ manger	nous mang**e**ons	je mang**e**ais

- Normalement, quand un verbe finit en **-er**, le '**e**' disparaît:

★ jouer	nous jouons	je jouais
★ regarder	nous regardons	je regardais

- Peux-tu deviner pourquoi **manger** est différent?

  C'est une question de prononciation: la lettre '**e**' change la prononciation de la lettre '**g**'. Par exemple, pense aux mots **gé**nial et **ga**rçon.

  Peux-tu recopier et compléter l'exemple suivant?

changer	nous _____	je _____
ranger	nous _____	je _____

4

Peux-tu trouver dans la lettre de Jean-Luc des réponses aux questions suivantes? Recopie-les dans ton cahier.

1 Est-ce que tu faisais du sport il y a cinq ans?

2 Est-ce que tu aimais la musique classique?

Peux-tu expliquer comment on parle des choses qu'on ne faisait pas dans le passé?

Le principe

- C'est très simple! Comme pour le présent, tu mets **ne** ou **n'** avant le verbe, et **pas** après le verbe.

★ Présent	★ Imparfait
je **ne** joue **pas** au tennis	je **ne** jouais **pas** au tennis
je **n'**aime **pas** le sport	je **n'**aimais **pas** le sport

5

Trouve trois choses que tu avais en commun avec ton/ta partenaire il y a cinq ans.

reflexive verbs (1)

Regarde ces illustrations. Une illustration n'est pas à la bonne place. Laquelle? Quelle est la bonne place?

 A Je me lève à 7h00.   **D** Je m'habille.

 B Je me lave.   **E** Je me réveille.

 C Je me brosse les dents.   **F** Je me couche à 10h30.

Le principe

- You use a special kind of verb, called a **reflexive verb**, to talk about certain things you do. Reflexive verbs often describe actions you do to yourself, although this is not always obvious in the English translation!
  - ★ **Je me lave**. I wash *myself*.
  - ★ **Je me couche**. I go to bed (I put *myself* to bed).
  - ★ **Tu te brosses les dents** tous les jours? Do you brush *your* teeth every day?
  - ★ **Il s'habille**. He dresses *himself*.
  - ★ **Nous nous entraînons** au même club. We train (*ourselves*) at the same club.
  - ★ **Vous vous maquillez** pour sortir? Do you make *yourselves* up to go out?
  - ★ **Ils s'amusent**. They are enjoying *themselves*.

- Can you see how reflexive verbs work?
  It is very simple. You just add an extra word before the verb: **me**, **te**, **se**, **nous**, **vous** or **se**. If the verb begins with a vowel (a,e,i,o,u) or h, **me**, **te** and **se** change to **m'**, **t'** and **s'**.

- For regular verbs, like the ones above, the endings follow the usual pattern:
  - ★ **se laver**

je **me** lave	nous **nous** lavons
tu **te** laves	vous **vous** lavez
il **se** lave	ils **se** lavent
elle **se** lave	elles **se** lavent
on **se** lave	

- You also already know some reflexive verbs:
  - ★ Je **m'**appelle Claude. I'm called/I call *myself* Claude.
  - ★ Tu **te** rappelles? Do you remember?

- You may come across some of these as non-reflexive verbs, too, if the action is being done to someone or something else:
  - ★ Je lave la voiture. I wash the car.
  - ★ Il couche le bébé. He is putting the baby to bed.

reflexive verbs (2)

 2

Ton correspondant te pose des questions. Réponds-lui:

1 Tu te réveilles à quelle heure?
2 Est-ce que tu te lèves immédiatement?
3 Tu te brosses les dents avant ou après le petit déjeuner?
4 A quelle heure est-ce que tu te couches?

3

Peux-tu deviner les questions qui correspondent à ces réponses?

1 Je me lève à sept heures et quart.
2 Je me lave avant le petit déjeuner.
3 Oui, je me brosse les dents tous les jours.
4 Le samedi, je me couche à onze heures.

✳

Jeu de logique! Monsieur et Madame Leclerc répondent aux questions: vous vous couchez à quelle heure? Et vos enfants?

'Julia et Sophie se couchent à la même heure. Nous nous couchons plus tard que les autres. Sophie se couche après Paul mais avant Sonia.'

A toi de trouver:

★ qui se couche(nt) à 8h30   ★ qui se couche(nt) à 11h
★ qui se couche(nt) à 10h   ★ qui se couche(nt) à 11h30.

Deuxième partie

Voici les réponses aux questions de ton correspondant:

Je me réveille à sept heures, mais je ne me lève pas immédiatement. Je me lave avant le petit déjeuner, mais je ne me brosse pas les dents. Le soir, je ne me couche pas avant onze heures.

Vois-tu comment dire ce que tu **ne fais pas**?

Le principe

It is easy! You just put **ne** and **pas** around the verb and the extra word:

je me lave → je **ne** me lave **pas**
il s'amuse → il **ne** s'amuse **pas**

5

Joue avec trois ou quatre amis. Recopie et complète ces quatre phrases, mais ne les montre pas aux autres:

Je me réveille à. . .   **Je m'habille à. . .**
        Je me couche à. . .   **Je me lève à. . .**

Jouez contre la montre. Les autres essaient de deviner à quelle heure tu fais chaque chose – en une minute! Tu dois répondre par une phrase complète:

Exemple

Les autres: Tu te réveilles à sept heures?
Toi: Oui, je me réveille à sept heures.
     ou Non, je ne me réveille pas à sept heures.

Est-ce que les autres arrivent à deviner tes quatre réponses en une minute? Changez de rôle.

reflexive verbs (3)

Comment parler du passé avec ces verbes?

> Quelle journée! Je me suis réveillé en retard. Je me suis levé immédiatement. J'ai réveillé ma soeur, qui était en retard, elle aussi. Elle s'est levée. Nous nous sommes lavés et habillés. Nous n'avons pas pris de petit déjeuner: nous sommes partis pour le collège. Mais quand nous sommes arrivés au collège, je me suis rappelé: on était le dimanche! Mes parents ont trouvé ça amusant. Ils se sont levés à dix heures!

Le principe

- Like some other verbs you know, reflexive verbs take **être** (and not avoir) in the perfect tense.

- Again like some other verbs, in these phrases, the second verb agrees with the person who did the action: if the person is female, an '**e**' is added:
  - ★ **je me suis** réveillé(**e**)
  - ★ **tu t'es** levé(**e**)
  - ★ **il s'est** lavé
  - ★ **elle s'est** lavé**e**
  - ★ **nous nous sommes** couché(**e**)**s**
  - ★ **vous vous êtes** amusé(**e**)(**s**)
  - ★ **ils se sont** entraîné**s**
  - ★ **elles se sont** entraîné**es**

- Talking about things you **did not** do is easy, too. Look at these examples:
  - ★ je **ne** me suis **pas** réveillé(e)
  - ★ tu **ne** t'es **pas** levé(e)
  - ★ il **ne** s'est **pas** lavé
  - ★ elle **ne** s'est **pas** lavée
  - ★ nous **ne** nous sommes **pas** couché(e)s
  - ★ vous **ne** vous êtes **pas** amusé(e)s
  - ★ ils **ne** se sont **pas** entraînés
  - ★ elles **ne** se sont **pas** entraînées

- As you see, you just put **ne** and **pas** around **me suis**, **t'es**, **s'est**, **nous sommes**, **vous êtes** and **se sont**.

 6 ►

Tu sais maintenant parler du passé! Recopie ces questions dans le bon ordre, et écris les réponses.

1 Tu hier? réveillé(e) à heure t'es quelle

2 tout de suite Tu levé(e) t'es?

3 après Tu déjeuner? avant t'es ou le petit lavé(e)

4 quelle t'es heure à hier? Tu couché(e)

reflexive verbs (4)

Quatrième partie

Le principe

- It is easy to use reflexives in the imperfect tense: they follow the same pattern as other verbs (see 4ème Etape) and just add, in front of the verb, **me**, **te**, **se**, **nous**, **vous**, **se**:
  - ★ Quand j'avais cinq ans **je me couchais** à sept heures.
  - ★ **Tu te levais** à quelle heure?
  - ★ Ma sœur **se réveillait** avant moi.
  - ★ Elle ne **se levait** pas avant moi.
  - ★ **Nous nous levions** à huit heures du soir.
  - ★ **Vous vous amusiez** ensemble?
  - ★ Mes parents **se couchaient** à minuit.

7

a Tu as changé tes habitudes? Réponds à ces questions:
  1 Tu te lèves et te couches à quelle heure, normalement?
  2 Il y a cinq ans, tu te levais et te couchais à quelle heure?
  3 Et il y a dix ans?

b Maintenant, pose ces questions à ton/ta partenaire. Vos réponses sont similaires?

Cinquième partie

Le principe

- The future tense is easy as well. Reflexive verbs just follow the usual pattern (see 1ère Etape), adding, in front of the verb, **me**, **te**, **se**, **nous**, **vous**, **se**:
  - ★ **Je me coucherai** à dix heures.
  - ★ **Tu te lèveras** à quelle heure?
  - ★ **Il s'amusera** bien en France.
  - ★ **Elle s'habillera** dans la chambre.
  - ★ **Nous nous entraînerons** ensemble.
  - ★ **Vous vous réveillerez** à l'heure?
  - ★ **Ils se brosseront** les dents après le dîner.
  - ★ **Elles se laveront** les cheveux demain.

8

Imagine! La semaine prochaine, tu seras en vacances. Quelle sera ta routine? Tu te coucheras à quelle heure? Tu te réveilleras à quelle heure? Tu te lèveras tout de suite?

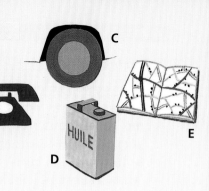

1

Que veulent-ils? Pour chaque question, trouve l'illustration qui correspond:

1 Voulez-vous vérifier l'huile, s'il vous plaît?
2 Est-ce que vous vendez des cartes routières?
3 Pouvez-vous vérifier la pression des pneus?
4 Il y a des toilettes ici?

Il y a trois façons de formuler une question en français. Tu les connais déjà.
Peux-tu les identifier? Pour t'aider, regarde les questions **1** à **4** ci-dessus.

Le principe

- **Turn a statement into a question by changing the intonation of your voice and, where appropriate, adding a question word.**
  This is the most common way of asking a question in speech.
  ★ Vous avez des sandwiches → Vous avez des sandwiches**?**
  ★ Tu habites où**?**

- **Add the words 'Est-ce que'.**
  This is the next most common form of question.
  ★ Vous avez des sandwiches. → **Est-ce que** vous avez des sandwiches?
  ★ Où **est-ce que** tu habites?

- **Change the order of the words, so that the verb comes before the person or thing**.
  This form is used less in speech than in writing, as it is more formal. However, it is often used in speech after question words, because it is easier and shorter.
  ★ Vous avez des sandwiches → **Avez-vous** des sandwiches?
  ★ Où **habites-tu**?

- Note: **Il y a** changes to **Y a-t-il**
  ★ Il y a des toilettes ici → **Y a-t-il** des toilettes ici?

2

Tu es dans une station-service. Comment vas-tu demander:

1 si on vend des cartes routières?
2 à quelle heure la station-service ferme?
3 s'il y a des toilettes?
4 si on peut vérifier l'huile?

3

Comment vas-tu demander à la mère de ton correspondant:

1 si elle aime le tennis?
2 où elle travaille?
3 si elle va souvent au cinéma?
4 l'heure du dîner?

4

Comment vas-tu demander à ton correspondant:

1 s'il veut aller au parc?
2 s'il aime le reggae?
3 quelles matières il préfère?
4 son âge?

à. . . km/à. . . minutes

Pour répondre à la question 'C'est loin?', tu peux donner une distance en kilomètres ou en minutes:

> *L'autoroute, c'est loin d'ici?*

> *Non, ce n'est pas loin. C'est à dix minutes.*

> *Pour aller à Chartres, c'est loin?*

> *C'est assez loin. C'est à trente kilomètres d'ici.*

Le principe

● Tu as remarqué? En français, on ajoute le mot **à**:

★ C'est **à** trente kilomètres d'ici.
It's thirty kilometres from here.

★ C'est **à** dix minutes.
It's ten minutes away.

★ C'est **à** un quart d'heure d'ici.
It's a quarter of an hour from here.

✱ **1** ▶

a Tu es à la Châtre. Réponds à ces questions. Utilise la carte pour calculer les distances.

1 Pour aller à Lignières, c'est loin?
2 Est-ce que Châteaumeillant est loin d'ici?
3 Pour aller à Culan, c'est loin?
4 Je vais à Issoudun. C'est loin d'ici?
5 Est-ce que Chârost est loin d'ici?

b Invente d'autres questions pour ton/ta partenaire.

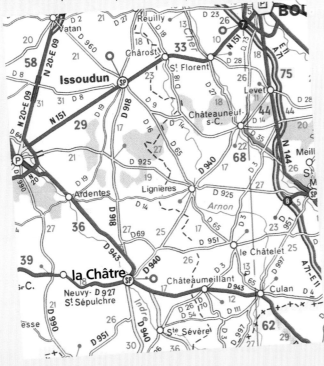

2 ▶

Quand les distances sont plus petites, par exemple en ville, on donne plutôt les distances en minutes.

Exemples:

> *La gare SNCF, c'est loin?*

> *Non, c'est à cinq minutes.*

> *L'hôtel de ville, c'est loin d'ici?*

> *C'est assez loin. C'est à vingt, vingt-cinq minutes.*

Ton correspondant est chez toi. Réponds à ses questions:

1 Il y a un parc près d'ici?
2 Pour aller à la piscine, c'est loin?
3 Le cinéma, c'est loin d'ici?
4 C'est loin, la gare routière?
5 Il y a une pharmacie près d'ici?
6 Chez toi, c'est près de la mer?

the conditional tense (1)

Trouve dans ce mini-dialogue des phrases qui veulent dire 'I **would** like. . .' et '**Could** I. . .?' :

– Je voudrais changer quarante livres sterling, s'il vous plaît.
– Oui, madame.
– Est-ce que je pourrais avoir des billets de cent francs?
– Bien sûr, madame.

Dans cette interview, un jeune homme, qui n'a pas beaucoup d'argent, parle des choses qu'il **ferait** s'il était riche. Et toi, est-ce que tu ferais aussi ces choses-là?

– *Qu'est-ce que tu ferais si tu étais très riche?*
– Si j'étais riche, je mangerais du caviar et je boirais du champagne. Des orchestres célèbres joueraient pour moi. Une actrice célèbre tomberait amoureuse de moi. Elle serait très belle. Nous partirions ensemble.
– *Où iriez-vous?*
– Nous visiterions toutes les grandes villes du monde.

Le principe

- To talk about what you **would** do (if the conditions were right!), you use the **conditional tense**.
  Look again at the examples above. Can you identify the verb endings of the conditional tense, and the part of the verb which they are added to? Tip: you will probably recognise both of these from previous units!

- The endings are the same as the imperfect tense:
  (je)   - **ais**
  (tu)   - **ais**
  (il, elle, on) - **ait**
  (nous)   - **ions**
  (vous)   - **iez**
  (ils, elles)   - **aient**

- The 'stem' you add them to is the same as for the **future tense**:
  ★ Take the infinitive form of the verb.
  ★ For verbs ending in **-er** or **-ir**, add the appropriate ending:
    manger → je manger**ais**
    partir → tu partir**ais**
  ★ For verbs ending in **-re**, remove the final 'e' before adding the ending:
    prendre → je prendr**ais**

- The verbs which are exceptions in the future tense are exceptions in the conditional, e.g.:
  ★ faire   je **fer**ais (I would do)
  ★ être   je **ser**ais (I would be)
  ★ avoir   j'**aur**ais (I would have)
  ★ aller   j'**ir**ais (I would go)

the conditional tense (2)

3

Et toi, si tu étais riche. . . :

. . . qu'est-ce que tu mangerais?

. . . qu'est-ce que tu boirais?

. . . qu'est-ce que tu achèterais?

. . . où est-ce que tu irais, et avec qui?

. . . qu'est-ce que tu ferais, le week-end?

✱ **4**

Que ferait Nadia, si elle était riche?

5

a On a posé ces questions à des jeunes Français. Peux-tu trouver leurs réponses?

Questions	Réponses
Imaginez! Qu'est-ce qui se passerait. . .	**A** Nous ferions des révisions.
1 si la télévision ne marchait pas?	**B** Les gens iraient partout à pied ou à vélo.
2 si l'essence coûtait dix fois plus cher?	**C** On jouerait aux cartes ou on écouterait de la musique.
3 si votre prof était absent(e)?	**D** Beaucoup de gens prendraient le bus.
4 si l'essence coûtait cent fois plus cher?	**E** Nous ne travaillerions pas.
5 si vous aviez un examen demain?	

b Et toi, comment est-ce que tu répondrais à ces questions?

Deuxième partie

6

Pour être poli(e), par exemple quand tu es invité(e) chez quelqu'un, tu peux utiliser le conditionnel:

Je voudrais. . .   I would like. . .

Est-ce que je pourrais. . .?   Could I. . .?

Je préférerais. . .   I would prefer. . .

Quelles questions sont les plus polies?

1 a Je voudrais du pain, s'il te plaît.

  b Je veux du pain, s'il te plaît.

2 a Je peux téléphoner à mes parents?

  b Est-ce que je pourrais téléphoner à mes parents?

3 a Nous voulons visiter le château.

  b Nous voudrions visiter le château.

7

Change ces phrases pour être un peu plus poli(e):

★ Je veux du thé.

★ Je peux regarder la télé?

★ Je préfère aller à la piscine.

★ Est-ce que nous pouvons faire du vélo?

★ Pouvez-vous me réveiller à huit heures?

the conditional tense (3)

8 ►

Si on demande quelque chose, on peut utiliser l'expression suivante pour être extrêmement poli:

Vous n'auriez pas de la monnaie, s'il vous plaît?
You wouldn't happen to have some change, please?

Tu n'aurais pas une pièce de deux francs, s'il te plaît?
You wouldn't happen to have a two franc piece, please?

Comment est-ce que tu demanderais ces choses à ton correspondant?

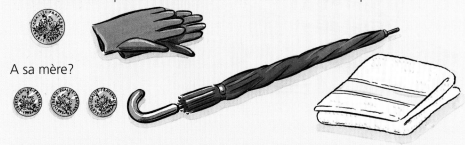

A sa mère?

Troisième partie

Le principe

● You can use the conditional tense to give advice in two ways:
  ★ by telling someone what you would do in their position
    A ta/votre place, j'irais chez le médecin.
  ★ by telling them what they should, or ought to do
    Tu devrais aller chez le dentiste.

9 ►

Trouve les conseils qui correspondent à chaque problème:

Problèmes	Conseils
1 Vendez-vous de l'aspirine? J'ai de la fièvre, et j'ai très mal à la gorge.	**A** A votre place, j'irais dans une banque: ils prennent moins de commission.
2 Est-ce que je peux changer de l'argent à l'hôtel?	**B** Tu devrais te coucher plus tôt.
3 Je suis toujours fatiguée.	**C** A votre place, je prendrais l'autoroute. C'est plus rapide.
4 J'ai mal aux dents.	**D** A ta place, j'irais chez le dentiste.
5 Pardon, madame, quelle est la meilleure route pour aller à Strasbourg?	**E** Vous devriez aller chez un médecin.

10 ►

Peux-tu donner des conseils à ces gens?

Est-ce que tu donnes les mêmes conseils que ton/ta partenaire?

le plus. . ./le moins. . . (1)

Première partie

1

a Des records de longueur! Peux-tu deviner les bonnes réponses?

1 Combien mesure le fleuve le plus long du monde?
- **a** 1 320 km
- **b** 4 460 km
- **c** 6 750 km

3 Combien mesurent les cheveux les plus longs du monde?
- **a** 137 cm
- **b** 252 cm
- **c** 386 cm

2 Combien mesure la route la plus longue du monde?
- **a** 10 470 km
- **b** 24 110 km
- **c** 32 490 km

4 Quel pays a les plages les plus longues du monde?
- **a** les Etats-Unis
- **b** la France
- **c** l'Espagne

b Peux-tu trouver quatre façons différentes d'écrire 'the longest. . .'? Peux-tu expliquer le principe?

Réponses: 1 c 2 b 3 c 4 a

Le principe

- As you know, words describing someone or something change their spelling depending on the person or thing being described. The same principle applies when talking about 'the most. . .', 'the longest. . .', and so on:
  - ★ masculine singular le film **le plus long**: the longest film
  - ★ feminine singular la rivière **la plus longue**: the longest river
  - ★ masculine plural les ponts **les plus longs**: the longest bridges
  - ★ feminine plural les rues **les plus longues**: the longest streets

- Most adjectives come *after* the nouns they describe. For example:
  - ★ une fille **intelligente** → la fille **la plus intelligente**
  - ★ un film **intéressant** → le film **le plus intéressant**

- With adjectives which come *before* the word they describe, there are two ways of talking about 'the most. . .':
  - ★ un **long** film → le film **le plus long**
  - ★ un **beau** monument → **le plus beau** monument

Deuxième partie

2

Es-tu d'accord avec ces points de vue?

A mon avis, le plus beau monument de Paris est l'Arc de Triomphe. Le moins beau, c'est le Centre Pompidou. Je ne l'aime pas du tout!

Je pense que le musée le plus intéressant est le Louvre. Il y a beaucoup de choses à voir. A mon avis, c'est le meilleur musée de Paris. Pour moi, le musée le moins intéressant est le Musée de l'Armée. Je ne m'intéresse pas aux uniformes militaires.

le plus. . ./le moins. . . (2)

Si **le plus**. . . veut dire 'the most. . .' comment dit-on, en français, 'the least. . .'? C'est facile!

Le principe

le plus: the most
le moins: the least

le musée **le plus** intéressant: **the most** interesting museum
le musée **le moins** intéressant: **the least** interesting museum
la matière **la moins** intéressante: **the least** interesting subject

3 ▶

A ton avis, quel est le plus beau monument à Paris? Et le moins beau?

la Grande Arche

la Pyramide du Louvre

l'Arc de Triomphe

la Tour Eiffel

Troisième partie

Le principe

● The words **plus** and **moins** are not used with **bon(ne)** (good) and **mauvais(e)** (bad). Instead, you say **meilleur(e)** (best) and **pire** (worst):

★ Mon **meilleur** souvenir de Paris, c'est le panorama du haut de la Tour Eiffel. Mon **pire** souvenir, c'est quand j'ai perdu mon appareil-photo!

4 ▶

a Recopie et complète ces phrases:

A mon avis. . .

. . . le meilleur disque du Top 50, c'est. . .
. . . le pire groupe, c'est. . .
. . . le film de science-fiction le moins intéressant, c'est. . .
. . . les plus belles voitures, ce sont les. . .
. . . la meilleure actrice, c'est. . .
. . . les vêtements les plus confortables, ce sont. . .
. . . l'émission de télévision la plus intéressante, c'est. . .

b Tu donnes les mêmes réponses que ton/ta partenaire?

5 ▶

Avec un(e) partenaire, ou en groupe, fais des recherches, et invente un jeu-test comme celui de l'activité . Faites faire ce test à vos amis!

y

* ▶ 1

Es-tu fort(e) en géographie? Peux-tu identifier ces capitales européennes?

1 On y va pour visiter la place Rouge.
2 On y trouve la Tour Eiffel.
3 On y trouve Big Ben.
4 On peut y voir les Jardins Tivoli.
5 Beaucoup de touristes y vont pour visiter le Vatican.

> Quelques capitales européennes
>
> **Bruxelles**   **Paris**   **Rome**
> **Edimbourg**   **Copenhague**   **Moscou**
> **Londres**   **Madrid**   **Oslo**

Le principe

- The word **y** means 'there'. It can be used to avoid repetition of the name of the place you are talking about, e.g.:
  - ★ Tu vas **à Paris**? Oui j'**y** vais la semaine prochaine.
    Are you going **to Paris**? Yes, I'm going **there** next week.
  - ★ Tu vas souvent **en France**? Non, je n'**y** vais pas très souvent.
    Do you often go **to France**? No, I don't go **there** very often.

- In English, we often miss out the word **there** (No, I don't go very often), but the word **y** is never missed out in French.

- The word **y** comes before the verb:
  - ★ Mon père **y** va souvent.
    My father goes **there** often.
  - ★ J'**y** suis allé(e) l'année dernière.
    I went **there** last year.
  - ★ Qu'est-ce que vous **y** faites?
    What do you do **there**?
  - ★ On peut **y** aller en avion.
    You can go **there** by plane.

- As you can see, **je** becomes **j'** in front of **y**.

- When talking in the negative, **ne** comes before **y**, and changes to **n'**.
  - ★ Je **n'y** vais **pas** cette année.
    I'm not going **there** this year.
  - ★ Je **n'y** suis **pas** allé(e) l'année dernière.
    I didn't go **there** last year.

▶ 2

Réponds à ces questions (✓ = oui; ✗ = non). Utilise le mot **y**.

1 Tu vas en France cette année? (✓)
2 Tu vas en France en train? (✗)
3 Tes parents vont à Paris? (✗)
4 Tu es allé(e) à Paris l'année dernière? (✓)

▶ 3

A toi de répondre à ces questions sur toi. Utilise le mot **y**.

1 Tu vas au collège à pied?
2 Tu arrives au collège à quelle heure?
3 Tu vas souvent au cinéma?
4 Tu vas souvent au parc?
5 Tu es déjà allé(e) en France?

using the imperfect and perfect tenses (1)

1

Ces jeunes parlent de leurs vacances de l'année dernière. Qui a pris quelle photo?

A

B

C

Sandrine: **Je suis allée** à Paris avec mes parents. **On a fait** du tourisme.

Cédric: J'habite au bord de la mer, alors **je suis resté** à la maison. **Je me suis très bien amusé**.

Noémie: **J'ai passé** trois semaines en colonie de vacances avec mes copains. **Il a fait** très beau. **On s'est bien amusé**.

Le principe

● The above descriptions all contain examples of the **perfect tense**. Remember, you use the perfect tense:

★ **to describe single, completed actions in the past**
On a visité la Tour Eiffel. We visited the Eiffel Tower.
J'ai fait du camping. I went camping.

★ **to sum up something as a whole**
Je me suis bien amusé(e). I enjoyed myself.
Il a fait mauvais. The weather was bad (throughout the holiday).

● Remember that most verbs work with **avoir** in the perfect tense:

★ **J'ai passé** mes vacances à l'étranger.
★ **Tu as visité** des monuments historiques?
★ **Il a fait** beau?
★ **On a joué** au volley.
★ **Nous avons fait** du camping.
★ **Vous avez dormi** dans un hôtel?
★ **Mes parents ont lu** des livres.

● Some verbs take **être**. Remember that the ending of these verbs changes, depending on the person who did the action.

★ **Tu es parti** en vacances, l'année dernière, Philippe?
★ Oui, **je suis allé** au bord de la mer.
★ **Tu t'es** bien **amusée**, Liliane?
★ Non, **je ne me suis pas** bien **amusée**!
★ **Nous sommes restés** chez nous.

2

Comment est-ce que ces deux jeunes décriraient leurs vacances?

Himdi:

Elisabeth:

using the imperfect and perfect tenses (2)

Deuxième partie

3 ▶

Qui a été le plus actif en vacances? Est-ce que tu préfères passer des vacances comme Yolande ou comme Frédéric?

Yolande: Pendant les vacances, je me levais à onze heures tous les jours. En général, je lisais un bon livre le matin. De temps en temps, j'allais faire les magasins, ou je me promenais en ville. Le soir, en général, je mangeais dans un bon restaurant. C'était très reposant.

Frédéric: Je me levais toujours assez tôt, parce que je jouais au tennis avant le petit déjeuner. Chaque jour, je bronzais sur la plage. Je faisais souvent de la planche à voile. J'allais en boîte tous les soirs. C'était fatigant, mais génial!

Le principe

- When describing a holiday you have had, you use the **imperfect tense**:
  - ★ **to describe your habits, the things you did regularly**
    Je me levais tôt tous les jours. I got up early every day.
    Chaque jour, je bronzais sur la plage. I used to sunbathe on the beach each day.
  - ★ **to say what it was like**
    C'était fatigant, mais génial! It was tiring, but great!
    C'était passionnant! It was exciting!
    Je m'ennuyais un peu. I was a bit bored.

- Remember that, to form the imperfect tense, you take the **nous** form of the present tense of the verb, remove the **-ons** ending, and add the imperfect endings:
  - ★ Normalement, je me lev**ais** tôt.
  - ★ Tu all**ais** souvent à la plage?
  - ★ Mon frère sort**ait** tous les soirs.
  - ★ On mange**ait** au restaurant.
  - ★ Nous jou**ions** quelquefois au foot.
  - ★ Vous all**iez** de temps en temps au cinéma?
  - ★ Mes parents visit**aient** des monuments historiques.

4 ▶

Jean-Pierre a envoyé cette carte postale à un copain, pendant ses vacances. Comment est-ce qu'il décrirait ses vacances maintenant, quelques mois plus tard?

Je fais du camping avec ma famille. C'est super ici! Normalement, l'après-midi je bronze sur la plage. Je vais en boîte tous les soirs, et je me couche tard.

Amitiés,

Jean-Pierre

2,80

RÉPUBLIQUE FRANÇAISE LA POSTE 1993

A. Pillier
21, avenue de la Gare
23000 Guéret
Creuse

10ème Etape

ne. . . personne/rien/jamais/que/ plus/ni. . . ni. . .

Une Française vient de passer ses vacances en Angleterre. A ton avis, elle exagère? Sur quoi?

> Les Anglais **ne** font **rien** comme tout le monde. Ils roulent à gauche et ils **ne** boivent **que** du thé. Ils **ne** parlent **ni** français, **ni** allemand: je **ne** connais **personne** en Angleterre qui parle une langue étrangère. Et il **ne** fait **jamais** beau! Dormir à l'hôtel en Angleterre, ça coûte cher – je n'ai **plus** d'argent! Non, je **ne** retournerai **plus** en Angleterre!

Peux-tu trouver comment dire en français 'no one', 'nothing', 'never', 'neither. . . nor. . .', 'no more', 'only' (nothing but), 'not again'?

Le principe

- You already know how to use **ne** and **pas** in negative sentences. You can use other words with **ne**, to mean different things:
  - ★ Je **ne** connais **personne**. I know **no-one**.
  - ★ Ils **ne** font **rien** à midi. They do **nothing** at mid-day.
  - ★ Je **ne** vais **jamais** à l'étranger. I **never** go abroad.
  - ★ Je **ne** parle **ni** allemand **ni** français. I speak **neither** German **nor** French.
  - ★ Je n'ai **plus** d'argent. I've got **no more** money.
  - ★ Ils **ne** mangent **que** des pizzas. They **only** eat pizzas.
  - ★ Je **ne** vais **plus** en France. I'm **not** going to France **again (not any more)**.
- In the present tense, these words take the same position around the verb as **ne** and **pas**.

✳ 2

Ces gens parlent de leurs vacances. Recopie et complète les phrases, en utilisant les mots suivants: personne; rien; jamais; ni. . . ni. . . ; plus; que.

1 Je ne pars _____ en vacances: je préfère rester chez moi.
2 J'aime me reposer. Je m'installe sur la plage, et je ne fais _____ .
3 Je ne vais _____ en Espagne _____ en Italie. Il y fait trop chaud pour moi.
4 Mes vacances ont coûté cher: je n'ai _____ d'argent.
5 Quand je vais chez mon ami au Danemark, je ne parle _____ danois.
6 L'année dernière, je suis allée au bord de la mer, mais je me suis ennuyée. Je n'y retournerai _____ .

✳ 3

Un élève passe trois mois à Paris, mais ça ne lui plaît pas. En fait, il ne sort jamais et ne fait aucun effort pour s'amuser. Imagine les réponses qu'il donnerait à ces questions:

1 Tu connais beaucoup de jeunes Français?
2 Tu vas au cinéma de temps en temps?
3 Les pizzas, c'est bien, mais tu ne manges jamais autre chose?
4 Tu regardes les films ou les comédies à la télé?
5 Qu'est-ce que tu fais le week-end?
6 Tu ne vas pas au club de jeunes?

✳ 4

Eric a passé ses vacances à Paris. Il est souvent allé dans les magasins, et il a acheté beaucoup de cadeaux. Il a parlé français avec plusieurs personnes. Il a visité la Tour Eiffel et le Louvre. Les vacances de son frère, Daniel, ont été tout à fait différentes. Change la description pour les décrire.

Le principe

- Note that in the perfect tense, like **pas**, most of these words go before the second part of the verb:
  - ★ Je n'ai **rien** acheté.
  - ★ Je ne suis **jamais** allé(e) à Paris.
- However, **personne**, **que** and **ni**. . . **ni**. . . come after the second part:
  - ★ Je n'ai vu **personne**.
  - ★ Je n'ai vu **que** lui.
  - ★ Je n'ai vu **ni** Paul, **ni** Anne.

11ème Etape
moi/toi/lui. . .

1 ▶

a Qui s'entend le mieux avec ses parents, Julie ou Olivier?

Julie: Tes sœurs et **toi**, vous vous entendez bien avec vos parents?

Olivier: Oui, on s'entend assez bien avec **eux**.

Julie: **Moi**, je m'entends mal avec ma mère. Mon père, **lui**, est plus raisonnable qu'**elle**. Je me dispute rarement avec **lui**. Mes parents sont très stricts avec **moi**. Vos parents sont stricts avec **vous**?

Olivier: Ils sont assez stricts avec **nous**, surtout avec mes sœurs. Ils sont plus stricts avec **elles** qu'avec **moi**.

b Peux-tu identifier des mots dans cette conversation qui veulent dire 'me', 'you', 'he', 'him', 'her', 'us', 'them'?

✱ **2** ▶

Recopie les questions avec les réponses qui correspondent.

Questions	Réponses
1 Dans ma famille, on se dispute rarement. Et chez vous?	**A** Je m'entends bien avec Carole, mais Andréa, elle, m'embête.
2 Tu t'entends bien avec tes sœurs?	**B** Mes parents, eux, ne m'écoutent pas.
3 Tu te confies à tes parents?	**C** Moi, je me confie plutôt à mon frère.
4 Je discute beaucoup avec mes parents. Et toi?	**D** Nous, on se dispute très souvent.

Le principe

B After *et, avec, sans, chez, pour* and *à*:

★ Vos parents sont stricts **avec vous**? Are your parents strict **with you**?

★ Ma sœur sort toujours **sans moi**. My sister is always going out **without me**.

★ Mes grands-parents viennent **chez nous** samedi. My grandparents are coming to **our house** on Saturday.

★ Voici un conseil **pour toi**. Here's some advice **for you**.

★ Je ne me confie pas **à eux**. Et toi? I don't confide **in them**. Do **you**?

✱ **3** ▶

Utilise les expressions de la boîte pour compléter ces phrases: ☞

1 Je ne m'entends pas avec mon frère. Je me dispute souvent _____.

2 Ta sœur se confie _____?

3 Mes parents font beaucoup _____.

4 Je m'entends bien avec Clara et Emilie. J'aime bien aller _____.

> chez elles
> à toi
> avec lui
> pour moi

Le principe

C Making comparisons

You already know how to make comparisons in French!

★ Je suis plus grand que **toi**, mais moins grand que **lui**.

✱ **4** ▶

Recopie et complète ces phrases:

1 Mon père est très actif. Ma mère est plus calme que _____.

2 Mes parents sont très nerveux. Moi, je suis beaucoup moins nerveux qu' _____.

3 Tu es assez optimiste. Moi, je suis moins optimiste que _____.

4 Mes sœurs ne sont pas très actives. Mon frère est plus actif qu' _____.

Le principe

● The following words are very useful when talking about yourself and others. They are used in a number of situations.

★ **moi**: I, me
★ **toi**: you
★ **lui**: he, him
★ **elle**: she, her
★ **nous**: we, us
★ **vous**: you
★ **eux**: they, them (masculine)
★ **elles**: they, them (feminine)

A To show extra emphasis:

★ **Moi**, je pense que. . . *I* think that. . .
★ Mon père, **lui**, est strict. My *father* is strict.
★ **Eux**, ils ne comprennent rien! *They* don't understand anything!

La grammaire: un résumé (1)

Un/une/des
(*Auto 1*, page 159)

Un and *une* both mean 'a' or 'an'.

- *un* + masculine nouns
  C'est **un** bon livre.
- *une* + feminine nouns
  Tu as **une** gomme?
- *des* means 'some'.
  Tu veux **des** fraises?

Du/de la/de l'/des
(*Auto 2*, page 171)

Du/de la/de l'/des mean 'some'.

- *de* + *le* = *du*
  Tu veux **du** café?
- *de* + *la* = *de la*
  Il y a **de la** confiture.
- *de* + *l'* = *de l'*
  Je voudrais **de l'**eau.
- *de* + *les* = *des*
  J'ai acheté **des** chips.

Attention!

- For a specific quantity, or a bottle or tin, or a little or a lot of something, you use *de*:
  un kilo **de** pommes
  une boîte **de** petits pois
- Before a word beginning with a vowel or an h, you use *d'*:
  une bouteille **d'**Orangina
- After *pas* you use *de* or *d'*:
  Il **n'**y a **pas de** biscuits.
  Je **n'**ai **pas d'**argent.
- For a musical instrument, you use *jouer de*:
  Elle **joue de la** guitare et **du** piano.

Le/la/l'/les
(*Auto 1*, pages 162, 167)

Le/la/l'/les mean 'the'.

- *le* + masculine nouns
  J'ai vu **le** film.
- *la* + feminine nouns
  La chambre est grande.
- *l'* + singular nouns that begin with a vowel or an h
  Tu connais **l'**hôtel?
- *les* + plural nouns
  J'adore **les** animaux.

Au/à la/à l'/aux
(*Auto 1*, page 168)

- *à* + *le* = *au*
  Elle est allée **au** cinéma.
- *à* + *la* = *à la*
  On va **à la** piscine?
- *à* + *l'* = *à l'*
  Ton frère va **à l'**école?
- *à* + *les* = *aux*
  Continuez jusqu'**aux** feux.

Attention!

- For a game or a sport, you use *jouer à*:
  Il adore **jouer au** tennis.
  Tu veux **jouer aux** échecs?

Ordinal numbers
(*Auto 1*, page 161)

un/une > premier/première
deux > deuxième
trois > troisième
quatre > quatrième
cinq > cinquième
neuf > neuvième
onze > onzième
vingt et un > vingt et unième

En/au/à
(*Auto 1*, page 158)

You use *en/au/à* when talking about where you live or where you are going.

- *en* + feminine countries
  la Belgique: j'habite **en** Belgique
- *au* + masculine countries
  le Portugal: il va **au** Portugal
- *aux* + masculine plural countries
  les Etats-Unis: elle habite **aux** Etats-Unis
- *à* + town/village
  Vous allez **à** Londres?

Adjectives
(*Auto 1*, page 175)

Words used to describe people, places and things in French change their spelling, depending on what is being described. Most adjectives work like this:

- masculine words
  Il est intelligent.
- feminine words, add an -e
  Elle est intelligent**e**.
- plural, masculine words, add an -s
  Ces livres sont intéressant**s**.
- plural, feminine words, add -es
  Ces vidéos sont intéressant**es**.
- Most adjectives come after the word they describe.
  Il a les yeux **bleus**.
- Some adjectives come before the word they describe, e.g. *grand/petit/beau/gros*.
  J'ai deux **petites** sœurs.
- Some adjectives change their spelling in irregular ways (*Auto 2*, page 156), e.g. *gros/grosse*; *beau/belle*.
  Mon cousin est assez **beau**, et ma cousine est très **belle**.
- Past participles are often used as adjectives.
  Elle habite au Royaume-**Uni**.
  J'adore les fraises **sucrées**.
  Bien **joué**!

Ne. . . pas
(*Auto 1*, page 173)

- You use *ne*. . . *pas* when making a negative statement.
  – Il pleut?
  – Non, il **ne** pleut **pas**.
- *Ne* is shortened to *n'* before a vowel or an h or y.
  Je **n'**ai **pas** joué au football.

Plus/moins/aussi. . . que
(*Auto 2*, page 185)

- *plus. . . que* means 'more. . . than'
  Elle est **plus** grande **que** toi.
- *moins. . . que* means 'less. . . than'
  Je suis **moins** fort **que** mon frère.
- *aussi. . . que* means 'as. . . as'
  Tu es **aussi** intelligente **que** ta sœur.

La grammaire: un résumé (2)

Quel/quelle/quels/quelles
(*Auto 3*, page 162)

Quel/quelle/quels/quelles are used to ask the question 'which?' or 'what?'.
They are also used to express your reactions.

- *Quel* + masculine words
  Le train part de **quel** quai?
- *Quelle* + feminine words
  Quelle heure est-il?
- *Quels* + plural, masculine words
  Quels films aimes-tu?
- *Quelles* + plural, feminine words
  Quelles jolies fleurs!

Prepositions
(*Auto 3*, page 170)

Prepositions are often used for saying where something is.

- *devant*: in front of
  Mon bureau est **devant** la fenêtre.
- *derrière*: behind
  Mon lit est **derrière** la porte.
- *sur*: on
  J'ai une lampe **sur** la table.
- *sous*: under
  Il y a des livres **sous** mon lit.
- *près de*: near
  Il y a un café **près de** la piscine.
- *à côté de*: next to
  A côté du collège, il y a un parc.
- *en face de*: opposite
  Il y a des posters **en face des** étagères.

Attention!

With the last three prepositions listed, you use *du*, *de la*, *de l'* or *des*. If you are unsure which, check the relevant section on page 178.

Me/te/vous pronouns (*Auto 2*, page 183)

- *Me*, *te* and *vous* refer to people. They come immediately before the verb.
  Les serpents, ça **me** fait peur.
  Ça **te** dit d'aller au cinéma?
  L'histoire **vous** intéresse?
- Before a vowel, *me* and *te* change to *m'* and *t'*.
  Ça **m'**embête!

Qui (*Auto 3*, page 164)

- When talking about people, *qui* means 'who'.
  Qui veut aller à la piscine?
  C'est Marc **qui** a gagné la compétition.
- When talking about things, *qui* means 'which'.
  Voilà un bus **qui** va à la gare.

Impersonal phrases (*Auto 3,* page 177)

- *Il est important de* + infinitive
  Il est important de vérifier l'horaire.
- *Il est obligatoire de* + infinitive
  Il est obligatoire de composter son billet.
- *Il faut* + infinitive
  Il faut acheter un billet avant de monter dans le train.

  When speaking, people use *c'est*, rather than *il est*.
  – **C'est** important de faire tes devoirs.

Possessives
(*Auto 1*, page 180)

The French words for showing who something belongs to depend on the thing, as well as on the person who owns it.

	+ masculine words	+ feminine words	+ plural words
my	**mon** lit	**ma** chambre	**mes** livres
your	**ton** stylo	**ta** gomme	**tes** crayons
his/her/its	**son** nez	**sa** bouche	**ses** yeux
our	**notre** oncle	**notre** tante	**nos** cousins
your	**votre** père	**votre** mère	**vos** parents
their	**leur** jardin	**leur** maison	**leurs** animaux

Attention!

- *Son nez* can mean 'his nose', 'her nose' or 'its nose'.
- You use *mon*, *ton* and *son* with feminine words in the singular when they begin with a vowel or h:
  Je te présente **mon** amie, Sophie.
  Donne-moi **ton** adresse.
  Son actrice préférée, c'est Sandrine Bonnaire.

La grammaire: un résumé (3)

VERBS

Regular verbs

(*Auto 3*, page 146)

There are three main groups of verbs in French:

- verbs with infinitives which end in **-er**

  aimer *(vt)* to love

- verbs with infinitives which end in **-re**

  répondre *(vt)* to reply

- verbs with infinitives which end in **-ir**

  finir *(vt, vi)* to finish

present tense

j'aim**e**	je répond**s**	je fin**is**
tu aim**es**	tu répond**s**	tu fin**is**
il aim**e**	il répond	il fin**it**
elle aim**e**	elle répond	elle fin**it**
on aim**e**	on répond	on fin**it**
nous aim**ons**	nous répond**ons**	nous fin**issons**
vous aim**ez**	vous répond**ez**	vous fin**issez**
ils aim**ent**	ils répond**ent**	ils fin**issent**
elles aim**ent**	elles répond**ent**	elles fin**issent**

perfect tense (see page 182)

j'ai aimé   **j'ai répondu**   **j'ai fini**

future tense (see pages 151–153)

j'aimerai   **je répondrai**   **je finirai**

imperfect tense (see pages 160–161)

j'aimais   **je répondais**   **je finissais**

conditional tense (see pages 168–170)

j'aimerais   **je répondrais**   **je finirais**

Other verbs in this group include:

arriver, jouer, habiter, parler, penser, regarder, rester, travailler.

Other verbs in this group include:

attendre, descendre, perdre, vendre.

Other verbs in this group include:

choisir, remplir.

Irregular verbs

Here are some other important verbs, which are irregular: they do not follow the usual patterns.

acheter *(vt)* to buy	**aller** *(vi)* to go	**avoir** *(vt)* to have
j'achète	je vais	j'ai
tu achètes	tu vas	tu as
il achète	il va	il a
elle achète	elle va	elle a
on achète	on va	on a
nous achetons	nous allons	nous avons
vous achetez	vous allez	vous avez
ils achètent	ils vont	ils ont
elles achètent	elles vont	elles ont
perfect j'ai acheté	**perfect** je suis allé(e)	**perfect** j'ai eu
future j'achèterai	**future** j'irai	**future** j'aurai
imperfect j'achetais	**imperfect** j'allais	**imperfect** j'avais
conditional j'achèterais	**conditional** j'irais	**conditional** j'aurais

La grammaire: un résumé (4)

boire *(vt)* *to drink*
je bois
tu bois
il boit
elle boit
on boit
nous buvons
vous buvez
ils boivent
elles boivent
perfect j'ai bu
future je boirai
imperfect je buvais
conditional je boirais

devoir *(vt)* *to have to; to owe*
je dois
tu dois
il doit
elle doit
on doit
nous devons
vous devez
ils doivent
elles doivent
perfect j'ai dû
future je devrai
imperfect je devais
conditional je devrais

dire *(vt)* *to say, to tell*
je dis
tu dis
il dit
elle dit
on dit
nous disons
vous dites
ils disent
elles disent
perfect j'ai dit
future je dirai
imperfect je disais
conditional je dirais

écrire *(vt, vi)* *to write*
j'écris
tu écris
il écrit
elle écrit
on écrit
nous écrivons
vous écrivez
ils écrivent
elles écrivent
perfect j'ai écrit
future j'écrirai
imperfect j'écrivais
conditional j'écrirais

être *(vi)* *to be*
je suis
tu es
il est
elle est
on est
nous sommes
vous êtes
ils sont
elles sont
perfect j'ai été
future je serai
imperfect j'étais
conditional je serais

faire *(vt)* *to make; to do*
je fais
tu fais
il fait
elle fait
on fait
nous faisons
vous faites
ils font
elles font
perfect j'ai fait
future je ferai
imperfect je faisais
conditional je ferais

lire *(vt, vi)* *to read*
je lis
tu lis
il lit
elle lit
on lit
nous lisons
vous lisez
ils lisent
elles lisent
perfect j'ai lu
future je lirai
imperfect je lisais
conditional je lirais

mettre *(vt)* *to put (on)*
je mets
tu mets
il met
elle met
on met
nous mettons
vous mettez
ils mettent
elles mettent
perfect j'ai mis
future je mettrai
imperfect je mettais
conditional je mettrais

ouvrir *(vt)* *to open*
j'ouvre
tu ouvres
il ouvre
elle ouvre
on ouvre
nous ouvrons
vous ouvrez
ils ouvrent
elles ouvrent
perfect j'ai ouvert
future j'ouvrirai
imperfect j'ouvrais
conditional j'ouvrirais

pouvoir *(vt)* *to be able*
je peux
tu peux
il peut
elle peut
on peut
nous pouvons
vous pouvez
ils peuvent
elles peuvent
perfect j'ai pu
future je pourrai
imperfect je pouvais
conditional je pourrais

préférer *(vt)* *to prefer*
je préfère
tu préfères
il préfère
elle préfère
on préfère
nous préférons
vous préférez
ils préfèrent
elles préfèrent
perfect j'ai préféré
future je préférerai
imperfect je préférais
conditional je préférerais

prendre *(vt)* *to take*
je prends
tu prends
il prend
elle prend
on prend
nous prenons
vous prenez
ils prennent
elles prennent
perfect j'ai pris
future je prendrai
imperfect je prenais
conditional je prendrais
(also *comprendre, apprendre*)

La grammaire: un résumé (5)

savoir *(vt)* *to know*
je sais
tu sais
il sait
elle sait
on sait
nous savons
vous savez
ils savent
elles savent
perfect j'ai su
future je saurai
imperfect je savais
conditional je saurais

sortir *(vi)* *to leave*
je sors
tu sors
il sort
elle sort
on sort
nous sortons
vous sortez
ils sortent
elles sortent
perfect je suis sorti(e)
future je sortirai
imperfect je sortais
conditional je sortirais

venir *(vi)* *to come*
je viens
tu viens
il vient
elle vient
on vient
nous venons
vous venez
ils viennent
elles viennent
perfect je suis venu(e)
future je viendrai
imperfect je venais
conditional je viendrais
(also *tenir, revenir, devenir*)

voir *(vt)* *to see*
je vois
tu vois
il voit
elle voit
on voit
nous voyons
vous voyez
ils voient
elles voient
perfect j'ai vu
future je verrai
imperfect je voyais
conditional je verrais

vouloir *(vt)* *to want*
je veux
tu veux
il veut
elle veut
on veut
nous voulons
vous voulez
ils veulent
elles veulent
perfect j'ai voulu
future je voudrai
imperfect je voulais
conditional je voudrais

The perfect tense

A To form the perfect tense, you usually use **avoir** and a past participle (see also *Auto 3*, page 165):

j'ai mangé
tu as regardé
il a choisi
elle a réservé
on a bu
nous avons fini
vous avez pris
ils ont vendu
elles ont fait

B With some verbs, you use **être** instead of avoir (see also *Auto 3*, page 167).

je suis sorti(e)
tu es allé(e)
il est parti
elle est restée
on est arrivé
nous sommes tombé(e)s
vous êtes arrivé(e)(s)
ils sont venus
elles sont entrées

Attention!

● Verbs which take **être** have to agree with the person who did the action.
To help you remember which verbs take **être**, just remember the sentence:
MR P. VANS TRAMPED.

Monter *(vi)* (monté)
Rester *(vi)* (resté)
Passer *(vi)* (passé)
Venir *(vi)* (venu)
Arriver *(vi)* (arrivé)
Naître *(vi)* (né)
Sortir *(vi)* (sorti)
Tomber *(vi)* (tombé)
Rentrer *(vi)* (rentré)
Aller *(vi)* (allé)
Mourir *(vi)* (mort)
Partir *(vi)* (parti)
Entrer *(vi)* (entré)
Descendre *(vi)* (descendu)

Past participles

● **-er** verbs
The **-er** changes to **-é**:
manger → **mangé**

● **-re** verbs
The **-re** changes to **-u**:
vendre → **vendu**

● **-ir** verbs
The **-ir** changes to **-i**:
finir → **fini**

● For some verbs, the past participle does not follow the usual pattern. See the list of irregular verbs for examples.

Aller + infinitive
(*Auto 3*, page 153)

● To talk about what people are going to do and things that are going to happen, you can use the verb **aller** and the infinitive of the main verb:
Je **vais faire** mes devoirs.
Il **va neiger**.

Le petit dictionnaire

(If there are any abbreviations that you do not understand, you can look them up on pages *VIII* and *IX* of the *Collins Paperback French Dictionary*.)

FRANÇAIS – ANGLAIS

A

abriter *vt (loger)* to accommodate.

accessoire *nm* accessory.

accrochage *nm (dispute)* clash, brush.

acerbe *a* caustic, acid.

achats *nmpl* purchases.

acheter *vt* to buy, purchase; **s'~** *vi* to be on sale.

actif, ive *a* active.

actuellement *ad* at present, at the present time.

admiratif, ive *a* admiring.

aérospatiale *nf* the aerospace industry.

affiche *nf* poster; *(officielle)* (public) notice.

affilié, e *a*: **être ~ à** to be affiliated to.

agence *nf* agency, office; **~ de voyages** travel agency.

agréable *a* pleasant, nice.

agrément *nm (plaisir)* pleasure.

aider *vt* to help.

aimable *a* kind, nice.

ainsi *ad (ce faisant)* thus ♦ *cj* thus, so; **~ que** *ad (comme)* (just) as; *(et aussi)* as well as.

air *nm* air; **avoir l'~** to look *ou* seem.

aire *nf* area; **~ de jeu** play area.

ajouter *vt* to add.

alors que *cj (opposition)* whereas, while.

amateur *nm* amateur; **~ de musique/sport** *etc* music/sport *etc* lover.

améliorer *vt* to improve.

amour *nm* love.

amusant, e *a (comique)* funny, amusing.

amuser *vt* to entertain, amuse; **s'~** *vi (jouer)* to amuse o.s., play; *(se divertir)* to enjoy o.s., have fun.

ancien, ne *a (précédent, ex-)* former, old.

animé, e *a* lively.

animer *vt (ville, soirée)* to liven up, enliven.

année *nf* year.

annonce *nf* announcement; *(aussi: ~ publicitaire)* advertisement.

appareil-photo *nm* camera.

apparence *nf* appearance.

appartement *nm* flat.

apporter *vt* to bring.

apprécier *vt* to appreciate.

apprendre *vt* to learn.

approvisionner *vt* to supply.

appuyer *vt (poser)*: **~ qch sur/contre** to lean or rest sth on/against; *vi* **~ sur** *(bouton, frein)* to press, push.

après-ski *nm inv (chaussure)* snow-boot.

argent *nm (monnaie)* money; **~ de poche** pocket money.

armée *nf* army.

armoire *nf* (tall) cupboard; *(penderie)* wardrobe.

arrêt *nm (de bus, etc)* stop.

arrêter *vt* to stop; **s'~** *vi* to stop; *(s'interrompre)* to stop o.s.

arriver *vi* to arrive; **~ à (faire) qch** *(réussir)* to manage (to do) sth.

arrogant, e *a* arrogant.

ascenseur *nm* lift.

assis, e *a pp de* **asseoir** ♦ *a* sitting (down), seated.

assurance *nf (confiance en soi)* (self-) confidence.

assuré, e *a (assurances)* insured.

assurer *vt (victoire etc)* to ensure, make certain.

athée *a* atheistic.

attirer *vt* to attract.

aucun, e *pronom* none, *tournure négative* + any.

autant (de) *ad* so much *(ou* many).

autoroute *nf* motorway.

autour de *prép* around.

avance *nf (de troupes etc)* advance; **à l'~** in advance.

avant *prép* before.

avenir *nm* : **l'~** the future.

averse *nf* shower.

avion *nm* (aero)plane.

B

baby-foot *nm inv* table football.

baie *nf (GÉO)* bay.

baignade *nf (action)* bathing.

balader *vt* to trail around; **se ~** *vi* to go for a walk or stroll.

balai *nm* broom, brush.

balnéaire *a* seaside.

banlieue *nf* suburbs *pl*.

barrage *nm* dam.

bas, basse *a* low.

basilique *nf* basilica.

bassin *nm (pièce d'eau)* pond, pool.

bateau, x *nm* boat.

bâtiment *nm* building.

beau-père *nm (remariage)* step-father

beauté *nf* beauty.

belge *a* Belgian.

belle-mère *nf (remariage)* step-mother.

besoin *nm* need; **avoir ~ de qch** to need sth.

bête *a* stupid, silly.

bizarre *a* strange, odd.

blague *nf (propos)* joke.

blanc *nm (espace non écrit)* blank.

boisé, e *a* woody, wooded.

boisson *nf* drink.

boîte *nf* box; **~ de nuit** night club.

bon, bonne *a* good; *(juste)* **le ~ ordre** the correct order.

bonbon *nm* (boiled) sweet.

bord *nm* edge: **au ~ de** on the banks of; **à ~** to go on board.

boule *nf (pour jouer)* bowl.

bout *nm (: d'une ficelle, table, rue, période)* end.

bouton *nm (de vêtement, électrique etc)* button.

Bretagne *nf:* **la ~** Brittany.

britannique *a* British.

brouillon *nm* (first) draft.

C

cachemire *nm* cashmere.

cadeau , x *nm* present, gift.

caisse *nf (: machine)* till.

calcul *nm* calculation.

camping *nm* camping; **(terrain de) ~** campsite, camping site.

car *nm* coach.

carburant *nm* (motor) fuel.

carrière *nf (métier)* career.

carte *nf (de géographie)* map; *(de fichier, d'abonnement etc, à jouer)* card; **~ bancaire** cash card.

cas *nm* case; **en ~ de** in case of; **en ce ~** in that case.

cause *nf* cause; **à ~ de** because of, owing to.

ce qui, ce que *pronom* what.

célèbre *a* famous.

chacun, e *pronom* each.

chance *nf:* **la ~** luck.

changer *vt (COMM)* to change.

chanter *vt,vi* to sing.

chapelle *nf* chapel.

chaque *dét* each, every.

charbon *nm* coal.

charger *vt* to load, charge; **se ~ de** *vt* to see to, to take care of.

charmant, e *a* charming.

chasse *nf* hunting.

chaussée *nf* road(way).

chemin *nm* path; **~ de fer** railway.

chéquier *nm* cheque book.

cher, ère *a (aimé)* dear; *(coûteux)* expensive.

chercher *vt* to look for; **(aller) ~** (to go and) fetch; **~ à faire (qch)** to try to do (sth).

chic *a inv* chic, smart.

choisir *vt* to choose.

choix *nm* choice, selection.

chose *nf* thing.

ci-dessous *ad* below.

ci-dessus *ad* above.

ci-joint, e *a, ad* enclosed.

ciel *nm* sky.

citadin, e *nm/f* city dweller.

citronnnier *nm* lemon tree.

clair, e *a* light; *(eau, son, fig)* clear.

client, e *nm/f (acheteur)* customer, client.

climatisé, e *a* air-conditioned.

cocher *vt* to tick off.

code *nm* code; **~ de la route** highway code.

cœur *nm* heart; **apprendre par ~** to learn by heart.

colline *nf* hill.

commerçant, e *nm/f* shopkeeper, trader.

comprendre *vt* to understand; *(inclure)* to include.

compter *vi (être non négligeable)* to count, matter

contemporain, e *a* contemporary.

concours *nm* competition.

conduire *vt (véhicule, passager)* to drive; *vi* **se ~** to behave.

confier *vt:* **~ à qn** to entrust to sb; **se ~ à qn** *vi* to confide in sb.

conflit *nm* conflict.

conjoint, e *nm/f* spouse.

connaître *vt* to know.

conscient, e *a* conscious; **~ de** aware *ou* conscious of.

conseil *nm (avis)* piece of advice.

conseiller *vt (personne)* to advise.

constater *vt (remarquer)* to note, notice.

construire *vt* to build.

contraire *a, nm* opposite.

contre *prép* against.

contredire *vt (personne)* to contradict.

controversé, e *a (personnage, question)* controversial.

coquillage *nm (mollusque)* shellfish.

correspondant, e *nm/f* penfriend.

corriger *vt (texte)* to correct, amend; *(erreur, défaut)* to correct, put right.

costume *nm (d'homme)* suit.

côte *nf* coast.

côté *nm (gén)* side.

couper *vt* to cut.

courrier *nm* mail, post; **~ électronique** electronic mail.

cours *nm (leçon)* lesson.

court, e *a* short.

couvert , e *pp de* **couvrir** ♦ *a (ciel)* cloudy, overcast.

couvert *nm* place setting; *(place à table)* place.

couverture *nf (de lit)* blanket.

crâne *nm* skull.

créer *vt* to create.

crevette *nf* shrimp.

croix *nf* cross.

cuisine *nf (art culinaire)* cookery, cooking; *(nourriture)* cooking, food.

cultivé, e *a (personne)* cultured, cultivated.

D

débat *nm* discussion, debate.

debout *ad:* **être ~** *(personne)* to be standing, stand.

début *nm* beginning, start.

déchiré, e *a* torn.

découvrir *vt* to discover.

décrire *vt* to describe.

décrocher *vt (dépendre)* to take down.

dédier *vt* to dedicate.

défendu, e *pp de* **défendre** ♦ *a* forbidden.

dehors *ad* outside; **en ~** outside.

déjà *ad* already.

déjeuner *vi* to (have) lunch.

deltaplane *nm* ® hang-glider.

demain *ad* tomorrow.

démaquillant *nm* make-up remover.

dépêcher *vt* to dispatch; **se ~** *vi* to hurry.

dépliant *nm* leaflet.

dernier, ière *a (le plus récent)* latest, last; *(final, ultime:effort)* final; **ce ~, cette dernière** the latter.

désagréable *a* unpleasant, disagreeable.

descendre *vt (escalier, montagne)* to go (ou come) down; *vi* to go (ou come) down.

désolé, e *a:* **je suis ~** I am sorry.

dessin *nm (œuvre, art)* drawing.

détente *nf* relaxation.

devant *prép* in front of.

devenir *vt* to become.

deviner *vt* to guess.

devises *nfpl (argent)* currency *sg.*

dîner *vi* to have dinner.

discuter *vt (débattre: prix)* to discuss; **~ de** to discuss.

disparu, e *pp de* **disparaître** ♦ *nm/f* missing person; *(défunt)* departed.

disponible *a* available.

disposer de *vt* to have (at one's disposal).

disque *nm (MUS)* record.

distraction *nf (passe-temps)* distraction, entertainment.

diviser *vt (morceler, subdiviser)* to divide (up), split (up).

dominer *vt (surplomber)* to tower above, dominate.

dont *pronom relatif*: **il y avait plusieurs personnes, ~ Gabrielle** there were several people, among them Gabrielle.

doucement *ad (à voix basse)* softly.

doux, douce *a (peu fort: moutarde etc, clément: climat)* mild; *(pas brusque)* gentle.

droit *nm (prérogative)* right.

droite *a (opposé à gauche)* right, right-hand.

drôle *a (amusant)* funny, amusing.

dur, e *a (pierre, siège, travail, problème)* hard.

durée *nf* length; **de courte ~** *(séjour, répit)* short-term; **de longue ~** long-term.

durer *vi* to last.

E

échange *nm* exchange.

échecs *nmpl (jeu)* chess.

écriteau, x *nm* notice, sign.

édifier *vt* to build, erect.

effacer *vt* to erase, rub out.

également *ad* equally; *(aussi)* too, as well.

élevé, e *a (prix, sommet)* high.

embouchure *nf (GÉO)* mouth.

émetteur *nm*: **poste ~** transmitter.

émission *nf (RADIO, TV)* programme, broadcast.

empêcher *vt* to prevent.

employer *vi (outil, moyen, méthode, mot)* to use.

emporter *vt* to take (with one).

emprunter *vt* to borrow.

enceinte *af*: **~ (de 6 mois)** (6 months) pregnant.

endroit *nm* place.

énerver *vt* to irritate, annoy.

enfer *nm* hell.

engager *vt*: **~ qch dans** to insert sth into.

ennuyer *vt* to bother; **s'~** *vi* to be bored.

enquête *nf (sondage d'opinion)* survey.

enrichir *vt (fig)* to enrich.

entendre *vt* to hear, *(comprendre)* understand; **s'~ (avec)** *vi (sympathiser)* to get on (with).

entraîner *vt* to pull; **s~** *vi (SPORT)* to train.

entier, ière *a (non entamé, en totalité)* whole; *(total, complet)* complete.

entraînement *nm* training.

entraîner *vt* to pull; **s~** *vi (SPORT)* to train.

entretenir *vt* to maintain.

envers *prép* towards, to.

envie *nf*: **avoir ~ de faire** to feel like doing; to want to do.

environ *ad* around, about.

épanouir: **s'~** *vi (fig: se développer)* to blossom (out).

épargner *vt* to save.

épeler *vt* to spell.

équestre *a* equestrian.

équipe *nf* team.

équitation *nf* (horse-)riding.

erreur *nf* mistake, error.

escargot *nm* snail.

espèces *nfpl (COMM)* cash *sg*.

espérer *vt* to hope for.

esprit *nm (pensée, intellect)* mind; *(mentalité, d'une loi etc, fantôme etc)* spirit.

essayer *vt (gén)* to try; **~ de faire** *vi* to try *ou* attempt to do.

étage *nm (d'immeuble)* storey, floor.

étape *nf* unit; stage; *(lieu d'arrivée)* stopping place.

état *nm* state.

étonnant, e *a* surprising.

étrange *a* strange.

étranger, ère *nm/f* foreigner; stranger ♦ *nm*: **à l'~** abroad.

éviter *vt* to avoid.

évoluer *vi* to develop.

excitant *nm* stimulant.

exiger *vt* to demand, require.

explication *nf* explanation.

expliquer *vt* to explain.

exposé *nm (écrit)* exposé; *(oral)* talk.

exposition *nf (manifestation)* exhibition.

expression *nf* expression, phrase; **~~-clé** key phrase.

exprimer *vt (sentiment, idée)* to express; **s'~** *vi (personne)* to express o.s.

F

fabriquer *vt* to make.

face *nf* face; **faire ~ à** to face.

fâché, e *a* angry.

facile *a* easy.

façon *nf (manière)* way.

fatigant, e *a* tiring.

fatigué, e *a* tired.

fatiguer *vt* to tire, make tired; **se ~** *vi* to get tired, to tire o.s. (out).

faute *nf* fault, mistake.

faux, fausse *a* false.

férié, e *a*: **jour ~** public holiday.

ferme *a* firm.

fermer *vi* to close, shut.

fermeture *nf* closing, shutting; **~ éclair** ® zip (fastener).

fête *nf (du nom)* name/saint's day; *(publique)* holiday; *(kermesse)* fête, fair, festival.

feu, x *nm (gén)* fire; **~x d'artifice** fireworks.

feuilleton *nm* serial.

fiche *nf (feuille)* sheet, slip; *(formulaire)* form.

fidélité *nf* faithfulness.

fier, fière *a* proud.

fin, e *a (cheveux, poudre, pointe, visage)* fine.

fin *nf* end.

fleur *nf* flower.

fondamental, e *a* fundamental, basic.

fondateur, trice *nm/f* founder.

fontaine *nf* fountain.

footing *nm* jogging.

force *nf* strength.

formation *nf (éducation)* training.

forme *nf*: **être en (bonne** *ou* **pleine) ~, avoir la ~** *(SPORT etc)* to be on form.

former *vt (éduquer)* to train.

fort, e *a* strong; *(doué)*; **être ~ (en)** to be good (at); *ad (sonner)* loud(ly).

fou (fol), folle *nm/f* madman/woman.

frais, fraîche *a (air, eau, acceuil)* cool.

fraternité *nf* brotherhood.

frites *nfpl* chips.

frontière *nf (GÉO)* border.

fruits de mer *nmpl (CULIN)* seafood(s).

fusée *nf* rocket.

fut *vb* was.

G

gagner *vt (concours, procès, pari)* to win; *(somme d'argent)* to earn; **~ sa vie** to earn one's living.

gamme *nf (fig)* range.

gardien, ne *nm/f (de domaine, réserve)* warden; *(de musée etc)* attendant.

gâté, e *a* spoilt.

gauche *a* left, left-hand; **à ~** on the left.

géant, e *nm/f* giant.

geler *vt, vi* to freeze.

genre *nm (espèce, sorte)* type, kind.

gens *nmpl* people *pl*.

gentil, le *a* kind; *(sympa: endroit etc)* nice.
gloire *nf* glory.
golf *nm (terrain)* golf course.
goût *nm* taste; *(fig: appréciation)* taste, liking.
grandir *vi (enfant, arbre)* to grow.
gros, se *a* big, large; *(obèse)* fat; *(problème, quantité)* great.
grotte *nf* cave.

H

habitant *nm/f* inhabitant.
habitude *nf* habit; **d'~** usually.
halte *nf (escale)* stopping place.
hameau, x *nm* hamlet.
hanté, e *a* haunted.
haras *nm* stud farm.
haut, e *a* high ; *(grand)* tall.
hébergement *nm* accommodation, lodging.
hier *ad* yesterday.
honnête *a* honest.
honnêteté *nf* honesty.
horaire *nm* timetable, schedule; **~s** *nmpl (heures de travail)* hours.
horodateur *nm* (parking) ticket machine.
hôte *nm (maître de maison)* host.
hôtel (particulier) *nm* (private) mansion.
hôtesse *nf* hostess; **~ de l'air** air hostess; **~ (d'acceuil)** receptionist.

I

il y a *(temporel)* ago.
image *nf (gén)* picture.
important, e *a* important; *(en quantité)* considerable, sizeable.
imposant, e *a* imposing.
inconvénient *nm (d'une situation, d'un projet)* disadvantage, drawback.
ingénieur *nm* engineer.
inoubliable *a* unforgettable.
inquiéter *vt* to worry, disturb; **s'~** *vi* to worry, become anxious.
installer *vt* to settle (down); **s'~** to set o.s. up, to settle down.
interdit, e *pp de* **interdire** ♦ *a (défendu)* forbidden, prohibited.
interrompre *vt* to interrupt.
invité, e *nm/f* guest.
irremplaçable *a* irreplaceable.

J

jaloux, ouse *a* jealous.
jamais *ad* never; *(sans négation)* ever.
jeter *vt* to throw; **se ~ sur** to throw o.s. onto.
jeu de rôles *nm* rôle-play.
jeune *a* young; **les ~s** young people, the young.
joli, e *a* pretty, attractive.
jouet *nm* toy.
jouir: ~ de *vt* to enjoy.
journée *nf* day.
Juif, ive *nm/f* Jew/Jewish woman.
jumeau,elle, x *a, nm/f* twin.
jumelé, e *a* twinned.
jusqu'à *(endroit)* as far as; *(prép) (limite)* up to.
juste *a (équitable)* just, fair; *(exact, vrai)* right.

L

lac *nm* lake.
laisser *vt* to leave.
laitage *nm* milk product.
langue *nf (LING)* language.
laverie *nf*: **~ (automatique)** launderette.
légume *nm* vegetable.
lentement *ad* slowly.
lentilles de contact *nfpl* contact lenses.
lequel, laquelle, *mpl* **lesquels,** *fpl* **lesquelles** *pronom (interrogatif)* which, which one; *(relatif: personne: sujet)* who; *(:objet, après préposition)* whom.
libérer *vt* to free, liberate.
libre *a* free.
lieu, x *nm* place.
lire *vt, vi* to read.
loger *vt* to accommodate.
loin *ad* far.
loisir *nm*: **~s** *nmpl* leisure *sg*; *(activités)* leisure activities.
longueur *nf* length.
lorqsue *cj* when, as.
louer *vt (maison: suj: propriétaire)* to let, rent (out) *(:locataire)* to rent.
lourd, e *a* heavy; *(chaleur, temps)* sultry.
loyauté *nf* loyalty, faithfulness.
luxe *nm* luxury.
lycéen, ne *nm/f* secondary school pupil.

M

machine *nf* machine; **~ à sous** fruit machine.

magasin *nm (boutique)* shop; **faire les ~s** to go (a)round the shops, do the shops.
main *nf* hand; **donner un coup de ~ à qn** to give sb a hand.
majeur, e *a (important)* major.
malédiction *nf* curse.
malgré *prép* in spite of, despite.
mammifère *nm* mammal.
manière *nf (façon)* way, manner; **~s** *nfpl (attitude)* manners.
manifestation *nf (fête etc)* event.
manoir *nm* country house, manor.
manquer *vi* to be lacking, to be missing ♦ *vb impersonnel*: **il (nous) manque encore 100F** we are still 100F short; **il/cela me manque** I miss him/that.
marcher *vi (fonctionner)* to work, run.
marée *nf* tide.
marque *nf* mark; **de ~** *a (COMM)* brand-name, designer.
matériel *nm* equipment.
matière *nf (SCOL)* subject.
mauvais, e *a* bad.
mazout *nm* (fuel) oil.
méchant, e *a* nasty, malicious, spiteful; *(enfant: passage)* naughty.
meilleur, e *a, ad* better.
mélanger *vt (substances)* to mix.
même *a* same.
menace *nf* threat.
ménager, ère *a* household, domestic.
mener *vt* to lead.
méridional, e, aux *nm/f* Southerner.
merveille *nf* marvel, wonder.
merveilleux, euse *a* marvellous, wonderful.
métier *nm (profession: gén)* job.
mettre *vt* to put; **se ~ en colère** *vi* to get angry.
millier *nm* thousand.
mineur *nm (travailleur)* miner.
mitoyen, ne *a* common; **maisons ~nes** semi-detached houses.
mode *nf* fashion; **à la ~** fashionable, in fashion ♦ *nm (manière)* form, mode, method; **~ de vie** way of life; **~ d'emploi** directions *pl* (for use).
modèle réduit *nm* small-scale model.
modéliste *nm/f (COUTURE)* fashion designer.
modéré, e *a* moderate.
moins *ad* less; **au ~** at least.
monde *nm* world; **beaucoup/peu de ~** many/few people.
mondial, e, aux *a* world.
mongolfière *nf* hot air balloon.

monnaie *nf (ECON, gén: moyen d'échange)* currency; *(petites pièces)*: **avoir de la ~** to have (some) change.
monotone *a* monotonous.
montant *nm (somme, total)* (sum) total; (total) amount.
monter *vt (escalier, côte)* to go (*ou* come) up; *vi* to go (*ou* come) up; *(brouillard, bruit)* to rise.
montre *nf* watch.
montrer *vt* to show.
moquer: **se ~ de** *vt* to make fun of, laugh at.
mort *nf* death.
mot *nm* word; **~-clé** key word.
mourir *vi* to die.
moyens *nmpl (capacités)* means.
municipal, e, aux *a* municipal; town.
musculation *nf*: **exercices de ~** muscle-developing exercises.
mystère *nm* mystery.
mystérieux, euse *a* mysterious.

N

nager *vi* to swim.
naître *vi* to be born.
natation *nf* swimming.
nautique *a* nautical, water *cpd*.
neuf, neuve *a* new.
n'importe *ad*: **~ qui** anybody; **~ quel/quelle** any.
noctambule *nm* night-bird.
nocturne *nf (d'un magasin)* late opening.
Noël *nm* Christmas.
note *nf (SCOL)* mark.
nôtre *pronom*: **le/la ~** ours; **les ~s** ours.
nourriture *nf* food.

O

obéissance *nf* obedience.
objet *nm (chose)* object.
obséder *vt* to obsess.
obtenir *vt* to obtain, get.
occuper *vt* to occupy; **s'~ de** *(se charger de: affaire)* to take charge of, deal with.
œuvre *nf (ouvrage achevé, livre, tableau etc)* work.
orage *nm* (thunder)storm.
oranger *nm* orange tree.
ordinateur *nm* computer.
ordonner *vt (donner un ordre)*: **~ à qn de faire** to order sb to do.
ordre *nm* order.
orthographe *nf* spelling.
ou *cj* or; **~ bien** or (else).
où *ad, pronom* where.

oublier *vt* to forget.
ouvrir *vt, vi* to open.

P

palais *nm* palace.
palmier *nm* palm tree.
panneau, x *nm* sign.
panorama *nm (vue)* all-round view, panorama.
Pâques *nm* Easter.
paradis *nm* heaven, paradise.
paraître *vb avec attribut* to seem, look, appear.
parapente *nm* paragliding; **faire du ~** to go paragliding.
pardonner *vt* to forgive.
paresseux, euse *a* lazy.
parfois *ad* sometimes.
parking *nm (lieu)* car park.
à part entier *a* full, complete.
partager *vt* to share.
particulier, ière *a (spécial)* special, particular.
partir *vi* to leave **~ en vacances** to go on holiday.
parvenir *vt*: **~ à faire** to manage to do, succeed in doing.
pas *ad* not; **~ mal de** quite a lot of.
passager, ère *nm/f* passenger.
passé *nm* past.
passer *vi (se rendre, aller)* to go ♦ *vt* to cross, go through; **se ~** *vi (avoir lieu: scène, action)* to take place; *(se dérouler: entretien etc)* to go; *(arriver)* to happen.
passionnant, e *a* fascinating.
passionné, e *a* passionate.
pasteur *nm (protestant)* minister.
patin *nm* skate; **~ à glace** ice-skating.
patrie *nf* homeland.
pause *nf (arrêt)* break.
pauvre *nm/f* poor man/woman.
pays *nm (territoire, habitants)* country, land.
paysan, ne *nm/f* country man/woman.
péage *nm* toll.
pêche *nf (sport, activité)* fishing.
pédestre *a*: **randonnée ~** *(activité)* rambling; **tourisme ~** hiking.
peintre *nm* painter.
peinture *nf* painting.
pelouse *nf* lawn.
pente *nf* slope.
perdre *vt* to lose.
permis *nm* permit, licence; **~ (de conduire)** driving licence.

personnage *nm (THÉATRE)* character.
perte *nf* loss.
pétanque *nf* type of bowls.
peu *ad* little, not very; **~ de** *(nombre)* few; **à ~ près** just about, more or less.
phrase *nf (LING)* sentence.
pièce *nf (d'un logement)* room; *(THÉATRE)* play; *(de monnaie)* coin; **dix francs (la) ~** ten francs each; *(de drap, fragment, d'une collection)* piece; **~ d'identité**: **avez-vous une ~ d'identité?** Have you got any (means of) identification?
pied *nm* foot: **à ~** on foot.
pierre *nf* stone.
pire *a (comparatif)* worse; *(superlatif)*: **le (la) ~ . . .** the worst. . .
piscine *nf* (swimming) pool.
pistolet *nm* petrol pump nozzle.
place *nf (emplacement, situation, classement)* place; *(de ville, village)* square; **sur ~** on the spot .
plaindre *vt* to pity, feel sorry for; **se ~ (à qn) (de)** *vi* to complain (to sb) (about).
plaire *vi* to please; **~ à: cela me plaît** I like it.
plaisance *nf* sailing, yachting; **port de ~** *(bassin)* sailing harbour, *(ville)* sailing resort.
plaisir *nm* pleasure.
plan *nm* plan, map.
plat *nm (CULIN)* dish.
plein, e *a* full.
plier *vt* to fold.
plongeon *nm* dive.
pluie *nf* rain.
plupart: **la ~** *pronom* the majority, most (of them).
plusieurs *pronom* several.
pluvieux, euse *a* rainy, wet.
pneu *nm* tyre.
poli, e *a* polite.
politesse *nf* politeness.
pompiste *nm/f* petrol pump attendant.
pont *nm* bridge; **faire le ~** to take the extra day off.
posséder *vt* to own, possess.
possibilité *nf* chance.
pour *prép* for.
pratiquant,e *a* practising.
pratique *a* practical.
pratiquer *vt* to practise.
précis, e *a* precise.
préjugé *nm* prejudice, preconceived idea.
prélever *vt* to deduct.

prendre *vt* to take.

pressé, e *a* in a hurry.

prestation *nf (d'une entreprise)* service provided.

prêt, e *a* ready.

principal, e, aux *a* principal, main.

priorité *nf:* **en ~** as a (matter of) priority; **avoir la ~ (sur)** to have right of way (over).

prix *nm (valeur)* price; *(récompense, SCOL)* prize.

prochain, e *a* next.

profiter *vi:* **~ de** to take advantage of, to make the most of.

projet *nm* plan.

promenade *nf* walk *(ou* drive *ou* ride).

promener *vt (personne, chien)* to take out for a walk; **se ~** *vi (à pied)* to go for *(ou* be out for) a walk.

prononcer: se ~ *vi* to reach a decision; **ne se prononce pas** *(sondage)* no response.

propre *a (possessif)* own ♦ *nm* : **au ~** *(LING)* literally.

provenir: ~ de *vt* to come from.

province *nf* province.

proximité *nf* nearness, closeness, proximity; **à ~** near *ou* close by.

publicité *nf (annonce)* advertisement.

puisque *cj* since.

Q

quand *cj, ad* when.

quartier *nm (de ville)* district, area.

quel, quelle *a:* **~ livre/homme?** what book/man?; *(parmi un certain choix)* which book/man?

qui *pronom (personne)* who; *(chose, animal)* which, that.

quotidien, ne *a (journalier)* daily.

R

raccrocher *vi (TÉL)* to hang up.

raison *nf* reason; **avoir ~** to be right.

randonnée *nf (à pied)* walk, hike.

ranger *vt (classer, grouper)* to order, arrange.

rapport *nm (compte rendu)* report; **~s** *nmpl (entre personnes, pays)* relations; **par ~ à** with regard to.

réagir *vi* to react.

réaliste *a* realistic ♦ *nm/f* realist.

recevoir *vt* to receive.

recherche *nf* research; **~s** *nfpl (scientifiques)* research.

réclamer *vt (aide, nourriture etc)* to ask for.

recommander *vt* to recommend.

recopier *vt (transcrire)* to copy out again, write out again.

recoudre *vt (bouton)* to sew back on.

récréation *nf (SCOL)* break.

réduit, e *a (prix, tarif, échelle)* reduced.

réécouter *vt* to listen again.

réel, le *a* real.

réfléchir *vi* to think.

refléter *vt* to reflect.

règle *nf (loi, prescription)* rule.

règne *nm (d'un roi etc)* reign.

régulièrement *ad* regularly.

reine *nf* queen.

rejoindre *vt (lieu)* to get (back) to.

relaxer *vt* to relax; **se ~** *vi* to relax.

relier *vt* to link up.

rembourser *vt* to pay back, repay.

remercier *vt* to thank.

remonter *vt* to go up; **~ le moral à qn** to raise sb's spirits.

remplir *vt* to fill (up); *(questionnaire)* to fill out.

rémunérer *vt* to remunerate, pay.

rencontrer *vt* to meet.

rendez-vous *nm (rencontre)* appointment; *(lieu)* meeting place.

rénover *vt (immeuble)* renovate, do up.

renseignements *nmpl* information.

renseigner: se ~ *vi* to ask for information, make inquiries.

rentrer *vi (entrer de nouveau)* to go *(ou* come) back in; *(entrer)* to go *(ou* come) in; *(revenir chez soi)* to go *(ou* come) (back home).

répartition *nf* sharing out; dividing up; distribution.

repas *nm* meal.

répondeur *nm:* **~ (automatique)** *(TÉL)* (telephone) answering machine.

répondre *vi* to answer, reply.

réponse *nf* answer, reply.

reposant, e *a* restful.

reposer *vt* to put down; to put back; to rest; **se ~** *vi* to rest.

réseau, x *nm* network.

réservoir *nm* petrol tank.

résoudre *vt* to solve.

ressentir *vt* to feel.

ressources *nfpl* resources.

restauration *nf (hôtellerie)* catering.

rester *vi (dans un lieu, un état, une position)* to stay, remain; *(subsister)* to remain, be left.

restes *nmpl* remains, leftovers.

résumé *nm* summary.

résumer *vt (texte)* to summarise.

retard *nm* lateness, delay ; **en ~** late.

retirer *vt* to withdraw; *(reprendre: bagages, billets)* to collect, pick up.

retour *nm* return.

retrait *nm (voir retirer)* withdrawal; collection.

réunion *nf (séance)* meeting.

réussite *nf* success.

rêve *nm* dream.

rien *pronom* nothing.

risque *nm* risk.

roi *nm* king.

roman, e *a (ARCHIT)* Romanesque.

rouler *vi (automobiliste)* to drive.

route *nf* road; *(fig: chemin)* way; *(itinéraire, parcours)* route.

royaume *nm* kingdom.

S

sable *nm* sand.

salle *nf* room; **~ d'eau** shower-room.

sanitaires *nmpl (salle de bain et w.c.)* bathroom *sg.*

sans *prép* without.

santé *nf* health.

sauf *prép* except.

sauter *vt* to jump (over), leap (over).

savoir *vt* to know; *(être capable de):* **il sait nager** he knows how to swim, he can swim.

sec, sèche *a* dry.

séduire *vt (femme: abuser de)* to seduce; *(suj: chose)* to appeal to.

séjour *nm* stay.

selon *prép* according to.

sens *nm (PHYSIOL, instinct)* sense; *(signification)* meaning, sense.

sentier *nm* path.

sentiment *nm* feeling.

sentir *vi* to smell: **se ~ bien** to feel good.

sérieux, euse *a* serious.

serrer *vt* to grip *ou* hold tight; **~ la main à qn** to shake sb's hand.

servir *vt* to serve; **se ~ de** *vi (plat)* to help o.s to; *(voiture, outil, relations)* to use.

siècle *nm* century.
siège *nm* seat.
siéger *vi (assemblée, tribunal)* to sit.
sieste *nf* (afternoon) snooze *ou* nap.
signification *nf* meaning.
signifier *vt (vouloir dire)* to mean.
singe *nm* monkey.
situé, e *a* situated.
ski *nm (objet)* ski; *(sport)* skiing; **~ alpin** Alpine skiing; **~ de fond** cross-country skiing.
soi-disant *ad* supposedly.
sois *vb* be.
soit ... soit either ... or.
somme *nf (argent)* sum, amount.
sondage *nm (enquête)* survey, sounding out of opinion.
sortie *nf (le soir: au restaurant etc)* night out.
sortir *vi* to come out; to go out; *vt* to take out;
souci *nm (inquiétude)* worry.
souligner *vt* to underline.
source *nf (pointe d'eau)* spring.
sous *prép* under.
sous-estimer *vt* underestimate.
soutenir *vt* to support.
souvenir *nm (réminiscence)* memory; *(cadeau)* souvenir.
souvent *ad* often.
souverain, e *nm/f* sovereign.
spectacle *nm (représentation)* show.
station *nf (de villégiature)* resort.
station-service *nf* service station.
stationnement *nm* parking.
suggérer *vt* to suggest.
suivant, e *a* next, following.
suivre *vt* to follow.
supplémentaire *a* additional, further; extra.
supplice *nm* torture.
sur *prép* on; **~ le tas** on the job.
sûr, e *a* sure, certain; *(sans danger)* safe.
sûrement *ad (certainement)* certainly.
surtout *ad (avant tout, d'abord)* above all; *(spécialement, particulièrement)* especially.
sweat *nm* sweat-shirt.

syndicaliste *nm/f* trade unionist.
syndicat *nm* union; **~ d'initiative** tourist office.

T

tâche *nf* task.
taire *vt* to keep to o.s., conceal; **se ~** *vi* to be silent *ou* quiet.
tandis: ~ que *cj* while.
tante *nf* aunt.
tard *ad* late.
tasse *nf* cup.
tâtonner *vi (fig)* to grope around (in the dark).
téléphérique *nm* cable car.
télésiège *nm* chairlift.
témoin *nm* witness.
temps *nm (atmosphérique)* weather; *(époque)* time, times.
tendance *nf (inclination)* tendency; **avoir ~ à** to have a tendency to, tend to.
tendresse *nf* tenderness.
terminer *vt* to end.
terre *nf*: **la T~** Earth.
thé *nm* tea.
thermal, e, aux *a*: **cure ~e** water cure; **station ~e** spa.
tiers, tierce *a* third.
timide *a* shy, timid.
tiroir *nm* drawer.
titre *nm* title.
tomber *vi* to fall.
tôt *ad* early.
toujours *ad* always; *(encore)* still.
tour *nf* tower.
tournoi *nm* tournament.
tout *nm* whole ♦ *ad* **~ le monde** everybody, everyone; **~ de suite** immediately, straightaway.
train *nm (allure)* pace: **être en ~ de faire qch** to be doing sth.
travail, aux *nm (gén)* work.
travailleur, euse *a* hard-working.
triste *a* sad.
trop *ad* too.
trou *nm* hole; *(fig)* gap.
tuer *vt* to kill.

U

uni, e *a (ton, tissu)* plain; *(pays)* united.
usine *nf* factory.
utile *a* useful.
utiliser *vt* to use.

V

vacances *nfpl* holiday(s *pl*).
vacancier, ière *nm/f* holiday-maker.
valeur *nf (gén)* value.
valise *nf* (suit)case.
vallonné, e *a* undulating.
véhicule *nm* vehicle.
veille *nf (garde)* watch: **la ~** the day before.
vélo *nm* bike, cycle; **~ tout terrain** mountain bike.
vendeur, euse *nm/f (de magasin)* shop *ou* sales assistant.
vendre *vt* to sell; "**á ~**" " for sale".
venir *vi* to come.
vérifier *vt* to check.
véritable *a* real.
vérité *nf* truth.
vestige *nm (objet)* relic; **~s** *nmpl (d'une ville)* remains; *(d'une civilisation, du passé)* remnants, relics.
vêtement *nm* garment, item of clothing; **~s** *nmpl* clothes.
vider *vt* to empty.
vie *nf* life.
vieux (vieil), vieille *a* old.
vignoble *nm (vignes d'une région)* vineyards *pl*.
visage *nm* face.
vitre *nf* (window) pane.
vitrine *nf* (shop) window.
vivifiant, e *a* invigorating.
vivre *vi, vt* to live.
voie *nf (AUTO)* lane (on motorway).
voile *nf* sail; *(sport)* sailing; *(sport)* **planche à ~** windsurfing.
voisin, e *a (proche)* neighbouring; *nm/f* neighbour.
voix *nf* voice.
vol *nm (mode d'appropriation)* theft, stealing; *(trajet, voyage, group d'oiseaux)* flight.
vouloir *vt* to want; **~ dire (que)** *(signifier)* to mean (that).
voyager *vi* to travel.
vrai, e *a (véridique: récit, faits)* true.
VTT = vélo tout terrain *nm* mountain bike.
vue *nf (panorama, image, photo)* view.

ANGLAIS – FRANÇAIS

A

abroad *ad* à l'étranger.
advise *vt* conseiller.
after *prep, ad* après.
against *prep* contre.
ago *ad*: **2 days ~** il y a 2 jours.
agree *vi*: **to ~ (with)** *(person)* être d'accord *(avec)*.
almost *ad* presque.
already *ad* déjà.
always *ad* toujours.
amusement arcade *n* luna-park *m*.
amusement park *n* parc *m* d'attractions.
answer *n* réponse *f*: ♦ *vi* répondre.
arrive *vi* arriver.
ash-tray *n* cendrier *m*.
ask *vt* demander.

B

badly *ad (work, dress etc)* mal.
bar *n (of chocolate)* tablette *f*.
because *cj* parce que; **~ of** *prep* à cause de.
before *prep (of time)* avant.
behind *prep* derrière.
believe *vt, vi* croire.
birthday *n* anniversaire *m*.
bit: **a ~ (of)** *n* un peu (de) *m*.
blackboard *n* tableau noir *m*.
boring *a* ennuyeux (euse).
borrow *vt* : **to ~ sth (from sb)** emprunter qch (à qn).
break *vt* casser, briser; *(law)* violer.
but *cj* mais.
buy *vt* acheter.

C

can *n (drink)* cannette *(de coca etc) f*.
chat *vi* bavarder, causer.
chocolate *n* chocolat *m*.
computer *n* ordinateur *m*.
cost *vi* coûter.
country *n* pays *m*.

D

difficult *a* difficile.
divorced *a* divorcé(e).
doll *n* poupée *f*.
drawing pin *n* punaise *f*.

E

easy *a* facile.
every *a* chaque.

everywhere *ad* partout.
excuse: **~ me!** excusez-moi! pardon!
expensive *a* cher (chère).

F

fast food *n* fast food *m*.
find *vt* trouver.
finish *vt* finir.
first *ad (before other things)* d'abord.
flat *n* appartement *m*.
football ground *n* terrain *m* de football.
foreigner *n* étranger/ère *m/f*.
forget *vt, vi* oublier.
fortunately *ad* heureuseument.
front: **in ~ (of)** devant.

G

give *vt* donner.
go *vi* aller.
guardian *n (of minor)* tuteur/trice *m/f*.

H

half *n* moitié *f*.
half-brother *n* demi-frère *m*.
half-sister *n* demi-sœur *f*.
headphones *npl* casque *m* (à écouteurs).
hobby *n* passe-temps (favori) *m*.
hope *vt, vi* espérer.
however *cj* cependant.

I

ice cream *n* glace *f*.
ice rink *n* patinoire *f*.
if *cj* si.
information *n* renseignements *mpl*.
insured *a* assuré(e).
interesting *a* intéressant(e).

J

jewellery *n* bijoux *mpl*.

K

key ring *n* porte-clés *m*.
know *vt* savoir; *(person, place)* connaître.

L

last *a* dernier(ière).
late *a (not on time)* en retard ♦ *ad* tard.

learn *vi* apprendre.
leave *vt* laisser; *(go away from)* quitter ♦ *vi* partir, s'en aller.
listen *vi* écouter; **to ~ to** écouter.
little *a (small)* petit(e) ♦ *ad* peu.
look *vt* regarder; *(seem)* sembler, paraître, avoir l'air.
lose *vt* perdre.
luxury *cpd* de luxe.

M

mean *vt (signify)* signifier, vouloir dire.
mouse *n* souris *f*.

N

near *prep (also: ~ to)* près de.
next *a* prochain(e) ♦ *ad (afterwards)* ensuite.
normally *ad* normalement.

O

obedient *a* obéissant(e).
obsessed *a*: **to be ~ by** *or* **with sb/sth** être obsédé(e) par qn/qch.
often *ad* souvent.
opinion *n* avis *m*; **in my ~** à mon avis.
opposite *n* contraire *m*.
overhead projector *n* rétro-projeteur *m*.

P

palace *n* palais *m*.
paper-clip *n* trombone *m*.
patient *a* patient(e).
perfume *n* parfum *m*.
perhaps *ad* peut-être.
phrase *n* expression *f*.
place *n* endroit *m*.
plug in *(ELEC) vt* brancher.
practise *vt* répéter.
present *n* cadeau *m*.
probably *ad* probablement.

Q

quite *ad (rather)* assez.

R

racecourse *n* champ *m* de courses.
ready *a* prêt(e).
really *ad* vraiment.
recommend *vt* recommander.

record *vt (MUS: song etc)*
  enregistrer.
repeat *vt* répéter.
rude *a (impolite: person)*
  impoli(e).
rule *n* règle *f*; *(regulation)*
  règlement *m*.
ruler *n (for measuring)* règle *f*.

S

save *vt (money)* mettre de côté.
see *vt* voir.
seem *vi* sembler.
sell *vt* vendre.
send *vt* envoyer.
sensitive *a* sensible.
sentence *n (LING)* phrase *f*.
separated *a* séparé(e).
several *a, pronoun* plusieurs
  m/fpl.
shopping centre *n* centre *m*
  commercial.
snack *n* casse-croûte *m inv*.
sometimes *ad* quelquefois.
soon *ad* bientôt.
sorry *a* désolé(e).
souvenir *n* souvenir *m*.
spend *vt (money)* dépenser.
sports car *n* voiture *f* de sport.
sports ground *n* terrain *m* de
  sport.
start *vt* commencer.
stepbrother *n* demi-frère *m*.

stepfather *n* beau-père *m*.
stepmother *n* belle-mère *f*.
stepsister *n* demi-sœur *f*.
still *ad (up to this time)* toujours.
street *n* rue *f*.
strong *a* fort(e).
sweet *n* bonbon *m*.
switch on *vt* allumer.

T

talk (about) *vi* parler (de).
tape-recorder *n* magnétophone
  m.
theatre *n* théâtre *m*.
thing *n* chose *f*.
think *vt,vi* penser.
time *n* temps *m*; *(by clock)* heure
  f; **on ~** à l'heure.
tomorrow *n* demain *m*
too *ad (excessively)* trop.
toy *n* jouet *m*.
travel *vi* voyager.
trust *vt (rely on)* avoir confiance
  en.
try: **to ~ to do** *vi* essayer de faire.
turn *n* tour *m*: **it's my ~** c'est à
  moi.

U

understand *vt,vi* comprendre.
unfortunately *ad*
  malheureusement.

useful *a* utile.
usually *ad* d'habitude.

V

video recorder *n* magnétoscope
  m.
visit *vt (person)* rendre visite à;
  (place) visiter.

W

wait *vi* attendre.
watch *vt (match, programme)*
  regarder.
weak *a* faible.
wear *vt (clothes)* porter.
well *a* bien.
where *ad,cj* où.
whether *cj* si.
whiteboard *n* tableau blanc *m*.
why *ad* pourquoi.
with *prep* avec.
without *prep* sans.
word *n* mot *m*.
work *vi* travailler; *(plan etc)*
  marcher.
write *vt,vi* écrire.

Y

yacht *n* yacht *m*.
yesterday *ad, n* hier *(m)*.
young *a* jeune.

Published by Collins Educational
An imprint of HarperCollins*Publishers*
77-85 Fulham Palace Road
Hammersmith
London
W6 8JB

© HarperCollins*Publishers* 1995
First published 1995
Reprinted 1995, 1997

ISBN 0 00 320067 1

Series planned by Kate Harris
Edited by Philippa Sawyer
Production by Mandy Inness
Cover design by Celia Hart
Book design by Bob Vickers
Printed in Hong Kong
Cover inset photo by Tim Booth

Acknowledgements

The Authors and Publishers would sincerely like to thank the many people in Paris who helped with material and photographs for *Auto Examen A*. We are particularly grateful to:

Camping du Bois de Boulogne; Carole Dorléans; Caroline Florin; Anne Gruneberg; Pascal Landré; Lycée Claude Monet; Céline Maurs; Isabelle Mignard; Printemps Italie; Pierre Reivé (Station Elf – Vincent Auriol); Samuel Saïz; Zoo de Vincennes.

We would also like to thank the following for their assistance during the writing and production of *Auto Examen A*:

Barrie Birch (Queens Park Community College)
Nina Boye and Dorothy Galloway for typing and checking the manuscript
Valérie Nollet, Université de Provence
Joaquim Nassar, Ecole Polytechnique
Lea and Lorraine for organising the handwritten extracts
Sydney Thorne
Allan Willey, Wesley College, Melbourne, Australia

The following are thanked for permission to reproduce copyright material:

Agence Touristique Savoie: p.96 (Chambéry); Airotels de France: p.28 (extracts from *Airotels de France*); Comité Régional de Tourisme de Bretagne: p.96 (Perros-Guirec); Frantour T.O: p.109 (Frantour Victoria); Galeries Lafayette: p.35 (tables); Hatier International/Eryica: pp.77, 87, 89; Map extracts reproduced with permission of Michelin from their map no. 989 (authorisation nos. 94-308 and 95-021): pp.68, 72, 167; Northern Examinations and Assessment Board (article and illustration from *Phosphore* used in Higher Reading paper, May 1993): p.134; Office du Tourisme de Caen: p.103 (extracts and photos); © *Okapi*, Bayard Presse: p.8 (extrait d'un sondage réalisé par l'institut Louis Harris, N° 500); p.119 (poem, N° 527); p.122 (Soyez tolérants, N° 509); p.130 (Une mère parle, N° 483); Paris Convention and Visitors Bureau: p.91; © *Phosphore*, Bayard Presse: p.129 (sondage, N° 143); p.134 (letter/illustration by Willem, N° 109); Terrain de Camping International «Les Falaises»: p.30; Union Départementale des Offices de Tourisme et Syndicats d'Initiative: p.96 (Annonay).

Artwork buyer: Lorraine Sennett

Illustrations

Kathy Baxendale: 20, 21, 45, 47, 85, 86, 90, 98, 138, 160, 162, 169, 170, 175.
Tim Beer: 84.
Peter Brown: 5, 13, 18, 22, 23, 26, 31, 62, 68, 69, 70, 71, 73, 74, 75, 76, 79, 80, 116, 140, 153, 155, 156, 166.
Phillip Burrows: 3, 30, 43, 54, 146, 157, 168, 170.
Peter Clark: 8, 126.
Joan Corlass: 11, 32, 33, 37, 41, 157, 158, 159.
Paul Gendrot: 8, 28, 29, 36, 46, 55, 97, 126, 127.

Ian Heard: 4, 9, 17, 84, 101, 104, 116, 137, 149, 152, 158, 161, 164, 171, 174.
Veronica Jones: 61, 67, 108, 118, 123, 128, 129, 133.
Mike Ormond: 6, 79, 92, 93, 148.
Patrice Nares: 117, 118, 125, 132.
Ben Radis: 82, 83, 84, 105, 124.
Bruno le Sourd: 24, 35, 38, 39, 42, 50, 91, 115, 121.

Photographs

L'Agence Photographique de la Réunion des Musées Nationaux: 94 (top right).
Image Bank: 114 (bottom right), 110 (top right, bottom left).
Tim James: 81 (bottom right).
Martin Sookias: 4 (bottom left).
Stockphotos Inc.: 102
Tony Stone: 49, 114 (bottom left).
World Pictures (Feature Pix Colour Library Ltd): 105, 110 (top left).

All other photographs taken on location by Tim Booth.